THE LOEB CLASSICAL LIBRARY

FOUNDED BY JAMES LOEB, LL.D.

EDITED BY

† T. E. PAGE, c.h., litt.d.

† E. CAPPS, ph.d., ll.d.   † W. H. D. ROUSE, litt.d.

L. A. POST, l.h.d.   E. H. WARMINGTON, m.a., f.r.hist.soc.

THUCYDIDES

III

BERNOULLI.   GR. IKON.

THUCYDIDES.
BUST IN HOLKHAM HALL.

THUCYDIDES

WITH AN ENGLISH TRANSLATION BY

CHARLES FORSTER SMITH

OF THE UNIVERSITY OF WISCONSIN

[works] /

IN FOUR VOLUMES

III

HISTORY OF THE PELOPONNESIAN WAR
BOOKS V AND VI

LONDON
WILLIAM HEINEMANN LTD
CAMBRIDGE, MASSACHUSETTS
HARVARD UNIVERSITY PRESS
MCMLIX

First Printed 1921
Reprinted 1951, 1952, 1959

Printed in Great Britain

CONTENTS

THUCYDIDES

BOOK V

ΘΟΥΚΥΔΙΔΟΥ ΙΣΤΟΡΙΩΝ

Ε

I. Τοῦ δὲ ἐπιγιγνομένου θέρους αἱ μὲν ἐνιαύσιοι σπονδαὶ διελέλυντο μέχρι Πυθίων· καὶ ἐν τῇ ἐκεχειρίᾳ Ἀθηναῖοι Δηλίους ἀνέστησαν ἐκ Δήλου, ἡγησάμενοι κατὰ παλαιάν τινα αἰτίαν οὐ καθαροὺς ὄντας ἱερῶσθαι, καὶ ἅμα ἐλλιπὲς σφίσιν εἶναι τοῦτο τῆς καθάρσεως, ᾗ πρότερόν μοι δεδήλωται ὡς ἀνελόντες τὰς θήκας τῶν τεθνεώτων ὀρθῶς ἐνόμισαν ποιῆσαι. καὶ οἱ μὲν Δήλιοι Ἀτραμύττειον Φαρνάκου δόντος αὐτοῖς ἐν τῇ Ἀσίᾳ ᾤκησαν, οὕτως ὡς ἕκαστος ὥρμητο.

II. Κλέων δὲ Ἀθηναίους πείσας ἐς τὰ ἐπὶ Θρᾴκης χωρία ἐξέπλευσε μετὰ τὴν ἐκεχειρίαν, Ἀθηναίων μὲν ὁπλίτας ἔχων διακοσίους καὶ χιλίους καὶ ἱππέας τριακοσίους, τῶν δὲ ξυμμάχων πλείους, 2 ναῦς δὲ τριάκοντα. σχὼν δὲ ἐς Σκιώνην πρῶτον ἔτι πολιορκουμένην καὶ προσλαβὼν αὐτόθεν ὁπλίτας τῶν φρουρῶν, κατέπλευσεν ἐς τὸν Κωφὸν λιμένα, τῶν Τορωναίων ἀπέχοντα οὐ πολὺ τῆς

---

1 The truce had really expired, according to IV. cxviii. 12, the 14th of the Attic month Elaphebolion (about the end of March), but hostilities were not renewed till after the Pythian games, which were celebrated in the Attic month Metageitnion (latter half of August and first of September). This seems the most natural interpretation of Thucydides'

THUCYDIDES

BOOK V

I. The next summer the one-year's truce con- tinued till, and ended with, the Pythian games.[1] During the suspension of arms the Athenians expelled the Delians from Delos, thinking that they had been consecrated [2] while in a state of pollution from some ancient crime, and besides, that they themselves had been responsible for this defect in the purification, in which, as I have before related, they believed they had acted rightly in removing the coffins of the dead. And the Delians settled, according as each man chose,[3] in Atramytteum in Asia, which had been given them by Pharnaces.

II. After the armistice had expired Cleon persuaded the Athenians to let him sail to the cities in Thrace, with twelve hundred Athenian hoplites and three hundred cavalry, and a larger force of the allies, and thirty ships. And touching first at Scione, which was still under siege, and taking on from there some hoplites of the garrison, he then sailed down to the port of Cophus, which is not far distant

language, but many editors render "The next summer the one-year's truce was ended and war was renewed till the Pythian games."

[2] Referring to their purification and consecration to Apollo four years before (iii. 107).

[3] Or, "was inclined" (*sc.* οἰκῆσαι).

3 πόλεως. ἐκ δ' αὐτοῦ, αἰσθόμενος ὑπ' αὐτομόλων
ὅτι οὔτε Βρασίδας ἐν τῇ Τορώνῃ οὔτε οἱ ἐνόντες
ἀξιόμαχοι εἶεν, τῇ μὲν στρατιᾷ τῇ πεζῇ ἐχώρει
ἐς τὴν πόλιν, ναῦς δὲ περιέπεμψε δέκα ἐς[1] τὸν
4 λιμένα περιπλεῖν. καὶ πρὸς τὸ περιτείχισμα
πρῶτον ἀφικνεῖται, ὃ προσπεριέβαλε τῇ πόλει ὁ
Βρασίδας ἐντὸς βουλόμενος ποιῆσαι τὸ προά-
στειον καὶ διελὼν τοῦ παλαιοῦ τείχους μίαν
αὐτὴν ἐποίησε πόλιν.

III. Βοηθήσαντες δὲ ἐς αὐτὸ Πασιτελίδας τε
ὁ Λακεδαιμόνιος ἄρχων καὶ ἡ παροῦσα φυλακὴ
προσβαλόντων τῶν Ἀθηναίων ἠμύνοντο. καὶ ὡς
ἐβιάζοντο καὶ αἱ νῆες ἅμα περιέπλεον αἱ[2] ἐς τὸν
λιμένα περιπεμφθεῖσαι, δείσας ὁ Πασιτελίδας μὴ
αἵ τε νῆες φθάσωσι λαβοῦσαι ἐρῆμον τὴν πόλιν
καὶ τοῦ τειχίσματος ἁλισκομένου ἐγκαταληφθῇ,
2 ἀπολιπὼν αὐτὸ δρόμῳ ἐχώρει ἐς τὴν πόλιν. οἱ
δὲ Ἀθηναῖοι φθάνουσιν οἵ τε ἀπὸ τῶν νεῶν ἑλόντες τὴν Τορώνην καὶ ὁ πεζὸς ἐπισπόμενος αὐτο-
βοεί, κατὰ τὸ διῃρημένον τοῦ παλαιοῦ τείχους
ξυνεσπεσών. καὶ τοὺς μὲν ἀπέκτειναν τῶν Πελοποννησίων καὶ Τορωναίων εὐθὺς ἐν χερσί, τοὺς δὲ
ζῶντας ἔλαβον καὶ Πασιτελίδαν τὸν ἄρχοντα.
3 Βρασίδας δὲ ἐβοήθει μὲν τῇ Τορώνῃ, αἰσθόμενος
δὲ καθ' ὁδὸν ἑαλωκυῖαν ἀνεχώρησεν, ἀποσχὼν
τεσσαράκοντα μάλιστα σταδίους μὴ φθάσαι
4 ἐλθών. ὁ δὲ Κλέων καὶ οἱ Ἀθηναῖοι τροπαῖά τε
ἔστησαν δύο, τὸ μὲν κατὰ τὸν λιμένα, τὸ δὲ πρὸς
τῷ τειχίσματι, καὶ τῶν Τορωναίων γυναῖκας μὲν
καὶ παῖδας ἠνδραπόδισαν, αὐτοὺς δὲ καὶ Πελοποννησίους καὶ εἴ τις ἄλλος Χαλκιδέων ἦν,

---

[1] ἐς added by Bekker.   [2] αἱ added by Haacke.

from the city of Torone. From there, on learning
from deserters that Brasidas was not in Torone and
that the inhabitants were not a match for him
in battle, he advanced with his land-force against
the city, but sent ten ships to sail round into the
harbour. And first he arrived at the new wall which
Brasidas had built round the city for the purpose
of taking in the suburb, having pulled down a
part of the old wall and made one city of Torone.

III. But Pasitelidas, the Lacedaemonian commander, and the garrison that was present came to
the defence of this wall and tried to ward off the
Athenian assault. But they were hard pressed and
the ships that had been sent round were now sailing
into the harbour; so Pasitelidas, in fear that the ships
might take the town, undefended as it was, before he
could get there, and that if the new fortifications
were carried he might be captured in them, left them
and hurried back into the town. But the Athenians
from the ships forestalled him and took Torone, and
their land-force, following close upon him, at the
first assault dashed in with him at the breach in the
old wall. And they slew some of the Peloponnesians
and Toronaeans on the spot in hand to hand fighting,
but others they took alive, including Pasitelidas the
commander. Brasidas meanwhile was coming to the
relief of Torone, but learning on the road that it
had fallen he retreated, having missed getting there
in time by just about forty stadia. Cleon and the
Athenians set up two trophies, one at the harbour,
the other at the new wall, and made slaves of the
women and children of the Toronaeans, but the men
of Torone along with the Peloponnesians, and any
that were Chalcidians, all together to the number of

ξύμπαντας ἐς ἑπτακοσίους, ἀπέπεμψαν ἐς τὰς
Ἀθήνας· καὶ αὐτοῖς τὸ μὲν Πελοποννήσιον
ὕστερον ἐν ταῖς γενομέναις σπονδαῖς ἀπῆλθε, τὸ
δὲ ἄλλο ἐκομίσθη ὑπ' Ὀλυνθίων, ἀνὴρ ἀντ'
5 ἀνδρὸς λυθείς. εἷλον δὲ καὶ Πάνακτον Ἀθηναίων ἐν μεθορίοις τεῖχος Βοιωτοὶ ὑπὸ τὸν αὐτὸν
6 χρόνον προδοσίᾳ. καὶ ὁ μὲν Κλέων φυλακὴν
καταστησάμενος τῆς Τορώνης ἄρας περιέπλει
τὸν Ἄθων ὡς ἐπὶ τὴν Ἀμφίπολιν.

IV. Φαίαξ δὲ ὁ Ἐρασιστράτου τρίτος αὐτὸς
Ἀθηναίων πεμπόντων ναυσὶ δύο ἐς Ἰταλίαν καὶ
Σικελίαν πρεσβευτὴς ὑπὸ τὸν αὐτὸν χρόνον ἐξέ-
2 πλευσεν. Λεοντῖνοι γὰρ ἀπελθόντων Ἀθηναίων
ἐκ Σικελίας μετὰ τὴν ξύμβασιν πολίτας τε ἐπε-
γράψαντο πολλοὺς καὶ ὁ δῆμος τὴν γῆν ἐπενόει
3 ἀναδάσασθαι. οἱ δὲ δυνατοὶ αἰσθόμενοι Συρακοσίους τε ἐπάγονται καὶ ἐκβάλλουσι τὸν δῆμον.
καὶ οἱ μὲν ἐπλανήθησαν ὡς ἕκαστοι· οἱ δὲ
δυνατοὶ ὁμολογήσαντες Συρακοσίοις καὶ τὴν
πόλιν ἐκλιπόντες καὶ ἐρημώσαντες Συρακούσας
4 ἐπὶ πολιτείᾳ ᾤκησαν. καὶ ὕστερον πάλιν αὐτῶν
τινες διὰ τὸ μὴ ἀρέσκεσθαι ἀπολιπόντες ἐκ τῶν
Συρακουσῶν Φωκέας τε, τῆς πόλεώς τι τῆς
Λεοντίνων χωρίον καλούμενον, καταλαμβάνουσι
καὶ Βρικιννίας, ὃν ἔρυμα ἐν τῇ Λεοντίνῃ. καὶ
τῶν τοῦ δήμου τότε ἐκπεσόντων οἱ πολλοὶ ἦλθον
ὡς αὐτούς, καὶ καταστάντες ἐκ τῶν τειχῶν ἐπο-
5 λέμουν. ἃ πυνθανόμενοι οἱ Ἀθηναῖοι τὸν Φαίακα
πέμπουσιν, εἴ πως πείσαντες τοὺς σφίσιν ὄντας

---

[1] i.e. in exchange for Athenian prisoners.
[2] cf. IV. lxv. init.

seven hundred, they sent to Athens. There, however, the Peloponnesians were afterwards set free in
the treaty that was made, but the rest were brought
back by the Olynthians, being ransomed man for
man.[1] About the same time Panactum, a fortress on
the frontier of Attica, was betrayed to the Boeotians.
As for Cleon, after setting a guard over Torone, he
weighed anchor and sailed round Athos with a view
to attacking Amphipolis.

IV. About the same time Phaeax son of
Erasistratus and two others were sent by the
Athenians with two ships on a mission to Italy and
Sicily. For the Leontines, on the departure of the
Athenians from Sicily after the general peace,[2] had
enrolled many new citizens,[3] and the people were
minded to make a redistribution of the land. But
the oligarchs, perceiving their intention, brought
over the Syracusans and expelled the people. And
the latter were scattered in every direction; but the
oligarchs, coming to an agreement with the
Syracusans and leaving their own city desolated,
settled at Syracuse on condition of having the rights
of citizenship. But later some of them, owing to
discontent, left Syracuse and occupied Phoceae, a
quarter so named of the city of Leontini, and
Bricinniae, a stronghold in Leontine territory. These
being joined by most of the members of the
popular party who had been expelled, they established themselves and carried on war from their
strongholds. Hearing of this, the Athenians sent
Phaeax to see if perchance they might persuade
their own allies there, and the rest of the Siceliots

[3] This was to strengthen the democratic party, and for
their benefit a new division of state lands was to be made.

αὐτόθι ξυμμάχους καὶ τοὺς ἄλλους, ἢν δύνωνται,
Σικελιώτας κοινῇ, ὡς Συρακοσίων δύναμιν περι-
ποιουμένων, ἐπιστρατεῦσαι, διασώσειαν τὸν
6 δῆμον τῶν Λεοντίνων. ὁ δὲ Φαίαξ ἀφικόμενος
τοὺς μὲν Καμαριναίους πείθει καὶ Ἀκραγαντί-
νους, ἐν δὲ Γέλα ἀντιστάντος αὐτῷ τοῦ πράγ-
ματος οὐκέτι ἐπὶ τοὺς ἄλλους ἔρχεται, αἰσθόμενος οὐκ ἂν πείθειν αὐτούς, ἀλλ᾽ ἀναχωρήσας
διὰ τῶν Σικελῶν ἐς Κατάνην, καὶ ἅμα ἐν τῇ
παρόδῳ καὶ ἐς τὰς Βρικιννίας ἐλθὼν καὶ παρα-
θαρσύνας, ἀπέπλει.

V. Ἐν δὲ τῇ παρακομιδῇ τῇ ἐς τὴν Σικελίαν
καὶ πάλιν ἀναχωρήσει καὶ ἐν τῇ Ἰταλίᾳ τισὶ
πόλεσιν ἐχρημάτισε περὶ φιλίας τοῖς Ἀθηναίοις
καὶ Λοκρῶν ἐντυγχάνει τοῖς ἐκ Μεσσήνης
ἐποίκοις ἐκπεπτωκόσιν, οἳ μετὰ τὴν Σικελιωτῶν ὁμολογίαν στασιασάντων Μεσσηνίων
καὶ ἐπαγαγομένων τῶν ἑτέρων Λοκροὺς ἔποικοι
ἐξεπέμφθησαν καὶ ἐγένετο Μεσσήνη Λοκρῶν
2 τινὰ χρόνον. τούτοις οὖν ὁ Φαίαξ ἐντυχὼν
κομιζομένοις [1] οὐκ ἠδίκησεν· ἐγεγένητο γὰρ τοῖς
Λοκροῖς πρὸς αὐτὸν ὁμολογία ξυμβάσεως πέρι
3 πρὸς τοὺς Ἀθηναίους. μόνοι γὰρ τῶν ξυμμάχων,
ὅτε Σικελιῶται ξυνηλλάσσοντο, οὐκ ἐσπείσαντο
Ἀθηναίοις, οὐδ᾽ ἂν τότε, εἰ μὴ αὐτοὺς κατεῖχεν
ὁ πρὸς Ἱπωνιᾶς [2] καὶ Μεδμαίους πόλεμος,
ὁμόρους τε ὄντας καὶ ἀποίκους. καὶ ὁ μὲν Φαίαξ
ἐς τὰς Ἀθήνας χρόνῳ ὕστερον ἀφίκετο.

---

[1] τοῖς of the MSS. before κομιζομένοις deleted by Dobree.
[2] So corrected by Beloch with the help of coins; MSS.
Ἰτωνέας.

if possible, to make a common expedition against the Syracusans on the ground of their continual aggression, and thus save the people of Leontini. Phaeax, on his arrival, persuaded the Camarinaeans and Agrigentines ; but since his undertaking did not prosper at Gela he did not go on to the other states, perceiving that he could not persuade them, but withdrew through the country of the Sicels to Catana, having visited Bricinniae on the way and encouraged its inhabitants. He then sailed back home.

V. On his voyage along the coast to and from Sicily and in Italy he negotiated with certain cities about friendship with the Athenians. He fell in also with the Locrian settlers who had been expelled from Messene ; for these, after the general agreement among the Siceliots, when the Messenians had fallen into discord and one faction had called in the Locrians, had been sent out as colonists, Messene thus coming for a time into the hands of the Locrians. Falling in, then, with these when they were on their way home, he did them no injury, as an agreement had been made with him[1] by the Locrians for a treaty with the Athenians. For they alone of the allies, when the Siceliots became reconciled, made no treaty with the Athenians, nor would they have done so then if they had not been pressed by the war with the Iponieans and Medmaeans, who lived on their borders and were colonists of theirs. And Phaeax some time after this returned to Athens.

[1] On his way to Sicily.

VI. Ὁ δὲ Κλέων ὡς τότε ἀπὸ τῆς Τορώνης περιέπλευσεν ἐπὶ τὴν Ἀμφίπολιν, ὁρμώμενος ἐκ τῆς Ἠιόνος Σταγίρῳ μὲν προσβάλλει Ἀνδρίων ἀποικίᾳ καὶ οὐχ εἷλε, Γαληψὸν δὲ τὴν Θασίων 2 ἀποικίαν λαμβάνει κατὰ κράτος. καὶ πέμψας ὡς Περδίκκαν πρέσβεις, ὅπως παραγένοιτο στρατιᾷ κατὰ τὸ ξυμμαχικόν, καὶ ἐς τὴν Θράκην ἄλλους παρὰ Πολλῆν τὸν Ὀδομάντων βασιλέα, ἄξοντας μισθοῦ Θρᾷκας ὡς πλείστους, αὐτὸς 3 ἡσύχαζε περιμένων ἐν τῇ Ἠιόνι. Βρασίδας δὲ πυνθανόμενος ταῦτα ἀντεκάθητο καὶ αὐτὸς ἐπὶ τῷ Κερδυλίῳ· ἔστι δὲ τὸ χωρίον τοῦτο Ἀργιλίων ἐπὶ μετεώρου πέραν τοῦ ποταμοῦ οὐ πολὺ ἀπέχον τῆς Ἀμφιπόλεως, καὶ κατεφαίνετο πάντα αὐτόθεν, ὥστε οὐκ ἂν ἔλαθεν αὐτὸν ὁρμώμενος ὁ Κλέων τῷ στρατῷ· ὅπερ προσεδέχετο ποιήσειν αὐτόν, ἐπὶ τὴν Ἀμφίπολιν ὑπεριδόντα σφῶν τὸ πλῆθος τῇ παρούσῃ στρατιᾷ ἀναβήσεσθαι. 4 ἅμα δὲ καὶ παρεσκευάζετο Θρᾷκάς τε μισθωτοὺς πεντακοσίους καὶ χιλίους καὶ τοὺς Ἠδῶνας πάντας παρακαλῶν, πελταστὰς καὶ ἱππέας· καὶ Μυρκινίων καὶ Χαλκιδέων χιλίους πελταστὰς 5 εἶχε πρὸς τοῖς ἐν Ἀμφιπόλει. τὸ δ᾽ ὁπλιτικὸν ξύμπαν ἠθροίσθη δισχίλιοι μάλιστα καὶ ἱππῆς Ἕλληνες τριακόσιοι. τούτων Βρασίδας μὲν ἔχων ἐπὶ Κερδυλίῳ ἐκάθητο ἐς πεντακοσίους καὶ χιλίους, οἱ δ᾽ ἄλλοι ἐν Ἀμφιπόλει μετὰ Κλεαρίδου ἐτετάχατο.

VII. Ὁ δὲ Κλέων τέως μὲν ἡσύχαζεν, ἔπειτα ἠναγκάσθη ποιῆσαι ὅπερ ὁ Βρασίδας προσε-

---

[1] cf. IV. lxxxviii. 2.   [2] cf. IV. cvii. 3.

Modern Roads

Ancient Roads

1. Thracian Gate

2. First brow of the Long Wall

3. Gate from the town into space enclosed by the Palisade

4. Gate in the Palisade

VI. Now when Cleon had sailed round from
Torone to Amphipolis, as mentioned above, taking
Eion as his base he made an unsuccessful attack
upon Stagirus,[1] an Andrian colony, but did take by
storm Galepsus,[2] a colony of the Thasians. Then
sending envoys to Perdiccas, with a request to join
him with an army in accordance with the terms
of alliance,[3] and other envoys to Thrace to Polles,
king of the Odomantians, to bring as many
Thracian mercenaries as possible, he himself kept
quiet at Eion. But Brasidas, on hearing of these
things, took post over against him at Cerdylium.
This place is in the territory of the Argilians, on
high ground across the river not far from Amphipolis,
and commands a view in all directions, so that
Cleon could not move his army without being observed; for Brasidas expected that Cleon in contempt
of the small numbers of the Lacedaemonians would go
up against Amphipolis, with his present army.[4] At
the same time he made further preparations, calling
to his aid fifteen hundred Thracian mercenaries and
all the Edonians, both targeteers and cavalry. And
he had also of the Myrcinians and the Chalcidians
one thousand targeteers, in addition to the troops in
Amphipolis. The whole body of hoplites collected by
him was about two thousand in number, and he had
three hundred Hellenic horsemen. Of these forces
Brasidas took about fifteen hundred and stationed
himself at Cerdylium; the rest were posted at
Amphipolis under the command of Clearidas.

VII. Cleon kept quiet for a while, then was forced
to do just what Brasidas had expected. For when

[3] cf. IV. cxxxii. 1.
[4] i.e. without waiting for reinforcements.

2 δέχετο. τῶν γὰρ στρατιωτῶν ἀχθομένων μὲν τῇ
ἕδρᾳ, ἀναλογιζομένων δὲ τὴν ἐκείνου ἡγεμονίαν
πρὸς οἵαν ἐμπειρίαν καὶ τόλμαν μετὰ οἵας ἀνεπι-
στημοσύνης καὶ μαλακίας γενήσοιτο καὶ οἴ-
κοθεν ὡς ἄκοντες αὐτῷ ξυνεξῆλθον, αἰσθόμενος
τὸν θροῦν καὶ οὐ βουλόμενος αὐτοὺς διὰ τὸ ἐν
τῷ αὐτῷ καθημένους βαρύνεσθαι, ἀναλαβὼν
3 ἦγεν. καὶ ἐχρήσατο τῷ τρόπῳ ᾧπερ καὶ ἐς τὴν
Πύλον εὐτυχήσας ἐπίστευσέ τι φρονεῖν· ἐς μάχην μὲν γὰρ οὐδὲ ἤλπισέν οἱ ἐπεξιέναι οὐδένα,
κατὰ θέαν δὲ μᾶλλον ἔφη ἀναβαίνειν τοῦ χωρίου,
καὶ τὴν μείζω παρασκευὴν περιέμεινεν, οὐχ ὡς
τῷ ἀσφαλεῖ, ἢν ἀναγκάζηται, περισχήσων, ἀλλ'
ὡς κύκλῳ περιστὰς βίᾳ αἱρήσων τὴν πόλιν.
4 ἐλθών τε καὶ καθίσας ἐπὶ λόφου καρτεροῦ πρὸ
τῆς Ἀμφιπόλεως τὸν στρατόν, αὐτὸς ἐθεᾶτο τὸ
λιμνῶδες τοῦ Στρυμόνος καὶ τὴν θέσιν τῆς πόλεως
5 ἐπὶ τῇ Θρᾴκῃ [1] ὡς ἔχοι. ἀπιέναι τε ἐνόμιζεν,
ὁπόταν βούληται, ἀμαχεί· καὶ γὰρ οὐδὲ ἐφαίνετο
οὔτ' ἐπὶ τοῦ τείχους οὐδεὶς οὔτε κατὰ πύλας
ἐξῄει, κεκλημέναι τε ἦσαν πᾶσαι. ὥστε καὶ μηχανὰς ὅτι οὐκ ἀνῆλθεν ἔχων, ἁμαρτεῖν ἐδόκει·
ἑλεῖν γὰρ ἂν τὴν πόλιν διὰ τὸ ἔρημον.

VIII. Ὁ δὲ Βρασίδας εὐθὺς ὡς εἶδε κινου-
μένους τοὺς Ἀθηναίους, καταβὰς καὶ αὐτὸς ἀπὸ
τοῦ Κερδυλίου ἐσέρχεται ἐς τὴν Ἀμφίπολιν.
2 καὶ ἐπέξοδον μὲν καὶ ἀντίταξιν οὐκ ἐποιήσατο
πρὸς τοὺς Ἀθηναίους, δεδιὼς τὴν αὐτοῦ παρα-

---

[1] With most MSS.; Hude reads τὴν Θρᾴκην with CGc₂.

the soldiers began to be annoyed at sitting still and
to discuss the quality of his leadership—what experience and daring there was on the other side and what
incompetence and cowardice would be pitted against
it, and how unwillingly they had come with him from
home—he became aware of their grumbling, and
unwilling that they should be exasperated by remaining inactive in the same place, marched out with them.
He adopted the same course in which he had been
successful at Pylos and so had acquired confidence
in his own wisdom; for he had no expectation that
anybody would come against him for battle, but he
was going up, he said, rather to reconnoitre the
place; and in fact he was waiting for the larger force,[1]
not with a view to gaining the victory without risk
should he be forced to fight, but to surrounding the
town and taking it by force of arms. Accordingly he
went and posted his force on a strong hill before
Amphipolis, and was himself surveying the marshy
part of the Strymon and the situation of the city in
respect to the surrounding Thracian country, and
he thought that he could withdraw whenever he
pleased without a battle; for no one was visible
on the wall or was seen coming out by the gates,
which were all closed. He therefore thought that
he had made a mistake in coming up without
storming-machines; for he might have taken the
town, since it was undefended.

VIII. But Brasidas, as soon as he saw the
Athenians stirring, went down himself from
Cerdylium and entered Amphipolis. But he did not
march out and draw up against the Athenians,
because he mistrusted his own force, believing them

[1] cf. ch. vi. 2.

σκευὴν καὶ νομίζων ὑποδεεστέρους εἶναι, οὐ τῷ
πλήθει (ἀντίπαλα γάρ πως ἦν), ἀλλὰ τῷ ἀξιώματι (τῶν γὰρ Ἀθηναίων ὅπερ ἐστράτευε κα-
θαρὸν ἐξῆλθε, καὶ Λημνίων καὶ Ἰμβρίων τὸ
κράτιστον), τέχνῃ δὲ παρεσκευάζετο ἐπιθησό-
3 μενος. εἰ γὰρ δείξειε τοῖς ἐναντίοις τό τε πλῆθος
καὶ τὴν ὅπλισιν ἀναγκαίαν οὖσαν τῶν μεθ'
ἑαυτοῦ, οὐκ ἂν ἡγεῖτο μᾶλλον περιγενέσθαι ἢ
ἄνευ προόψεώς τε αὐτῶν καὶ μὴ ἀπὸ τοῦ ὄντος
4 καταφρονήσεως. ἀπολεξάμενος οὖν αὐτὸς πεντήκοντα καὶ ἑκατὸν ὁπλίτας, καὶ τοὺς ἄλλους
Κλεαρίδᾳ προστάξας, ἐβουλεύετο ἐπιχειρεῖν
αἰφνιδίως, πρὶν ἀπελθεῖν τοὺς Ἀθηναίους, οὐκ
ἂν νομίζων ὁμοίως αὐτοὺς ἀπολαβεῖν αὖθις
μεμονωμένους, εἰ τύχοι ἐλθοῦσα αὐτοῖς ἡ βοή-
5 θεια. ξυγκαλέσας δὲ τοὺς πάντας στρατιώτας
καὶ βουλόμενος παραθαρσῦναί τε καὶ τὴν ἐπί-
νοιαν φράσαι ἔλεγε τοιάδε.

IX. "Ἄνδρες Πελοποννήσιοι, ἀπὸ μὲν οἵας
χώρας ἥκομεν, ὅτι αἰεὶ διὰ τὸ εὔψυχον ἐλευθέρας,
καὶ ὅτι Δωριῆς μέλλετε Ἴωσι μάχεσθαι, ὧν
εἰώθατε κρείσσους εἶναι, ἀρκείτω βραχέως δεδη-
2 λωμένον· τὴν δὲ ἐπιχείρησιν ᾧ τρόπῳ διανοοῦμαι
ποιεῖσθαι διδάξω, ἵνα μή τῳ τὸ κατ' ὀλίγον καὶ
μὴ ἅπαντας κινδυνεύειν ἐνδεὲς φαινόμενον ἀτολ-
3 μίαν παράσχῃ. τοὺς γὰρ ἐναντίους εἰκάζω
καταφρονήσει τε ἡμῶν καὶ οὐκ ἂν ἐλπίσαντας
ὡς ἂν ἐπεξέλθοι τις αὐτοῖς ἐς μάχην, ἀναβῆναί
τε πρὸς τὸ χωρίον καὶ νῦν ἀτάκτως κατὰ θέαν
4 τετραμμένους ὀλιγωρεῖν. ὅστις δὲ τὰς τοιαύτας
ἁμαρτίας τῶν ἐναντίων κάλλιστα ἰδὼν καὶ ἅμα

to be inferior, not in numbers—as they were about
equal—but in quality; for the force that was in the
field were Athenians of pure blood and the pick of
the Lemnians and Imbrians. So he was preparing to
attack by means of a stratagem; for he thought that
if he showed the enemy the number and the barely
sufficient equipment of the troops with him he
should be less likely to gain a victory than if they
had no previous sight of his forces and did not look
upon them with contempt from seeing their real
character. Accordingly, picking out for himself one
hundred and fifty hoplites and assigning the rest to
Clearidas, he determined to make a sudden attack
before the Athenians withdrew, thinking that he could
not again cut them off thus isolated if once
reinforcements should reach them. So calling
together all the soldiers, wishing to encourage them
and explain his plan, he spoke to them as follows:

IX. "Men of the Peloponnesus, let it suffice to
remind you briefly from what manner of country we
have come, that it has ever been free because of its
courage, and that you are going to fight, Dorians
against Ionians, whom you have been accustomed to
vanquish. I will, however, explain to you in what
way I intend to make the attack, in order that my
plan of fighting in detachments and not in a body may
not seem to anyone poor tactics and thus cause dis-
couragement. For I imagine that the enemy ascended
the hill in contempt of us and because they could
not have expected that anybody would come out
for battle against them, and now, with broken ranks
and intent upon reconnoitring, are taking small
account of us. Now when an assailant having most
clearly observed such errors in the enemy also makes

πρὸς τὴν ἑαυτοῦ δύναμιν τὴν ἐπιχείρησιν ποιεῖται
μὴ ἀπὸ τοῦ προφανοῦς μᾶλλον καὶ ἀντιπαρα-
ταχθέντος ἢ ἐκ τοῦ πρὸς τὸ παρὸν ξυμφέροντος,
5 πλεῖστ᾽ ἂν ὀρθοῖτο· καὶ τὰ κλέμματα ταῦτα
καλλίστην δόξαν ἔχει ἃ τὸν πολέμιον μάλιστ᾽
ἄν τις ἀπατήσας τοὺς φίλους μέγιστ᾽ ἂν ὠφε-
6 λήσειεν. ἕως οὖν ἔτι ἀπαράσκευοι θαρσοῦσι καὶ
τοῦ ὑπαπιέναι πλέον ἢ τοῦ μένοντος, ἐξ ὧν ἐμοὶ
φαίνονται, τὴν διάνοιαν ἔχουσιν, ἐν τῷ ἀνειμένῳ
αὐτῶν τῆς γνώμης καὶ πρὶν ξυνταθῆναι[1] μᾶλλον
τὴν δόξαν, ἐγὼ μὲν ἔχων τοὺς μετ᾽ ἐμαυτοῦ καὶ
φθάσας, ἢν δύνωμαι, προσπεσοῦμαι δρόμῳ κατὰ
7 μέσον τὸ στράτευμα· σὺ δέ, Κλεαρίδα, ὕστερον,
ὅταν ἐμὲ ὁρᾷς ἤδη προσκείμενον καὶ κατὰ τὸ εἰκὸς
φοβοῦντα αὐτούς, τοὺς μετὰ σεαυτοῦ τούς τ᾽
Ἀμφιπολίτας καὶ τοὺς ἄλλους ξυμμάχους ἄγων
αἰφνιδίως τὰς πύλας ἀνοίξας ἐπεκθεῖν καὶ ἐπεί-
8 γεσθαι ὡς τάχιστα ξυμμεῖξαι. ἐλπὶς γὰρ μάλιστα αὐτοὺς οὕτως φοβηθῆναι· τὸ γὰρ ἐπιὸν
ὕστερον δεινότερον τοῖς πολεμίοις τοῦ παρόντος
9 καὶ μαχομένου. καὶ αὐτός τε ἀνὴρ ἀγαθὸς γί-
γνου, ὥσπερ σε εἰκὸς ὄντα Σπαρτιάτην, καὶ ὑμεῖς,
ὦ ἄνδρες ξύμμαχοι, ἀκολουθήσατε ἀνδρείως, καὶ
νομίσατε τρία[2] εἶναι τοῦ καλῶς πολεμεῖν, τὸ ἐθέ-
λειν καὶ τὸ αἰσχύνεσθαι καὶ τὸ[3] τοῖς ἄρχουσι
πείθεσθαι, καὶ τῇδε ὑμῖν τῇ ἡμέρᾳ ἢ ἀγαθοῖς
γενομένοις ἐλευθερίαν τε ὑπάρχειν καὶ Λακεδαιμονίων ξυμμάχοις κεκλῆσθαι, ἢ Ἀθηναίων τε
δούλοις, ἢν τὰ ἄριστα ἄνευ ἀνδραποδισμοῦ ἢ

---

[1] Krüger's emendation for ξυνταχθῆναι of the MSS.
[2] Omitted by MSS. but rightly restored by Stahl from
Stobaeus and schol.   [3] Added by Krüger.

his attack in accordance with the force at his own
disposal, not openly and in array of battle, but as
may be advantageous under present circumstances,
then he would be most likely to succeed. And those
stratagems have won the highest credit by which
a man most completely deceives the enemy and
helps his friends. While, then, the Athenians, still
unprepared, are full of confidence and are thinking,
so far as I can see, more of withdrawing than of
staying where they are, while their tension of mind
is relaxed and before they have got their thoughts
together, I will take my own troops and if possible
surprise them by a dash upon the centre of their
army. Then, Clearidas, the moment you see me
pressing on and in all likelihood striking terror into
them, do you suddenly throw open the gates and at
the head of your own men and the Amphipolitans
and the rest of our allies rush out upon them and
make all haste to close with them at once. In this
way there is the best hope to put them in a panic;
for a force that comes up afterwards has always
more terror for an enemy than that with which he is
already engaged. As for yourself, shew yourself a
brave man, as becomes a Spartan; and do you, men
of the allies, follow him bravely, and bear in mind
that the three virtues of a good soldier are zeal,
sense of honour, and obedience to his leaders; and
that on this day there is in store for you, if you are
brave, freedom and to be called allies of the
Lacedaemonians—or else vassals of the Athenians (if
you be so fortunate as to escape death or being sold

THUCYDIDES

θανατώσεως πράξητε, καὶ δουλείαν χαλεπωτέραν
ἢ πρὶν εἴχετε, τοῖς δὲ λοιποῖς Ἕλλησι κωλυταῖς
10 γενέσθαι ἐλευθερώσεως. ἀλλὰ μήτε ὑμεῖς μαλα-
κισθῆτε, ὁρῶντες περὶ ὅσων ὁ ἀγών ἐστιν, ἐγώ τε
δείξω οὐ παραινέσαι οἷός τε ὢν μᾶλλον τοῖς πέλας ἢ καὶ αὐτὸς ἔργῳ ἐπεξελθεῖν."

X. Ὁ μὲν Βρασίδας τοσαῦτα εἰπὼν τήν τε
ἔξοδον παρεσκευάζετο αὐτὸς καὶ τοὺς ἄλλους
μετὰ τοῦ Κλεαρίδα καθίστη ἐπὶ τὰς Θρᾳκίας
καλουμένας τῶν πυλῶν, ὅπως ὥσπερ εἴρητο ἐπ-
2 εξίοιεν. τῷ δὲ Κλέωνι, φανεροῦ γενομένου αὐτοῦ
ἀπὸ τοῦ Κερδυλίου καταβάντος καὶ ἐν τῇ πόλει,
ἐπιφανεῖ οὔσῃ ἔξωθεν, περὶ τὸ ἱερὸν τῆς Ἀθη-
ναίας θυομένου καὶ ταῦτα πράσσοντος, ἀγγέλ-
λεται (προυκεχωρήκει γὰρ τότε κατὰ τὴν θέαν)
ὅτι ἥ τε στρατιὰ ἅπασα φανερὰ τῶν πολεμίων ἐν
τῇ πόλει καὶ ὑπὸ τὰς πύλας ἵππων τε πόδες
πολλοὶ καὶ ἀνθρώπων ὡς ἐξιόντων ὑποφαίνονται.
3 ὁ δὲ ἀκούσας ἐπῆλθε, καὶ ὡς εἶδεν, οὐ βουλόμενος
μάχῃ διαγωνίσασθαι πρίν οἱ καὶ τοὺς βοηθοὺς
ἥκειν καὶ οἰόμενος φθήσεσθαι ἀπελθών, σημαίνειν
τε ἅμα ἐκέλευεν ἀναχώρησιν καὶ παρήγγελλε
τοῖς ἀπιοῦσιν ἐπὶ τὸ εὐώνυμον κέρας, ὥσπερ
4 μόνον οἷόν τ' ἦν, ὑπάγειν ἐπὶ τῆς Ἠιόνος. ὡς δ'
αὐτῷ ἐδόκει σχολῇ γίγνεσθαι, αὐτὸς ἐπιστρέψας
τὸ δεξιὸν καὶ τὰ γυμνὰ πρὸς τοὺς πολεμίους δοὺς
5 ἀπῆγε τὴν στρατιάν. κἂν τούτῳ Βρασίδας ὡς
ὁρᾷ τὸν καιρὸν καὶ τὸ στράτευμα τῶν Ἀθηναίων
18

into slavery) and that, too, in a harsher vassalage
than you had before, while for the rest of the
Hellenes you will prove a barrier to their liberation.
Nay, then, seeing how much is at stake, do you
on your part not play the coward; and I, for my
part, will show that I am not better able to exhort
others than to carry out myself in action the advice
I give to my fellows."

X. After this brief speech, Brasidas himself
prepared for the sally and placed the rest with
Clearidas at the gate called Thracian, in order that
they might come out to his support according to his
orders. But he had been seen when he came down
from Cerdylium, and again in the city—which is in
full view from outside—while sacrificing at the
temple of Athena and busied about these matters;
and word was brought to Cleon, who had gone
forward at that time for the reconnaissance, that the
whole army of the enemy could be clearly seen
inside the city, and the feet of men and horses in
great numbers were visible under the gates, as
though ready for a sally. Hearing this Cleon came
nearer; and when he saw it, being unwilling to risk
a battle before his reinforcements arrived, and thinking that he could get away in time, he gave orders
to sound a retreat and at the same time passed along
word to the troops as they set off to go to the left
—as alone was possible—upon the road to Eion. But
as it seemed to him this was being done too slowly,
he himself wheeled the right wing, thus exposing
the unarmed side [1] to the enemy, and began to lead
off his army. At this moment Brasidas, seeing his
opportunity and the army of the Athenians on the

[1] i.e. the right side, the left being covered by the shield.

κινούμενον, λέγει τοῖς μεθ' ἑαυτοῦ καὶ τοῖς ἄλλοις
ὅτι "Οἱ ἄνδρες ἡμᾶς οὐ μένουσιν· δῆλοι δὲ τῶν τε
δοράτων τῇ κινήσει καὶ τῶν κεφαλῶν· οἷς γὰρ ἂν
τοῦτο γίγνηται, οὐκ εἰώθασι μένειν τοὺς ἐπιόντας.
ἀλλὰ τάς τε πύλας τις ἀνοιγέτω ἐμοὶ ἃς εἴρηται,
6 καὶ ἐπεξίωμεν ὡς τάχιστα θαρσοῦντες." καὶ ὁ
μὲν κατὰ τὰς ἐπὶ τὸ σταύρωμα πύλας καὶ τὰς
πρώτας τοῦ μακροῦ τείχους τότε ὄντος ἐξελθὼν
ἔθει δρόμῳ τὴν ὁδὸν ταύτην εὐθεῖαν ᾗπερ νῦν
κατὰ τὸ καρτερώτατον τοῦ χωρίου ἰόντι τροπαῖον
ἕστηκε, καὶ προσβαλὼν τοῖς Ἀθηναίοις, πεφοβη-
μένοις τε ἅμα τῇ σφετέρᾳ ἀταξίᾳ καὶ τὴν τόλμαν
αὐτοῦ ἐκπεπληγμένοις, κατὰ μέσον τὸ στράτευμα,
7 τρέπει· καὶ ὁ Κλεαρίδας, ὥσπερ εἴρητο, ἅμα
κατὰ τὰς Θρᾳκίας πύλας ἐπεξελθὼν τῷ στρατῷ
ἐπεφέρετο. ξυνέβη τε τῷ ἀδοκήτῳ καὶ ἐξαπίνης
8 ἀμφοτέρωθεν τοὺς Ἀθηναίους θορυβηθῆναι· καὶ
τὸ μὲν εὐώνυμον κέρας αὐτῶν, τὸ πρὸς τὴν Ἠιόνα
ὅπερ δὴ καὶ προυκεχωρήκει, εὐθὺς ἀπορραγὲν
ἔφευγε (καὶ ὁ Βρασίδας ὑποχωροῦντος ἤδη αὐτοῦ
ἐπιπαριὼν τῷ δεξιῷ τιτρώσκεται, καὶ πεσόντα
αὐτὸν οἱ μὲν Ἀθηναῖοι οὐκ αἰσθάνονται, οἱ δὲ
πλησίον ἄραντες ἀπήνεγκαν), τὸ δὲ δεξιὸν τῶν
9 Ἀθηναίων ἔμενε μᾶλλον. καὶ ὁ μὲν Κλέων, ὡς
τὸ πρῶτον οὐ διενοεῖτο μένειν, εὐθὺς φεύγων καὶ
καταληφθεὶς ὑπὸ Μυρκινίου πελταστοῦ ἀποθνῄσκει, οἱ δὲ αὐτοῦ ξυστραφέντες ὁπλῖται ἐπὶ
τὸν λόφον τόν τε Κλεαρίδαν ἠμύνοντο καὶ δὶς ἢ
τρὶς προσβαλόντα, καὶ οὐ πρότερον ἐνέδοσαν

move, said to those immediately about him [1] and to
the rest of the troops: "These men will not stand
before us; they show it by the wagging of their
spears and of their heads; men who do that never
await an attack. Somebody open the gates for me
as I have ordered and let us boldly get at them as
quickly as possible." He went out then by the gate
that led to the palisade and by the first gate of the
long wall, which was then standing, and advanced at
full speed up the straight road where now, as one
comes to the steepest part of the hill, a trophy
stands, and attacking the centre of the Athenians,
who were amazed at his audacity, as well as panic-
stricken because of their own disorder, he routed
them. At the same moment Clearidas, as he had
been ordered, went out at the Thracian gate and
bore down with his troops. And so it came to pass
that owing to the unexpected and sudden nature of
the attack from both sides at once the Athenians
were thrown into confusion; and the left wing, on
the side toward Eion, which had already gone
some distance in advance, was at once cut off, and
fled. (It was just when it began to retire that
Brasidas, who was pressing forward against the right
wing, was wounded, and the Athenians did not observe that he had fallen, but those who were near
took him up and carried him from the field.) The
right wing of the Athenians stood its ground better.
Cleon, indeed, as he had not intended from the first
to stand his ground, fled at once, and was overtaken
and slain by a Myrcinian targeteer; but the hoplites,
rallying at their first position on the hill, twice or
thrice repulsed the attack of Clearidas, and did not

---

[1] *i.e.* the hundred and fifty (ch. viii. 4).

πρὶν ἥ τε Μυρκινία καὶ ἡ Χαλκιδικὴ ἵππος καὶ
οἱ πελτασταὶ περιστάντες καὶ ἐσακοντίζοντες
10 αὐτοὺς ἔτρεψαν. οὕτω δὴ¹ τὸ στράτευμα πᾶν ἤδη
τῶν Ἀθηναίων φυγὸν χαλεπῶς καὶ πολλὰς ὁδοὺς
τραπόμενοι κατὰ ὄρη, ὅσοι μὴ διεφθάρησαν ἢ
αὐτίκα ἐν χερσὶν ἢ ὑπὸ τῆς Χαλκιδικῆς ἵππου
καὶ τῶν πελταστῶν, οἱ λοιποὶ ἀπεκομίσθησαν ἐς
11 τὴν Ἠιόνα. οἱ δὲ τὸν Βρασίδαν ἄραντες ἐκ τῆς
μάχης καὶ διασώσαντες ἐς τὴν πόλιν ἔτι ἔμπνουν
ἐσεκόμισαν· καὶ ᾔσθετο μὲν ὅτι νικῶσιν οἱ μεθ'
12 αὐτοῦ, οὐ πολὺ δὲ διαλιπὼν ἐτελεύτησεν· καὶ ἡ
ἄλλη στρατιὰ ἀναχωρήσασα μετὰ τοῦ Κλεαρίδου
ἐκ τῆς διώξεως νεκρούς τε ἐσκύλευσε καὶ τροπαῖον
ἔστησεν.

XI. Μετὰ δὲ ταῦτα τὸν Βρασίδαν οἱ ξύμμαχοι
πάντες ξὺν ὅπλοις ἐπισπόμενοι δημοσίᾳ ἔθαψαν
ἐν τῇ πόλει πρὸ τῆς νῦν ἀγορᾶς οὔσης· καὶ τὸ
λοιπὸν οἱ Ἀμφιπολῖται περιείρξαντες αὐτοῦ τὸ
μνημεῖον ὡς ἥρῳ τε ἐντέμνουσι καὶ τιμὰς δεδώ-
κασιν ἀγῶνας καὶ ἐτησίους θυσίας, καὶ τὴν ἀποικίαν ὡς οἰκιστῇ προσέθεσαν καταβαλόντες τὰ
Ἁγνώνεια² οἰκοδομήματα καὶ ἀφανίσαντες εἴ τι
μνημόσυνόν που ἔμελλεν αὐτοῦ τῆς οἰκίσεως
περιέσεσθαι, νομίσαντες τὸν μὲν Βρασίδαν σω-
τῆρά τε σφῶν γεγενῆσθαι καὶ ἐν τῷ παρόντι ἅμα
τὴν τῶν Λακεδαιμονίων ξυμμαχίαν φόβῳ τῶν
Ἀθηναίων θεραπεύοντες, τὸν δὲ Ἅγνωνα κατὰ τὸ
πολέμιον τῶν Ἀθηναίων οὐκ ἂν ὁμοίως σφίσι
ξυμφόρως οὐδ' ἂν ἡδέως τὰς τιμὰς ἔχειν. καὶ
2 τοὺς νεκροὺς τοῖς Ἀθηναίοις ἀπέδοσαν. ἀπέθανον

¹ δὴ, Krüger's correction for δὲ of the MSS.
² cf. IV. cii. 3, 4.

22

give way till the Myrcinian and Chalcidian horse and
the targeteers, who surrounded and hurled javelins
at them, put them to flight.   Then at last the whole
Athenian army took to flight, making their way with
difficulty and by many routes over the hills, until
finally the survivors—all that were not destroyed
either at once in hand to hand conflict or by the
Chalcidian horse and targeteers—got back to Eion.
Brasidas was taken up by his followers and carried
safely from the battlefield to the city, still breathing;
and he learned that his men were victorious, but
after a little interval he died.   The rest of the army,
after returning with Clearidas from the pursuit, de-
spoiled the dead and set up a trophy.

XI.   After this all the allies gave Brasidas a public
burial in the city at a spot facing what is now the
market-place, following his body in full armour.   And
the Amphipolitans fenced in his monument and have
ever since made offerings to him as a hero, giving
honours and instituting games and yearly sacrifices.
They also adopted him as founder of the colony,
pulling down the edifices of Hagnon and obliterating
whatever was likely, if left standing, to be a reminder
of his settlement,[1] for at the present moment they
courted the alliance of the Lacedaemonians through
fear of the Athenians, thinking Brasidas to have been
their saviour, whereas Hagnon, in consequence of
their hostile attitude towards Athens, would not in
like manner as before [2] receive their honours either
with benefit to themselves or with pleasure to himself.   The dead they gave back to the Athenians.

[1] cf. IV. cii. 3, 4.
[2] i.e. as formerly, when their relations with Athens were
pleasant.   Or the meaning may be, "so advantageously for
them as Brasidas would."

δὲ Ἀθηναίων μὲν περὶ ἑξακοσίους, τῶν δ' ἐναντίων ἑπτά, διὰ τὸ μὴ ἐκ παρατάξεως, ἀπὸ δὲ
τοιαύτης ξυντυχίας καὶ προεκφοβήσεως τὴν μά-
3 χην μᾶλλον γενέσθαι. μετὰ δὲ τὴν ἀναίρεσιν οἱ
μὲν ἐπ' οἴκου ἀπέπλευσαν, οἱ δὲ μετὰ τοῦ Κλεαρίδου τὰ περὶ τὴν Ἀμφίπολιν καθίσταντο.

XII. Καὶ ὑπὸ τοὺς αὐτοὺς χρόνους τοῦ θέρους
τελευτῶντος Ῥαμφίας καὶ Αὐτοχαρίδας καὶ Ἐπι-
κυδίδας Λακεδαιμόνιοι ἐς τὰ ἐπὶ Θρᾴκης χωρία
βοήθειαν ἦγον ἐνακοσίων ὁπλιτῶν, καὶ ἀφικόμενοι ἐς Ἡράκλειαν τὴν ἐν Τραχῖνι καθίσταντο ὅ
2 τι αὐτοῖς ἐδόκει μὴ καλῶς ἔχειν. ἐνδιατριβόντων
δὲ αὐτῶν ἔτυχεν ἡ μάχη αὕτη γενομένη, καὶ τὸ
θέρος ἐτελεύτα.

XIII. Τοῦ δ' ἐπιγιγνομένου χειμῶνος εὐθὺς μέχρι μὲν Πιερίου τῆς Θεσσαλίας διῆλθον οἱ περὶ
τὸν Ῥαμφίαν, κωλυόντων δὲ τῶν Θεσσαλῶν καὶ
ἅμα Βρασίδου τεθνεῶτος, ᾧπερ ἦγον τὴν στρατιάν, ἀπετράποντο ἐπ' οἴκου, νομίσαντες οὐδένα
καιρὸν ἔτι εἶναι, τῶν τε Ἀθηναίων ἥσσῃ ἀπελη-
λυθότων καὶ οὐκ ἀξιόχρεων αὐτῶν ὄντων δρᾶν τι
2 ὧν κἀκεῖνος ἐπενόει. μάλιστα δὲ ἀπῆλθον εἰδότες
τοὺς Λακεδαιμονίους, ὅτε ἐξῇσαν, πρὸς τὴν εἰρήνην μᾶλλον τὴν γνώμην ἔχοντας.

XIV. Ξυνέβη τε εὐθὺς μετὰ τὴν ἐν Ἀμφιπόλει
μάχην καὶ τὴν Ῥαμφίου ἀναχώρησιν ἐκ Θεσσαλίας ὥστε πολέμου μὲν μηδὲν ἔτι ἅψασθαι μηδετέρους, πρὸς δὲ τὴν εἰρήνην μᾶλλον τὴν γνώμην
εἶχον, οἱ μὲν Ἀθηναῖοι πληγέντες ἐπί τε τῷ

---

[1] cf. IV. c., ci.

About six hundred of these had been killed, but of their adversaries only seven; for the fight had been made, not as a regular battle, but as the result of such an accident and previous panic as has been described. After taking up the dead the Athenians sailed back home, but Clearidas and his followers remained and set in order the affairs of Amphipolis.

XII. About the same time, towards the close of this summer, Rhamphias, Autocharidas, and Epicydidas, who were Lacedaemonians, were on their way with reinforcements, consisting of nine hundred hoplites, to the strongholds in Thrace, and arriving at Heracleia in Trachis they set in order whatever seemed to them amiss. It was while they were staying there that the battle at Amphipolis occurred; and so the summer ended.

XIII. As soon as winter came on Rhamphias and his followers advanced as far as Pierium in Thessaly; but as the Thessalians hindered their progress and Brasidas, to whom they were bringing the army, was now dead, they turned back homeward. They thought the favourable moment was past, for the Athenians had gone away in consequence of their defeat, and they were not competent by themselves to carry out any of Brasidas' plans. But the chief reason for their return was that they knew that the Lacedaemonians, at the time when they set out, were more than ever inclined to peace.

XIV. It so happened, too, that directly after the battle at Amphipolis and the withdrawal of Rhamphias from Thessaly neither side undertook any further military operations, and both were more inclined to peace. The Athenians were so inclined because they had been beaten at Delium,[1] and again

25

Δηλίῳ καὶ δι' ὀλίγου αὖθις ἐν Ἀμφιπόλει, καὶ
οὐκ ἔχοντες τὴν ἐλπίδα τῆς ῥώμης πιστὴν ἔτι,
ἥπερ οὐ προσεδέχοντο πρότερον τὰς σπονδάς,
δοκοῦντες τῇ παρούσῃ εὐτυχίᾳ καθυπέρτεροι γε-
2 νήσεσθαι (καὶ τοὺς ξυμμάχους ἅμα ἐδέδισαν
σφῶν μὴ διὰ τὰ σφάλματα ἐπαιρόμενοι ἐπὶ πλέον
ἀποστῶσι, μετεμέλοντό τε ὅτι μετὰ τὰ ἐν Πύλῳ
3 καλῶς παρασχὸν οὐ ξυνέβησαν), οἱ δ' αὖ Λακεδαιμόνιοι παρὰ γνώμην μὲν ἀποβαίνοντος σφίσι
τοῦ πολέμου, ἐν ᾧ ᾤοντο ὀλίγων ἐτῶν καθαι-
ρήσειν τὴν τῶν Ἀθηναίων δύναμιν εἰ τὴν γῆν τέμ-
νοιεν, περιπεσόντες δὲ τῇ ἐν τῇ νήσῳ ξυμφορᾷ,
οἵα οὔπω ἐγεγένητο τῇ Σπάρτῃ, καὶ λῃστευομένης
τῆς χώρας ἐκ τῆς Πύλου καὶ Κυθήρων, αὐτομο-
λούντων τε τῶν Εἱλώτων καὶ αἰεὶ προσδοκίας
οὔσης μή τι καὶ οἱ ὑπομένοντες τοῖς ἔξω πίσυνοι
πρὸς τὰ παρόντα σφίσιν, ὥσπερ καὶ πρότερον,
4 νεωτερίσωσιν· ξυνέβαινε δὲ καὶ πρὸς τοὺς Ἀργείους αὐτοῖς τὰς τριακοντούτεις σπονδὰς ἐπ'
ἐξόδῳ εἶναι, καὶ ἄλλας οὐκ ἤθελον σπένδεσθαι οἱ
Ἀργεῖοι, εἰ μή τις αὐτοῖς τὴν Κυνουρίαν γῆν ἀπο-
δώσει (ἀδύνατα δ'[1] εἶναι ἐφαίνετο Ἀργείοις καὶ
Ἀθηναίοις ἅμα πολεμεῖν), τῶν τε ἐν Πελοποννήσῳ πόλεων ὑπώπτευόν τινας ἀποστήσεσθαι
πρὸς τοὺς Ἀργείους, ὅπερ καὶ ἐγένετο.

XV. Ταῦτ' οὖν ἀμφοτέροις αὐτοῖς λογιζομένοις
ἐδόκει ποιητέα εἶναι ἡ ξύμβασις, καὶ οὐχ ἧσσον

---

[1] Stahl's emendation for ὥστ' ἀδύνατα of the MSS.

---

[1] *i.e.* those who had escaped.
[2] The great revolt of the Helots, called the Third Mes-
senian War; *cf.* I. ci.–ciii.

at Amphipolis a little later, and consequently had no longer that confidence in their strength in reliance upon which they had earlier refused to accept the truce, as they then thought that with their existing good luck they would prove superior. They were afraid, too, of their allies, lest, elated over these failures of theirs, the revolt among them might spread, and they repented that they had not come to terms when a good opportunity offered after the affair at Pylos. The Lacedaemonians, on the other hand, favoured peace because the war was turning out contrary to their hopes. They had expected that in a few years, if they should ravage their territory, they could pull down the power of the Athenians; whereas they had met with the calamity on the island of Sphacteria, such an one as had never before befallen Sparta; their territory was ravaged from Pylos and Cythera; the Helots were deserting, and always there was apprehension that those who remained, relying on those beyond the border,[1] might revolt in the present state of affairs, just as they had done before.[2] It happened also that the thirty years' truce with the Argives was on the point of expiring,[3] and the Argives were unwilling to make another treaty unless the territory of Cynuria[4] were restored to them; and it seemed impossible to carry on the war with the Argives and the Athenians at the same time. Besides, they suspected that some of the cities in the Peloponnesus would revolt to the Argives, as indeed did happen.

XV. In consideration of these things, both parties thought it advisable to come to an agreement,

[3] It expired the next year (*cf.* ch. xxviii. 2), and therefore dated from 457 B.C.   [4] *cf.* IV. lvi. 2.

τοῖς Λακεδαιμονίοις, ἐπιθυμίᾳ τῶν ἀνδρῶν τῶν ἐκ
τῆς νήσου κομίσασθαι· ἦσαν γὰρ οἱ Σπαρτιᾶται
αὐτῶν πρῶτοί τε καὶ ὁμοίως σφίσι ξυγγενεῖς.
2 ἤρξαντο μὲν οὖν καὶ εὐθὺς μετὰ τὴν ἅλωσιν
αὐτῶν πράσσειν, ἀλλ' οἱ Ἀθηναῖοι οὔπως ἤθελον,
εὖ φερόμενοι, ἐπὶ τῇ ἴσῃ καταλύεσθαι. σφαλέντων δὲ αὐτῶν ἐπὶ τῷ Δηλίῳ παραχρῆμα οἱ Λακεδαιμόνιοι γνόντες νῦν μᾶλλον ἂν ἐνδεξαμένους
ποιοῦνται τὴν ἐνιαύσιον ἐκεχειρίαν, ἐν ᾗ ἔδει
ξυνιόντας καὶ περὶ τοῦ πλείονος χρόνου βουλεύεσθαι.

XVI. Ἐπειδὴ δὲ καὶ ἡ ἐν Ἀμφιπόλει ἧσσα
τοῖς Ἀθηναίοις ἐγεγένητο καὶ ἐτεθνήκει Κλέων τε
καὶ Βρασίδας, οἵπερ ἀμφοτέρωθεν μάλιστα ἠναντιοῦντο τῇ εἰρήνῃ, ὁ μὲν διὰ τὸ εὐτυχεῖν τε καὶ
τιμᾶσθαι ἐκ τοῦ πολεμεῖν, ὁ δὲ γενομένης ἡσυχίας
καταφανέστερος νομίζων ἂν εἶναι κακουργῶν καὶ
ἀπιστότερος διαβάλλων, τότε δὲ[1] ἑκατέρᾳ τῇ
πόλει σπεύδοντες τὰ μάλιστ' αὐτὴν[2] Πλειστοάναξ τε ὁ Παυσανίου, βασιλεὺς Λακεδαιμονίων,
καὶ Νικίας ὁ Νικηράτου, πλεῖστα τῶν τότε εὖ
φερόμενος ἐν στρατηγίαις, πολλῷ δὴ μᾶλλον
προυθυμοῦντο, Νικίας μὲν βουλόμενος, ἐν ᾧ ἀπα-
θὴς ἦν καὶ ἠξιοῦτο, διασώσασθαι τὴν εὐτυχίαν,

---

[1] So all the better MSS.; Hude reads δή.
[2] The vulgate has μάλιστα τὴν ἡγεμονίαν : Stahl deletes
ἡγεμονίαν and corrects τὴν to αὐτήν. The vulgate would
mean : "then those who in either country were most desirous of taking the lead, namely . . ."

especially the Lacedaemonians, because of their
desire to recover the men captured at Sphacteria;
for the Spartiates among these were men of high
rank and all alike kinsmen of theirs.[1]   Accordingly,
they began negotiations directly after their capture,
but the Athenians were not at all inclined, as long
as they were getting on well, to make a settlement
on fair terms.   When, however, the Athenians were
defeated at Delium, the Lacedaemonians knew immediately that they would now be more ready to
accept offers, and they concluded the truce for a
year, during which they were to come together and
consult about a treaty for a longer period.

XVI.   But when the Athenians had met defeat at
Amphipolis also and both Cleon and Brasidas had
been killed—the men who on either side had been
most opposed to peace, the one because of his
success and the reputation he had derived from the
war, the other because he thought if quiet were
restored he would be more manifest in his villainies
and less credited in his calumnies—then it was that
Pleistoanax son of Pausanias, king of the Lacedaemonians, and Nicias son of Niceratus, who had been
of all the generals of his day most successful in his
commands—men who had most zealously supported
the cause of peace each in the interest of his own
state—urged this course with greater zeal than
ever.   Nicias wished, while his record was still free
from disaster and he was held in esteem, to pre-

---

[1] *i.e.* of the Lacedaemonians in authority.   The Spartiates
formed a clan; besides their common descent, they were
closely connected by intermarriage.   Or reading, with the
schol., ἦσαν γὰρ οἱ Σπαρτιᾶται αὐτῶν κτλ., "for there were
among them *some* Spartiates of the first rank and related to
the most distinguished families."

καὶ ἔς τε τὸ αὐτίκα πόνων πεπαῦσθαι καὶ αὐτὸς
καὶ τοὺς πολίτας παῦσαι, καὶ τῷ μέλλοντι χρόνῳ
καταλιπεῖν ὄνομα ὡς οὐδὲν σφήλας τὴν πόλιν
διεγένετο, νομίζων ἐκ τοῦ ἀκινδύνου τοῦτο ξυμβαίνειν καὶ ὅστις ἐλάχιστα τύχῃ αὐτὸν παρα-
δίδωσι, τὸ δὲ ἀκίνδυνον τὴν εἰρήνην παρέχειν·
Πλειστοάναξ δὲ ὑπὸ τῶν ἐχθρῶν διαβαλλόμενος
περὶ τῆς καθόδου καὶ ἐς ἐνθυμίαν τοῖς Λακεδαιμονίοις αἰεὶ προβαλλόμενος ὑπ᾽ αὐτῶν, ὁπότε τι
πταίσειαν, ὡς διὰ τὴν ἐκείνου κάθοδον παρανο-
2 μηθεῖσαν ταῦτα ξυμβαίνοι. τὴν γὰρ πρόμαντιν
τὴν ἐν Δελφοῖς ἐπῃτιῶντο αὐτὸν πεῖσαι μετ᾽
Ἀριστοκλέους τοῦ ἀδελφοῦ ὥστε χρῆσαι Λακεδαιμονίοις ἐπὶ πολὺ τάδε θεωροῖς ἀφικνουμένοις,
Διὸς υἱοῦ ἡμιθέου τὸ σπέρμα ἐκ τῆς ἀλλοτρίας ἐς
τὴν ἑαυτῶν ἀναφέρειν· εἰ δὲ μή, ἀργυρέᾳ εὐλάκᾳ
3 εὐλαξεῖν· χρόνῳ δὲ προτρέψαι τοὺς Λακεδαιμονίους φεύγοντα αὐτὸν ἐς Λύκαιον διὰ τὴν ἐκ
τῆς Ἀττικῆς ποτε μετὰ δώρων δοκοῦσαν ἀναχώρησιν καὶ ἥμισυ τῆς οἰκίας τοῦ ἱεροῦ τότε τοῦ
Διὸς οἰκοῦντα φόβῳ τῷ Λακεδαιμονίων, ἔτει ἑνὸς
δέοντι εἰκοστῷ τοῖς ὁμοίοις χοροῖς καὶ θυσίαις
καταγαγεῖν ὥσπερ ὅτε τὸ πρῶτον Λακεδαίμονα
κτίζοντες τοὺς βασιλέας καθίσταντο.

---

[1] i.e. as the schol. explains, there would be a pestilence,
and they would buy food at a very high price, as it were
using silver tools.

[2] 427 B.C., since he had left the country in 446. cf. I.
cxiv. 2 and II. xxi. 1.

serve his good luck to the end, and not only at
present both to rest from toil himself and to give
his fellow-citizens a rest, but also to hand down to
after times a name as of one who had lived his life
through without injuring the state; and he thought
that a man might achieve such a result by keeping
out of danger and by least exposing himself to the
caprices of fortune, and that it was peace only that
offered freedom from danger. Pleistoanax, on the
other hand, was for peace, because he was constantly maligned by his enemies about his return
from exile, and because, whenever any reverses
occurred, he was always spitefully recalled to their
thoughts by these persons as though these misfortunes were due to his illegal restoration. For
they charged that he, along with his brother Aristocles, had bribed the priestess at Delphi constantly to answer the Lacedaemonians, whenever
they came to consult the oracle: " Bring back
the seed of the demigod, son of Zeus, from the
foreign land to your own; otherwise you shall
plough with a silver plough-share "[1]; and that in
course of time she had induced the Lacedaemonians
to bring him back from banishment in the twentieth
year[2] with like dances and sacrifices as when at the
founding of Lacedaemon they had first enthroned
their kings. For he had fled for refuge to Mt.
Lycaeum,[3] on account of his retreat from Attica,
that was thought to be due to bribery, and through
fear of the Lacedaemonians had occupied at that
time a house whereof the half was within the
sanctuary of Zeus.

[3] A mountain in Arcadia on which was an ancient sanctuary
of Zeus.

XVII. Ἀχθόμενος οὖν τῇ διαβολῇ ταύτῃ καὶ νομίζων ἐν εἰρήνῃ μὲν οὐδενὸς σφάλματος γιγνομένου καὶ ἅμα τῶν Λακεδαιμονίων τοὺς ἄνδρας κομιζομένων κἂν αὐτὸς τοῖς ἐχθροῖς ἀνεπίληπτος εἶναι, πολέμου δὲ καθεστῶτος αἰεὶ ἀνάγκην εἶναι τοὺς προύχοντας ἀπὸ τῶν ξυμφορῶν διαβάλλεσθαι, προυθυμήθη τὴν ξύμβασιν.

2 Καὶ τόν τε χειμῶνα τοῦτον ἦσαν ἐς λόγους, καὶ πρὸς τὸ ἔαρ ἤδη παρασκευή τε προεπανεσείσθη ἀπὸ τῶν Λακεδαιμονίων, περιαγγελλομένη κατὰ πόλεις ὡς ἐς ἐπιτειχισμόν,[1] ὅπως οἱ Ἀθηναῖοι μᾶλλον ἐσακούοιεν, καὶ ἐπειδὴ ἐκ τῶν ξυνόδων ἅμα πολλὰς δικαιώσεις προενεγκόντων ἀλλήλοις ξυνεχωρεῖτο ὥστε ἃ ἑκάτεροι πολέμῳ ἔσχον ἀποδόντας τὴν εἰρήνην ποιεῖσθαι, Νίσαιαν δ' ἔχειν Ἀθηναίους (ἀνταπαιτούντων γὰρ Πλάταιαν οἱ Θηβαῖοι ἔφασαν οὐ βίᾳ, ἀλλ' ὁμολογίᾳ αὐτῶν προσχωρησάντων καὶ οὐ προδόντων ἔχειν τὸ χωρίον, καὶ οἱ Ἀθηναῖοι τῷ αὐτῷ τρόπῳ τὴν Νίσαιαν), τότε δὴ παρακαλέσαντες τοὺς ἑαυτῶν ξυμμάχους οἱ Λακεδαιμόνιοι καὶ ψηφισαμένων πλὴν Βοιωτῶν καὶ Κορινθίων καὶ Ἠλείων καὶ Μεγαρέων τῶν ἄλλων ὥστε καταλύεσθαι (τούτοις δὲ οὐκ ἤρεσκε τὰ πρασσόμενα), ποιοῦνται τὴν ξύμβασιν καὶ ἐσπείσαντο πρὸς τοὺς Ἀθηναίους καὶ ὤμοσαν, ἐκεῖνοί τε πρὸς τοὺς Λακεδαιμονίους, τάδε.

---

[1] Poppo's conjecture for ὡς ἐπὶ τειχισμόν of MSS.

[1] cf. ᾽ν. lxix.　　[2] cf. iii. lii. 2.

XVII. Vexed, therefore, by this calumny, and
thinking that in time of peace, when no calamity
would occur and, moreover, the Lacedaemonians
would be recovering their men, he himself would
not be exposed to the attack of his enemies, whereas
so long as there was war it must always be that the
leading men would be maligned in the event of any
misfortunes, he became very ardent for the agreement.

During this winter they kept attending conferences; and toward spring there was a menace of
warlike preparation on the part of the Lacedaemonians, orders being sent to the cities as though for
the erection of a fortress to overawe the territory of
the Athenians, that they might be more inclined to
listen to terms; and at the same time as the result
of their conferences, in which each party had filed
many claims against the other, an agreement was
finally reached that they should make peace, each
party to restore to the other the territories which
they had gained by war, though the Athenians were
to keep Nisaea.[1] (For when they had demanded
back Plataea, the Thebans protested that they had
obtained possession of the place, not by force, but
because the Plataeans had come over to them by
agreement and not through betrayal[2]; and the
Athenians claimed to have obtained Nisaea in the
same way.)   At this time the Lacedaemonians summoned their own allies, and when all the rest had
voted to stop hostilities, except the Boeotians,
Corinthians, Eleans, and Megarians—to whom the
negotiations were displeasing—they made the agreement, ratifying it by libations and oaths with the
Athenians, and the Athenians with them, on the
following terms:—

33

THUCYDIDES

XVIII. "Σπονδὰς ἐποιήσαντο Ἀθηναῖοι καὶ Λακεδαιμόνιοι καὶ οἱ ξύμμαχοι κατὰ τάδε, καὶ ὤμοσαν κατὰ πόλεις.

"Περὶ μὲν τῶν ἱερῶν τῶν κοινῶν, θύειν ἐξεῖναι[1] καὶ μαντεύεσθαι καὶ θεωρεῖν κατὰ τὰ πάτρια τὸν βουλόμενον καὶ κατὰ γῆν καὶ κατὰ θάλασσαν ἀδεῶς.

2 "Τὸ δ' ἱερὸν καὶ τὸν νεὼν τὸν ἐν Δελφοῖς τοῦ Ἀπόλλωνος καὶ Δελφοὺς αὐτονόμους εἶναι καὶ αὐτοτελεῖς καὶ αὐτοδίκους καὶ αὑτῶν καὶ τῆς γῆς τῆς ἑαυτῶν κατὰ τὰ πάτρια.

3 "Ἔτη δὲ εἶναι τὰς σπονδὰς πεντήκοντα Ἀθηναίοις καὶ τοῖς ξυμμάχοις τοῖς Ἀθηναίων καὶ Λακεδαιμονίοις καὶ τοῖς ξυμμάχοις τοῖς Λακεδαιμονίων ἀδόλους καὶ ἀβλαβεῖς καὶ κατὰ γῆν καὶ κατὰ θάλασσαν.

4 "Ὅπλα δὲ μὴ ἐξέστω ἐπιφέρειν ἐπὶ πημονῇ μήτε Λακεδαιμονίους καὶ τοὺς ξυμμάχους ἐπ' Ἀθηναίους καὶ τοὺς ξυμμάχους μήτε Ἀθηναίους καὶ τοὺς ξυμμάχους ἐπὶ Λακεδαιμονίους καὶ τοὺς ξυμμάχους, μήτε τέχνῃ μήτε μηχανῇ μηδεμιᾷ. ἢν δέ τι διάφορον ᾖ πρὸς ἀλλήλους, δίκαις χρήσθων καὶ ὅρκοις, καθ' ὅ τι ἂν ξυνθῶνται.

5 "Ἀποδόντων δὲ Ἀθηναίοις Λακεδαιμόνιοι καὶ οἱ ξύμμαχοι Ἀμφίπολιν. ὅσας δὲ πόλεις παρέδοσαν Λακεδαιμόνιοι Ἀθηναίοις ἐξέστω ἀπιέναι ὅποι ἂν βούλωνται αὐτοὺς καὶ τὰ ἑαυτῶν ἔχοντας. τὰς δὲ πόλεις φερούσας τὸν φόρον τὸν ἐπ' Ἀριστείδου αὐτονόμους εἶναι. ὅπλα δὲ μὴ ἐξέστω ἐπιφέρειν Ἀθηναίους μηδὲ τοὺς

---

[1] Kirchhoff's emendation for καὶ ἰέναι of MSS.

34

XVIII. "The Athenians and the Lacedaemonians and their respective allies have concluded a treaty and sworn to it state by state upon the following terms :

1. "With regard to the common sanctuaries,[1] whoever wishes may offer sacrifices and consult the oracles and attend as a deputy according to the customs of the fathers, both by land and sea, without fear.

2. "The precinct and the temple of Apollo at Delphi and the people of Delphi shall be independent, having their own system of taxation and their own courts of justice, both as regards themselves and their own territory, according to the customs of the fathers.

3. "The truce shall be in force for fifty years between the Athenians and their allies and the Lacedaemonians and their allies, without fraud or hurt, both by land and sea.

4. "It shall not be lawful to bear arms with harmful intent, either for the Lacedaemonians and their allies against the Athenians and their allies, or for the Athenians and their allies against the Lacedaemonians and their allies, by any art or device. And if there be any dispute with one another, they shall have recourse to courts and oaths, according as they shall agree.

5. "The Lacedaemonians and their allies shall restore Amphipolis to the Athenians. But in the case of cities delivered by the Lacedaemonians to the Athenians, their inhabitants shall be allowed to go away wherever they wish, having their own possessions ; and these cities, so long as they pay the tribute that was fixed in the time of Aristeides, shall be independent. And it shall not be lawful for the Athenians and their allies, after the ratification of the treaty,

---

[1] With reference especially to Delphi and Olympia.

ξυμμάχους ἐπὶ κακῷ, ἀποδιδόντων τὸν φόρον,
ἐπειδὴ αἱ σπονδαὶ ἐγένοντο. εἰσὶ δὲ ᾿Αργι-
λος, Στάγιρος, ῎Ακανθος, Στῶλος,[1] ῎Ολυνθος,
Σπάρτωλος. ξυμμάχους δ᾿ εἶναι μηδετέρων, μήτε
Λακεδαιμονίων μήτε ᾿Αθηναίων· ἢν δὲ ᾿Αθηναῖοι
πείθωσι τὰς πόλεις, βουλομένας ταύτας ἐξέστω
ξυμμάχους ποιεῖσθαι αὐτοῖς ᾿Αθηναίους.

6   " Μηκυβερναίους δὲ καὶ Σαναίους καὶ Σιγγίους[2]
οἰκεῖν τὰς πόλεις τὰς ἑαυτῶν, καθάπερ ᾿Ολύνθιοι
καὶ ᾿Ακάνθιοι.

7   " ᾿Αποδόντων δὲ ᾿Αθηναίοις Λακεδαιμόνιοι καὶ
οἱ ξύμμαχοι Πάνακτον. ἀποδόντων δὲ καὶ ᾿Αθη-
ναῖοι Λακεδαιμονίοις Κορυφάσιον καὶ Κύθηρα
καὶ Μέθανα[3] καὶ Πτελεὸν καὶ ᾿Αταλάντην,
καὶ τοὺς ἄνδρας ὅσοι εἰσὶ Λακεδαιμονίων ἐν
τῷ δημοσίῳ τῷ ᾿Αθηναίων ἢ ἄλλοθί που ὅσης
᾿Αθηναῖοι ἄρχουσιν ἐν δημοσίῳ καὶ τοὺς ἐν
Σκιώνῃ πολιορκουμένους Πελοποννησίων ἀφεῖναι,
καὶ τοὺς ἄλλους ὅσοι Λακεδαιμονίων ξύμμαχοι ἐν
Σκιώνῃ εἰσὶ καὶ ὅσους Βρασίδας ἐσέπεμψε, καὶ εἴ
τις τῶν ξυμμάχων τῶν Λακεδαιμονίων ἐν ᾿Αθή-
ναις ἐστὶν ἐν τῷ δημοσίῳ ἢ ἄλλοθί που ἧς ᾿Αθη-
ναῖοι ἄρχουσιν ἐν δημοσίῳ. ἀποδόντων δὲ καὶ
Λακεδαιμόνιοι καὶ οἱ ξύμμαχοι οὕστινας ἔχουσιν
᾿Αθηναίων καὶ τῶν ξυμμάχων κατὰ ταὐτά.

8   " Σκιωναίων δὲ καὶ Τορωναίων καὶ Σερμυλιῶν
καὶ εἴ τινα ἄλλην πόλιν ἔχουσιν ᾿Αθηναῖοι, ᾿Αθη-

---

[1] Kirchhoff's correction after inscriptions; MSS. Σκῶλος.
[2] Kirchhoff's correction for Σιγγαίους of the MSS.
[3] Stahl's correction for Μεθώνη of MSS.

36

to bear arms against the cities to their hurt, so long as they pay the tribute. These cities are Argilus,[1] Stagirus,[2] Acanthus,[3] Stolus, Olynthus,[4] Spartolus.[5] These shall be allies neither of the Lacedaemonians nor of the Athenians; but if the Athenians can persuade these cities it shall be lawful for the Athenians to make them, with their own free will and consent, allies to themselves.

6. "The Mecybernaeans and Sanaeans[6] and Sin-gians shall dwell in their own towns on the same terms as the Olynthians and Acanthians.

7. "The Lacedaemonians and their allies shall restore Panactum[7] to the Athenians. The Athenians shall restore to the Lacedaemonians, Coryphasium,[8] Cythera,[9] Methana,[10] Pteleum, and Atalante[11]; also they shall set at liberty the Lacedaemonian captives who are in the public prison at Athens or in public prison anywhere else that the Athenians hold sway, and the men of the Peloponnesus who are being besieged in Scione, and all besides who are allies of the Lacedaemonians in Scione,[12] and those whom Brasidas sent into the place,[13] as likewise any of the allies of the Lacedaemonians who are in the public prison in Athens, or in public prison anywhere else that the Athenians have sway. In like manner the Lacedaemonians and their allies shall restore whomsoever they have of the Athenians and their allies.

8. "As to Scione, Torone,[14] Sermyle, or any other city which the Athenians hold, the Athenians shall

---

[1] cf. iv. ciii. 4.
[2] cf. iv. lxxxviii. 2.
[3] cf. iv. lxxxviii. 1.
[4] cf. i. lviii. 2.
[5] cf. ii. lxxix.
[6] cf. iv. cix. 3, 5.
[7] cf. ch. iii. 5.
[8] cf. iv. iii. 2.
[9] cf. iv. liv.
[10] cf. iv. xlv. 2.
[11] cf. ii. xxxii.
[12] cf. iv. cxxxi.
[13] cf. iv. cxxiii. 4.
[14] cf. ch. iii. 2.

ναίους βουλεύεσθαι περὶ αὐτῶν καὶ τῶν ἄλλων
πόλεων ὅ τι ἂν δοκῇ αὐτοῖς.

9 "῞Ορκους δὲ ποιήσασθαι Ἀθηναίους πρὸς Λακεδαιμονίους καὶ τοὺς ξυμμάχους κατὰ πόλεις·
ὀμνύντων δὲ τὸν ἐπιχώριον ὅρκον ἑκάτεροι τὸν
μέγιστον, ἑπτὰ καὶ δέκα[1] ἑκάστης πόλεως. ὁ
δ᾽ ὅρκος ἔστω ὅδε· ‘Ἐμμενῶ ταῖς ξυνθήκαις καὶ
ταῖς σπονδαῖς ταῖσδε δικαίως καὶ ἀδόλως.’ ἔστω
δὲ Λακεδαιμονίοις καὶ τοῖς ξυμμάχοις κατὰ ταὐτὰ
ὅρκος πρὸς Ἀθηναίους. τὸν δὲ ὅρκον ἀνανεοῦσθαι
κατ᾽ ἐνιαυτὸν ἀμφοτέρους.

10 "Στήλας δὲ στῆσαι Ὀλυμπίασι καὶ Πυθοῖ καὶ
Ἰσθμοῖ καὶ Ἀθήνησιν ἐν πόλει καὶ ἐν Λακεδαίμονι ἐν Ἀμυκλαίῳ.

11 "Εἰ δέ τι ἀμνημονοῦσιν ὁποτεροιοῦν καὶ ὅτου
πέρι, λόγοις δικαίοις χρωμένοις εὔορκον εἶναι
ἀμφοτέροις ταύτῃ μεταθεῖναι ὅπῃ ἂν δοκῇ ἀμφοτέροις, Ἀθηναίοις καὶ Λακεδαιμονίοις.

XIX. "῎Αρχει δὲ τῶν σπονδῶν ἔφορος Πλειστόλας, Ἀρτεμισίου μηνὸς τετάρτῃ φθίνοντος, ἐν
δὲ Ἀθήναις ἄρχων Ἀλκαῖος, Ἐλαφηβολιῶνος
2 μηνὸς ἕκτῃ φθίνοντος. ὤμνυον δὲ οἵδε καὶ ἐσπέν-
δοντο· Λακεδαιμονίων μὲν Πλειστοάναξ, ῎Αγις,[2]
Πλειστόλας, Δαμάγητος, Χίονις, Μεταγένης,
῎Ακανθος, Δάιθος, Ἰσχαγόρας, Φιλοχαρίδας,
Ζευξίδας, ῎Αντιππος, Τέλλις, Ἀλκινάδας, Ἐμ-
πεδίας, Μηνᾶς, Λάφιλος· Ἀθηναίων δὲ οἵδε·
Λάμπων, Ἰσθμιόνικος, Νικίας, Λάχης, Εὐθύδη-

---

[1] ἑπτὰ καὶ δέκα, Classen and Stahl assume that ιζ᾽ has
fallen out of the MSS.

[2] Πλειστοάναξ, ῎Αγις, wanting in all MSS., added from inscriptions.

determine about these and the other cities as they
may think best.

9. "The Athenians shall bind themselves by oaths
with the Lacedaemonians and their allies, city by city ;
and either party shall swear its customary oath in
the form that is most binding,[1] seventeen men repre-
senting each city. The oath shall be as follows : ' I
will abide by this agreement and this treaty, justly
and without deceit.' For the Lacedaemonians and
their allies there shall be an oath, in the same terms,
with the Athenians. And both parties shall renew
the oath year by year.

10. "They shall erect pillars at Olympia, Delphi,
the Isthmus, and on the Acropolis at Athens, and
at Lacedaemon in the temple of Apollo of Amyclae.[2]

11. "If either party forgets anything about any
matter whatsoever, it shall be consistent with their
oath for both, by means of fair discussion, to make a
change at any point where it may seem good to both
parties, the Athenians and the Lacedaemonians.

XIX. "The treaty begins at Lacedaemon in the
ephorate of Pleistolas, on the fourth day from the end
of the month Artemisium, and at Athens in the
archonship of Alcaeus, on the sixth day from the end
of the month Elaphebolion. The following persons
took oaths and ratified the treaty : on behalf of the
Lacedaemonians, Pleistoanax, Agis, Pleistolas, Damagetus, Chionis, Metagenes, Acanthus, Daïthus, Ischagoras, Philocharidas, Zeuxidas, Antippus, Tellis, Al-
cinadas, Empedias, Menas, Laphilus ; on behalf of the
Athenians, Lampon, Isthmionicus, Nicias, Laches,

---

[1] The Athenians, in ratifying treaties, swore by Zeus,
Demeter and Apollo. See Fränkel, *Hermes*, xiii. 460.
Ullrich suggests for Sparta the Dioscuri.

[2] Two or three miles from Sparta.

μος, Προκλῆς, Πυθόδωρος, Ἅγνων, Μυρτίλος,
Θρασυκλῆς, Θεαγένης, Ἀριστοκρατης, Ἰώλκιος,
Τιμοκράτης, Λέων, Λάμαχος, Δημοσθένης."

XX. Αὗται αἱ σπονδαὶ ἐγένοντο τελευτῶντος
τοῦ χειμῶνος ἅμα ἦρι ἐκ Διονυσίων εὐθὺς τῶν
ἀστικῶν, αὐτόδεκα ἐτῶν διελθόντων καὶ ἡμερῶν
ὀλίγων παρενεγκουσῶν ἢ ὡς τὸ πρῶτον ἡ ἐσβολὴ
ἐς τὴν Ἀττικὴν καὶ ἡ ἀρχὴ τοῦ πολέμου τοῦδε
2 ἐγένετο. σκοπείτω δέ τις κατὰ τοὺς χρόνους καὶ μὴ
τῶν ἑκασταχοῦ ἢ ἀρχόντων ἢ ἀπὸ τιμῆς τινος ἐς
τὰ προγεγενημένα σημαινόντων[1] τὴν ἀπαρίθμησιν
τῶν ὀνομάτων πιστεύσας[2] μᾶλλον. οὐ γὰρ ἀκριβές
ἐστιν, οἷς καὶ ἀρχομένοις καὶ μεσοῦσι καὶ ὅπως
3 ἔτυχέ τῳ ἐπεγένετό τι. κατὰ θέρη δὲ καὶ χειμῶνας ἀριθμῶν, ὥσπερ γέγραπται, εὑρήσει, ἐξ
ἡμισείας ἑκατέρου τοῦ ἐνιαυτοῦ τὴν δύναμιν
ἔχοντος, δέκα μὲν θέρη, ἴσους δὲ χειμῶνας τῷ
πρώτῳ πολέμῳ τῷδε γεγενημένους.

XXI. Λακεδαιμόνιοι δέ (ἔλαχον γὰρ πρότεροι
ἀποδιδόναι ἃ εἶχον) τούς τε ἄνδρας εὐθὺς τοὺς
παρὰ σφίσιν αἰχμαλώτους ἀφίεσαν καὶ πέμψαντες ἐς τὰ ἐπὶ Θράκης πρέσβεις Ἰσχαγόραν καὶ
Μηνᾶν καὶ Φιλοχαρίδαν ἐκέλευον τὸν Κλεαρίδαν
τὴν Ἀμφίπολιν παραδιδόναι τοῖς Ἀθηναίοις καὶ
τοὺς ἄλλους τὰς σπονδάς, ὡς εἴρητο ἑκάστοις,
2 δέχεσθαι. οἱ δ᾽ οὐκ ἤθελον, νομίζοντες οὐκ ἐπι-

---

[1] ἐς τὰ . . . σημαινόντων, the order is according to Arnold's
suggestion ; in MSS. these words come after ὀνομάτων.

[2] Hude corrects to ποιήσας.

Euthydemus, Procles, Pythodorus, Hagnon, Myrtilus, Thrasycles, Theagenes, Aristocrates, Iolcius, Timocrates, Leon, Lamachus, Demosthenes."

XX. This treaty was concluded at the end of the winter and the opening of spring immediately after the City Dionysia.[1] Just ten years and a few days had passed since the first invasion of Attica and the beginning of this war. But one must reckon according to the natural divisions of the year, not according to the catalogue of the names of officials in each place, be they archons or others who in consequence of some office mark the dates for past events, in the belief that this method is more to be trusted; for it is really inexact, since an event may have occurred in the beginning of their term of office, or in the middle, or at any other point as it happened. But reckoning by summers and winters, as has been done in this history—inasmuch as each of these divisions is to be reckoned as half a year—it will be found that there have been ten summers and as many winters in this first war.[2]

XXI. Now since the lot fell to the Lacedaemonians to make restoration first of the positions they held, they straightway set at liberty the prisoners of war that were in their hands, and sending Ischagoras, Menas, and Philocharidas as envoys to Thrace ordered Clearidas to give up Amphipolis to the Athenians, and the rest of the allies to accept the treaty, as it had been prescribed for each. But the latter were unwilling to do so, as they thought that the terms were unfavourable to them;

[1] The City or Greater Dionysia began before the vernal equinox and lasted several days.

[2] Commonly referred to by the Attic orators as the Archidamian War. See Introduction, vol. i., p. xiii.

τηδείας εἶναι· οὐδὲ ὁ Κλεαρίδας παρέδωκε τὴν
πόλιν χαριζόμενος τοῖς Χαλκιδεῦσι, λέγων ὡς οὐ
3 δυνατὸς εἴη κατὰ βίᾳ ἐκείνων παραδιδόναι. ἐλθὼν δὲ
αὐτὸς κατὰ τάχος μετὰ πρέσβεων αὐτόθεν ἀπο-
λογησόμενός τε ἐς τὴν Λακεδαίμονα, ἢν κατηγο-
ρῶσιν οἱ περὶ τὸν Ἰσχαγόραν ὅτι οὐκ ἐπείθετο,
καὶ ἅμα βουλόμενος εἰδέναι εἰ ἔτι μετακινητὴ εἴη
ἡ ὁμολογία, ἐπειδὴ ηὗρε κατειλημμένους,[1] αὐτὸς
μὲν πάλιν πεμπόντων τῶν Λακεδαιμονίων καὶ
κελευόντων μάλιστα μὲν καὶ τὸ χωρίον παραδοῦναι, εἰ δὲ μή, ὁπόσοι Πελοποννησίων ἔνεισιν
ἐξαγαγεῖν, κατὰ τάχος ἐπορεύετο.

XXII. Οἱ δὲ ξύμμαχοι ἐν τῇ Λακεδαίμονι
αὐτοὶ[2] ἔτι ἔτυχον ὄντες, καὶ αὐτῶν τοὺς μὴ
δεξαμένους τὰς σπονδὰς ἐκέλευον οἱ Λακεδαιμόνιοι ποιεῖσθαι. οἱ δὲ τῇ αὐτῇ προφάσει, ἧπερ
καὶ τὸ πρῶτον ἀπεώσαντο, οὐκ ἔφασαν δέξεσθαι,
2 ἢν μή τινας δικαιοτέρας τούτων ποιῶνται. ὡς δ᾽
αὐτῶν οὐκ ἐσήκουον, ἐκείνους μὲν ἀπέπεμψαν,
αὐτοὶ δὲ πρὸς τοὺς Ἀθηναίους ξυμμαχίαν ἐποιοῦντο, νομίζοντες ἥκιστα ἂν σφίσι τούς τε Ἀργείους,[3] ἐπειδὴ οὐκ ἤθελον Ἀμπελίδου καὶ Λίχου
ἐλθόντων ἐπισπένδεσθαι, νομίσαντες αὐτοὺς ἄνευ
Ἀθηναίων οὐ δεινοὺς εἶναι καὶ τὴν ἄλλην Πελοπόννησον μάλιστ᾽ ἂν ἡσυχάζειν· πρὸς γὰρ ἂν

---

[1] Krüger's correction for κατειλημμένας of the MSS.
[2] αὐτοῦ, Krüger's correction for αὐτοί of the MSS., is
adopted by Hude. ἔτι was added by Stahl.
[3] Hude inserts ἐπιτίθεσθαι after Ἀργείους, with Madvig.

---

[1] The narrative recurs to the end of ch. xvii.
[2] cf. ch. xvii. (end).

and Clearidas, to oblige the Chalcidians, did not give up Amphipolis, saying that he was unable to give it up against their will. And he hastened in person, with envoys from the place, to Lacedaemon, in order to defend himself in case Ischagoras and his colleagues should accuse him of disobedience ; and he wished also to learn whether the agreement could still be changed. But when he found that they were already bound by oath, he himself went back again in haste, with orders from the Lacedaemonians to give up Amphipolis if possible, or at all events to fetch away whatsoever Peloponnesians were in it.

XXII. The representatives of the allies [1] happened to be still present in person at Lacedaemon, and as many of them as had not accepted the treaty were ordered by the Lacedaemonians to adopt it. But they, on the same pretext for which they had at first [2] rejected it, still refused to accept it unless a fairer treaty were made. Since, then, they would not hearken to them, the Lacedaemonians dismissed them, and proceeded to make an alliance with the Athenians by themselves, thinking that the Argives would by no means make an alliance with Sparta— since they had refused to renew the treaty with them when Ampelidas and Lichas went to Argos—and believing that they would not be dangerous to them without the Athenians, and that the rest of the Peloponnesians would be most likely to remain quiet; [3] for, had it been possible, they might have gone over

---

[3] The text is surely not in order and numerous emendations have been offered. The rendering above assumes ξυμμαχίαν ποιεῖσθαι as predicate of νομίζοντες, and adds καί, before νομίσαντες, as correlative to τε—or, possibly, νομίσαντες may be causal.

3 τοὺς Ἀθηναίους, εἰ ἐξῆν, χωρεῖν. παρόντων οὖν
πρέσβεων ἀπὸ τῶν Ἀθηναίων καὶ γενομένων
λόγων ξυνέβησαν, καὶ ἐγένοντο ὅρκοι καὶ ξυμμαχία ἥδε·

XXIII. "Κατὰ τάδε ξύμμαχοι ἔσονται Ἀθηναῖοι καὶ[1] Λακεδαιμόνιοι πεντήκοντα ἔτη·

"Ἢν[2] τινες ἴωσιν ἐς τὴν γῆν πολέμιοι τὴν Λακεδαιμονίων καὶ κακῶς ποιῶσι Λακεδαιμονίους, ὠφελεῖν Ἀθηναίους Λακεδαιμονίους τρόπῳ ὁποίῳ ἂν
δύνωνται ἰσχυροτάτῳ κατὰ τὸ δυνατόν· ἢν δὲ
δῃώσαντες οἴχωνται, πολεμίαν εἶναι ταύτην τὴν
πόλιν Λακεδαιμονίοις καὶ Ἀθηναίοις καὶ κακῶς
πάσχειν ὑπὸ ἀμφοτέρων, καταλύειν δὲ ἅμα ἄμφω
τὼ πόλει. ταῦτα δ᾽ εἶναι δικαίως καὶ προθύμως
καὶ ἀδόλως.

2 "Καὶ ἤν τινες ἐς τὴν Ἀθηναίων γῆν ἴωσι πολέμιοι καὶ κακῶς ποιῶσιν Ἀθηναίους, ὠφελεῖν Λακεδαιμονίους Ἀθηναίους[3] τρόπῳ ὅτῳ ἂν δύνωνται
ἰσχυροτάτῳ κατὰ τὸ δυνατόν. ἢν δὲ δῃώσαντες
οἴχωνται, πολεμίαν εἶναι ταύτην τὴν πόλιν
Λακεδαιμονίοις καὶ Ἀθηναίοις καὶ κακῶς πάσχειν
ὑπ᾽ ἀμφοτέρων, καταλύειν δὲ ἅμα ἄμφω τὼ
πόλει. ταῦτα δ᾽ εἶναι δικαίως καὶ προθύμως
καὶ ἀδόλως.

3 "Ἢν δὲ ἡ δουλεία ἐπανιστῆται, ἐπικουρεῖν
Ἀθηναίους Λακεδαιμονίοις παντὶ σθένει κατὰ
τὸ δυνατόν.

4 "Ὀμοῦνται δὲ ταῦτα οἵπερ καὶ τὰς ἄλλας

---

[1] Ἀθηναῖοι καί, wanting in MSS., added by Krüger.
[2] δέ, after ἤν, deleted by Boehme.
[3] Ἀθηναίους added by Ullrich.

to the Athenians.[1] Accordingly since envoys were present from the Athenians, a conference was held and they came to an agreement, and oaths were sworn and an alliance made on the following terms:

XXIII. "The Lacedaemonians and Athenians shall be allies for fifty years on the following conditions:

1. "If any enemy invade the territory of the Lacedaemonians and be doing them harm, the Athenians shall help the Lacedaemonians in whatever way they can most effectively, with all their might; but if the enemy, after ravaging the country, shall have departed, that city shall be the enemy of the Lacedaemonians and Athenians, and shall suffer at the hands of both, and neither city shall make peace with it without the other. These conditions shall be observed honestly, zealously, and without fraud.

2. "If any enemy invade the territory of the Athenians and be doing them harm, the Lacedaemonians shall help the Athenians in whatever way they can most effectively, with all their might; but if the enemy, after ravaging the country, shall have departed, that city shall be the enemy of the Lacedaemonians and Athenians, and shall suffer at the hands of both, and neither city shall make peace with it without the other. These conditions shall be observed honestly, zealously, and without fraud.

3. "If there shall be an insurrection of slaves, the Athenians shall aid the Lacedaemonians with all their might, to the utmost of their power.

4. "These articles shall be sworn to by the same

[1] *i.e.* if there should be no treaty between Athens and Sparta, any dissatisfied state in the Peloponnesus might join the Athenian alliance and cause trouble. This danger would be removed by entering into the treaty, and also Argos, whose relations continued hostile, would be isolated.

σπονδὰς ὤμνυον ἑκατέρων. ἀνανεοῦσθαι δὲ κατ᾽
ἐνιαυτὸν Λακεδαιμονίους μὲν ἰόντας ἐς ᾿Αθήνας
πρὸς τὰ Διονύσια, ᾿Αθηναίους δὲ ἰόντας ἐς Λακεδαίμονα πρὸς τὰ ῾Υακίνθια.

5 "Στήλην δὲ ἑκατέρους στῆσαι, τὴν μὲν ἐν
Λακεδαίμονι παρ᾽ ᾿Απόλλωνι ἐν ᾿Αμυκλαίῳ, τὴν
δὲ ἐν ᾿Αθήναις ἐν πόλει παρ᾽ ᾿Αθηναίᾳ.

6 "῍Ην δέ τι δοκῇ Λακεδαιμονίοις καὶ ᾿Αθηναίοις
προσθεῖναι καὶ ἀφελεῖν περὶ τῆς ξυμμαχίας, ὅ
τι ἂν δοκῇ, εὔορκον ἀμφοτέροις εἶναι.

XXIV. "Τὸν δὲ ὅρκον ὤμνυον Λακεδαιμονίων
μὲν οἵδε· Πλειστοάναξ, ῍Αγις, Πλειστόλας, Δα-
μάγητος, Χίονις, Μεταγένης, ῍Ακανθος, Δάιθος,
᾿Ισχαγόρας, Φιλοχαρίδας, Ζευξίδας, ῍Αντιππος,
᾿Αλκινάδας, Τέλλις, ᾿Εμπεδίας, Μηνᾶς, Λάφιλος·
᾿Αθηναίων δὲ Λάμπων, ᾿Ισθμιόνικος, Λάχης,
Νικίας, Εὐθύδημος, Προκλῆς, Πυθόδωρος, ῍Αγ-
νων, Μυρτίλος, Θρασυκλῆς, Θεαγένης, ᾿Αριστο-
κράτης, ᾿Ιώλκιος, Τιμοκράτης, Λέων, Λάμαχος,
Δημοσθένης."

2 Αὕτη ἡ ξυμμαχία ἐγένετο μετὰ τὰς σπονδὰς
οὐ πολλῷ ὕστερον, καὶ τοὺς ἄνδρας τοὺς ἐκ τῆς
νήσου ἀπέδοσαν οἱ ᾿Αθηναῖοι τοῖς Λακεδαιμονίοις,
καὶ τὸ θέρος ἦρχε τοῦ ἑνδεκάτου ἔτους. ταῦτα
δὲ τὰ δέκα ἔτη ὁ πρῶτος πόλεμος ξυνεχῶς
γενόμενος γέγραπται.

XXV. Μετὰ δὲ τὰς σπονδὰς καὶ τὴν ξυμμαχίαν
τῶν Λακεδαιμονίων καὶ τῶν ᾿Αθηναίων, αἳ ἐγένοντο μετὰ τὸν δεκέτη πόλεμον ἐπὶ Πλειστόλα
μὲν ἐν Λακεδαίμονι ἐφόρου, ᾿Αλκαίου δ᾽ ἄρχοντος

---

[1] The City Dionysia; cf. ch. xx. 1.

persons who swore to the other treaty on both sides.
They shall be renewed every year, the Lacedaemonians going to Athens at the Dionysia,[1] the Athenians to Lacedaemon at the Hyacinthia.[2]

5. "Each party shall erect a pillar, that in Lacedaemon by the temple of Apollo of Amyclae, that at
Athens on the Acropolis by the temple of Athena.

6. "If it shall seem good to the Lacedaemonians
and Athenians to add or take away anything pertaining to the alliance, it shall be consistent with
the oaths of both to do whatever may seem good
to both.

XXIV. "For the Lacedaemonians the following
persons took the oath : Pleistoanax, Agis, Pleistolas,
Damagetus, Chionis, Metagenes, Acanthus, Daïthus,
Ischagoras, Philocharidas, Zeuxidas, Antippus, Alci-
nadas, Tellis, Empedias, Menas, Laphilus ; for the
Athenians, Lampon, Isthmionicus, Laches, Nicias,
Euthydemus, Procles, Pythodorus, Hagnon, Myrti-
lus, Thrasycles, Theagenes, Aristocrates, Iolcius,
Timocrates, Leon, Lamachus, Demosthenes."

This alliance was made not long after the treaty,
and the Athenians restored to the Lacedaemonians
the captives taken on the island ; and thus began the
summer of the eleventh year. During these ten
years the first war, of which the history has now been
written, was waged continuously.

XXV. After the treaty and the alliance between
the Lacedaemonians and Athenians, which were
concluded at the end of the ten years' war, in the
ephorate of Pleistolas at Lacedaemon and the archonship of Alcaeus at Athens, those who accepted these

[2] The festival of Apollo of Amyclae in the month Hya-
cinthius (Attic Hecatombaion).

Ἀθήνησι, τοῖς μὲν δεξαμένοις αὐτὰς εἰρήνη ἦν,
οἱ δὲ Κορίνθιοι καὶ τῶν ἐν Πελοποννήσῳ πόλεων
τινες διεκίνουν τὰ πεπραγμένα· καὶ εὐθὺς ἄλλη [1]
ταραχὴ καθίστατο τῶν ξυμμάχων πρὸς τὴν Λακε-
2 δαίμονα, καὶ ἅμα καὶ τοῖς Ἀθηναίοις οἱ Λακεδαιμόνιοι προϊόντος τοῦ χρόνου ὕποπτοι ἐγένοντο
ἔστιν ἐν οἷς οὐ ποιοῦντες ἐκ τῶν ξυγκειμένων
3 ἃ εἴρητο. καὶ ἐπὶ ἓξ ἔτη μὲν καὶ δέκα μῆνας
ἀπέσχοντο μὴ ἐπὶ τὴν ἑκατέρων γῆν στρατεῦσαι,
ἔξωθεν δὲ μετ' ἀνοκωχῆς οὐ βεβαίου ἔβλαπτον
ἀλλήλους τὰ μάλιστα· ἔπειτα μέντοι καὶ ἀναγ-
κασθέντες λῦσαι τὰς μετὰ τὰ δέκα ἔτη σπονδὰς
αὖθις ἐς πόλεμον φανερὸν κατέστησαν.

XXVI. Γέγραφε δὲ καὶ ταῦτα ὁ αὐτὸς Θουκυδίδης Ἀθηναῖος ἑξῆς, ὡς ἕκαστα ἐγένετο, κατὰ
θέρη καὶ χειμῶνας, μέχρι οὗ τήν τε ἀρχὴν κατέ-
παυσαν τῶν Ἀθηναίων Λακεδαιμόνιοι καὶ οἱ
ξύμμαχοι καὶ τὰ μακρὰ τείχη καὶ τὸν Πειραιᾶ
κατέλαβον. ἔτη δὲ ἐς τοῦτο τὰ ξύμπαντα ἐγέ-
2 νοντο τῷ πολέμῳ ἑπτὰ καὶ εἴκοσι. καὶ τὴν διὰ
μέσου ξύμβασιν εἴ τις μὴ ἀξιώσει πόλεμον
νομίζειν, οὐκ ὀρθῶς δικαιώσει. τοῖς τε γὰρ ἔργοις
ὡς διῄρηται ἀθρείτω καὶ εὑρήσει οὐκ εἰκὸς ὂν
εἰρήνην αὐτὴν κριθῆναι, ἐν ᾗ οὔτε ἀπέδοσαν
πάντα οὔτ' ἀπεδέξαντο ἃ ξυνέθεντο, ἔξω τε
τούτων πρὸς τὸν Μαντινικὸν καὶ Ἐπιδαύριον

---

[1] τε, after ἄλλη, inserted by Hude after Stahl.

---

[1] This chapter forms a kind of second introduction, and
was probably written after the author enlarged his plan
from a history of the first ten years to that of the whole
war.

were at peace; but the Corinthians and some of the
cities in the Peloponnesus attempted to disturb the
agreements, and at once other trouble also began between Lacedaemon and her allies. At the same
time, too, the Lacedaemonians, as time went on,
incurred the suspicion of the Athenians, by not
acting in some matters in accordance with the articles
of the agreement. For six years and ten months the
two powers abstained from invading each other's
territory; in other regions, however, there was only
an unstable cessation of arms and they kept on
doing each other the greatest possible damage. But
at last they were forced to break the treaty which had
been concluded after the first ten years, and again
engaged in open war.

XXVI. ¹ The history of these events, also, has been
written by the same Thucydides, an Athenian, in the
chronological order of events, by summers and winters, up to the time when the Lacedaemonians and
their allies put an end to the dominion of the Athenians and took the Long Walls and Peiraeus.² Up to
that event the war lasted twenty-seven years in all;
and if anyone shall not deem it proper to include the
intervening truce in the war, he will not judge
aright. For let him but look at the question in the
light of the facts as they have been set forth ³ and he
will find that that can not fitly be judged a state of
peace in which neither party restored or received all
that had been agreed upon. And, apart from that,
there were violations of the treaty on both sides in

² According to Plutarch, *Lysander* 15, this took place in
April 404.
³ Or, taking ἡ διὰ μέσου ξύμβασις as subject of διῄρηται,
"For if he will but observe how the truce was interrupted
by actual military operations"

49

πόλεμον καὶ ἐς ἄλλα ἀμφοτέροις ἁμαρτήματα
ἐγένοντο, καὶ οἱ ἐπὶ Θράκης ξύμμαχοι οὐδὲν
ἧσσον πολέμιοι ἦσαν, Βοιωτοί τε ἐκεχειρίαν
3 δεχήμερον ἦγον. ὥστε ξὺν τῷ πρώτῳ πολέμῳ
τῷ δεκέτει καὶ τῇ μετ᾽ αὐτὸν ὑπόπτῳ ἀνοκωχῇ
καὶ τῷ ὕστερον ἐξ αὐτῆς πολέμῳ εὑρήσει τις
τοσαῦτα ἔτη, λογιζόμενος κατὰ τοὺς χρόνους, καὶ
ἡμέρας οὐ πολλὰς παρενεγκούσας, καὶ τοῖς ἀπὸ
χρησμῶν τι ἰσχυρισαμένοις μόνον δὴ τοῦτο
4 ἐχυρῶς ξυμβάν. αἰεὶ γὰρ ἔγωγε μέμνημαι, καὶ
ἀρχομένου τοῦ πολέμου καὶ μέχρι οὗ ἐτελεύτησε,
προφερόμενον ὑπὸ πολλῶν ὅτι τρὶς ἐννέα ἔτη
5 δέοι γενέσθαι αὐτόν. ἐπεβίων δὲ διὰ παντὸς
αὐτοῦ, αἰσθανόμενός τε τῇ ἡλικίᾳ καὶ προσέχων
τὴν γνώμην ὅπως ἀκριβές τι εἴσομαι· καὶ ξυνέβη
μοι φεύγειν τὴν ἐμαυτοῦ ἔτη εἴκοσι μετὰ τὴν ἐς
Ἀμφίπολιν στρατηγίαν, καὶ γενομένῳ παρ᾽ ἀμφοτέροις τοῖς πράγμασι, καὶ οὐχ ἧσσον τοῖς Πελοποννησίων διὰ τὴν φυγήν, καθ᾽ ἡσυχίαν τι αὐτῶν
6 μᾶλλον αἰσθέσθαι. τὴν οὖν μετὰ τὰ δέκα ἔτη
διαφοράν τε καὶ ξύγχυσιν τῶν σπονδῶν καὶ τὰ
ἔπειτα ὡς ἐπολεμήθη ἐξηγήσομαι.

XXVII. Ἐπειδὴ γὰρ αἱ πεντηκοντούτεις σπονδαὶ ἐγένοντο καὶ ὕστερον ἡ ξυμμαχία, καὶ αἱ ἀπὸ
τῆς Πελοποννήσου πρεσβεῖαι, αἵπερ παρεκλή-
θησαν ἐς αὐτά, ἀνεχώρουν ἐκ τῆς Λακεδαίμονος.
2 καὶ οἱ μὲν ἄλλοι ἐπ᾽ οἴκου ἀπῆλθον, Κορίνθιοι δὲ
ἐς Ἄργος τραπόμενοι πρῶτον λόγους ποιοῦνται

the Mantinean and Epidaurian wars,[1] as well as in other matters; the allies in Thrace, too, were no less hostile to Athens than before, and the Boeotians observed a truce which had to be renewed every ten days. So that, including the first ten-years' war, the suspicious truce succeeding that, and the war which followed the truce, one will find that, reckoning according to natural seasons, there were just so many years as I have stated, and some few days over. He will also find, in the case of those who have made any assertion in reliance upon oracles, that this fact alone proved true; for always, as I remember, from the beginning of the war until its close, it was said by many that it was fated to last thrice nine years. I lived through the whole war, being of an age to form judgments, and followed it with close attention, so as to acquire accurate information. It befell me also to be banished from my own country for twenty years after my command at Amphipolis,[2] and being conversant with affairs on both sides, especially with those of the Peloponnesians by reason of my banishment, to gain at my leisure a better acquaintance with the course of events. The difference, then, which arose after the ten years, and the breaking of the truce and the subsequent hostilities, I will now proceed to relate.

XXVII. After the conclusion of the fifty years' treaty and the subsequent alliance, the embassies from the Peloponnesus, which had been summoned for this business, withdrew from Lacedaemon. The rest went home; but the Corinthians proceeded first to Argos and entered into communication with certain

---

[1] For these wars, see chs. xxxiii. f. and liii. f.
[2] cf. IV. civ. 4.

πρός τινας τῶν ἐν τέλει ὄντων Ἀργείων ὡς χρη,
ἐπειδὴ Λακεδαιμόνιοι οὐκ ἐπ' ἀγαθῷ ἀλλ' ἐπὶ
καταδουλώσει τῆς Πελοποννήσου σπονδὰς καὶ
ξυμμαχίαν πρὸς Ἀθηναίους τοὺς πρὶν ἐχθίστους
πεποίηνται, ὁρᾶν τοὺς Ἀργείους ὅπως σωθήσεται
ἡ Πελοπόννησος, καὶ ψηφίσασθαι τὴν βουλομένην πόλιν τῶν Ἑλλήνων, ἥτις αὐτόνομός
τέ ἐστι καὶ δίκας ἴσας καὶ ὁμοίας δίδωσι, πρὸς
Ἀργείους ξυμμαχίαν ποιεῖσθαι ὥστε τῇ ἀλλήλων
ἐπιμαχεῖν, ἀποδεῖξαι δὲ ἄνδρας ὀλίγους ἀρχὴν
αὐτοκράτορας καὶ μὴ πρὸς τὸν δῆμον τοὺς λόγους
εἶναι, τοῦ μὴ καταφανεῖς γίγνεσθαι τοὺς μὴ
πείσαντας τὸ πλῆθος. ἔφασαν δὲ πολλοὺς
3 προσχωρήσεσθαι μίσει τῶν Λακεδαιμονίων. καὶ
οἱ μὲν Κορίνθιοι διδάξαντες ταῦτα ἀνεχώρησαν
ἐπ' οἴκου.

XXVIII. Οἱ δὲ τῶν Ἀργείων ἄνδρες ἀκούσαντες ἐπειδὴ ἀνήνεγκαν τοὺς λόγους ἔς τε τὰς
ἀρχὰς καὶ τὸν δῆμον, ἐψηφίσαντο Ἀργεῖοι, καὶ
ἄνδρας εἵλοντο δώδεκα πρὸς οὓς τὸν βουλόμενον
τῶν Ἑλλήνων ξυμμαχίαν ποιεῖσθαι πλὴν Ἀθηναίων καὶ Λακεδαιμονίων· τούτων δὲ μηδετέροις
ἐξεῖναι ἄνευ τοῦ δήμου τοῦ Ἀργείων σπείσασθαι.
2 ἐδέξαντό τε ταῦτα οἱ Ἀργεῖοι μᾶλλον, ὁρῶντες τόν
τε Λακεδαιμονίων σφίσι πόλεμον ἐσόμενον (ἐπ'
ἐξόδῳ γὰρ πρὸς αὐτοὺς αἱ σπονδαὶ ἦσαν) καὶ
ἅμα ἐλπίσαντες τῆς Πελοποννήσου ἡγήσεσθαι.
κατὰ γὰρ τὸν χρόνον τοῦτον ἥ τε Λακεδαίμων
μάλιστα δὴ κακῶς ἤκουσε καὶ ὑπερώφθη διὰ τὰς

of the Argive magistrates, saying that, since the Lacedaemonians had made a treaty and alliance with the Athenians, hitherto their bitterest enemies, not for the good of the Peloponnesus but for its enslavement, the Argives ought to be considering how the Peloponnesus could be saved; and should pass a decree, that any Hellenic city which is autonomous and offers settlement of disputes by fair and impartial trials, may, if it so wishes, make an alliance with the Argives for mutual defence of their territories; and that they should appoint a few men with absolutely full powers, and not discuss matters before the people, so that any who may fail to persuade the popular assembly may not become known to the Lacedaemonians. And they asserted that many would join them through hatred of the Lacedaemonians. The Corinthians, then, having suggested these things, went home.

XXVIII. The Argive magistrates, on hearing the proposals, reported them to their government and people, and the Argives passed the decree and chose twelve men with whom any of the Hellenes who pleased might conclude an alliance, except the Athenians and the Lacedaemonians; neither of these should be allowed to make a treaty with Argos without the express consent of the Argive people. These proposals the Argives accepted the more readily, in the first place because they saw that they should have war with the Lacedaemonians—for the treaty with them was on the point of expiring—and, moreover, because they had hoped to secure the hegemony of the Peloponnesus. For at this time Lacedaemon had fallen into very ill repute and was despised on account of its misfortunes, while

ξυμφοράς, οἵ τε Ἀργεῖοι ἄριστα ἔσχον τοῖς
πᾶσιν, οὐ ξυναράμενοι τοῦ Ἀττικοῦ πολέμου,
ἀμφοτέροις δὲ μᾶλλον ἔνσπονδοι ὄντες ἐκκαρπω-
σάμενοι. οἱ μὲν οὖν Ἀργεῖοι οὕτως ἐς τὴν ξυμμαχίαν προσεδέχοντο τοὺς ἐθέλοντας τῶν
Ἑλλήνων.

XXIX. Μαντινῆς δ' αὐτοῖς καὶ οἱ ξύμμαχοι
αὐτῶν πρῶτοι προσεχώρησαν δεδιότες τοὺς
Λακεδαιμονίους. τοῖς γὰρ Μαντινεῦσι μέρος τι
τῆς Ἀρκαδίας κατέστραπτο ὑπήκοον, ἔτι τοῦ
πρὸς Ἀθηναίους πολέμου ὄντος, καὶ ἐνόμιζον οὐ
περιόψεσθαι σφᾶς τοὺς Λακεδαιμονίους ἄρχειν,
ἐπειδὴ καὶ σχολὴν ἦγον· ὥστε ἄσμενοι πρὸς τοὺς
Ἀργείους ἐτράποντο, πόλιν τε μεγάλην νομίζοντες
καὶ Λακεδαιμονίοις αἰεὶ διάφορον δημοκρατου-
2 μένην τε ὥσπερ καὶ αὐτοί. ἀποστάντων δὲ τῶν
Μαντινέων καὶ ἡ ἄλλη Πελοπόννησος ἐς θροῦν
καθίστατο ὡς καὶ σφίσι ποιητέον τοῦτο, νομίσαντες πλέον τέ τι εἰδότας μεταστῆναι αὐτοὺς
καὶ τοὺς Λακεδαιμονίους ἅμα δι' ὀργῆς ἔχοντες ἐν
ἄλλοις τε καὶ ὅτι ἐν ταῖς σπονδαῖς ταῖς Ἀττικαῖς
ἐγέγραπτο εὔορκον εἶναι προσθεῖναι καὶ ἀφελεῖν
ὅ τι ἂν ἀμφοῖν τοῖν πόλεοιν δοκῇ, Λακεδαιμονίοις
3 καὶ Ἀθηναίοις. τοῦτο γὰρ τὸ γράμμα μάλιστα
τὴν Πελοπόννησον διεθορύβει καὶ ἐς ὑποψίαν
καθίστη μὴ μετὰ Ἀθηναίων σφᾶς βούλωνται
Λακεδαιμόνιοι δουλώσασθαι· δίκαιον γὰρ εἶναι
πᾶσι τοῖς ξυμμάχοις γεγράφθαι τὴν μετάθεσιν.

the Argives had attained an excellent position in all respects, having had no part of the burden of the war with Athens, but rather, as they were at peace with both parties, having reaped a harvest from it. Thus the Argives were ready to receive into their alliance any of the Hellenes that were so inclined.

XXIX. The Mantineans and their allies were the first to join them, through fear of the Lacedaemonians. For a part of Arcadia had been reduced to subjection by the Mantineans, while the war with the Athenians was still going on, and they thought that the Lacedaemonians, now that they had leisure, would not suffer them to retain their sovereignty. So they turned gladly to Argos, regarding it as a powerful state, one always at variance with the Lacedaemonians, and under a democratic form of government like themselves. And when the Mantineans had revolted, the rest of the Peloponnesus also began to mutter that they must do the like, thinking that the Mantineans had changed sides because they possessed some superior knowledge. At the same time they were angry with the Lacedaemonians on other grounds, and especially because it was written in the treaty with Athens that it would be consistent with their oaths to add or take away whatever shall seem good to both states, that is, to the Lacedaemonians and Athenians. For it was this article especially that was disturbing the Peloponnesus far and wide and causing suspicion that the Lacedaemonians wished in concert with the Athenians to reduce them all to slavery; for it would have been just, they thought, that the clause should have given the power to alter the articles to all the allies. And

4 ὥστε φοβούμενοι οἱ πολλοὶ ὥρμηντο πρὸς τοὺς
᾿Αργείους καὶ αὐτοὶ ἕκαστοι ξυμμαχίαν ποιεῖσθαι.

XXX. Λακεδαιμόνιοι δὲ αἰσθόμενοι τὸν θροῦν
τοῦτον ἐν τῇ Πελοποννήσῳ καθεστῶτα καὶ τοὺς
Κορινθίους διδασκάλους τε γενομένους καὶ αὐτοὺς
μέλλοντας σπείσασθαι πρὸς τὸ Ἄργος, πέμπουσι
πρέσβεις ἐς τὴν Κόρινθον, βουλόμενοι προκατα-
λαβεῖν τὸ μέλλον, καὶ ᾐτιῶντο τήν τε ἐσήγησιν
τοῦ παντὸς καὶ εἰ ᾿Αργείοις σφῶν ἀποστάντες
ξύμμαχοι ἔσονται, παραβήσεσθαί τε ἔφασαν
αὐτοὺς τοὺς ὅρκους, καὶ ἤδη ἀδικεῖν ὅτι οὐ
δέχονται τὰς ᾿Αθηναίων σπονδάς, εἰρημένον κύριον
εἶναι ὅ τι ἂν τὸ πλῆθος τῶν ξυμμάχων ψηφίσηται,
2 ἢν μή τι θεῶν ἢ ἡρώων κώλυμα ᾖ.   Κορίνθιοι δὲ
παρόντων σφίσι τῶν ξυμμάχων, ὅσοι οὐδ᾽ αὐτοὶ
ἐδέξαντο τὰς σπονδάς (παρεκάλεσαν δὲ αὐτοὺς
αὐτοὶ πρότερον), ἀντέλεγον τοῖς Λακεδαιμονίοις, ἃ
μὲν ἠδικοῦντο, οὐ δηλοῦντες ἄντικρυς, ὅτι οὔτε
Σόλλιον σφίσιν ἀπέλαβον παρ᾽ ᾿Αθηναίων οὔτε
᾿Ανακτόριον, εἴ τέ τι ἄλλο ἐνόμιζον ἐλασσοῦσθαι,
πρόσχημα δὲ ποιούμενοι τοὺς ἐπὶ Θρᾴκης μὴ προ-
δώσειν· ὀμόσαι γὰρ αὐτοῖς ὅρκους ἰδίᾳ τε, ὅτε
μετὰ Ποτειδεατῶν τὸ πρῶτον ἀφίσταντο, καὶ
3 ἄλλους ὕστερον.   οὔκουν παραβαίνειν τοὺς τῶν
ξυμμάχων ὅρκους ἔφασαν οὐκ ἐσιόντες ἐς τὰς τῶν

---

[1] In Acarnania, taken by the Athenians in the first year
of the war (II. xxx. 1).

so most of them were afraid and were eager on their own part also to make a separate alliance with the Argives.

XXX. The Lacedaemonians, aware of this murmuring that was going on in the Peloponnesus, and that the Corinthians had been the instigators in this matter and were themselves going to make a treaty with Argos, sent envoys to Corinth, wishing to forestall what was about to happen. And they charged them with starting the whole movement, and said that if they should revolt from them and become allies of the Argives, they would be violating the explicit terms of their oaths, and indeed were already doing wrong in not accepting the treaty with the Athenians, inasmuch as it had been declared that whatever the majority of the allies decreed should be binding, unless there should be some hindrance on the part of gods or heroes. But the Corinthians, in the presence of all their allies who had not themselves accepted the treaty—for they had on their own responsibility summoned them beforehand— in reply to the Lacedaemonians said in what respects they had been wronged, not stating outright that the Lacedaemonians had failed to recover from the Athenians for them Sollium [1] or Anactorium,[2] nor mentioning any other matter in which they thought they were getting less than their rights, but making a pretext that they could not give up their allies in Thrace; for they said they had given their oaths to these people, both privately, when they had first revolted along with the Potidaeans,[3] and afterwards. They were therefore, they said, not violating their oaths to their allies by refusing to join in

[2] *cf.* iv. xlix.   [3] *cf.* i. lviii. 1.

Ἀθηναίων σπονδάς· θεῶν γὰρ πίστεις ὁμόσαντες
ἐκείνοις οὐκ ἂν εὐορκεῖν προδιδόντες αὑτούς.
εἰρῆσθαι δ' ὅτι " ἢν μὴ θεῶν ἢ ἡρώων κώλυμα ᾖ."
4 φαίνεσθαι οὖν σφίσι κώλυμα θεῖον τοῦτο. καὶ περὶ
μὲν τῶν παλαιῶν ὅρκων τοσαῦτα εἶπον, περὶ δὲ
τῆς Ἀργείων ξυμμαχίας μετὰ τῶν φίλων βουλευ-
5 σάμενοι ποιήσειν ὅ τι ἂν δίκαιον ᾖ. καὶ οἱ μὲν
Λακεδαιμονίων πρέσβεις ἀνεχώρησαν ἐπ' οἴκου.
ἔτυχον δὲ παρόντες ἐν Κορίνθῳ καὶ Ἀργείων
πρέσβεις, οἳ ἐκέλευον τοὺς Κορινθίους ἰέναι ἐς
τὴν ξυμμαχίαν καὶ μὴ μέλλειν· οἱ δὲ ἐς τὸν
ὕστερον ξύλλογον αὐτοῖς τὸν παρὰ σφίσι προεῖπον
ἥκειν.

XXXI. Ἦλθε δὲ καὶ Ἠλείων πρεσβεία εὐθὺς καὶ ἐποιήσατο πρὸς Κορινθίους ξυμμαχίαν
πρῶτον, ἔπειτα ἐκεῖθεν ἐς Ἄργος ἐλθόντες,
καθάπερ προείρητο, Ἀργείων ξύμμαχοι ἐγένοντο·
διαφερόμενοι γὰρ ἐτύγχανον τοῖς Λακεδαιμονίοις
2 περὶ Λεπρέου. πολέμου γὰρ γενομένου ποτὲ πρὸς
Ἀρκάδων τινὰς Λεπρεάταις καὶ Ἠλείων παρα-
κληθέντων ὑπὸ Λεπρεατῶν ἐς ξυμμαχίαν ἐπὶ τῇ
ἡμισείᾳ τῆς γῆς καὶ λυσάντων τὸν πόλεμον,
Ἠλεῖοι τὴν γῆν νεμομένοις αὐτοῖς τοῖς Λεπρεάταις
τάλαντον ἔταξαν τῷ Διὶ τῷ Ὀλυμπίῳ ἀποφέρειν.
3 καὶ μέχρι τοῦ Ἀττικοῦ πολέμου ἀπέφερον, ἔπειτα
παυσαμένων διὰ πρόφασιν τοῦ πολέμου οἱ Ἠλεῖοι
ἐπηνάγκαζον, οἱ δ' ἐτράποντο πρὸς τοὺς Λακε-

the treaty with the Athenians; for since they had
bound themselves to those allies by pledges sworn
in the name of the gods, it would not be consistent
with their oaths to betray them. Besides, the words
of the agreement were, "if there be no hindrance on
the part of gods or heroes"; and it seemed to them
that this was a hindrance on the part of the gods.
So much they said in regard to their ancient oaths,
but as to the Argive alliance they would consult with
their friends and do whatever was right. So the
envoys of the Lacedaemonians returned home. But
there happened to be at Corinth Argive envoys,
who urged the Corinthians to come into the alliance
without delay; the latter, however, told them to
come to their next assembly.

XXXI. Soon after there also came an embassy of
the Eleans and first concluded an alliance with the
Corinthians, and then they proceeded to Argos, as
they had been instructed, and made an alliance with
the Argives. It seems that at one time the Eleans
were at variance with the Lacedaemonians about
Lepreum.[1] For when there had been a war between the Lepreates and some of the Arcadians,
and the Eleans had been invited by the Lepreates
to make an alliance with them, with the offer
of half their territory, on the conclusion of the
war the Eleans left the Lepreates in possession
of their land, but assessed upon them a tax of a
talent to be paid to Olympian Zeus. Now up to the war
with Athens they regularly paid the tribute; then
on the pretext of the war they ceased to pay the
tribute, and the Eleans tried to enforce payment,
whereupon they had recourse to the Lacedaemonians.

[1] In Triphylia, not far from the boundaries of Elis and
Laconia (ch. xxxiv. 1).

δαιμονίους. καὶ δίκης Λακεδαιμονίοις ἐπιτρα-
πείσης, ὑποτοπήσαντες οἱ Ἠλεῖοι μὴ ἴσον ἕξειν,
ἀνέντες τὴν ἐπιτροπὴν Λεπρεατῶν τὴν γῆν ἔτεμον.
4 οἱ δὲ Λακεδαιμόνιοι οὐδὲν ἧσσον ἐδίκασαν αὐτονόμους εἶναι Λεπρεάτας καὶ ἀδικεῖν Ἠλείους, καὶ
ὡς οὐκ ἐμμεινάντων τῇ ἐπιτροπῇ φρουρὰν ὁπλιτῶν
5 ἐσέπεμψαν ἐς Λέπρεον. οἱ δὲ Ἠλεῖοι νομίζοντες
πόλιν σφῶν ἀφεστηκυῖαν δέξασθαι τοὺς Λακεδαιμονίους καὶ τὴν ξυνθήκην προφέροντες ἐν ᾗ
εἴρητο, ἃ ἔχοντες ἐς τὸν Ἀττικὸν πόλεμον καθί-
σταντό τινες, ταῦτα ἔχοντας καὶ ἐξελθεῖν, ὡς οὐκ
ἴσον ἔχοντες ἀφίστανται πρὸς τοὺς Ἀργείους, καὶ
τὴν ξυμμαχίαν, ὥσπερ ποείρητο, καὶ οὗτοι ἐποιή-
6 σαντο. ἐγένοντο δὲ καὶ οἱ Κορίνθιοι εὐθὺς μετ᾽
ἐκείνους καὶ οἱ ἐπὶ Θράκης Χαλκιδῆς Ἀργείων
ξύμμαχοι. Βοιωτοὶ δὲ καὶ Μεγαρῆς τὸ αὐτὸ
λέγοντες ἡσύχαζον, περιορώμενοι [1] καὶ νομίζοντες
σφίσι τὴν Ἀργείων δημοκρατίαν, αὐτοῖς
ὀλιγαρχουμένοις, ἧσσον ξύμφορον εἶναι τῆς
Λακεδαιμονίων πολιτείας.

XXXII. Περὶ δὲ τοὺς αὐτοὺς χρόνους τοῦ
θέρους τούτου Σκιωναίους μὲν Ἀθηναῖοι ἐκπο-
λιορκήσαντες ἀπέκτειναν τοὺς ἡβῶντας, παῖδας
δὲ καὶ γυναῖκας ἠνδραπόδισαν καὶ τὴν γῆν
Πλαταιεῦσιν ἔδοσαν νέμεσθαι· Δηλίους δὲ κατή-
γαγον πάλιν ἐς Δῆλον, ἐνθυμούμενοι τάς τε ἐν

---

[1] ὑπὸ τῶν Λακεδαιμονίων, in the MSS. after περιορώμενοι,
deleted by Dobree. The sense of the verb, "jealously
watched" (Jowett), required with that reading, does not
occur in Thucydides.

The case having been referred to the Lacedaemonians
for arbitration, the Eleans, suspecting that they would
not receive fair treatment, renounced the arbitration
and ravaged the land of the Lepreates. The Lacedaemonians, nevertheless, gave judgment, to the
effect that the Lepreates were independent and the
Eleans the aggressors, and as the latter did not abide
by the arbitration, sent a garrison of hoplites to
Lepreum. But the Eleans, considering that the
Lacedaemonians had taken under their protection
a city of theirs that was in revolt, cited the agreement
in which it was stipulated that whatever places any
of the confederates had when they entered the
war with Athens they should retain when they came
out of it ; and on the ground that they had not received
fair treatment went over to the Argives, their envoys
making the alliance as they had been instructed to do.
Immediately after them the Corinthians also and the
Chalcidians in Thrace became allies of the Argives.
But the Boeotians and Megarians, though holding the
same views, kept quiet, awaiting events and thinking
the Argive democracy not so advantageous for them,
with their oligarchical form of government, as the
political constitution of the Lacedaemonians.

XXXII. About the same time during this summer,
the Athenians reduced the Scionaeans by siege, slew
the adult males,[1] made slaves of the women and
children, and gave the land to the Plataeans to
occupy ; and they brought back the Delians to Delos,[2]
taking to heart their mishaps in the battles[3] and

---

[1] In accordance with the decree moved by Cleon two years
before (IV. cxxii. 6). At the conclusion of peace they had
been left at the mercy of the Athenians (ch. xviii. 8).

[2] cf. ch. i.   [3] At Delium and Amphipolis.

ταῖς μάχαις ξυμφορὰς καὶ τοῦ ἐν Δελφοῖς θεοῦ
2 χρήσαντος. καὶ Φωκῆς καὶ Λοκροὶ ἤρξαντο
3 πολεμεῖν. καὶ Κορίνθιοι καὶ Ἀργεῖοι ἤδη ξύμμαχοι ὄντες ἔρχονται ἐς Τεγέαν ἀποστήσοντες
Λακεδαιμονίων, ὁρῶντες μέγα μέρος ὄν, καὶ εἰ
σφίσι προσγένοιτο, νομίζοντες ἅπασαν ἂν ἔχειν
4 Πελοπόννησον. ὡς δὲ οὐδὲν ἂν ἔφασαν ἐναν-
τιωθῆναι οἱ Τεγεᾶται Λακεδαιμονίοις, οἱ Κορίνθιοι
μέχρι τούτου προθύμως πράσσοντες ἀνεῖσαν τῆς
φιλονικίας καὶ ὠρρώδησαν μὴ οὐδεὶς σφίσιν ἔτι
5 τῶν ἄλλων προσχωρῇ. ὅμως δὲ ἐλθόντες ἐς τοὺς
Βοιωτοὺς ἐδέοντο σφῶν τε καὶ Ἀργείων γίγνεσθαι
ξυμμάχους καὶ τἆλλα κοινῇ πράσσειν· τάς τε
δεχημέρους ἐπισπονδάς, αἳ ἦσαν Ἀθηναίοις καὶ
Βοιωτοῖς πρὸς ἀλλήλους οὐ πολλῷ ὕστερον γενό-
μεναι αὐτῶν τῶν πεντηκοντουτίδων σπονδῶν,
ἐκέλευον οἱ Κορίνθιοι τοὺς Βοιωτοὺς ἀκολουθή-
σαντας Ἀθήναζε καὶ σφίσι ποιῆσαι, ὥσπερ
Βοιωτοὶ εἶχον, μὴ δεχομένων δὲ Ἀθηναίων
ἀπειπεῖν τὴν ἐκεχειρίαν καὶ τὸ λοιπὸν μὴ σπέν-
6 δεσθαι ἄνευ αὐτῶν. Βοιωτοὶ δὲ δεομένων τῶν
Κορινθίων περὶ μὲν τῆς Ἀργείων ξυμμαχίας
ἐπισχεῖν αὐτοὺς ἐκέλευον, ἐλθόντες δὲ Ἀθήναζε
μετὰ Κορινθίων οὐχ ηὕροντο τὰς δεχημέρους
σπονδάς, ἀλλ᾽ ἀπεκρίναντο οἱ Ἀθηναῖοι Κορινθίοις εἶναι σπονδάς, εἴπερ Λακεδαιμονίων εἰσὶ
7 ξύμμαχοι. Βοιωτοὶ μὲν οὖν οὐδὲν μᾶλλον ἀπεῖπον
τὰς δεχημέρους, ἀξιούντων καὶ αἰτιωμένων Κοριν-

---

¹ It had always maintained an independent position in
Arcadia, and in earlier times had been a powerful opponent
of Sparta.

62

obeying an oracle of the god at Delphi. Meanwhile
the Phocians and the Locrians began hostilities.
And the Corinthians and the Argives, being now allies,
came to Tegea,[1] hoping to induce it to revolt from the
Lacedaemonians, seeing that it was an important
part of the Peloponnesus, and thinking if it should be
gained to their side they would soon have the whole
Peloponnesus. But when the Tegeates refused to
oppose the Lacedaemonians, the Corinthians, who up
to that time had been working zealously, became slack
in their ardour and full of dread that none of the other
Peloponnesians would henceforth come over to them.
Nevertheless they went to the Boeotians and requested them to become allies of themselves and the
Argives, and to act generally in concert with them.
And the Corinthians further requested the Boeotians
to accompany them to Athens and procure for them
also the ten days' truce[2] which had been made between the Athenians and Boeotians not long after the
conclusion of the fifty years' treaty, on the same terms
as the Boeotians had obtained, and, if the Athenians
did not agree, to renounce the armistice and for the
future to make no truce without the Corinthians. The
Boeotians, when the Corinthians made these requests,
desired them to wait awhile in regard to the Argive
alliance, but they went with them to Athens, where
however they failed to obtain the ten days' truce, the
Athenians answering them that there was already a
truce with the Corinthians, if they were allies of the
Lacedaemonians. But the Boeotians did not any the
more give up the ten days' truce, although the Corinthians demanded it and accused them of having

[2] *i.e.* a truce which had to be renewed every ten days;
or, perhaps, "terminable at ten days' notice," as Jowett
thinks. *cf.* ch. xxvi. 3.

θίων ξυνθέσθαι σφίσι· Κορινθίοις δὲ ἀνοκωχὴ
ἄσπονδος ἦν πρὸς Ἀθηναίους.

XXXIII. Λακεδαιμόνιοι δὲ τοῦ αὐτοῦ θέρους
πανδημεὶ ἐστράτευσαν, Πλειστοάνακτος τοῦ
Παυσανίου Λακεδαιμονίων βασιλέως ἡγουμένου,
τῆς Ἀρκαδίας ἐς Παρρασίους Μαντινέων ὑπηκόους ὄντας, κατὰ στάσιν ἐπικαλεσαμένων σφᾶς,
ἅμα δὲ καὶ τὸ ἐν Κυψέλοις τεῖχος ἀναιρήσοντες,
ἢν δύνωνται, ὃ ἐτείχισαν Μαντινῆς καὶ αὐτοὶ
ἐφρούρουν, ἐν τῇ Παρρασικῇ κείμενον ἐπὶ τῇ
2 Σκιρίτιδι τῆς Λακωνικῆς. καὶ οἱ μὲν Λακεδαιμόνιοι τὴν γῆν τῶν Παρρασίων ἐδῄουν, οἱ δὲ
Μαντινῆς τὴν πόλιν Ἀργείοις φύλαξι παραδόν-
τες αὐτοὶ τὴν ξυμμαχίαν ἐφρούρουν· ἀδύνατοι
δ᾽ ὄντες διασῶσαι τό τε ἐν Κυψέλοις τεῖχος καὶ
3 τὰς ἐν Παρρασίοις πόλεις ἀπῆλθον. Λακεδαιμόνιοι δὲ τούς τε Παρρασίους αὐτονόμους ποιήσαντες καὶ τὸ τεῖχος καθελόντες ἀνεχώρησαν
ἐπ᾽ οἴκου.

XXXIV. Καὶ τοῦ αὐτοῦ θέρους, ἤδη ἡκόντων
αὐτοῖς τῶν ἀπὸ Θρᾴκης μετὰ Βρασίδου ἐξελθόντων στρατιωτῶν, οὓς ὁ Κλεαρίδας μετὰ τὰς
σπονδὰς ἐκόμισεν, οἱ Λακεδαιμόνιοι ἐψηφίσαντο
τοὺς μὲν μετὰ Βρασίδου Εἵλωτας μαχεσαμένους
ἐλευθέρους εἶναι καὶ οἰκεῖν ὅπου ἂν βούλωνται·
καὶ ὕστερον οὐ πολλῷ αὐτοὺς μετὰ τῶν νεοδαμώ-
δων ἐς Λέπρεον κατέστησαν, κείμενον ἐπὶ τῆς
Λακωνικῆς καὶ τῆς Ἠλείας, ὄντες ἤδη διάφοροι

---

[1] The mountainous region between the upper Eurotas and
the valley of the Oenus, one of the most important districts
of the Perioeci.

agreed with themselves to do so. Between the Corinthians, however, and the Athenians there was a cessation of activities without an actual truce.

XXXIII. The same summer the Lacedaemonians, under the command of Pleistoanax, son of Pausanias, king of the Lacedaemonians, made an expedition with all their forces into the territory of the Parrhasians of Arcadia, who were subjects of the Mantineans. They had been called in by the Parrhasians on account of a factional quarrel, and intended also to demolish, if possible, the fort at Cypsela, which, being situated in Parrhasian territory, the Mantineans had constructed and themselves garrisoned for the annoyance of the district Sciritis [1] in Laconia. The Lacedaemonians proceeded to ravage the land of the Parrhasians, and the Mantineans, giving over the custody of their city to the Argives, tried themselves to guard the territory of their Parrhasian allies. Being unable, however, to save the fort at Cypsela and the towns in Parrhasia, they withdrew. And the Lacedaemonians, after making the Parrhasians independent and pulling down the fort, then returned home.

XXXIV. During the same summer, on the return from Thrace of the troops which had gone out with Brasidas [2] and which Clearidas [3] had brought back after the treaty was made, the Lacedaemonians voted that the Helots who had fought with Brasidas should be free and dwell wherever they preferred; and not long afterwards they settled them with the Neodamodes [4] at Lepreum on the borders of Laconia and Elis, for they were by this time at variance with

[2] cf. IV. lxxviii. 1; lxxx. 5.   [3] cf. xxi. 3.
[4] The clans of new citizens formed of Helots emancipated for service in war.

2 Ἠλείοις· τοὺς δὲ ἐκ τῆς νήσου ληφθέντας σφῶν
καὶ τὰ ὅπλα παραδόντας, δείσαντες μή τι διὰ τὴν
ξυμφορὰν νομίσαντες ἐλασσωθήσεσθαι καὶ ὄντες
ἐπίτιμοι νεωτερίσωσιν, ἤδη καὶ ἀρχάς τινας ἔχοντας ἀτίμους ἐποίησαν, ἀτιμίαν δὲ τοιάνδε ὥστε
μήτε ἄρχειν μήτε πριαμένους τι ἢ πωλοῦντας
κυρίους εἶναι. ὕστερον δὲ αὖθις χρόνῳ ἐπίτιμοι
ἐγένοντο.

XXXV. Τοῦ δ᾽ αὐτοῦ θέρους καὶ Θυσσὸν τὴν
ἐν τῇ Ἀθωίδι Ἀκτῇ Διῆς[1] εἷλον, Ἀθηναίων οὖσαν
ξύμμαχον.

2 Καὶ τὸ θέρος τοῦτο πᾶν ἐπιμειξίαι μὲν ἦσαν
τοῖς Ἀθηναίοις καὶ Πελοποννησίοις, ὑπώπτευον
δὲ ἀλλήλους εὐθὺς μετὰ τὰς σπονδὰς οἵ τε
Ἀθηναῖοι καὶ Λακεδαιμόνιοι κατὰ τὴν τῶν
3 χωρίων ἀλλήλοις οὐκ ἀπόδοσιν. τὴν γὰρ Ἀμφίπολιν πρότεροι λαχόντες οἱ Λακεδαιμόνιοι ἀποδιδόναι καὶ τὰ ἄλλα οὐκ ἀπεδεδώκεσαν, οὐδὲ τοὺς
ἐπὶ Θρᾴκης παρεῖχον ξυμμάχους τὰς σπονδὰς
δεχομένους οὐδὲ Βοιωτοὺς οὐδὲ Κορινθίους, λέγοντες αἰεὶ ὡς μετ᾽ Ἀθηναίων τούτους, ἢν μὴ
᾽θέλωσι, κοινῇ ἀναγκάσουσιν· χρόνους τε πρού-
θεντο ἄνευ ξυγγραφῆς ἐν οἷς χρῆν τοὺς μὴ ἐσι-
4 όντας ἀμφοτέροις πολεμίους εἶναι. τούτων οὖν
ὁρῶντες οἱ Ἀθηναῖοι οὐδὲν ἔργῳ γιγνόμενον,
ὑπώπτευον τοὺς Λακεδαιμονίους μηδὲν δίκαιον
διανοεῖσθαι, ὥστε οὔτε Πύλον ἀπαιτούντων αὐ-

---

[1] Ἀκτῇ Διῆς, Meineke's conjecture for Δικτηδιῆς of nearly
all MSS.

the Eleans. But as to their men who had been taken on the island and had given up their arms, fearing that these might expect to suffer some degradation because of their misfortune and if they continued in possession of the franchise might attempt a revolution, they disfranchised them, though some of them now held office, and with such a disfranchisement that they could neither hold office nor have the legal right to buy or sell anything. In the course of time, however, they were again enfranchised.

XXXV. During the same summer also the Dians took Thyssus, a town on the promontory of Athos, which was in alliance with the Athenians.

All this summer there was intercourse between the Athenians and Lacedaemonians, but both parties began to suspect one another directly after the conclusion of the treaty, owing to their failure to give back to one another the places specified. The Lacedaemonians, though they had drawn the lot to make restoration first, had not restored Amphipolis and the other places; nor had they made their allies in Thrace accept the treaty, nor the Boeotians, nor the Corinthians, though they continually professed that they would join the Athenians in coercing these states, if they were unwilling; and they proposed dates, without making a written agreement, on which those who did not accede to the treaty were to be enemies of both. Seeing, then, that none of these things was actually being done, the Athenians suspected the Lacedaemonians of having no just intentions, and so not only did not restore Pylos when the Lacedaemonians demanded

τῶν ἀπεδίδοσαν, ἀλλὰ καὶ τοὺς ἐκ τῆς νήσου
δεσμώτας μετεμέλοντο ἀποδεδωκότες, τά τε ἄλλα
χωρία εἶχον, μένοντες ἕως σφίσι κἀκεῖνοι ποιή-
5 σειαν τὰ εἰρημένα. Λακεδαιμόνιοι δὲ τὰ μὲν
δυνατὰ ἔφασαν πεποιηκέναι· τοὺς γὰρ παρὰ
σφίσι δεσμώτας ὄντας Ἀθηναίων ἀποδοῦναι καὶ
τοὺς ἐπὶ Θρᾴκης στρατιώτας ἀπαγαγεῖν καὶ εἴ
του ἄλλου ἐγκρατεῖς ἦσαν· Ἀμφιπόλεως δὲ οὐκ
ἔφασαν κρατεῖν ὥστε παραδοῦναι, Βοιωτοὺς δὲ
πειράσεσθαι καὶ Κορινθίους ἐς τὰς σπονδὰς
ἐσαγαγεῖν καὶ Πάνακτον ἀπολαβεῖν, καὶ Ἀθηναίων ὅσοι ἦσαν ἐν Βοιωτοῖς αἰχμάλωτοι κομιεῖν.
6 Πύλον μέντοι ἠξίουν σφίσιν ἀποδοῦναι· εἰ δὲ μή,
Μεσσηνίους γε καὶ τοὺς Εἵλωτας ἐξαγαγεῖν,
ὥσπερ καὶ αὐτοὶ τοὺς ἀπὸ Θρᾴκης, Ἀθηναίους
δὲ φρουρεῖν τὸ χωρίον αὐτούς, εἰ βούλονται.
7 πολλάκις δὲ καὶ πολλῶν λόγων γενομένων ἐν τῷ
θέρει τούτῳ ἔπεισαν τοὺς Ἀθηναίους ὥστε ἐξαγαγεῖν ἐκ Πύλου Μεσσηνίους καὶ τοὺς ἄλλους
Εἵλωτάς τε καὶ ὅσοι ηὐτομολήκεσαν ἐκ τῆς
Λακωνικῆς· καὶ κατῴκισαν αὐτοὺς ἐν Κρανίοις
8 τῆς Κεφαλληνίας. τὸ μὲν οὖν θέρος τοῦτο ἡσυχία
ἦν καὶ ἔφοδοι παρ' ἀλλήλους.

XXXVI. Τοῦ δὲ ἐπιγιγνομένου χειμῶνος (ἔτυχον γὰρ ἔφοροι ἕτεροι καὶ οὐκ ἐφ' ὧν αἱ σπονδαὶ
ἐγένοντο ἄρχοντες ἤδη καί τινες αὐτῶν καὶ
ἐναντίοι σπονδαῖς) ἐλθουσῶν πρεσβειῶν ἀπὸ τῆς
ξυμμαχίδος καὶ παρόντων Ἀθηναίων καὶ Βοιωτῶν καὶ Κορινθίων καὶ πολλὰ ἐν ἀλλήλοις εἰπόν-

it, but even repented that they had restored the
prisoners taken on the island, and they continued to
hold the other places, waiting until the Lacedaemonians should have fulfilled their part of the contract.
The Lacedaemonians said that they had done what
was possible ; for they had restored the prisoners of
the Athenians that were in their hands, had brought
back their troops in Thrace, and had done whatever
else had been in their power. As to Amphipolis,
however, they said that they were not in control of it,
so as to deliver it up ; but they would try to bring
the Boeotians and Corinthians into the treaty and to
get back Panactum, and would recover all Athenian
prisoners that were in the hands of the Boeotians.
Pylos, however, they insisted the Athenians should
restore to them ; or at any rate, they should
withdraw the Messenians and the Helots, as they
themselves had withdrawn their troops from Thrace,
and the Athenians themselves might garrison the
place if they wished. After many and frequent
conferences had been held during this summer, they
persuaded the Athenians to withdraw from Pylos the
Messenians, the rest of the Helots, and all who had
deserted from Laconia ; and these the Athenians
settled at Cranii in Cephallenia. This summer, then,
there was peace and mutual intercourse.

XXXVI. The following winter the ephors who
happened to be in office at Sparta were other
than those under whom the treaty had been made,
and some of them were even opposed to it. Embassies had come from their allies, and there were
present also Athenians, Boeotians, and Corinthians ;
and after much discussion, without coming to an

421–420
B.C.

THUCYDIDES

των καὶ οὐδὲν ξυμβάντων, ὡς ἀπῆσαν ἐπ᾽ οἴκου,
τοῖς Βοιωτοῖς καὶ Κορινθίοις Κλεόβουλος καὶ
Ξενάρης, οὗτοι οἵπερ τῶν ἐφόρων ἐβούλοντο
μάλιστα διαλῦσαι τὰς σπονδάς, λόγους ποιοῦνται
ἰδίους, παραινοῦντες ὅτι μάλιστα ταῦτά τε γιγνώ-
σκειν καὶ πειρᾶσθαι Βοιωτούς, Ἀργείων γενομένους πρῶτον αὐτοὺς ξυμμάχους, αὖθις μετὰ
Βοιωτῶν Ἀργείους Λακεδαιμονίοις ποιῆσαι ξυμμάχους (οὕτω γὰρ ἥκιστ᾽ ἂν ἀναγκασθῆναι Βοιωτοὺς ἐς τὰς Ἀττικὰς σπονδὰς ἐσελθεῖν)· ἑλέσθαι
γὰρ Λακεδαιμονίους πρὸ τῆς Ἀθηναίων ἔχθρας
καὶ διαλύσεως τῶν σπονδῶν Ἀργείους σφίσι
φίλους καὶ ξυμμάχους γενέσθαι. τὸ γὰρ Ἄργος
αἰεὶ ἠπίσταντο ἐπιθυμοῦντας τοὺς Λακεδαιμονίους καλῶς σφίσι φίλιον γενέσθαι, ἡγουμένους τὸν
2 ἔξω Πελοποννήσου πόλεμον ῥᾷω ἂν εἶναι. τὸ
μέντοι Πάνακτον ἐδέοντο Βοιωτοὺς ὅπως παραδώ-
σουσι Λακεδαιμονίοις, ἵνα ἀντ᾽ αὐτοῦ Πύλον, ἢν
δύνωνται, ἀπολαβόντες ῥᾷον καθιστῶνται Ἀθηναίοις ἐς πόλεμον.

XXXVII. Καὶ οἱ μὲν Βοιωτοὶ καὶ Κορίνθιοι
ταῦτα ἐπεσταλμένοι ἀπό τε τοῦ Ξενάρους καὶ
Κλεοβούλου καὶ ὅσοι φίλοι ἦσαν αὐτοῖς τῶν
Λακεδαιμονίων ὥστε ἀπαγγεῖλαι ἐπὶ τὰ κοινά,
2 ἑκάτεροι ἀνεχώρουν. Ἀργείων δὲ δύο ἄνδρες τῆς
ἀρχῆς τῆς μεγίστης ἐπετήρουν ἀπιόντας αὐτοὺς
καθ᾽ ὁδὸν καὶ ξυγγενόμενοι ἐς λόγους ἦλθον, εἴ
πως οἱ Βοιωτοὶ σφίσι ξύμμαχοι γένοιντο, ὥσπερ
Κορίνθιοι καὶ Ἠλεῖοι καὶ Μαντινῆς· νομίζειν γὰρ

agreement, as the envoys were on the point of departing for home, Cleobulus and Xenares, the ephors who most desired to annul the treaty, made private proposals to the Boeotians and Corinthians, advising them to adopt as far as possible the same policy, and that the Boeotians should first become allies of the Argives and then try to make the Argives along with themselves allies of the Lacedaemonians. For in this way the Boeotians would be least likely to be forced to come into the treaty with Athens, since the Lacedaemonians would prefer gaining the friendship and alliance of the Argives, counting that more important than the enmity of the Athenians and the disruption of the treaty. For they knew that the Lacedaemonians were always desirous that Argos should be friendly to them on fair terms, thinking that war outside of the Peloponnesus would then be an easier matter for them. Panactum, however, they begged the Boeotians to give up to the Lacedaemonians, in order that they might, if possible, get back Pylos in exchange for it, and so be in a safer position for renewing the war with the Athenians.

XXXVII. The Boeotians and Corinthians, being charged by Xenares and Cleobulus and the Lacedaemonians that were friendly to them with these instructions, which they were to announce to their governments, now returned to their respective cities. But two Argive men of highest official position, who were watching for them by the way as they went off, joined them and made a proposal to them, in the hope that the Boeotians might become allies to them, just as the Corinthians, Eleans, and Mantineans had done; for they thought, if this

ἂν τούτου προχωρήσαντος ῥᾳδίως ἤδη καὶ πολεμεῖν καὶ σπένδεσθαι καὶ πρὸς Λακεδαιμονίους, εἰ
βούλοιντο, κοινῷ λόγῳ χρωμένους, καὶ εἴ τινα
3 πρὸς ἄλλον δέοι. τοῖς δὲ τῶν Βοιωτῶν πρέσβεσιν ἀκούουσιν ἤρεσκεν· κατὰ τύχην γὰρ
ἐδέοντο τούτων ὧνπερ καὶ οἱ ἐκ τῆς Λακεδαίμονος αὐτοῖς φίλοι ἐπεστάλκεσαν. καὶ οἱ τῶν
Ἀργείων ἄνδρες ὡς ᾔσθοντο αὐτοὺς δεχομένους
τὸν λόγον, εἰπόντες ὅτι πρέσβεις πέμψουσιν ἐς
4 Βοιωτούς, ἀπῆλθον. ἀφικόμενοι δὲ οἱ Βοιωτοὶ
ἀπήγγειλαν τοῖς βοιωτάρχαις τά τε ἐκ τῆς Λακεδαίμονος καὶ τὰ ἀπὸ τῶν ξυγγενομένων Ἀργείων·
καὶ οἱ βοιωτάρχαι ἠρέσκοντό τε καὶ πολλῷ προ-
θυμότεροι ἦσαν, ὅτι ἀμφοτέρωθεν ξυνεβεβήκει
αὐτοῖς τούς τε φίλους τῶν Λακεδαιμονίων τῶν
αὐτῶν δεῖσθαι καὶ τοὺς Ἀργείους ἐς τὰ ὁμοῖα
5 σπεύδειν. καὶ οὐ πολλῷ ὕστερον πρέσβεις
παρῆσαν Ἀργείων τὰ εἰρημένα προκαλούμενοι·
καὶ αὐτοὺς ἀπέπεμψαν ἐπαινέσαντες τοὺς λόγους
οἱ βοιωτάρχαι καὶ πρέσβεις ὑποσχόμενοι ἀπο-
στελεῖν περὶ τῆς ξυμμαχίας ἐς Ἄργος.

XXXVIII. Ἐν δὲ τούτῳ ἐδόκει πρῶτον τοῖς
βοιωτάρχαις καὶ Κορινθίοις καὶ Μεγαρεῦσι καὶ
τοῖς ἀπὸ Θρᾴκης πρέσβεσιν ὀμόσαι ὅρκους ἀλλήλοις ἦ μὴν ἔν τε τῷ παρατυχόντι ἀμυνεῖν τῷ
δεομένῳ καὶ μὴ πολεμήσειν τῳ μηδὲ ξυμβήσεσθαι
ἄνευ κοινῆς γνώμης, καὶ οὕτως ἤδη τοὺς Βοιωτοὺς
καὶ Μεγαρέας (τὸ γὰρ αὐτὸ ἐποίουν) πρὸς τοὺς
2 Ἀργείους σπένδεσθαι. πρὶν δὲ τοὺς ὅρκους γενέσθαι οἱ βοιωτάρχαι ἐκοίνωσαν ταῖς τέσσαρσι

---

[1] cf. ch. xxxi. 6.

succeeded, they might then readily, all pursuing a common policy, carry on war or make peace with the Lacedaemonians, if they should wish, or with anyone else with whom it might be necessary. The Boeotian envoys were pleased at hearing these things; for by good luck these men were asking the same things as their friends at Lacedaemon had enjoined upon them. And the Argive men, seeing that they were inclined to accept the proposal, told them they would send envoys to the Boeotians and went away. On coming home the Boeotians reported to the boeotarchs the proposal made at Lacedaemon and also that of the Argives who had met them on the way; and the boeotarchs were pleased and were now far more eager for this arrangement, because matters had turned out to their liking in both directions—their friends among the Lacedaemonians wanting the same things as they did, and the Argives striving for a like end. Not long after this envoys came from the Argives with the proposals that have been mentioned; and the boeotarchs assented to their proposals and sent them away with a promise to dispatch envoys to Argos to negotiate the alliance.

XXXVIII. In the meantime it was determined by the boeotarchs and the Corinthians, the Megarians, and the envoys from Thrace, first, to bind themselves by oaths one to another, that assuredly when occasion offered they would assist the one that needed help and would not go to war with anyone or make peace without a common agreement; and that then and only then the Boeotians and the Megarians—for they were acting in concert [1]—should make a treaty with the Argives. But before the oaths were sworn the boeotarchs communicated

βουλαῖς τῶν Βοιωτῶν ταῦτα, αἵπερ ἅπαν τὸ
κῦρος ἔχουσι, καὶ παρήνουν γενέσθαι ὅρκους ταῖς
πόλεσιν, ὅσαι βούλονται ἐπ' ὠφελίᾳ σφίσι ξυνο-
3 μνύναι. οἱ δ' ἐν ταῖς βουλαῖς τῶν Βοιωτῶν ὄντες
οὐ προσδέχονται τὸν λόγον, δεδιότες μὴ ἐναντία
Λακεδαιμονίοις ποιήσωσι τοῖς ἐκείνων ἀφεστῶσι
Κορινθίοις ξυνομνύντες· οὐ γὰρ εἶπον αὐτοῖς οἱ
βοιωτάρχαι τὰ ἐκ τῆς Λακεδαίμονος, ὅτι τῶν τε
ἐφόρων Κλεόβουλος καὶ Ξενάρης καὶ οἱ φίλοι
παραινοῦσιν Ἀργείων πρῶτον καὶ Κορινθίων
γενομένους ξυμμάχους ὕστερον μετ' αὐτῶν τῶν[1]
Λακεδαιμονίων γίγνεσθαι, οἰόμενοι τὴν βουλήν,
κἂν μὴ εἴπωσιν, οὐκ ἄλλα ψηφιεῖσθαι ἢ ἃ σφίσι
4 προδιαγνόντες παραινοῦσιν. ὡς δὲ ἀντέστη τὸ
πρᾶγμα, οἱ μὲν Κορίνθιοι καὶ οἱ ἀπὸ Θρᾴκης
πρέσβεις ἄπρακτοι ἀπῆλθον, οἱ δὲ βοιωτάρχαι,
μέλλοντες πρότερον, εἰ ταῦτα ἔπεισαν, καὶ τὴν
ξυμμαχίαν πειράσεσθαι πρὸς Ἀργείους ποιεῖν,
οὐκέτι ἐσήνεγκαν περὶ Ἀργείων ἐς τὰς βουλάς,
οὐδὲ ἐς τὸ Ἄργος τοὺς πρέσβεις οὓς ὑπέσχοντο
ἔπεμπον, ἀμέλεια δέ τις ἐνῆν καὶ διατριβὴ τῶν
πάντων.

XXXIX. Καὶ ἐν τῷ αὐτῷ χειμῶνι τούτῳ
Μηκύβερναν Ὀλύνθιοι Ἀθηναίων φρουρούντων
ἐπιδραμόντες εἷλον.

2 Μετὰ δὲ ταῦτα (ἐγίγνοντο γὰρ αἰεὶ λόγοι τοῖς
τε Ἀθηναίοις καὶ Λακεδαιμονίοις περὶ ὧν εἶχον

---

[1] μετ' αὐτῶν with Stahl, for μετὰ τῶν of MSS. as Hude
reads.

these resolutions to the four councils of the Boeotians which have supreme authority, and recommended that oaths be exchanged with such cities as wished to take oaths with them for mutual assistance. But the members of the Boeotian council did not accept the proposal, fearing that they might offend the Lacedaemonians by taking oaths with the Corinthians who had seceded from their confederacy. For the boeotarchs did not tell them what had happened at Lacedaemon—that it was the ephors, Cleobulus and Xenares, and their own friends who advised them first to become allies of the Argives and Corinthians, and then in conjunction with these to become allies of the Lacedaemonians ; for they thought that the council,[1] without their making any such statement, would not vote for any other course than that which they had previously resolved upon and now recommended. But now, when this difficulty arose, the Corinthians and the envoys from Thrace went away without accomplishing their purpose ; and the boeotarchs, who had before intended, if they carried these measures, to try to effect also the alliance with the Argives, did not now bring before the councils the matter concerning the Argives, nor did they send to Argos the envoys they had promised ; and there was neglect and delay in the whole business.

XXXIX. In the course of this same winter, the Olynthians by a sudden attack captured Mecyberna[2] which was garrisoned by the Athenians.

After this, while conferences were continually going on between the Athenians and Lacedae-

---

[1] The four councils here doubtless considered as one body.
[2] A port town of Olynthus ; cf. ch. xviii. 7.

ἀλλήλων) ἐλπίζοντες οἱ Λακεδαιμόνιοι, εἰ Πάνακτον Ἀθηναῖοι παρὰ Βοιωτῶν ἀπολάβοιεν,
κομίσασθαι ἂν αὐτοὶ Πύλον, ἦλθον ἐς τοὺς Βοιωτοὺς πρεσβευόμενοι καὶ ἐδέοντο σφίσι Πάνακτόν
τε καὶ τοὺς Ἀθηναίων δεσμώτας παραδοῦναι,
3 ἵνα ἀντ' αὐτῶν Πύλον κομίσωνται. οἱ δὲ Βοιωτοὶ
οὐκ ἔφασαν ἀποδώσειν, ἢν μὴ σφίσι ξυμμαχίαν
ἰδίαν ποιήσωνται ὥσπερ Ἀθηναίοις. Λακεδαιμόνιοι δὲ εἰδότες μὲν ὅτι ἀδικήσουσιν Ἀθηναίους,
εἰρημένον ἄνευ ἀλλήλων μήτε σπένδεσθαί τῳ
μήτε πολεμεῖν, βουλόμενοι δὲ τὸ Πάνακτον
παραλαβεῖν ὡς τὴν Πύλον ἀντ' αὐτοῦ κομιού-
μενοι, καὶ ἅμα τῶν ξυγχέαι σπευδόντων τὰς
σπονδὰς προθυμουμένων τὰ ἐς Βοιωτούς, ἐποιήσαντο τὴν ξυμμαχίαν, τοῦ χειμῶνος τελευτῶντος
ἤδη καὶ πρὸς ἔαρ· καὶ τὸ Πάνακτον εὐθὺς καθη-
ρεῖτο. καὶ ἑνδέκατον ἔτος τῷ πολέμῳ ἐτελεύτα.

XL. Ἅμα δὲ τῷ ἦρι εὐθὺς τοῦ ἐπιγιγνομένου
θέρους οἱ Ἀργεῖοι, ὡς οἵ τε πρέσβεις τῶν Βοιωτῶν οὓς ἔφασαν πέμψειν οὐχ ἧκον, τό τε Πάνακτον ᾔσθοντο καθαιρούμενον καὶ ξυμμαχίαν
ἰδίαν γεγενημένην τοῖς Βοιωτοῖς πρὸς τοὺς Λακεδαιμονίους, ἔδεισαν μὴ μονωθῶσι καὶ ἐς Λακεδαι-
2 μονίους πᾶσα ἡ ξυμμαχία χωρήσῃ· τοὺς γὰρ
Βοιωτοὺς ᾤοντο πεπεῖσθαι ὑπὸ Λακεδαιμονίων τό
τε Πάνακτον καθελεῖν καὶ ἐς τὰς Ἀθηναίων
σπονδὰς ἐσιέναι, τούς τε Ἀθηναίους εἰδέναι ταῦτα

monians about places belonging to one or the other
which they respectively held, the Lacedaemonians,
in the hope that, if the Athenians should get back
Panactum from the Boeotians, they themselves
might recover Pylos, sent envoys to the Boeotians
and begged them to deliver up Panactum and the
Athenian prisoners to themselves, in order that they
might recover Pylos in exchange for these. But the
Boeotians refused to give them up, unless they
would make a separate alliance with them just as
with the Athenians. Now the Lacedaemonians
knew that they would thereby be wronging the
Athenians, inasmuch as it was stipulated not to make
either peace or war with anyone without mutual
consent, yet they wished to obtain Panactum in
order to recover Pylos in exchange for it. Besides,
the party that was eager to break the treaty was
zealous for the connection with the Boeotians. So
they concluded the alliance, when the winter was
closing and the spring at hand; and the demolition
of Panactum was immediately begun. So ended the
eleventh year of the war.

XL. At the very beginning of the following March,
summer, when the envoys whom the Boeotians 420 B.C.
promised to send did not come, the Argives,
perceiving that Panactum was being demolished and
a private alliance had been made by the Boeotians
with the Lacedaemonians, began to fear that they
would be left alone and the whole confederacy
would go over to the Lacedaemonians. For they
thought that the Boeotians had been persuaded by
the Lacedaemonians to raze Panactum and to accede
to the treaty with the Athenians, and that the
Athenians knew these things, so that it was no

ὥστε οὐδὲ πρὸς 'Αθηναίους ἔτι σφίσιν εἶναι ξυμμαχίαν ποιήσασθαι, πρότερον ἐλπίζοντες ἐκ τῶν διαφορῶν, εἰ μὴ μείνειαν αὐτοῖς αἱ πρὸς Λακεδαιμονίους σπονδαί, τοῖς γοῦν 'Αθηναίοις ξύμμαχοι
3 ἔσεσθαι. ἀποροῦντες οὖν ταῦτα οἱ 'Αργεῖοι καὶ φοβούμενοι μὴ Λακεδαιμονίοις καὶ Τεγεάταις, Βοιωτοῖς καὶ 'Αθηναίοις ἅμα πολεμῶσι, πρότερον οὐ δεχόμενοι τὰς Λακεδαιμονίων σπονδάς, ἀλλ' ἐν φρονήματι ὄντες τῆς Πελοποννήσου ἡγήσεσθαι, ἔπεμπον ὡς ἐδύναντο τάχιστα ἐς τὴν Λακεδαίμονα πρέσβεις Εὔστροφον καὶ Αἴσωνα, οἳ ἐδόκουν προσφιλέστατοι αὐτοῖς εἶναι, ἡγούμενοι ἐκ τῶν παρόντων κράτιστα, πρὸς Λακεδαιμονίους σπονδὰς ποιησάμενοι ὅπῃ ἂν ξυγχωρῇ, ἡσυχίαν ἔχειν.

XLI. Καὶ οἱ πρέσβεις ἀφικόμενοι αὐτῶν λόγους ἐποιοῦντο πρὸς τοὺς Λακεδαιμονίους ἐφ' ᾧ ἂν
2 σφίσιν αἱ σπονδαὶ γίγνοιντο. καὶ τὸ μὲν πρῶτον οἱ 'Αργεῖοι ἠξίουν δίκης ἐπιτροπὴν σφίσι γενέσθαι ἢ ἐς πόλιν τινὰ ἢ ἰδιώτην περὶ τῆς Κυνουρίας γῆς, ἧς αἰεὶ πέρι διαφέρονται μεθορίας οὔσης (ἔχει δὲ ἐν αὐτῇ Θυρέαν καὶ 'Ανθήνην πόλιν, νέμονται δ' αὐτὴν Λακεδαιμόνιοι)· ἔπειτα δ' οὐκ ἐώντων Λακεδαιμονίων μεμνῆσθαι περὶ αὐτῆς, ἀλλ' εἰ βούλονται σπένδεσθαι ὥσπερ πρότερον, ἑτοῖμοι εἶναι, οἱ 'Αργεῖοι πρέσβεις τάδε ὅμως ἐπηγάγοντο τοὺς Λακεδαιμονίους ξυγχωρῆσαι, ἐν μὲν τῷ παρόντι σπονδὰς ποιήσασθαι ἔτη πεντήκοντα, ἐξεῖναι δ' ὁποτεροισοῦν προκαλεσαμένοις, μήτε νόσου οὔσης μήτε πολέμου Λακεδαίμονι καὶ "Αργει, διαμά-

---

[1] i.e. of the Lacedaemonians and Athenians.

longer possible for them to make an alliance even
with the Athenians; whereas they had formerly
hoped that if their treaty with the Lacedaemonians
should not continue they might at any rate, in
consequence of the differences,[1] become allies of
the Athenians. Being then in such perplexity and
fearing lest they might have war at once with the
Lacedaemonians and Tegeates, the Boeotians and
the Athenians, the Argives, who before this had not
accepted the treaty with the Lacedaemonians but
proudly hoped to have the hegemony of the
Peloponnesus, now sent to Lacedaemon in all haste
two envoys, Eustrophus and Aeson, who seemed
likely to be most acceptable to them, thinking it
best under the present circumstances to make a
treaty with the Lacedaemonians in whatever way
might be feasible and to have quiet.

XLI. On their arrival their envoys made proposals
to the Lacedaemonians as to the terms on which the
treaty should be concluded. At first the Argives
claimed that they should be allowed to submit to the
arbitration of some city or private person the matter
of the Cynurian territory—a district containing the
towns of Thyrea and Anthene and occupied by the
Lacedaemonians—which being border ground they
were always disputing about. Afterwards, however,
although the Lacedaemonians would not permit
them to make mention of that district, but said that,
if they wished to make a treaty on the same terms
as before, they were ready to do so, the Argive envoys
did induce the Lacedaemonians to agree to the following terms: for the present that a treaty should
be made for fifty years; that, however, either Lacedaemon or Argos, provided there were at the time

χεσθαι περὶ τῆς γῆς ταύτης, ὥσπερ καὶ πρότερόν
ποτε, ὅτε αὐτοὶ ἑκάτεροι ἠξίωσαν νικᾶν, διώκειν
δὲ μὴ ἐξεῖναι περαιτέρω τῶν πρὸς Ἄργος καὶ
3 Λακεδαίμονα ὅρων· τοῖς δὲ Λακεδαιμονίοις τὸ
μὲν πρῶτον ἐδόκει μωρία εἶναι ταῦτα, ἔπειτα
(ἐπεθύμουν γὰρ τὸ Ἄργος πάντως φίλον ἔχειν)
ξυνεχώρησαν ἐφ' οἷς ἠξίουν καὶ ξυνεγράψαντο.
ἐκέλευον δ' οἱ Λακεδαιμόνιοι, πρὶν τέλος τι αὐτῶν
ἔχειν, ἐς τὸ Ἄργος πρῶτον ἐπαναχωρήσαντας
αὐτοὺς δεῖξαι τῷ πλήθει, καὶ ἢν ἀρέσκοντα ᾖ,
ἥκειν ἐς τὰ Ὑακίνθια τοὺς ὅρκους ποιησομένους.
καὶ οἱ μὲν ἀνεχώρησαν.

XLII. Ἐν δὲ τῷ χρόνῳ τούτῳ ᾧ οἱ Ἀργεῖοι
ταῦτα ἔπρασσον, οἱ πρέσβεις τῶν Λακεδαιμονίων
Ἀνδρομένης καὶ Φαίδιμος καὶ Ἀντιμενίδας, οὓς
ἔδει τὸ Πάνακτον καὶ τοὺς ἄνδρας τοὺς παρὰ
Βοιωτῶν παραλαβόντας Ἀθηναίοις ἀποδοῦναι, τὸ
μὲν Πάνακτον ὑπὸ τῶν Βοιωτῶν αὐτῶν καθῃρη-
μένον ηὗρον, ἐπὶ προφάσει ὡς ἦσάν ποτε Ἀθηναίοις καὶ Βοιωτοῖς ἐκ διαφορᾶς περὶ αὐτοῦ ὅρκοι
παλαιοὶ μηδετέρους οἰκεῖν τὸ χωρίον ἀλλὰ κοινῇ
νέμειν, τοὺς δ' ἄνδρας οὓς εἶχον αἰχμαλώτους
Βοιωτοὶ Ἀθηναίων παραλαβόντες οἱ περὶ τὸν
Ἀνδρομένη ἐκόμισαν τοῖς Ἀθηναίοις καὶ ἀπέδοσαν, τοῦ τε Πανάκτου τὴν καθαίρεσιν ἔλεγον
αὐτοῖς, νομίζοντες καὶ τοῦτο ἀποδιδόναι· πολέμιον γὰρ οὐκέτι ἐν αὐτῷ Ἀθηναίοις οἰκήσειν

---

[1] 550 B.C. ; cf. Hdt. I. lxxxii.

neither pestilence nor war in either place, might challenge the other to decide by battle the question about this territory—just as once before,[1] when each had claimed to be victorious—but pursuit must not be made beyond the boundaries, between Argos and Lacedaemon. At first this seemed to the Lacedaemonians mere folly, but afterwards, as they desired under any circumstances to have Argos friendly to them, they accepted the conditions demanded and joined in a written agreement. But the Lacedaemonians urged the envoys first, before any of the provisions should be regarded as settled, to return to Argos and lay the matter before the people, and then, if it should be satisfactory to them, to come to the Hyacinthian festival and take the oaths. So they withdrew.

XLII. In the meantime, while the Argives were negotiating these matters, the Lacedaemonian envoys, Andromenes, Phaedimus and Antimenidas, who were to take over Panactum and the prisoners from the Thebans and restore them to the Athenians, found that Panactum had been destroyed by the Boeotians themselves, on the pretext that once in former times, when there had been a quarrel about Panactum, oaths had been exchanged between the Athenians and Boeotians, that neither should inhabit the district, but they should graze it in common. As for the men of the Athenians, however, whom the Boeotians held as prisoners, Andromenes and his colleagues received these from them, and bringing them back restored them to the Athenians. They also told them of the demolition of Panactum, claiming that this, too, was a restoration; for thereafter no one hostile to the Athenians would

2 οὐδένα. λεγομένων δὲ τούτων οἱ Ἀθηναῖοι δεινὰ
ἐποίουν, νομίζοντες ἀδικεῖσθαι ὑπὸ Λακεδαιμονίων
τοῦ τε Πανάκτου τῇ καθαιρέσει, ὃ ἔδει ὀρθὸν
παραδοῦναι, καὶ πυνθανόμενοι ὅτι καὶ Βοιωτοῖς
ἰδίᾳ ξυμμαχίαν πεποίηνται φάσκοντες πρότερον
κοινῇ τοὺς μὴ δεχομένους τὰς σπονδὰς προσαναγ-
κάσειν. τά τε ἄλλα ἐσκόπουν ὅσα ἐξελελοίπεσαν
τῆς ξυνθήκης καὶ ἐνόμιζον ἐξηπατῆσθαι, ὥστε
χαλεπῶς πρὸς τοὺς πρέσβεις ἀποκρινάμενοι
ἀπέπεμψαν.

XLIII. Κατὰ τοιαύτην δὴ διαφορὰν ὄντων τῶν
Λακεδαιμονίων πρὸς τοὺς Ἀθηναίους οἱ ἐν ταῖς
Ἀθήναις αὖ βουλόμενοι λῦσαι τὰς σπονδὰς εὐθὺς
2 ἐνέκειντο. ἦσαν δὲ ἄλλοι τε καὶ Ἀλκιβιάδης ὁ
Κλεινίου, ἀνὴρ ἡλικίᾳ μὲν ἔτι τότε ὢν νέος ὡς ἐν
ἄλλῃ πόλει, ἀξιώματι δὲ προγόνων τιμώμενος· ᾧ
ἐδόκει μὲν καὶ ἄμεινον εἶναι πρὸς τοὺς Ἀργείους
μᾶλλον χωρεῖν, οὐ μέντοι ἀλλὰ καὶ φρονήματι
φιλονικῶν ἠναντιοῦτο, ὅτι Λακεδαιμόνιοι διὰ
Νικίου καὶ Λάχητος ἔπραξαν τὰς σπονδάς, ἑαυτὸν κατά τε τὴν νεότητα ὑπεριδόντες καὶ κατὰ
τὴν παλαιὰν προξενίαν ποτὲ οὖσαν οὐ τιμήσαν-
τες, ἣν τοῦ πάππου ἀπειπόντος αὐτὸς τοὺς ἐκ τῆς
νήσου αὐτῶν αἰχμαλώτους θεραπεύων διενοεῖτο
3 ἀνανεώσασθαι. πανταχόθεν τε νομίζων ἐλασ-

---

[1] cf. ch. xxxv. 3.
[2] Born about 450 B.C., and so now about thirty years of age.

dwell in it. The moment this was said the
Athenians were very indignant, thinking that they
were wronged by the Lacedaemonians, both in the
demolition of Panactum, which ought to have been
restored to them intact, and because they heard that
the Lacedaemonians had made a separate alliance
with the Boeotians, although they had said before [1]
that they would join in coercing any that did not
accept the treaty. And they took into consideration
the other matters wherein the Lacedaemonians had
failed in their contract and in which they thought
they had been deceived; and so they gave the
envoys an angry answer and sent them away.

XLIII. As now the Lacedaemonians were thus
at variance with the Athenians, the party at Athens
that wished to annul the treaty at once became
urgent in pressing their views. To this party belonged, among others, Alcibiades son of Cleinias, a
man who, though as regards his age he would in any
other city have been accounted even at that time as
still young,[2] was held in honour on account of the
worth of his ancestors. To him it seemed really
to be better to side with the Argives; it was not
that alone, however, for he also opposed the treaty
because he was piqued in his pride because the Lacedaemonians had negotiated it through Nicias and
Laches, overlooking him on account of his youth
and not showing him the respect that was due him
on account of the old proxeny that once existed [3]
in his family. This relationship, though his grandfather had renounced it, he himself was by his at-
tentions to their captives from Sphacteria now
planning to renew. And so considering himself in

[3] cf. vi. lxxxix. 2; Plut. *Alcib.* xiv.

σοῦσθαι τό τε πρῶτον ἀντεῖπεν, οὐ βεβαίους
φάσκων εἶναι Λακεδαιμονίους, ἀλλ' ἵνα Ἀργείους
σφίσι σπεισάμενοι ἐξέλωσι καὶ αὖθις ἐπ' Ἀθηναίους μόνους ἴωσι, τούτου ἕνεκα σπένδεσθαι
αὐτούς, καὶ τότε, ἐπειδὴ ἡ διαφορὰ ἐγεγένητο,
πέμπει εὐθὺς ἐς Ἄργος ἰδίᾳ, κελεύων ὡς τάχιστα
ἐπὶ τὴν ξυμμαχίαν προκαλουμένους ἥκειν μετὰ
Μαντινέων καὶ Ἠλείων, ὡς καιροῦ ὄντος καὶ
αὐτὸς ξυμπράξων τὰ μάλιστα.

XLIV. Οἱ δὲ Ἀργεῖοι ἀκούσαντες τῆς τε
ἀγγελίας καὶ ἐπειδὴ ἔγνωσαν οὐ μετ' Ἀθηναίων
πραχθεῖσαν τὴν τῶν Βοιωτῶν ξυμμαχίαν, ἀλλ'
ἐς διαφορὰν μεγάλην καθεστῶτας αὐτοὺς πρὸς
τοὺς Λακεδαιμονίους, τῶν μὲν ἐν Λακεδαίμονι
πρέσβεων, οἳ σφίσι περὶ τῶν σπονδῶν ἔτυχον
ἀπόντες, ἠμέλουν, πρὸς δὲ τοὺς Ἀθηναίους μᾶλλον τὴν γνώμην εἶχον, νομίζοντες πόλιν τε σφίσι
φιλίαν ἀπὸ παλαιοῦ καὶ δημοκρατουμένην ὥσπερ
καὶ αὐτοὶ καὶ δύναμιν μεγάλην ἔχουσαν τὴν κατὰ
θάλασσαν ξυμπολεμήσειν σφίσιν, ἢν καθιστῶν-
2 ται ἐς πόλεμον. ἔπεμπον οὖν εὐθὺς πρέσβεις ὡς
τοὺς Ἀθηναίους περὶ τῆς ξυμμαχίας· ξυνεπρεσ-
3 βεύοντο δὲ καὶ Ἠλεῖοι καὶ Μαντινῆς. ἀφίκοντο
δὲ καὶ Λακεδαιμονίων πρέσβεις κατὰ τάχος,
δοκοῦντες ἐπιτήδειοι εἶναι τοῖς Ἀθηναίοις, Φιλοχαρίδας τε καὶ Λέων καὶ Ἔνδιος, δείσαντες μὴ
τήν τε ξυμμαχίαν ὀργιζόμενοι πρὸς τοὺς Ἀργείους
ποιήσωνται, καὶ ἅμα Πύλον ἀπαιτήσοντες ἀντὶ

every way slighted, he both spoke against the treaty in the first instance, alleging that the Lacedaemonians were not to be trusted, but that their object in making the treaty was, that by concluding a treaty with the Athenians they might utterly overthrow the Argives and then proceed against the Athenians when thus isolated; and at the present time, after the difference had occurred, he promptly dispatched a message to Argos privately, bidding them come as quickly as possible, along with the Mantineans and Eleans, and invite the Athenians to form an alliance, as the moment was favourable and he himself would cooperate to the utmost.

XLIV. When the Argives received this message and realized that the alliance with the Boeotians had been made without the consent of the Athenians, but that these were involved in a serious quarrel with the Lacedaemonians, they took no further thought about their envoys at Lacedaemon, who had gone thither on the matter of the treaty, and gave their attention rather to the Athenians, thinking that a city which had been of old friendly to them and was governed by a democracy, just as they were, and possessed great power on sea, would enter the war along with them, should they be involved in war. Accordingly, they at once sent envoys to Athens to negotiate the alliance; and there went with them also envoys of the Eleans and Mantineans. But thither came, too, in all haste, envoys of the Lacedaemonians who were thought to be acceptable to the Athenians, Philocharidas, Leon, and Endius, for there was fear that the Athenians in their anger might make the alliance with the Argives; and the envoys were also to demand the restoration of Pylos in place of

THUCYDIDES

Πανάκτου, καὶ περὶ τῆς Βοιωτῶν ξυμμαχίας ἀπο-
λογησόμενοι ὡς οὐκ ἐπὶ κακῷ τῶν Ἀθηναίων
ἐποιήσαντο.

XLV. Καὶ λέγοντες ἐν τῇ βουλῇ περί τε τούτων καὶ ὡς αὐτοκράτορες ἥκουσι περὶ πάντων
ξυμβῆναι τῶν διαφόρων, τὸν Ἀλκιβιάδην ἐφό-
βουν μὴ καί, ἢν ἐς τὸν δῆμον ταὐτὰ λέγωσιν,
ἐπαγάγωνται τὸ πλῆθος καὶ ἀπωσθῇ ἡ Ἀργείων
2 ξυμμαχία. μηχανᾶται δὲ πρὸς αὐτοὺς τοιόνδε τι
ὁ Ἀλκιβιάδης· τοὺς Λακεδαιμονίους πείθει πίστιν
αὐτοῖς δούς, ἢν μὴ ὁμολογήσωσιν ἐν τῷ δήμῳ
αὐτοκράτορες ἥκειν, Πύλον τε αὐτοῖς ἀποδώσειν
(πείσειν γὰρ αὐτὸς Ἀθηναίους, ὥσπερ καὶ νῦν
3 ἀντιλέγειν) καὶ τἆλλα ξυναλλάξειν. βουλόμενος
δὲ αὐτοὺς Νικίου τε ἀποστῆσαι ταῦτα ἔπρασσε
καὶ ὅπως, ἐν τῷ δήμῳ διαβαλὼν αὐτοὺς ὡς οὐδὲν
ἀληθὲς ἐν νῷ ἔχουσιν οὐδὲ λέγουσιν οὐδέποτε
ταὐτά, τοὺς Ἀργείους καὶ Ἠλείους καὶ Μαν-
4 τινέας ξυμμάχους ποιήσῃ. καὶ ἐγένετο οὕτως.
ἐπειδὴ γὰρ ἐς τὸν δῆμον παρελθόντες καὶ ἐπερω-
τώμενοι οὐκ ἔφασαν ὥσπερ ἐν τῇ βουλῇ αὐτοκράτορες ἥκειν, οἱ Ἀθηναῖοι οὐκέτι ἠνείχοντο,
ἀλλὰ τοῦ Ἀλκιβιάδου πολλῷ μᾶλλον ἢ πρότερον
καταβοῶντος τῶν Λακεδαιμονίων ἐσήκουόν τε καὶ
ἕτοιμοι ἦσαν εὐθὺς παραγαγόντες τοὺς Ἀργείους
καὶ τοὺς μετ᾽ αὐτῶν ξυμμάχους ποιεῖσθαι· σεισμοῦ δὲ γενομένου πρίν τι ἐπικυρωθῆναι, ἡ
ἐκκλησία αὕτη ἀνεβλήθη.

XLVI. Τῇ δ᾽ ὑστεραίᾳ ἐκκλησίᾳ ὁ Νικίας,

Panactum, and to say at the same time, in excuse for the Boeotian alliance, that it had not been made with a view to injuring the Athenians.

XLV. Speaking in the senate on these points, and saying that they had come with full power to settle all their differences, they filled Alcibiades with alarm lest, if they should say the same things to the assembly, they should win over the people and the Argive alliance might be rejected. So he adopted the following device against them: He persuaded the Lacedaemonians, by pledging them his faith, that, if they would not admit before the assembly that they had come with full powers, he would restore Pylos to them—for he himself would use his influence with the Athenians for them as now he opposed them—and would settle the other points at issue. He resorted to such methods because he wished to detach them from Nicias, and in order that he might accuse them before the assembly of having no sincere intentions and of never saying the same things, and thereby might effect an alliance with the Argives, Mantineans, and Eleans. And so it turned out. For when, on coming before the popular assembly and being asked whether they had come with full powers, they answered " No," contrary to what they had said in the senate, the Athenians could endure it no longer, but hearkened to Alcibiades, who inveighed against the Lacedaemonians far more than before, and were ready at once to bring in the Argives and their confederates and conclude an alliance. But before anything was ratified an earthquake occurred, and this assembly was adjourned.

XLVI. In the assembly on the next day, however,

καίπερ, τῶν Λακεδαιμονίων αὐτῶν ἠπατημένων,
καὶ αὐτὸς ἐξηπατημένος περὶ τοῦ μὴ αὐτοκράτορας ὁμολογῆσαι ἥκειν, ὅμως τοῖς Λακεδαιμονίοις
ἔφη χρῆναι φίλους μᾶλλον γίγνεσθαι, καὶ ἐπι-
σχόντας τὰ πρὸς Ἀργείους πέμψαι ἔτι ὡς αὐτοὺς
καὶ εἰδέναι ὅ τι διανοοῦνται, λέγων ἐν μὲν τῷ
σφετέρῳ καλῷ, ἐν δὲ τῷ ἐκείνων ἀπρεπεῖ τὸν
πόλεμον ἀναβάλλεσθαι· σφίσι μὲν γὰρ εὖ
ἑστώτων τῶν πραγμάτων ὡς ἐπὶ πλεῖστον
ἄριστον εἶναι διασώσασθαι τὴν εὐπραγίαν,
ἐκείνοις δὲ δυστυχοῦσιν ὅτι τάχιστα εὕρημα
2 εἶναι διακινδυνεῦσαι. ἔπεισέ τε πέμψαι πρέσβεις, ὧν καὶ αὐτὸς ἦν, κελεύσοντας Λακεδαιμονίους, εἴ τι δίκαιον διανοοῦνται, Πάνακτόν
τε ὀρθὸν ἀποδιδόναι καὶ Ἀμφίπολιν, καὶ τὴν
Βοιωτῶν ξυμμαχίαν ἀνεῖναι, ἢν μὴ ἐς τὰς σπονδὰς
ἐσίωσι, καθάπερ εἴρητο ἄνευ ἀλλήλων μηδενὶ
3 ξυμβαίνειν. εἰπεῖν τε ἐκέλευον ὅτι καὶ σφεῖς, εἰ
ἐβούλοντο ἀδικεῖν, ἤδη ἂν Ἀργείους ξυμμάχους
πεποιῆσθαι, ὡς παρεῖναί γ' αὐτοὺς αὐτοῦ
τούτου ἕνεκα· εἴ τέ τι ἄλλο ἐνεκάλουν, πάντα
ἐπιστείλαντες ἀπέπεμψαν τοὺς περὶ τὸν Νικίαν
4 πρέσβεις. καὶ ἀφικομένων αὐτῶν καὶ ἀπαγγει-
λάντων τά τε ἄλλα καὶ τέλος εἰπόντων ὅτι, εἰ μὴ

Nicias, although, as the Lacedaemonians had themselves been deceived, so he too had been deceived in
the matter of their admission that they had not
come with full powers, nevertheless still maintained
that they ought to become friends with the Lacedaemonians rather than with the Argives; and accordingly he proposed that, deferring the question
of the Argive alliance, they should again send envoys
to the Lacedaemonians and find out what their intentions were.   He urged the view that the post-
ponement of hostile operations was honourable for
themselves but humiliating for the Lacedaemonians;
for as matters stood well for themselves, it was best
to preserve their good fortune as long as possible,
whereas for the Lacedaemonians, who were in hard
luck, it would be clear gain to risk a decisive contest
as quickly as possible.   So he persuaded them to
send envoys, himself being one, to urge the Lacedaemonians, if they had any just intentions, to restore
Panactum intact and Amphipolis, and to give up the
alliance with the Boeotians—unless these should
accede to the treaty—in accordance with the
stipulation which had been arrived at that neither
should enter into an agreement with any third party
without the consent of the other.   The ambassadors
were instructed also to say that, if the Athenians
had wished to do wrong, they would already have
made the Argives allies, as their envoys were present
for that very purpose; and any other complaints
which they had to make they included in their
instructions to Nicias and his colleagues and then
despatched them to Sparta.   When these had arrived
and had finished reciting their other demands, they
said in conclusion that, unless the Lacedaemonians

τὴν ξυμμαχίαν ἀνήσουσι Βοιωτοῖς μὴ ἐσιοῦσιν ἐς
τὰς σπονδάς, ποιήσονται καὶ αὐτοὶ Ἀργείους καὶ
τοὺς μετ᾽ αὐτῶν ξυμμάχους, τὴν μὲν ξυμμαχίαν
οἱ Λακεδαιμόνιοι Βοιωτοῖς, οὐκ ἔφασαν ἀνήσειν,
ἐπικρατούντων τῶν περὶ τὸν Ξενάρη τὸν ἔφορον
ταῦτα γίγνεσθαι καὶ ὅσοι ἄλλοι τῆς αὐτῆς γνώμης
ἦσαν, τοὺς δὲ ὅρκους δεομένου Νικίου ἀνενεώ-
σαντο· ἐφοβεῖτο γὰρ μὴ πάντα ἀτελῆ ἔχων
ἀπέλθῃ καὶ διαβληθῇ, ὅπερ καὶ ἐγένετο, αἴτιος
δοκῶν εἶναι τῶν πρὸς Λακεδαιμονίους σπονδῶν.
5 ἀναχωρήσαντός τε αὐτοῦ ὡς ἤκουσαν οἱ Ἀθηναῖοι
οὐδὲν ἐκ τῆς Λακεδαίμονος πεπραγμένον, εὐθὺς δι᾽
ὀργῆς εἶχον, καὶ νομίζοντες ἀδικεῖσθαι (ἔτυχον
γὰρ παρόντες οἱ Ἀργεῖοι καὶ οἱ ξύμμαχοι, παρα-
γαγόντος Ἀλκιβιάδου) ἐποιήσαντο σπονδὰς καὶ
ξυμμαχίαν πρὸς αὐτοὺς τήνδε.

XLVII. Σπονδὰς ἐποιήσαντο ἑκατὸν Ἀθηναῖοι
ἔτη καὶ Ἀργεῖοι καὶ Μαντινῆς καὶ Ἠλεῖοι πρὸς
ἀλλήλους,[1] ὑπὲρ σφῶν αὐτῶν καὶ τῶν ξυμμάχων
ὧν ἄρχουσιν ἑκάτεροι, ἀδόλους καὶ ἀβλαβεῖς καὶ
κατὰ γῆν καὶ κατὰ θάλασσαν.

2   Ὅπλα δὲ μὴ ἐξέστω ἐπιφέρειν ἐπὶ πημονῇ μήτε
Ἀργείους καὶ Ἠλείους καὶ Μαντινέας καὶ τοὺς
ξυμμάχους ἐπὶ Ἀθηναίους καὶ τοὺς ξυμμάχους
ὧν ἄρχουσιν Ἀθηναῖοι, μήτε Ἀθηναίους καὶ τοὺς
ξυμμάχους ὧν ἄρχουσιν Ἀθηναῖοι[2] ἐπὶ Ἀργείους
καὶ Ἠλείους καὶ Μαντινέας καὶ τοὺς ξυμμάχους,
τέχνῃ μηδὲ μηχανῇ μηδεμιᾷ.

3   Κατὰ τάδε ξυμμάχους εἶναι Ἀθηναίους καὶ

[1] πρὸς ἀλλήλους, restored from the inscription recording
this treaty (C.I.A. iv. p. 15 f., No. 46 b). See note, p. 96.
[2] ὧν ἄρχουσιν Ἀθηναῖοι restored by Kirchhoff from the
inscription.

BOOK V. xlvi. 4–xlvii. 3

should give up the alliance with the Boeotians, in case these would not accede to the treaty, they themselves would make an alliance with the Argives and their confederates. But the Lacedaemonians refused to give up the alliance with the Boeotians— the party of Xenares the ephor and all the rest that were of that view carrying their point to this effect—but the oaths they renewed on Nicias' request; for he was afraid that he would return with nothing accomplished and be exposed to calumny, as indeed happened, since he was generally regarded as having been responsible for the treaty with the Lacedaemonians. On his return, when the Athenians heard that nothing had been done at Lacedaemon, they flew into a rage, and thinking they had been wronged, when Alcibiades brought in the Argives and their allies, who chanced to be present, they made an alliance with them on the following terms :

XLVII. 1. "The Athenians, Argives, Mantineans, and Eleans have made a treaty with one another for a hundred years, on behalf of themselves and the allies over whom they have authority respectively, to be observed without fraud or hurt both by land and sea.

2. "It shall not be allowed to bear arms with harmful intent, either for the Argives, Eleans, Mantineans and their allies against the Athenians and the allies over whom the Athenians have authority, or for the Athenians and the allies over whom the Athenians have authority against the Argives, Eleans, Mantineans and their allies, by any art or device.

3. "The Athenians, Argives, Eleans, and Mantineans

'Αργείους καὶ 'Ηλείους καὶ Μαντινέας ἑκατὸν
ἔτη· ἢν πολεμιοι ἴωσιν ἐς τὴν γῆν τὴν 'Αθηναίων,
βοηθεῖν 'Αργείους καὶ 'Ηλείους καὶ Μαντινέας
'Αθήναζε, καθ' ὅ τι ἂν ἐπαγγέλλωσιν 'Αθηναῖοι,
τρόπῳ ὁποίῳ ἂν δύνωνται ἰσχυροτάτῳ κατὰ τὸ
δυνατόν· ἢν δὲ δῃώσαντες οἴχωνται, πολεμίαν
εἶναι ταύτην τὴν πόλιν 'Αργείοις καὶ Μαντινεῦσι
καὶ 'Ηλείοις καὶ 'Αθηναίοις καὶ κακῶς πάσχειν
ὑπὸ ἀπασῶν τῶν πόλεων τούτων· καταλύειν δὲ
μὴ ἐξεῖναι τὸν πόλεμον πρὸς ταύτην τὴν πόλιν
μηδεμιᾷ τῶν πόλεων, ἢν μὴ ἀπάσαις δοκῇ.

4   "Βοηθεῖν δὲ καὶ 'Αθηναίους ἐς "Αργος καὶ ἐς[1]
Μαντίνειαν καὶ ἐς[2] 'Ηλιν, ἢν πολέμιοι ἴωσιν ἐπὶ
τὴν γῆν τὴν 'Ηλείων ἢ τὴν Μαντινέων ἢ τὴν 'Αργείων, καθ' ὅ τι ἂν ἐπαγγέλλωσιν αἱ πόλεις
αὗται, τρόπῳ ὁποίῳ ἂν δύνωνται ἰσχυροτάτῳ κατὰ
τὸ δυνατόν· ἢν δὲ δῃώσαντες οἴχωνται, πολεμίαν
εἶναι ταύτην τὴν πόλιν 'Αθηναίοις καὶ 'Αργείοις
καὶ Μαντινεῦσι καὶ 'Ηλείοις καὶ κακῶς πάσχειν
ὑπὸ ἀπασῶν τούτων τῶν πόλεων· καταλύειν δὲ
μὴ ἐξεῖναι τὸν πόλεμον πρὸς ταύτην τὴν πόλιν μηδεμιᾷ τῶν πόλεων,[3] ἢν μὴ ἀπάσαις δοκῇ.[4]

5   "'Όπλα δὲ μὴ ἐᾶν ἔχοντας διιέναι ἐπὶ πολέμῳ
διὰ τῆς γῆς τῆς σφετέρας αὐτῶν καὶ τῶν ξυμμάχων ὧν ἄρχουσιν ἕκαστοι, μηδὲ κατὰ θάλασσαν,
ἢν μὴ ψηφισαμένων τῶν πόλεων ἀπασῶν τὴν
δίοδον εἶναι, 'Αθηναίων καὶ 'Αργείων καὶ Μαντινέων καὶ 'Ηλείων.

[1] Added by Stahl.   [2] Added by Stahl.
[3] μηδεμιᾷ τῶν πόλεων restored by Kirchhoff from the
inscription.
[4] ταῖς πόλεσιν, after δοκῇ, deleted by Kirchhoff according
to the inscription.

shall be allies for a hundred years on the following terms: If an enemy invade the territory of the Athenians, the Argives, Eleans and Mantineans shall bring aid to Athens, according as the Athenians may send them word, in whatever way they can most effectually, to the limit of their power; but if the invaders shall have ravaged the land and gone, that city shall be hostile to the Argives, Mantineans, Eleans, and Athenians, and shall suffer at the hands of all these states; and to discontinue hostilities against that state shall not be allowed to any one of these states, unless all agree.

4. "Likewise the Athenians shall bring aid to Argos and to Mantinea and Elis, if an enemy come against the territory of the Eleans or that of the Mantineans or that of the Argives, according as these states send word, in whatever way they can most effectually, to the limit of their power; but if the invader shall have ravaged the land and gone, that city shall be hostile to the Athenians, Argives, Mantineans, and Eleans, and shall suffer ill at the hands of all these states; and to discontinue hostilities against that state shall not be allowed to any one of these states, unless all agree.

5. "It shall not be permitted to pass under arms with hostile intent through their own territory or that of the allies over whom they severally have authority, nor by sea, unless passage shall have been voted by all of these states, Athenians, Argives, Mantineans, and Eleans.

6 "Τοῖς δὲ βοηθοῦσιν ἡ πόλις ἡ πέμπουσα παρ-
εχέτω μέχρι μὲν τριάκοντα ἡμερῶν σῖτον ἐπὴν
ἔλθωσιν ἐς τὴν πόλιν τὴν ἐπαγγείλασαν βοηθεῖν,
καὶ ἀπιοῦσι κατὰ ταὐτά· ἢν δὲ πλέονα βούλωνται χρόνον τῇ στρατιᾷ χρῆσθαι, ἡ πόλις ἡ
μεταπεμψαμένη διδότω σῖτον, τῷ μὲν ὁπλίτῃ
καὶ ψιλῷ καὶ τοξότῃ τρεῖς ὀβολοὺς Αἰγιναίους
τῆς ἡμέρας ἑκάστης, τῷ δ᾽ ἱππεῖ δραχμὴν Αἰγι-
ναίαν.

7 "'Η δὲ πόλις ἡ μεταπεμψαμένη τὴν στρατιὰν[1]
τὴν ἡγεμονίαν ἐχέτω, ὅταν ἐν τῇ αὑτῆς ὁ πόλεμος
ᾖ. ἢν δέ ποι δόξῃ ἀπάσαις[2] ταῖς πόλεσι κοινῇ
στρατεύεσθαι, τὸ ἴσον τῆς ἡγεμονίας μετεῖναι
ἀπάσαις ταῖς πόλεσιν.

8 "'Ομόσαι δὲ τὰς σπονδὰς Ἀθηναίους μὲν ὑπέρ
τε σφῶν αὐτῶν καὶ τῶν ξυμμάχων, Ἀργεῖοι δὲ
καὶ Μαντινῆς καὶ Ἠλεῖοι καὶ οἱ ξύμμαχοι τούτων
κατὰ πόλεις ὀμνύντων. ὀμνύντων δὲ τὸν ἐπιχώριον ὅρκον ἕκαστοι τὸν μέγιστον κατὰ ἱερῶν
τελείων. ὁ δὲ ὅρκος ἔστω ὅδε· 'Εμμενῶ τῇ
ξυμμαχίᾳ κατὰ τὰ ξυγκείμενα δικαίως καὶ ἀβλα-
βῶς καὶ ἀδόλως, καὶ οὐ παραβήσομαι τέχνῃ οὐδὲ
μηχανῇ οὐδεμιᾷ.'

9 "'Ομνύντων δὲ Ἀθήνησι μὲν ἡ βουλὴ καὶ αἱ
ἔνδημοι ἀρχαί, ἐξορκούντων δὲ οἱ πρυτάνεις· ἐν
Ἄργει δὲ ἡ βουλὴ καὶ οἱ ὀγδοήκοντα καὶ οἱ
ἀρτῦναι, ἐξορκούντων δὲ οἱ ὀγδοήκοντα· ἐν δὲ
Μαντινείᾳ οἱ δημιουργοὶ καὶ ἡ βουλὴ καὶ αἱ
ἄλλαι ἀρχαί, ἐξορκούντων δὲ οἱ θεωροὶ καὶ οἱ

---

[1] τὴν στρατιὰν added by van Herwerden.
[2] ἀπάσαις according to the inscription ; MSS. omit.

6. "For the relieving force the state which sends for them shall furnish provisions for thirty days after their arrival in the state which sent for succour, and in like manner on their return; but if they wish to use the army for a longer period, the city which sends for it shall furnish provisions for heavy-armed or light-armed troops or bowmen, three Aeginetan obols [1] per day, and for a cavalryman one Aeginetan drachma.[2]

7. "The state which sent for the troops shall have command whenever the war is in its territory. But if it shall seem good to all the states to make a joint expedition anywhere, all the states shall share the command equally.

8. "The Athenians shall swear to the treaty for themselves and their allies, but the Argives, Mantineans, Eleans, and their allies shall swear to it individually by states. And they shall severally swear the oath that is most binding in their own country, over full-grown victims. And the oath shall be as follows: 'I will abide by the alliance in accordance with its stipulations, justly and without injury and without guile, and will not transgress it by any art or device.'

9. "The oath shall be sworn at Athens by the senate and the home [3] magistrates, the prytanes administering it; at Argos by the senate and the eighty and the artynae, the eighty administering the oath; at Mantinea by the demiurgi and the senate and the other magistrates, the theori and the

---

[1] About 8*d.* or 16 cents.
[2] About 1*s.* 4*d.* or 32 cents.
[3] *i.e.* those whose functions were restricted to the city.

πολέμαρχοι· ἐν δὲ Ἤλιδι οἱ δημιουργοὶ[1] καὶ οἱ
ἐξακόσιοι, ἐξορκούντων δὲ οἱ δημιουργοὶ καὶ οἱ
θεσμοφύλακες.

10 "'Ανανεοῦσθαι δὲ τοὺς ὅρκους 'Αθηναίους μὲν
ἰόντας ἐς Ἤλιν καὶ ἐς Μαντίνειαν καὶ ἐς "Αργος
τριάκοντα ἡμέραις πρὸ 'Ολυμπίων, 'Αργείους δὲ
καὶ 'Ηλείους καὶ Μαντινέας ἰόντας 'Αθήναζε δέκα
ἡμέραις πρὸ Παναθηναίων τῶν μεγάλων.

11 "Τὰς δὲ ξυνθήκας τὰς περὶ τῶν σπονδῶν καὶ
τῶν ὅρκων καὶ τῆς ξυμμαχίας ἀναγράψαι ἐν
στήλῃ λιθίνῃ 'Αθηναίους μὲν ἐν πόλει, 'Αργείους
δὲ ἐν ἀγορᾷ ἐν τοῦ 'Απόλλωνος τῷ ἱερῷ, Μαντινέας δὲ ἐν τοῦ Διὸς τῷ ἱερῷ ἐν τῇ ἀγορᾷ·
καταθέντων δὲ καὶ 'Ολυμπίασι στήλην χαλκῆν
κοινῇ 'Ολυμπίοις τοῖς νυνί.

12 "'Εὰν δέ τι δοκῇ ἄμεινον εἶναι ταῖς πόλεσι
ταύταις προσθεῖναι πρὸς τοῖς ξυγκειμένοις, ὅ τι
ἂν[2] δόξῃ ταῖς πόλεσιν ἁπάσαις κοινῇ βουλευο-
μέναις, τοῦτο κύριον εἶναι."

XLVIII. Αἱ μὲν σπονδαὶ καὶ ἡ ξυμμαχία
οὕτως ἐγένοντο. καὶ αἱ τῶν Λακεδαιμονίων καὶ
'Αθηναίων οὐκ ἀπείρηντο τούτου ἕνεκα οὐδ' ὑφ'
2 ἑτέρων. Κορίνθιοι δὲ 'Αργείων ὄντες ξύμμαχοι οὐκ
ἐσῆλθον ἐς αὐτάς, ἀλλὰ καὶ γενομένης πρὸ
τούτου 'Ηλείοις καὶ 'Αργείοις καὶ Μαντινεῦσι
ξυμμαχίας, τοῖς αὐτοῖς πολεμεῖν καὶ εἰρήνην
ἄγειν, οὐ ξυνώμοσαν, ἀρκεῖν δ' ἔφασαν σφίσι τὴν

---

[1] καὶ οἱ τὰ τέλη ἔχοντες, in MSS. after δημιουργοί, deleted
by Kirchhoff as gloss on that word.
[2] ὅ τι δ' ἄν MSS., δ' deleted by Bekker.

---

[1] A fragment of the official document recording this treaty
was found by the Archaeological Society at Athens in the

polemarchs administering the oath; at Elis by the
demiurgi and the six hundred, the demiurgi and the
thesmophylaces administering the oath.

10. "For renewal of the oath the Athenians shall
go to Elis, to Mantinea, and to Argos, thirty days
before the Olympic games; and the Argives, Eleans,
and Mantineans shall go to Athens ten days before
the great Panathenaea.

11. "The stipulations respecting the treaty, the
oaths, and the alliance shall be inscribed on a stone
column, by the Athenians on the Acropolis,[1] by the
Argives in the market-place, in the temple of
Apollo, by the Mantineans in the market-place, in
the temple of Zeus; and a brazen pillar shall be set
up by them jointly at the Olympic games of this
year.

12. "If it shall seem advisable to these states to add
anything further to these agreements, whatever shall
seem good to all the states in joint deliberation shall
be binding."

XLVIII. Thus the treaty and the alliance were
completed; but the treaty between the Lacedaemonians and Athenians was not on this account
renounced by either party. The Corinthians,
however, although allies of the Argives, did not
accede to the new treaty—even before this when an
alliance, offensive and defensive, had been made
between the Eleans, Argives, and Mantineans, they
had not joined it—but said they were content with
the first defensive alliance that had been made,

spring of 1877 upon a marble slab on the southern slope of
the Acropolis. The text of the inscription has been restored
by Kirchhoff, Schöne, Foucart, and Stahl in substantial
agreement.

πρώτην γενομένην ἐπιμαχίαν, ἀλλήλοις βοηθεῖν,
3 ξυνεπιστρατεύειν δὲ μηδενί. οἱ μὲν Κορίνθιοι
οὕτως ἀπέστησαν τῶν ξυμμάχων καὶ πρὸς τοὺς
Λακεδαιμονίους πάλιν τὴν γνώμην εἶχον.

XLIX. Ὀλύμπια δ᾽ ἐγένετο τοῦ θέρους τούτου,
οἷς Ἀνδροσθένης Ἀρκὰς παγκράτιον τὸ πρῶτον
ἐνίκα· καὶ Λακεδαιμόνιοι τοῦ ἱεροῦ ὑπὸ Ἠλείων
εἴρχθησαν ὥστε μὴ θύειν μηδ᾽ ἀγωνίζεσθαι, οὐκ
ἐκτίνοντες τὴν δίκην αὐτοῖς ἣν ἐν τῷ Ὀλυμπικῷ
νόμῳ Ἠλεῖοι κατεδικάσαντο αὐτῶν, φάσκοντες
σφῶν ἐπὶ Φύρκον τε τεῖχος ὅπλα ἐπενεγκεῖν καὶ
ἐς Λέπρεον αὐτῶν ὁπλίτας ἐν ταῖς Ὀλυμπικαῖς
σπονδαῖς ἐσπέμψαι. ἡ δὲ καταδίκη δισχίλιαι
μναῖ ἦσαν, κατὰ τὸν ὁπλίτην ἕκαστον δύο μναῖ,
2 ὥσπερ ὁ νόμος ἔχει. Λακεδαιμόνιοι δὲ πρέσβεις
πέμψαντες ἀντέλεγον μὴ δικαίως σφῶν καταδεδι-
κάσθαι, λέγοντες μὴ ἐπηγγέλθαι πω ἐς Λακεδαίμονα τὰς σπονδάς, ὅτ᾽ ἐσέπεμψαν τοὺς ὁπλίτας.
3 Ἠλεῖοι δὲ τὴν παρ᾽ αὐτοῖς ἐκεχειρίαν ἤδη ἔφασαν
εἶναι (πρώτοις γὰρ σφίσιν αὐτοῖς ἐπαγγέλλουσι),
καὶ ἡσυχαζόντων σφῶν καὶ οὐ προσδεχομένων ὡς
4 ἐν σπονδαῖς, αὐτοὺς λαθεῖν ἀδικήσαντας. οἱ δὲ
Λακεδαιμόνιοι ὑπελάμβανον οὐ χρεὼν εἶναι αὐτοὺς
ἐπαγγεῖλαι ἔτι ἐς Λακεδαίμονα, εἰ ἀδικεῖν γε ἤδη
ἐνόμιζον αὐτούς, ἀλλ᾽ οὐχ ὡς νομίζοντας τοῦτο
δρᾶσαι, καὶ ὅπλα οὐδαμόσε ἔτι αὐτοῖς ἐπενεγκεῖν.

---

[1] The month of the festival was sacred (ἱερομηνία) and all
warfare was stopped for that time. To enter the territory of
Elis with an armed force during that month was sacrilegious.

namely to aid one another, but not to join in attacking any other party. Thus, then, the Corinthians held aloof from their allies and were turning their thoughts again to the Lacedaemonians.

XLIX. This summer the Olympic games were held, in which Androsthenes an Arcadian won his first victory in the pancratium. The Lacedaemonians were excluded from the sanctuary by the Eleans, and so could neither sacrifice nor contend in the games, as they refused to pay the fine which had been assessed against them according to Olympic law by the Eleans, who alleged that they had attacked the Elean fortress of Phyrcus, and sent a force of their hoplites into Lepreum during the Olympic truce.[1] The fine was two thousand minas,[2] two minas[3] for each hoplite, as the law ordains. The Lacedaemonians sent envoys and urged that the fine had been unfairly imposed upon them, claiming that the treaty had not been announced at Lacedaemon when they sent the hoplites into Elis. But the Eleans said that the truce was already in force in their country—for they proclaim it among themselves first —and while they were keeping quiet and not expecting any attack, as in time of truce, the Lacedaemonians had done the wrong, taking them by surprise. The Lacedaemonians replied that they should not have gone on and announced the truce at Lacedaemon if they were of the opinion that the Lacedaemonians were already wronging them, but they had done this as though they did not think so, and they themselves had not kept on bearing arms against them anywhere after the announcement of the truce.

Ol. 90, 1; July, 420 B.C.

---

[2] About £8,125 or $38,840.
[3] About £8 2s. 6d. or $39.

5 Ἠλεῖοι δὲ τοῦ αὐτοῦ λόγου εἴχοντο, ὡς μὲν οὐκ
ἀδικοῦσι μὴ ἂν πεισθῆναι, εἰ δὲ βούλονται σφίσι
Λέπρεον ἀποδοῦναι, τό τε αὐτῶν μέρος ἀφιέναι
τοῦ ἀργυρίου καὶ ὃ τῷ θεῷ γίγνεται αὐτοὶ ὑπὲρ
ἐκείνων ἐκτείσειν.

L. Ὡς δ᾽ οὐκ ἐσήκουον, αὖθις τάδε ἠξίουν,
Λέπρεον μὲν μὴ ἀποδοῦναι, εἰ μὴ βούλονται,
ἀναβάντας δὲ ἐπὶ τὸν βωμὸν τοῦ Διὸς τοῦ Ὀλυμ-
πίου, ἐπειδὴ προθυμοῦνται χρῆσθαι τῷ ἱερῷ,
ἐπομόσαι ἐναντίον τῶν Ἑλλήνων ἦ μὴν ἀποδώσειν
2 ὕστερον τὴν καταδίκην. ὡς δὲ οὐδὲ ταῦτα ἤθελον,
Λακεδαιμόνιοι μὲν εἴργοντο τοῦ ἱεροῦ θυσίας καὶ
ἀγώνων[1] καὶ οἴκοι ἔθυον, οἱ δὲ ἄλλοι Ἕλληνες ἐθεώ-
3 ρουν πλὴν Λεπρεατῶν. ὅμως δὲ οἱ Ἠλεῖοι δεδιότες
μὴ βίᾳ θύσωσι, ξὺν ὅπλοις τῶν νεωτέρων φυλακὴν
εἶχον· ἦλθον δὲ αὐτοῖς καὶ Ἀργεῖοι καὶ Μαντινῆς,
χίλιοι ἑκατέρων, καὶ Ἀθηναίων ἱππῆς, οἳ ἐν Ἁρ-
4 πίνῃ[2] ὑπέμενον τὴν ἑορτήν. δέος δ᾽ ἐγένετο τῇ
πανηγύρει μέγα μὴ ξὺν ὅπλοις ἔλθωσιν οἱ Λακεδαιμόνιοι, ἄλλως τε καὶ ἐπειδὴ καὶ Λίχας ὁ
Ἀρκεσιλάου, Λακεδαιμόνιος, ἐν τῷ ἀγῶνι ὑπὸ τῶν
ῥαβδούχων πληγὰς ἔλαβεν, ὅτι νικῶντος τοῦ ἑαυτοῦ ζεύγους καὶ ἀνακηρυχθέντος Βοιωτῶν δημοσίου
κατὰ τὴν οὐκ ἐξουσίαν τῆς ἀγωνίσεως, προελθὼν
ἐς τὸν ἀγῶνα ἀνέδησε τὸν ἡνίοχον, βουλόμενος

---

[1] θυσίας καὶ ἀγώνων bracketed by Hude following Krüger.
[2] Michaelis' correction for Ἄργει of the MSS.

But the Eleans persisted in the same statement, saying that they could never be persuaded that the Lacedaemonians were not guilty; if, however, they were willing to restore Lepreum to them, they would give up their own half of the fine, and what was due to the gods they would themselves pay on their behalf.

L. When the Lacedaemonians refused this offer, the Eleans proposed that they should not restore Lepreum, if they objected to that, but, as they eagerly desired to have access to the sanctuary, that they should go up to the altar of Olympian Zeus and swear in the presence of the Hellenes that they would assuredly pay the fine later. But as they were unwilling to do even this, the Lacedaemonians were excluded from the temple, from the sacrifice and the contests, and sacrificed at home; while the rest of the Hellenes, except the Lepreates, sent representatives to the festival. Still the Eleans, fearing that the Lacedaemonians would force their way and offer sacrifice, kept guard with the young men under arms; and there came to their aid also some Argives and Mantineans, a thousand of each, and some Athenian cavalry that were at Arpina[1] awaiting the festival. And great fear came upon the assembly that the Lacedaemonians might come with arms, especially as Lichas son of Arcesilaus, a Lacedaemonian, received blows from the umpires on the course, because, when his own team won and was proclaimed as belonging to the Boeotian state on account of his having no right to contend, he had come upon the course and crowned the charioteer, wishing to show that the

[1] In the valley of the Alpheus, twenty stadia above Olympia

δηλῶσαι ὅτι ἑαυτοῦ ἦν τὸ ἅρμα· ὥστε πολλῷ δὴ
μᾶλλον ἐπεφόβηντο πάντες καὶ ἐδόκει τι νέον
ἔσεσθαι. οἱ μέντοι Λακεδαιμόνιοι ἡσύχασάν τε
5 καὶ ἡ ἑορτὴ αὐτοῖς οὕτω διῆλθεν. ἐς δὲ Κόρινθον
μετὰ τὰ Ὀλύμπια Ἀργεῖοί τε καὶ οἱ ξύμμαχοι
ἀφίκοντο δεησόμενοι αὐτῶν παρὰ σφᾶς ἐλθεῖν (καὶ
Λακεδαιμονίων πρέσβεις ἔτυχον παρόντες)· καὶ
πολλῶν λόγων γενομένων τέλος οὐδὲν ἐπράχθη,
ἀλλὰ σεισμοῦ γενομένου διελύθησαν ἕκαστοι ἐπ'
οἴκου. καὶ τὸ θέρος ἐτελεύτα.

LI. Τοῦ δ' ἐπιγιγνομένου χειμῶνος Ἡρακλεώ-
ταις τοῖς ἐν Τραχῖνι μάχη ἐγένετο πρὸς Αἰνιᾶνας
καὶ Δόλοπας καὶ Μηλιᾶς καὶ Θεσσαλῶν τινας·
2 προσοικοῦντα γὰρ τὰ ἔθνη ταῦτα τῇ πόλει πολέμια ἦν· οὐ γὰρ ἐπ' ἄλλῃ τινὶ γῇ ἢ τῇ τούτων τὸ
χωρίον ἐτειχίσθη. καὶ εὐθύς τε καθισταμένη τῇ
πόλει ἠναντιοῦντο, ἐς ὅσον ἐδύναντο φθείροντες,
καὶ τότε τῇ μάχῃ ἐνίκησαν τοὺς Ἡρακλεώτας, καὶ
Ξενάρης ὁ Κνίδιος, Λακεδαιμόνιος, ἄρχων αὐτῶν
ἀπέθανε, διεφθάρησαν δὲ καὶ ἄλλοι τῶν Ἡρα-
κλεωτῶν. καὶ ὁ χειμὼν ἐτελεύτα, καὶ δωδέκατον
ἔτος τῷ πολέμῳ ἐτελεύτα.

LII. Τοῦ δ' ἐπιγιγνομένου θέρους εὐθὺς ἀρχομένου
τὴν Ἡράκλειαν, ὡς μετὰ τὴν μάχην κακῶς ἐφθεί-
ρετο, Βοιωτοὶ παρέλαβον, καὶ Ἡγησιππίδαν τὸν
Λακεδαιμόνιον ὡς οὐ καλῶς ἄρχοντα ἐξέπεμψαν.
δείσαντες δὲ παρέλαβον τὸ χωρίον μὴ Λακεδαιμονίων τὰ κατὰ Πελοπόννησον θορυβουμένων
Ἀθηναῖοι λάβωσιν· Λακεδαιμόνιοι μέντοι ὠργί-
ζοντο αὐτοῖς.

2 Καὶ τοῦ αὐτοῦ θέρους Ἀλκιβιάδης ὁ Κλεινίου,

chariot was his. And so everybody was much more afraid, and it seemed that there would be some disturbance. The Lacedaemonians, however, kept quiet, and the festival went through in this way, as far as they were concerned. But after the Olympic games the Argives and their allies came to Corinth, to ask them to join their league. Lacedaemonian envoys also happened to be present. Many proposals were made, but nothing was done; for an earthquake occurred and they dispersed severally to their homes. And the summer ended.

LI. During the following winter, there was a battle between the people of Heracleia in Trachis and the Aenianians, Dolopians, Malians, and some of the Thessalians. For these were neighbouring tribes and hostile to the city of Heracleia, since the fortress there was established as a menace to no other territory but theirs. Accordingly, as soon as the city was founded, they began to show opposition to it, harassing it as much as they could; and at this time they defeated the Heracleotes, Xenares son of Cnidis, a Lacedaemonian and their commander, being killed, as well as some of the Heracleotes. And the winter ended, and with it the twelfth year of this war.

LII. At the very beginning of the following 419 B.C. summer, as Heracleia was in a grievous plight after the battle, the Boeotians took possession of it and dismissed Hegesippidas, the Lacedaemonian, for misgovernment. They occupied the place through fear that, while the Lacedaemonians were disturbed about matters in the Peloponnesus, the Athenians might take it; the Lacedaemonians, however, were angry at them for this.

During the same summer Alcibiades son of

THUCYDIDES

στρατηγὸς ὢν Ἀθηναίων, Ἀργείων καὶ τῶν ξυμμάχων ξυμπρασσόντων ἐλθὼν ἐς Πελοπόννησον μετ᾽
ὀλίγων Ἀθηναίων ὁπλιτῶν καὶ τοξοτῶν καὶ τῶν
αὐτόθεν ξυμμάχων παραλαβὼν τά τε ἄλλα
ξυγκαθίστη περὶ τὴν ξυμμαχίαν διαπορευόμενος
Πελοπόννησον τῇ στρατιᾷ καὶ Πατρέας τε τείχη
καθεῖναι ἔπεισεν ἐς θάλασσαν καὶ αὐτὸς ἕτερον
διενοεῖτο τειχίσαι ἐπὶ τῷ Ῥίῳ τῷ Ἀχαϊκῷ.
Κορίνθιοι δὲ καὶ Σικυώνιοι καὶ οἷς ἦν ἐν
βλάβῃ τειχισθὲν βοηθήσαντες διεκώλυσαν.

LIII. Τοῦ δ᾽ αὐτοῦ θέρους Ἐπιδαυρίοις καὶ
Ἀργείοις πόλεμος ἐγένετο, προφάσει μὲν περὶ τοῦ
θύματος τοῦ Ἀπόλλωνος τοῦ Πυθαιῶς,[1] ὃ δέον
ἀπαγαγεῖν οὐκ ἀπέπεμπον ὑπὲρ βοτανῶν[2] Ἐπιδαύριοι (κυριώτατοι δὲ τοῦ ἱεροῦ ἦσαν Ἀργεῖοι)·
ἐδόκει δὲ καὶ ἄνευ τῆς αἰτίας τὴν Ἐπίδαυρον τῷ
τε Ἀλκιβιάδῃ καὶ τοῖς Ἀργείοις προσλαβεῖν, ἢν
δύνωνται, τῆς τε Κορίνθου ἕνεκα ἡσυχίας καὶ ἐκ
τῆς Αἰγίνης βραχυτέραν ἔσεσθαι τὴν βοήθειαν ἢ
Σκύλλαιον περιπλεῖν τοῖς Ἀθηναίοις. παρεσκευάζοντο οὖν οἱ Ἀργεῖοι ὡς αὐτοὶ ἐς τὴν

---

[1] Correction of C_1, Πυθέως AEFM, Πιθέως B.
[2] Stahl's correction for βοταμίων of MSS.

---

[1] A low point of land at the mouth of the Corinthian
Gulf; on the opposite side of the strait was the Molycreian
Rhium. The fort would have given the Athenians entire
control of the entrance to the Gulf.

Cleinias, who was then a general of the Athenians, acting in concert with the Argives and their allies went into the Peloponnesus with a few Athenian hoplites and bowmen, and taking with him some of the allies from that region helped to settle matters pertaining to the alliance as he passed through the Peloponnesus with his army; coming to Patrae he persuaded the inhabitants to carry their walls down to the sea, and intended himself to build another fort at the Achaean Rhium.[1] But the Corinthians, Sicyonians, and all those to whom the fortification of Rhium would have been a menace, went in force and prevented it.

LIII. During the same summer war broke out between the Epidaurians and Argives. The alleged ground for this was that the Epidaurians were not sending the sacrifice to Apollo Pythaeus, which it was incumbent on them to render in payment for pasturage, and the Argives exercised chief authority over the sanctuary;[2] but even apart from this motive Alcibiades and the Argives deemed it advisable, if they could, to bring Epidaurus into the Argive alliance, both for the sake of keeping Corinth quiet, and because they thought the Athenians would be able to bring aid to Argos by a shorter way, from Aegina as base, than by sailing round Scyllaeum.[3] The Argives, then, were preparing, as

[2] Probably the temple of Apollo Pythaeus referred to is that which alone of all the buildings in Asine the Argives spared when they destroyed that town; cf. Paus. II. xxxvi. 5.

[3] A promontory between Hermione and Troezene. The short route was from Aegina to the neighbouring coast of Epidaurus and thence to Argos; if Epidaurus was hostile or neutral, reinforcements had to be carried round Scyllaeum to the Gulf of Nauplia and thence by land to Argos.

Ἐπίδαυρον διὰ τοῦ θύματος τὴν ἔσπραξιν
ἐσβαλοῦντες.

LIV. Ἐξεστράτευσαν δὲ καὶ οἱ Λακεδαιμόνιοι
κατὰ τοὺς αὐτοὺς χρόνους πανδημεὶ ἐς Λεῦκτρα
τῆς ἑαυτῶν μεθορίας πρὸς τὸ Λύκαιον, Ἄγιδος τοῦ
Ἀρχιδάμου βασιλέως ἡγουμένου· ᾔδει δὲ οὐδεὶς
ὅποι στρατεύουσιν, οὐδὲ αἱ πόλεις ἐξ ὧν ἐπέμ-
2 φθησαν. ὡς δ' αὐτοῖς τὰ διαβατήρια θυομένοις οὐ
προυχώρει, αὐτοί τε ἀπῆλθον ἐπ' οἴκου καὶ τοῖς
ξυμμάχοις περιήγγειλαν μετὰ τὸν μέλλοντα (Καρ-
νεῖος δ' ἦν μήν, ἱερομηνία Δωριεῦσι) παρασκευά-
3 ζεσθαι ὡς στρατευσομένους. Ἀργεῖοι δ' ἀναχωρησάντων αὐτῶν, τοῦ πρὸ τοῦ Καρνείου μηνὸς
ἐξελθόντες τετράδι φθίνοντος καὶ ἄγοντες τὴν
ἡμέραν ταύτην πάντα τὸν χρόνον, ἐσέβαλον ἐς
4 τὴν Ἐπιδαυρίαν καὶ ἐδῄουν. Ἐπιδαύριοι δὲ
τοὺς ξυμμάχους ἐπεκαλοῦντο· ὧν τινες οἱ μὲν
τὸν μῆνα προυφασίσαντο, οἱ δὲ καὶ ἐς μεθορίαν
τῆς Ἐπιδαυρίας ἐλθόντες ἡσύχαζον.

LV. Καὶ καθ' ὃν χρόνον ἐν τῇ Ἐπιδαύρῳ οἱ
Ἀργεῖοι ἦσαν, ἐς Μαντίνειαν πρεσβεῖαι ἀπὸ τῶν
πόλεων ξυνῆλθον, Ἀθηναίων παρακαλεσάντων.
καὶ γενομένων [1] λόγων Εὐφαμίδας ὁ Κορίνθιος οὐκ
ἔφη τοὺς λόγους τοῖς ἔργοις ὁμολογεῖν· σφεῖς μὲν
γὰρ περὶ εἰρήνης ξυγκαθῆσθαι, τοὺς δ' Ἐπιδαυρίους καὶ τοὺς ξυμμάχους καὶ τοὺς Ἀργείους μεθ'
ὅπλων ἀντιτετάχθαι· διαλῦσαι οὖν πρῶτον χρῆ-

---

[1] MSS. γινομένων, Hude γενομένων.

---

[1] The sacrifices offered to Zeus by the Spartan kings before
crossing the border.
[2] Corresponding to the Attic Metageitnion, nearly our
August.

of their own motion, to invade Epidaurus for the exaction of the offering.

LIV. About the same time the Lacedaemonians, too, marched out with all their forces to Leuctra, a place on their own borders opposite Mt. Lycaeum, under the command of King Agis son of Archidamus; and no one knew whither they were marching, not even the cities from which they were sent. But as the sacrifices for crossing the border [1] were not favourable, they went back home themselves, and sent word to their allies, after the coming month— the Carneian month,[2] a holiday among the Dorians—to prepare to take the field. When they withdrew, the Argives set out on the twenty-seventh of the month preceding the Carneian, and continuing to observe that day during the whole time,[3] invaded Epidaurus and proceeded to ravage it. The Epidaurians called upon their allies for help; but some of these made the month an excuse, while the rest went merely to the borders of Epidauria and there remained quiet.

LV. While the Argives were in Epidaurian territory envoys from the different cities came together at Mantinea, on the invitation of the Athenians. And in the course of the conference Euphamidas the Corinthian said that their words did not agree with their deeds; for they were sitting in council on the question of peace, while the Epidaurians with their allies and the Argives were arrayed in arms against each other; they ought to go

---

[3] They called every day the 27th as long as they were in Epidaurian territory and thus postponed the beginning of the following month until their work was done. Probably the Argives, on religious grounds (as Dorians), took holiday as soon as the Carneian month began.

ναι ἐφ᾿[1] ἑκατέρων ἐλθόντας τὰ στρατόπεδα, καὶ
2 οὕτω πάλιν λέγειν περὶ τῆς εἰρήνης. καὶ πεισθέντες ᾤχοντο καὶ τοὺς Ἀργείους ἀπήγαγον ἐκ
τῆς Ἐπιδαυρίας. ὕστερον δὲ ἐς τὸ αὐτὸ ξυνελ-
θόντες οὐδ᾿ ὡς ἐδυνήθησαν ξυμβῆναι, ἀλλ᾿ οἱ
Ἀργεῖοι πάλιν ἐς τὴν Ἐπιδαυρίαν ἐσέβαλον καὶ
3 ἐδῄουν. ἐξεστράτευσαν δὲ καὶ οἱ Λακεδαιμόνιοι
ἐς Καρύας· καὶ ὡς οὐδ᾿ ἐνταῦθα τὰ διαβατήρια
4 αὐτοῖς ἐγένετο, ἐπανεχώρησαν. Ἀργεῖοι δὲ τεμόν-
τες τῆς Ἐπιδαυρίας ὡς τὸ τρίτον μέρος ἀπῆλθον
ἐπ᾿ οἴκου. καὶ Ἀθηναίων αὐτοῖς χίλιοι ἐβοήθησαν ὁπλῖται καὶ Ἀλκιβιάδης στρατηγός, πυθόμενοι δὴ[2] τοὺς Λακεδαιμονίους ἐξεστρατεῦσθαι·
καὶ ὡς οὐδὲν ἔτι αὐτῶν ἔδει, ἀπῆλθον. καὶ τὸ
θέρος οὕτω διῆλθεν.

LVI. Τοῦ δ᾿ ἐπιγιγνομένου χειμῶνος Λακεδαιμόνιοι λαθόντες Ἀθηναίους φρουρούς τε τριακοσίους καὶ Ἀγησιππίδαν ἄρχοντα κατὰ θάλασσαν
2 ἐς Ἐπίδαυρον ἐσέπεμψαν. Ἀργεῖοι δ᾿ ἐλθόντες
παρ᾿ Ἀθηναίους ἐπεκάλουν ὅτι, γεγραμμένον ἐν
ταῖς σπονδαῖς διὰ τῆς ἑαυτῶν ἑκάστους μὴ ἐᾶν
πολεμίους διιέναι, ἔασειαν κατὰ θάλασσαν παρα-
πλεῦσαι· καὶ εἰ μὴ κἀκεῖνοι ἐς Πύλον κομιοῦσιν
ἐπὶ Λακεδαιμονίους τοὺς Μεσσηνίους καὶ Εἵλωτας,
3 ἀδικήσεσθαι αὐτοί. Ἀθηναῖοι δὲ Ἀλκιβιάδου
πείσαντος τῇ μὲν Λακωνικῇ στήλῃ ὑπέγραψαν ὅτι
οὐκ ἐνέμειναν οἱ Λακεδαιμόνιοι τοῖς ὅρκοις, ἐς δὲ

---

[1] suprascr. g₂, all other MSS. ἀφ᾿.
[2] Hude's correction for δὲ of the MSS.

---

[1] Or, reading πυθόμενοι δέ, with the MSS., "but learning that
the Lacedaemonians *had left the field*"—which the verb means
nowhere else—"and that there was no further need of them."

first to the camps of the two parties and disband
them, and then they might come back and talk about
peace. Adopting this suggestion, they went and
induced the Argives to depart from Epidauria.
Afterwards they came together again, but not even
then were they able to agree, and the Argives again
invaded Epidauria and began to ravage it. The
Lacedaemonians, too, marched out to Caryae; but
as not even there the sacrifices for crossing the
boundaries proved favourable, they returned. And
the Argives, having ravaged about a third part of
Epidauria, also went back home. Moreover, there
had come to their aid one thousand Athenian hoplites,
under the command of Alcibiades, on learning that
the Lacedaemonians had taken the field; as now
there was no longer any need of them these withdrew.[1] And so the summer ended.

LVI. During the following winter, the Lacedaemonians, eluding the vigilance of the Athenians,
sent a garrison of three hundred men, under the
command of Agesippidas, by sea to Epidaurus. And
the Argives, coming to Athens, made complaint that,
although it was written in the treaty that they were
not to allow enemies to go through their respective
territories,[2] the Athenians had permitted the Lacedaemonians to go past their territory [3] by sea; unless,
then, the Athenians should bring the Messenians and
Helots to Pylos to annoy the Lacedaemonians, they
themselves would feel aggrieved. So the Athenians,
on the advice of Alcibiades, inscribed at the bottom
of the Laconian column that the Lacedaemonians
had not kept their oaths, and they brought to Pylos

---

[2] *cf.* ch. xlvii. 5.
[3] *i.e.* past Aegina, now Athenian territory.

Πύλον ἐκόμισαν τοὺς ἐκ Κρανίων Εἴλωτας λή-
4 ζεσθαι, τὰ δ' ἄλλα ἡσύχαζον. τὸν δὲ χειμῶνα
τοῦτον πολεμούντων Ἀργείων καὶ Ἐπιδαυρίων
μάχη μὲν οὐδεμία ἐγένετο ἐκ παρασκευῆς, ἐνέδραι
δὲ καὶ καταδρομαί, ἐν αἷς ὡς τύχοιεν ἑκατέρων
5 τινὲς διεφθείροντο. καὶ τελευτῶντος τοῦ χειμῶνος
πρὸς ἔαρ ἤδη κλίμακας ἔχοντες οἱ Ἀργεῖοι ἦλθον
ἐπὶ τὴν Ἐπίδαυρον ὡς ἐρήμου οὔσης διὰ τὸν πόλεμον βίᾳ αἱρήσοντες· καὶ ἄπρακτοι ἀπῆλθον.
καὶ ὁ χειμὼν ἐτελεύτα, καὶ τρίτον καὶ δέκατον
ἔτος τῷ πολέμῳ ἐτελεύτα.

LVII. Τοῦ δ' ἐπιγιγνομένου θέρους μεσοῦντος
Λακεδαιμόνιοι, ὡς αὐτοῖς οἵ τε Ἐπιδαύριοι ξύμμαχοι ὄντες ἐταλαιπώρουν καὶ τἆλλα ἐν τῇ Πελοποννήσῳ τὰ μὲν ἀφειστήκει, τὰ δ' οὐ καλῶς εἶχε,
νομίσαντες, εἰ μὴ προκαταλήψονται ἐν τάχει, ἐπὶ
πλέον χωρήσεσθαι αὐτά, ἐστράτευον αὐτοὶ καὶ οἱ
Εἴλωτες πανδημεὶ ἐπ' Ἄργος· ἡγεῖτο δὲ Ἆγις ὁ
Ἀρχιδάμου, Λακεδαιμονίων βασιλεύς. ξυνεστρά-
2 τευον δ' αὐτοῖς Τεγεᾶταί τε καὶ ὅσοι ἄλλοι Ἀρκάδων Λακεδαιμονίοις ξύμμαχοι ἦσαν. οἱ δ' ἐκ τῆς
ἄλλης Πελοποννήσου ξύμμαχοι καὶ οἱ ἔξωθεν ἐς
Φλειοῦντα ξυνελέγοντο, Βοιωτοὶ μὲν πεντακισχί-
λιοι ὁπλῖται καὶ τοσοῦτοι ψιλοὶ καὶ ἱππῆς πεντακόσιοι καὶ ἄμιπποι ἴσοι, Κορίνθιοι δὲ δισχίλιοι
ὁπλῖται, οἱ δ' ἄλλοι ὡς ἕκαστοι, Φλειάσιοι δὲ
πανστρατιᾷ, ὅτι ἐν τῇ ἐκείνων ἦν τὸ στράτευμα.

the Helots from Cranii,[1] to plunder the country; but in other respects they kept quiet. During this winter, although the Argives and Epidaurians were at war, there was no pitched battle, but there were ambuscades and forays, in which some perished on either side as the chance might be. As winter was closing and spring at hand, the Argives came with scaling-ladders against Epidaurus, supposing, as it was stripped of its defenders by the war, that they could take it by assault; but they accomplished nothing and went back home. And the winter ended and with it the thirteenth year of the war.

LVII. In the middle of the following summer, the Lacedaemonians, seeing that their Epidaurian allies were in distress, and of the other states in the Peloponnesus some had revolted, while others were not well-disposed, and thinking that if measures of precaution were not taken quickly the evil would go yet further, marched against Argos with all their forces, themselves and their Helots, under the leadership of Agis son of Archidamus, king of the Lacedaemonians. And with them went the Tegeates and all the rest of the Arcadians that were allies of the Lacedaemonians. But the allies from the rest of the Peloponnesus and those from outside mustered at Phlius—five thousand Boeotian hoplites and as many light-armed troops, with five hundred cavalry each with his foot-soldier;[2] two thousand Corinthian hoplites; the rest of the allies in varying numbers, but the Phliasians with their whole force, since the armament was assembled in their territory.

418 B.C.

---

[1] cf. ch. xxxv. 7.

[2] ἄμιπποι, light-armed men, one with each horseman, running alongside or riding behind.

LVIII. Ἀργεῖοι δὲ προαισθόμενοι τό τε πρῶτον
τὴν παρασκευὴν τῶν Λακεδαιμονίων καὶ ἐπειδὴ ἐς
τὸν Φλειοῦντα βουλόμενοι τοῖς ἄλλοις προσμεῖξαι
ἐχώρουν, τότε δὴ ἐξεστράτευσαν καὶ αὐτοί. ἐβοήθησαν δ' αὐτοῖς καὶ Μαντινῆς ἔχοντες τοὺς
σφετέρους ξυμμάχους καὶ Ἠλείων τρισχίλιοι
2 ὁπλῖται. καὶ προϊόντες ἀπαντῶσι τοῖς Λακεδαιμονίοις ἐν Μεθυδρίῳ τῆς Ἀρκαδίας. καὶ κατα-
λαμβάνουσιν ἑκάτεροι λόφον· καὶ οἱ μὲν Ἀργεῖοι
ὡς μεμονωμένοις τοῖς Λακεδαιμονίοις παρεσκευάζοντο μάχεσθαι, ὁ δὲ Ἆγις τῆς νυκτὸς ἀναστήσας
τὸν στρατὸν καὶ λαθὼν ἐπορεύετο ἐς Φλειοῦντα
3 παρὰ τοὺς ἄλλους ξυμμάχους. καὶ οἱ Ἀργεῖοι
αἰσθόμενοι ἅμα ἕῳ ἐχώρουν, πρῶτον μὲν ἐς Ἄργος,
ἔπειτα δὲ ᾗ προσεδέχοντο τοὺς Λακεδαιμονίους
μετὰ τῶν ξυμμάχων καταβήσεσθαι, τὴν κατὰ
4 Νεμέαν ὁδόν. Ἆγις δὲ ταύτην μὲν ἣν προσεδέχοντο οὐκ ἐτράπετο, παραγγείλας δὲ τοῖς Λακεδαιμονίοις καὶ Ἀρκάσι καὶ Ἐπιδαυρίοις ἄλλην
ἐχώρησε χαλεπὴν καὶ κατέβη ἐς τὸ Ἀργείων
πεδίον· καὶ Κορίνθιοι καὶ Πελληνῆς καὶ Φλειάσιοι
ὄρθιον ἑτέραν ἐπορεύοντο· τοῖς δὲ Βοιωτοῖς καὶ
Μεγαρεῦσι καὶ Σικυωνίοις εἴρητο τὴν ἐπὶ Νεμέας
ὁδὸν καταβαίνειν, ᾗ οἱ Ἀργεῖοι ἐκάθηντο, ὅπως,
εἰ οἱ Ἀργεῖοι ἐπὶ σφᾶς ἰόντας[1] ἐς τὸ πεδίον
5 βοηθοῖεν, ἐφεπόμενοι τοῖς ἵπποις χρῷντο. καὶ ὁ
μὲν οὕτω διατάξας καὶ ἐσβαλὼν ἐς τὸ πεδίον
ἐδῄου Σάμινθόν τε καὶ ἄλλα.

LIX. Οἱ δὲ Ἀργεῖοι γνόντες ἐβοήθουν ἡμέρας
ἤδη ἐκ τῆς Νεμέας, καὶ περιτυχόντες τῷ Φλειασίων

Badham's correction for ἰόντες of the MSS.

LVIII. The Argives had been aware of the preparations of the Lacedaemonians from the first, and when the latter were on the march to Phlius where they intended to join the rest, they now took the field themselves. And the Mantineans came to their aid with their own allies and three thousand Elean hoplites. As they were going forward they came upon the Lacedaemonians at Methydrium in Arcadia. Each party took position on a hill, and the Argives prepared to fight with the Lacedaemonians, thinking to find them still isolated; but Agis, rousing up his force during the night and eluding detection, marched to Phlius to join the rest of the allies. The Argives, perceiving this, set out at daybreak, marching first to Argos and then taking the road to Nemea, where they expected the Lacedaemonians with their allies to come down. Agis, however, did not take the way they were expecting him to follow, but giving the word to the Lacedaemonians, Arcadians, and Epidaurians, he advanced by a more difficult route and descended to the Argive plain. The Corinthians, Pellenians, and Phliasians advanced by another steep road; while the Boeotians, Megarians and Sicyonians had been told to come down by the road to Nemea, where the Argives were posted, in order that if the Argives should attack their main force as it advanced into the plain, they might hang on their rear and use their cavalry against them. Having, then, so disposed his troops, Agis came down into the plain and proceeded to ravage Saminthus and other places.

LIX. The Argives discovered this and, it being now day, came to the rescue from Nemea, and falling in with the force of the Phliasians and Corinthians

καὶ Κορινθίων στρατοπέδῳ τῶν μὲν Φλειασίων
ὀλίγους ἀπέκτειναν, ὑπὸ δὲ τῶν Κορινθίων αὐτοὶ οὐ
2 πολλῷ πλείους διεφθάρησαν. καὶ οἱ Βοιωτοὶ καὶ οἱ
Μεγαρῆς καὶ οἱ Σικυώνιοι ἐχώρουν, ὥσπερ εἴρητο
αὐτοῖς, ἐπὶ τῆς Νεμέας, καὶ τοὺς Ἀργείους οὐκέτι
κατέλαβον, ἀλλὰ καταβάντες, ὡς ἑώρων τὰ ἑαυτῶν
δῃούμενα, ἐς μάχην παρετάσσοντο. ἀντιπαρε-
3 σκευάζοντο δὲ καὶ οἱ Λακεδαιμόνιοι. ἐν μέσῳ δὲ
ἀπειλημμένοι ἦσαν οἱ Ἀργεῖοι· ἐκ μὲν γὰρ τοῦ
πεδίου οἱ Λακεδαιμόνιοι εἶργον τῆς πόλεως καὶ οἱ
μετ' αὐτῶν, καθύπερθεν δὲ Κορίνθιοι καὶ Φλειάσιοι
καὶ Πελληνῆς, τὸ δὲ πρὸς Νεμέας Βοιωτοὶ καὶ
Σικυώνιοι καὶ Μεγαρῆς. ἵπποι δὲ αὐτοῖς οὐ παρ-
ῆσαν· οὐ γάρ πω οἱ Ἀθηναῖοι, μόνοι τῶν ξυμ-
4 μάχων, ἥκον. τὸ μὲν οὖν πλῆθος τῶν Ἀργείων
καὶ τῶν ξυμμάχων οὐχ οὕτω δεινὸν τὸ παρὸν
ἐνόμιζον, ἀλλ' ἐν καλῷ ἐδόκει ἡ μάχη ἔσεσθαι,
καὶ τοὺς Λακεδαιμονίους ἀπειληφέναι ἐν τῇ αὐτῶν
τε καὶ πρὸς τῇ πόλει. τῶν δὲ Ἀργείων δύο
ἄνδρες, Θράσυλλός τε, τῶν πέντε στρατηγῶν εἷς
ὤν, καὶ Ἀλκίφρων, πρόξενος Λακεδαιμονίων, ἤδη
τῶν στρατοπέδων ὅσον οὐ ξυνιόντων προσελθόντε
Ἄγιδι διελεγέσθην μὴ ποιεῖν μάχην· ἑτοίμους
γὰρ εἶναι Ἀργείους δίκας δοῦναι καὶ δέξασθαι
ἴσας καὶ ὁμοίας, εἴ τι ἐπικαλοῦσιν Ἀργείοις
Λακεδαιμόνιοι, καὶ τὸ λοιπὸν εἰρήνην ἄγειν σπονδὰς ποιησαμένους.

LX. Καὶ οἱ μὲν ταῦτα εἰπόντες τῶν Ἀργείων
ἀφ' ἑαυτῶν καὶ οὐ τοῦ πλήθους κελεύσαντος εἶπον·

slew a few of the Phliasians, but had rather more
of their own men slain by the Corinthians. Meanwhile the Boeotians, Megarians and Sicyonians advanced toward Nemea as they had been ordered, but
found the Argives no longer there; for these had
gone down and, seeing their country being ravaged,
were forming for battle, while the Lacedaemonians
were preparing to meet them. The Argives were
hemmed in on all sides: in the direction of the plain
the Lacedaemonians and their associates shut them
off from the city; above were the Corinthians,
Phliasians and Pellenians; towards Nemea were the
Boeotians, Sicyonians, and Megarians. They had no
cavalry at hand, for the Athenians[1] alone of their allies
had not yet arrived. The main body of the Argives
and their allies thought their present situation was
not so very dangerous, but that the battle was likely
to be fought under favourable circumstances, and that
the Lacedaemonians had been cut off in their
country and close to the city of Argos. But two of
the Argives—Thrasyllus, one of the five generals,
and Alciphron, proxenus of the Lacedaemonians—
when the two armies were all but in collision, went
to Agis and urged him not to bring on a battle;
for the Argives were ready to offer as well as to accept
a fair and impartial arbitration of any complaint
which the Lacedaemonians had against the Argives,
and for the future to make a treaty and keep the
peace.

LX. Those of the Argives who said these things
spoke on their own authority and not by order of

---

[1] Upon their cavalry the Argives had relied. Their coming
is announced ch. lxi. 1.

καὶ ὁ Ἆγις δεξάμενος τοὺς λόγους αὐτός, καὶ οὐ
μετὰ τῶν πλειόνων οὐδὲ αὐτὸς βουλευσάμενος
ἀλλ᾽ ἢ ἑνὶ ἀνδρὶ κοινώσας τῶν ἐν τέλει ξυστρα-
τευομένων, σπένδεται τέσσαρας μῆνας ἐν οἷς ἔδει
ἐπιτελέσαι αὐτοὺς τὰ ῥηθέντα. καὶ ἀπήγαγε τὸν
στρατὸν εὐθύς, οὐδενὶ φράσας τῶν ἄλλων ξυμ-
2 μάχων.¹ οἱ δὲ Λακεδαιμόνιοι καὶ οἱ ξύμμαχοι
εἵποντο μὲν ὡς ἡγεῖτο διὰ τὸν νόμον, ἐν αἰτίᾳ δ᾽
εἶχον κατ᾽ ἀλλήλους πολλῇ τὸν Ἆγιν, νομίζοντες,
ἐν καλῷ παρατυχὸν σφίσι ξυμβαλεῖν καὶ πανταχόθεν αὐτῶν ἀποκεκλῃμένων καὶ ὑπὸ ἱππέων
καὶ πεζῶν, οὐδὲν δράσαντες ἄξιον τῆς παρασκευῆς
3 ἀπιέναι. στρατόπεδον γὰρ δὴ τοῦτο κάλλιστον
Ἑλληνικὸν τῶν μέχρι τοῦδε ξυνῆλθεν· ὤφθη δὲ
μάλιστα ἕως ἔτι ἦν ἀθρόον ἐν Νεμέᾳ, ἐν ᾧ Λακε-
δαιμόνιοί τε πανστρατιᾷ ἦσαν καὶ Ἀρκάδες καὶ
Βοιωτοὶ καὶ Κορίνθιοι καὶ Σικυώνιοι καὶ Πελληνῆς
καὶ Φλειάσιοι καὶ Μεγαρῆς, καὶ οὗτοι πάντες
λογάδες ἀφ᾽ ἑκάστων, ἀξιόμαχοι δοκοῦντες εἶναι
οὐ τῇ Ἀργείων μόνον ξυμμαχίᾳ, ἀλλὰ κἂν ἄλλῃ
4 ἔτι προσγενομένῃ. τὸ μὲν οὖν στρατόπεδον οὕτως
ἐν αἰτίᾳ ἔχοντες τὸν Ἆγιν ἀνεχώρουν τε καὶ
5 διελύθησαν ἐπ᾽ οἴκου ἕκαστοι· Ἀργεῖοι δὲ καὶ
αὐτοὶ ἔτι ἐν πολλῷ πλείονι αἰτίᾳ εἶχον τοὺς σπει-
σαμένους ἄνευ τοῦ πλήθους, νομίζοντες κἀκεῖνοι
μὴ ἂν σφίσι ποτὲ κάλλιον παρασχὸν Λακεδαιμονίους διαπεφευγέναι· πρός τε γὰρ τῇ σφετέρᾳ
πόλει καὶ μετὰ πολλῶν καὶ ἀγαθῶν ξυμμάχων

¹ ξυμμάχων, Hude deletes, after Krüger.

the people; and Agis, receiving the proposals for
himself alone, not conferring with the majority, and
without any deliberation on his own part further
than to communicate the matter to a single one of
the magistrates who accompanied the expedition,
made a truce with the Argives for four months,
within which time they were to fulfil their agreement. And so he led off his army at once, without
explanation to any of the allies. The Lacedaemonians and their allies followed his guidance out of
respect for the law, but among themselves they
loudly blamed Agis, considering that when there
was opportunity for them to join battle under
favourable conditions, and the Argives were cut off
on all sides both by cavalry and infantry, they were
going back home without doing anything worthy of
their preparations. For this was indeed the finest
Hellenic force that had come together up to that
time; and this was seen especially while it was still
united at Nemea, including the Lacedaemonians in
full force, the Arcadians, Boeotians, Corinthians,
Sicyonians, Pellenians, Phliasians, and Megarians,
all of them picked men from each nation, who felt
themselves to be a match, not for the Argive
confederacy only, but even for another such force
in addition. The army, then, thus blaming Agis,
withdrew and dispersed severally to their homes.
But the Argives also on their part held in far
greater blame those who had made the truce without
consulting the people, as they too thought that the
Lacedaemonians had escaped, though circumstances
could never be more favourable for themselves; for
the contest would have been near their own city and

6 τὸν ἀγῶνα ἂν γίγνεσθαι. τόν τε Θράσυλλον
ἀναχωρήσαντες ἐν τῷ Χαράδρῳ, οὗπερ τὰς ἀπὸ
στρατείας δίκας πρὶν ἐσιέναι κρίνουσιν, ἤρξαντο
λεύειν. ὁ δὲ καταφυγὼν ἐπὶ τὸν βωμὸν περιγίγνε-
ται· τὰ μέντοι χρήματα ἐδήμευσαν αὐτοῦ.

LXI. Μετὰ δὲ τοῦτο Ἀθηναίων βοηθησάντων
χιλίων ὁπλιτῶν καὶ τριακοσίων ἱππέων, ὧν
ἐστρατήγουν Λάχης καὶ Νικόστρατος, οἱ Ἀργεῖοι
(ὅμως γὰρ τὰς σπονδὰς ὤκνουν λῦσαι πρὸς τοὺς
Λακεδαιμονίους) ἀπιέναι ἐκέλευον αὐτοὺς καὶ
πρὸς τὸν δῆμον οὐ προσῆγον βουλομένους χρη-
ματίσαι, πρὶν δὴ Μαντινῆς καὶ Ἠλεῖοι (ἔτι γὰρ
2 παρῆσαν) κατηνάγκασαν δεόμενοι. καὶ ἔλεγον οἱ
Ἀθηναῖοι Ἀλκιβιάδου πρεσβευτοῦ παρόντος ἔν
τε τοῖς Ἀργείοις καὶ ξυμμάχοις ταῦτα, ὅτι οὐκ
ὀρθῶς αἱ σπονδαὶ ἄνευ τῶν ἄλλων ξυμμάχων καὶ
γένοιντο, καὶ νῦν (ἐν καιρῷ γὰρ παρεῖναι σφεῖς)
3 ἅπτεσθαι χρῆναι τοῦ πολέμου. καὶ πείσαντες ἐκ
τῶν λόγων τοὺς ξυμμάχους εὐθὺς ἐχώρουν ἐπὶ
Ὀρχομενὸν τὸν Ἀρκαδικὸν πάντες πλὴν Ἀρ-
γείων· οὗτοι δὲ ὅμως καὶ πεισθέντες ὑπελείποντο
4 πρῶτον, ἔπειτα δ᾽ ὕστερον καὶ οὗτοι ἦλθον. καὶ
προσκαθεζόμενοι τὸν Ὀρχομενὸν πάντες ἐπολιόρκουν καὶ προσβολὰς ἐποιοῦντο, βουλόμενοι
ἄλλως τε προσγενέσθαι σφίσι καὶ ὅμηροι ἐκ τῆς
Ἀρκαδίας ἦσαν αὐτόθι ὑπὸ Λακεδαιμονίων κεί-
5 μενοι. οἱ δὲ Ὀρχομένιοι δείσαντες τήν τε τοῦ
τείχους ἀσθένειαν καὶ τοῦ στρατοῦ τὸ πλῆθος,
καὶ ὡς οὐδεὶς αὐτοῖς ἐβοήθει, μὴ προαπόλωνται,

in concert with numerous and brave allies. And so on their return they began to stone Thrasyllus in the bed of the Charadrus,[1] where before they enter the city all causes are tried that arise from an expedition. But he fled for refuge to the altar and was saved; his property however was confiscated.

LXI. After this, when Athenian reinforcements arrived, consisting of one thousand hoplites and three hundred cavalry, under the command of Laches and Nicostratus, the Argives—for they shrunk in spite of all from breaking off the truce with the Lacedaemonians—bade them go away, and would not comply with their wish to be brought before the people for negotiations, until the Mantineans and Eleans, who were still present, constrained them by their entreaties to do so. The Athenians, then, through Alcibiades, who was present as ambassador, protested before the Argives and their allies that it was not right even to have made the truce without the consent of the rest of the allies, and now, since they themselves were present opportunely, they ought to resume the war. Having persuaded the allies by their arguments, all of them except the Argives proceeded at once against Orchomenus in Arcadia; the Argives, though convinced, remained behind at first, then later came on too. Taking post before Orchomenus, they all proceeded to besiege it and to make assaults, being especially desirous of getting possession of it because hostages from Arcadia were deposited there by the Lacedaemonians. But the Orchomenians, fearing the weakness of the wall and the number of the enemy, and being apprehensive lest they might perish before relief came, capitulated on

[1] Close under the north-east wall of the city.

ξυνέβησαν ὥστε ξύμμαχοί τε εἶναι καὶ ὁμήρους
σφῶν τε αὐτῶν δοῦναι Μαντινεῦσι καὶ οὓς
κατέθεντο Λακεδαιμόνιοι παραδοῦναι.

LXII. Μετὰ δὲ τοῦτο ἔχοντες ἤδη τὸν Ὀρχομενὸν ἐβουλεύοντο οἱ ξύμμαχοι ἐφ᾽ ὅ τι χρὴ
πρῶτον ἰέναι τῶν λοιπῶν. καὶ Ἠλεῖοι μὲν ἐπὶ
Λέπρεον ἐκέλευον, Μαντινῆς δὲ ἐπὶ Τεγέαν· καὶ
προσέθεντο οἱ Ἀργεῖοι καὶ Ἀθηναῖοι τοῖς Μαν-
2 τινεῦσιν. καὶ οἱ μὲν Ἠλεῖοι ὀργισθέντες ὅτι οὐκ
ἐπὶ Λέπρεον ἐψηφίσαντο, ἀνεχώρησαν ἐπ᾽ οἴκου·
οἱ δὲ ἄλλοι ξύμμαχοι παρεσκευάζοντο ἐν τῇ
Μαντινείᾳ ὡς ἐπὶ Τεγέαν ἰόντες, καί τινες αὐτοῖς
καὶ αὐτῶν τῶν¹ ἐν τῇ πόλει ἐνεδίδοσαν τὰ
πράγματα.

LXIII. Λακεδαιμόνιοι δὲ ἐπειδὴ ἀνεχώρησαν ἐξ
Ἄργους τὰς τετραμήνους σπονδὰς ποιησάμενοι,
Ἆγιν ἐν μεγάλῃ αἰτίᾳ εἶχον οὐ χειρωσάμενον
σφίσιν Ἄργος, παρασχὸν καλῶς ὡς οὔπω πρότερον αὐτοὶ ἐνόμιζον· ἀθρόους γὰρ τοσούτους
ξυμμάχους καὶ τοιούτους οὐ ῥάδιον εἶναι λαβεῖν.
2 ἐπειδὴ δὲ καὶ περὶ Ὀρχομενοῦ ἠγγέλλετο ἑαλω-
κέναι, πολλῷ δὴ μᾶλλον ἐχαλέπαινον καὶ ἐβού-
λευον εὐθὺς ὑπ᾽ ὀργῆς παρὰ τὸν τρόπον τὸν
ἑαυτῶν ὡς χρὴ τήν τε οἰκίαν αὐτοῦ κατασκάψαι
3 καὶ δέκα μυριάσι δραχμῶν ζημιῶσαι. ὁ δὲ
παρῃτεῖτο μηδὲν τούτων δρᾶν· ἔργῳ γὰρ ἀγαθῷ
ῥύσεσθαι τὰς αἰτίας στρατευσάμενος, ἢ τότε
4 ποιεῖν αὐτοὺς ὅ τι βούλονται. οἱ δὲ τὴν μὲν
ζημίαν καὶ τὴν κατασκαφὴν ἐπέσχον, νόμον δὲ
ἔθεντο ἐν τῷ παρόντι, ὃς οὔπω πρότερον ἐγένετο

¹ Stahl and van Herwerden's correction for αὐτῶν Τεγεατῶν
of the MSS.

condition that they should be received as allies, should give hostages for themselves to the Mantineans, and should deliver up those whom the Lacedaemonians had deposited with them.

LXII. After this, being now in possession of Orchomenus, the allies deliberated which of the remaining places they should next proceed against. The Eleans were urging them to go against Lepreum, the Mantineans against Tegea; and the Argives and Athenians sided with the Mantineans. The Eleans, then, becoming angry because they did not vote to go against Lepreum, went off home; but the rest of the allies began to make preparations at Mantinea to go against Tegea; and there were even some of the inhabitants of the town who were in favour of yielding the place to them.

LXIII. But the Lacedaemonians, on their return from Argos after making the four months' truce, blamed Agis severely for not subduing Argos, when, in their judgment, the happy opportunity was such as had never been offered before; for it was not an easy matter to get together allies so many and so good. But when the tidings came about the capture of Orchomenus also, they were far more angry, and in their wrath, contrary to their habit, at once resolved to raze his house and to fine him in the sum of ten thousand drachmas.[1] But he besought them to do none of these things, promising that he would wipe out the charges by some brave deed when he took the field again; if not, they might then do what they wished. So they refrained from the fine and the razing of his house, but for the present enacted a law which had no precedent

---

[1] About £6,730, $32,000.

αὐτοῖς· δέκα γὰρ ἄνδρας Σπαρτιατῶν προσείλοντο αὐτῷ ξυμβούλους, ἄνευ ὧν μὴ κύριον εἶναι ἀπάγειν στρατιὰν ἐκ τῆς πόλεως.

LXIV. Ἐν τούτῳ δ' ἀφικνεῖται αὐτοῖς ἀγγελία παρὰ τῶν ἐπιτηδείων ἐκ Τεγέας ὅτι, εἰ μὴ παρέσονται ἐν τάχει, ἀποστήσεται αὐτῶν Τεγέα πρὸς Ἀργείους καὶ τοὺς ξυμμάχους καὶ ὅσον οὐκ ἀφέ2 στηκεν. ἐνταῦθα δὴ βοήθεια τῶν Λακεδαιμονίων γίγνεται αὐτῶν τε καὶ τῶν Εἱλώτων πανδημεὶ 3 ὀξεῖα καὶ οἵα οὔπω πρότερον. ἐχώρουν δὲ ἐς Ὀρέσθειον τῆς Μαιναλίας· καὶ τοῖς μὲν Ἀρκάδων σφετέροις οὖσι ξυμμάχοις προεῖπον ἀθροισθεῖσιν ἱέναι κατὰ πόδας αὐτῶν ἐς Τεγέαν, αὐτοὶ δὲ μέχρι μὲν τοῦ Ὀρεσθείου πάντες ἐλθόντες, ἐκεῖθεν δὲ τὸ ἕκτον μέρος σφῶν αὐτῶν ἀποπέμψαντες ἐπ' οἴκου, ἐν ᾧ τὸ πρεσβύτερόν τε καὶ τὸ νεώτερον ἦν, ὥστε τὰ οἴκοι φρουρεῖν, τῷ λοιπῷ στρατεύματι ἀφικνοῦνται ἐς Τεγέαν. καὶ οὐ πολλῷ ὕστερον οἱ ξύμμαχοι ἀπ' Ἀρκάδων παρῆσαν. 4 πέμπουσι δὲ καὶ ἐς τὴν Κόρινθον καὶ Βοιωτοὺς καὶ Φωκέας καὶ Λοκρούς, βοηθεῖν κελεύοντες κατὰ τάχος ἐς Μαντίνειαν. ἀλλὰ τοῖς μὲν ἐξ ὀλίγου τε ἐγίγνετο καὶ οὐ ῥᾴδιον ἦν μὴ ἁθρόοις καὶ ἀλλήλους περιμείνασι διελθεῖν τὴν πολεμίαν (ξυνέκλῃε γὰρ διὰ μέσου), ὅμως δὲ ἠπείγοντο. 5 Λακεδαιμόνιοι δὲ ἀναλαβόντες τοὺς παρόντας Ἀρκάδων ξυμμάχους ἐσέβαλον ἐς τὴν Μαντινικήν, καὶ στρατοπεδευσάμενοι πρὸς τῷ Ἡρακλείῳ ἐδῄουν τὴν γῆν.

---

[1] Compare similar proceedings in II. lxxxv. 1 ; III. lxix. 1 ; VIII. xxxix. 2.

among them; for they chose ten of the Spartiates as counsellors [1] for him without whose consent it was not lawful for him to lead an army out of the city.

LXIV. Meanwhile word came from their friends [2] in Tegea that, unless they should come quickly, Tegea would go over to the Argives and their allies, and already had all but done so. Whereupon succour was sent, both of the Lacedaemonians themselves and of the Helots, in full force, promptly and on such a scale as never before. These advanced to Orestheum in Maenalia, and gave orders to their allies among the Arcadians to get together and come close upon their heels to Tegea. After going, all together, as far as the Orestheum, they sent home from there a sixth part of their force—in which were included the older and younger men—to keep guard at home, and with the remainder of their army reached Tegea, where not long afterwards the allies from Arcadia arrived. They sent also to Corinth and to the Boeotians, Phocians and Locrians, bidding them bring aid in all haste to Mantinea. But to some this was a sudden call, and it was not easy for them, except in a body and after waiting for one another, to go through the enemy's country; for that closed the way, lying just between. Nevertheless they hurried on. But the Lacedaemonians, taking up the allies of the Arcadians that were present, invaded Mantinea, and encamping at the sanctuary of Heracles proceeded to ravage the country.

[2] As opposed to the faction mentioned at the end of ch. lxii.

LXV. Οἱ δ' Ἀργεῖοι καὶ οἱ ξύμμαχοι ὡς εἶδον αὐτούς, καταλαβόντες χωρίον ἐρυμνὸν καὶ δυσ-
2 πρόσοδον παρετάξαντο ὡς ἐς μάχην. καὶ οἱ Λακεδαιμόνιοι εὐθὺς αὐτοῖς ἐπῆσαν· καὶ μέχρι μὲν λίθου καὶ ἀκοντίου βολῆς ἐχώρησαν· ἔπειτα τῶν πρεσβυτέρων τις Ἄγιδι ἐπεβόησεν, ὁρῶν πρὸς χωρίον καρτερὸν ἰόντας σφᾶς, ὅτι διανοεῖται κακὸν κακῷ ἰᾶσθαι, δηλῶν τῆς ἐξ Ἄργους ἐπαι-τίου ἀναχωρήσεως τὴν παροῦσαν ἄκαιρον προ-
3 θυμίαν ἀνάληψιν βουλομένην εἶναι. ὁ δέ, εἴτε καὶ διὰ τὸ ἐπιβόημα εἴτε καὶ αὐτῷ ἄλλο τι ἢ [1] κατὰ τὸ αὐτὸ δόξαν ἐξαίφνης, πάλιν τὸ στρά-
4 τευμα κατὰ τάχος πρὶν ξυμμεῖξαι ἀπῆγεν. καὶ ἀφικόμενος πρὸς τὴν Τεγεᾶτιν τὸ ὕδωρ ἐξέτρεπεν ἐς τὴν Μαντινικήν, περὶ οὗπερ ὡς τὰ πολλὰ βλάπτοντος ὁποτέρωσε ἂν ἐσπίπτῃ Μαντινῆς καὶ Τεγεᾶται πολεμοῦσιν· ἐβούλετο δὲ τοὺς ἀπὸ τοῦ λόφου βοηθοῦντας ἐπὶ τὴν τοῦ ὕδατος ἐκτροπήν, ἐπειδὰν πύθωνται, καταβιβάσαι [2] καὶ ἐν τῷ ὁμαλῷ
5 τὴν μάχην ποιεῖσθαι. καὶ ὁ μὲν τὴν ἡμέραν ταύτην μείνας αὐτοῦ περὶ τὸ ὕδωρ ἐξέτρεπεν· οἱ δ' Ἀργεῖοι καὶ οἱ ξύμμαχοι τὸ μὲν πρῶτον κατα-πλαγέντες τῇ ἐξ ὀλίγου αἰφνιδίῳ αὐτῶν ἀναχω-ρήσει οὐκ εἶχον ὅ τι εἰκάσωσιν· εἶτ' ἐπειδὴ ἀναχωροῦντες ἐκεῖνοί τε ἀπέκρυψαν καὶ σφεῖς ἡσύχαζον καὶ οὐκ ἐπηκολούθουν, ἐνταῦθα τοὺς ἑαυτῶν στρατηγοὺς αὖθις ἐν αἰτίᾳ εἶχον τό τε

---

[1] But Hude deletes ἤ, making the sense to be, "had altered his views in a like manner."

[2] τοὺς Ἀργείους καὶ τοὺς ξυμμάχους, in MSS. after καταβιβά-σαι, deleted by van Herwerden.

LXV. But the Argives and their allies, on seeing them, took up a position that was steep and difficult of access, and drew up for battle. The Lacedaemonians went against them at once, advancing within a stone's throw or a javelin's cast; then one of the older men, seeing that they were going against a strong place, called out to Agis that he thought to cure one ill with another, meaning that the motive of his present unseasonable eagerness was to make amends for the culpable retreat from Argos.[1] Agis, then, whether on account of this call, or because it suddenly struck him, too, that some other course was better than the one he was following, led his army back again in all haste without coming into conflict. Then when he had reached Tegean territory he set about diverting into Mantinean territory the stream of water about which the Mantineans and Tegeates are always warring, on account of the harm it commonly does to whichever country it empties into. He wished to make the troops on the hill[2] come down to prevent the diversion of the water as soon as they should hear about it, and thus force them to fight the battle in the plain. So he lingered for that day in the neighbourhood of the stream and set about diverting it; but the Argives and their allies were at first amazed at their opponents' sudden withdrawal after coming close, and were at a loss what to make of it; afterwards, however, when the enemy had withdrawn out of sight, while they themselves kept quiet and did not follow after them, they began again to find fault with their own generals

---

[1] cf. ch. lxi. 1 ; lxiii. 2.
[2] i.e. χωρίον ἐρυμνόν mentioned above.

πρότερον καλῶς ληφθέντας πρὸς Ἄργει Λακεδαιμονίους ἀφεθῆναι καὶ νῦν ὅτι ἀποδιδράσκοντας
οὐδεὶς ἐπιδιώκει, ἀλλὰ καθ᾽ ἡσυχίαν οἱ μὲν
6 σῴζονται, σφεῖς δὲ προδίδονται. οἱ δὲ στρατηγοὶ
ἐθορυβήθησαν μὲν τὸ παραυτίκα, ὕστερον δὲ
ἀπάγουσιν αὐτοὺς ἀπὸ τοῦ λόφου καὶ προελθόντες
ἐς τὸ ὁμαλὸν ἐστρατοπεδεύσαντο ὡς ἰόντες ἐπὶ
τοὺς πολεμίους.

LXVI. Τῇ δ᾽ ὑστεραίᾳ οἵ τε Ἀργεῖοι καὶ οἱ
ξύμμαχοι ξυνετάξαντο, ὡς ἔμελλον μαχεῖσθαι,
ἢν περιτύχωσιν· οἵ τε Λακεδαιμόνιοι ἀπὸ τοῦ
ὕδατος πρὸς τὸ Ἡράκλειον πάλιν ἐς τὸ αὐτὸ
στρατόπεδον ἰόντες ὁρῶσι δι᾽ ὀλίγου τοὺς ἐναντίους ἐν τάξει τε ἤδη πάντας καὶ ἀπὸ τοῦ λόφου
2 προεληλυθότας. μάλιστα δὲ Λακεδαιμόνιοι ἐς
ὃ ἐμέμνηντο ἐν τούτῳ τῷ καιρῷ ἐξεπλάγησαν (διὰ
βραχείας γὰρ μελλήσεως ἡ παρασκευὴ αὐτοῖς
ἐγίγνετο), καὶ εὐθὺς ὑπὸ σπουδῆς καθίσταντο ἐς
κόσμον τὸν ἑαυτῶν, Ἅγιδος τοῦ βασιλέως ἕκαστα
3 ἐξηγουμένου κατὰ τὸν νόμον. βασιλέως γὰρ
ἄγοντος ὑπ᾽ ἐκείνου πάντα ἄρχεται, καὶ τοῖς μὲν
πολεμάρχοις αὐτὸς φράζει τὸ δέον, οἱ δὲ τοῖς
λοχαγοῖς, ἐκεῖνοι δὲ τοῖς πεντηκοντῆρσιν, αὖθις
δ᾽ οὗτοι τοῖς ἐνωμοτάρχαις, καὶ οὗτοι τῇ ἐνωμοτίᾳ.
4 καὶ αἱ παραγγέλσεις, ἤν τι βούλωνται, κατὰ τὰ
αὐτὰ χωροῦσι καὶ ταχεῖαι ἐπέρχονται· σχεδὸν
γάρ τι πᾶν πλὴν ὀλίγου[1] τὸ στρατόπεδον τῶν

---

[1] πλὴν ὀλίγου, deleted by Hude, after Badham.

because on a previous occasion the Lacedaemonians, when fairly caught near Argos, had been allowed to escape, and now when they were running away no one pursued them; on the contrary, the enemy were quietly making good their safety, while they themselves were being betrayed. The generals were confounded for the moment by the outcry, but afterwards they moved the troops from the hill and going forward into the plain encamped there, with the intention of advancing against the enemy.

LXVI. On the next day the Argives and their allies drew up in the order in which they intended to fight if they fell in with the enemy; and the Lacedaemonians, going away from the stream and back to their old camp at the sanctuary of Heracles, suddenly saw the enemy close at hand, all by that time in order of battle and occupying an advanced position away from the hill. Never had the Lacedaemonians, as far back as they remembered, been in such consternation as on this occasion. Their preparation had to be made on short notice; and at once in haste they fell into their own array, king Agis directing each movement as the law prescribed. For when a king leads all orders are given by him: he himself gives the necessary order to the polemarchs,[1] they to the commanders of battalions, these to the captains of companies, these again to the commanders of platoons, and these to the platoons. So the special orders, if they wish to give any, proceed in the same way, and reach their destination quickly; for almost the whole army of the Lacedaemonians consists of officers over

[1] Commanders of the six morae, according to Xen. *Resp. Lac.* XI. iv.

Λακεδαιμονίων ἄρχοντες ἀρχόντων εἰσί, καὶ τὸ
ἐπιμελὲς τοῦ δρωμένου πολλοῖς προσήκει.

LXVII. Τότε δὲ κέρας μὲν εὐώνυμον Σκιρῖται
αὐτοῖς καθίσταντο, αἰεὶ ταύτην τὴν τάξιν μόνοι
Λακεδαιμονίων ἐπὶ σφῶν αὐτῶν ἔχοντες· παρὰ
δ' αὐτοῖς οἱ ἀπὸ Θράκης Βρασίδειοι στρατιῶται
καὶ νεοδαμώδεις μετ' αὐτῶν· ἔπειτ' ἤδη Λακεδαιμόνιοι αὐτοὶ ἑξῆς καθίστασαι τοὺς λόχους καὶ
παρ' αὐτοὺς Ἀρκάδων Ἡραιῆς, μετὰ δὲ τούτους
Μαινάλιοι, καὶ ἐπὶ τῷ δεξιῷ κέρᾳ Τεγεᾶται καὶ
Λακεδαιμονίων ὀλίγοι τὸ ἔσχατον ἔχοντες, καὶ οἱ
2 ἱππῆς αὐτῶν ἐφ' ἑκατέρῳ τῷ κέρᾳ.   Λακεδαιμόνιοι μὲν οὕτως ἐτάξαντο· οἱ δ' ἐναντίοι αὐτοῖς
δεξιὸν μὲν κέρας Μαντινῆς εἶχον, ὅτι ἐν τῇ ἐκείνων
τὸ ἔργον ἐγίγνετο, παρὰ δ' αὐτοῖς οἱ ξύμμαχοι
Ἀρκάδων ἦσαν, ἔπειτα Ἀργείων οἱ χίλιοι λογάδες,
οἷς ἡ πόλις ἐκ πολλοῦ ἄσκησιν τῶν ἐς τὸν πόλεμον
δημοσίᾳ παρεῖχε, καὶ ἐχόμενοι αὐτῶν οἱ ἄλλοι
Ἀργεῖοι, καὶ μετ' αὐτοὺς οἱ ξύμμαχοι αὐτῶν,
Κλεωναῖοι καὶ Ὀρνεᾶται, ἔπειτα Ἀθηναῖοι ἔσχατοι
τὸ εὐώνυμον κέρας ἔχοντες καὶ ἱππῆς μετ' αὐτῶν
οἱ οἰκεῖοι.

LXVIII. Τάξις μὲν ἤδε καὶ παρασκευὴ ἀμφοτέρων ἦν, τὸ δὲ στρατόπεδον τῶν Λακεδαι-
2 μονίων μεῖζον ἐφάνη.   ἀριθμὸν δὲ γράψαι, ἢ καθ'
ἑκάστους ἑκατέρων ἢ ξύμπαντας, οὐκ ἂν ἐδυνάμην
ἀκριβῶς· τὸ μὲν γὰρ Λακεδαιμονίων πλῆθος διὰ τῆς
πολιτείας τὸ κρυπτὸν ἠγνοεῖτο, τῶν δ' αὖ διὰ τὸ
ἀνθρώπειον κομπῶδες ἐς τὰ οἰκεῖα πλήθη ἠπι-

officers, and the responsibility for the execution of orders devolves upon many.

LXVII. On this occasion there were posted on the left wing the Sciritae,[1] who alone of the Lacedaemonians always have that post by themselves; next to them the soldiers who had served with Brasidas in Thrace, and with them the Neodamodes; next the Lacedaemonians themselves, with their battalions posted one after another, and by them the Heraeans of Arcadia; after these the Maenalians; on the right wing the Tegeates, with a few of the Lacedaemonians holding the end of the line; and on either wing the cavalry. The Lacedaemonians were thus arrayed. On their enemy's side the Mantineans had the right wing, because the action was to be fought in their country; by their side were their Arcadian allies; then the thousand picked men of the Argives, for whom the state had for a long time furnished at public expense training in matters pertaining to war; next to them the rest of the Argives; after these their allies, the Cleonaeans and Orneates; then the Athenians last, on the left wing, and with them their own cavalry.

LXVIII. Such was the order and the composition of the two sides. The army of the Lacedaemonians appeared the larger; but the number, either of the separate contingents or of the total on either side, I could not possibly state accurately. For on account of the secrecy of their polity the number of the Lacedaemonians was unknown; and that claimed for the others, on account of men's tendency to boast with regard to their own numbers, was discredited.

---

[1] Inhabitants of the rough hilly country towards the territory of Tegea.

στεῖτο. ἐκ μέντοι τοιοῦδε λογισμοῦ ἔξεστί τῳ σκοπεῖν τὸ Λακεδαιμονίων τότε παραγενόμενον πλῆ-
3 θος· λόχοι μὲν γὰρ ἐμάχοντο ἑπτὰ ἄνευ Σκιριτῶν
ὄντων ἑξακοσίων, ἐν δὲ ἑκάστῳ λόχῳ πεντηκοστύες
ἦσαν τέσσαρες, καὶ ἐν τῇ πεντηκοστύι ἐνωμοτίαι
τέσσαρες. τῆς τε ἐνωμοτίας ἐμάχοντο ἐν τῷ
πρώτῳ ζυγῷ τέσσαρες· ἐπὶ δὲ βάθος ἐτάξαντο
μὲν οὐ πάντες ὁμοίως, ἀλλ᾽ ὡς λοχαγὸς ἕκαστος
ἐβούλετο, ἐπὶ πᾶν δὲ κατέστησαν ἐπὶ ὀκτώ. παρὰ
δὲ ἅπαν πλὴν Σκιριτῶν τετρακόσιοι καὶ δυοῖν
δέοντες πεντήκοντα ἄνδρες ἡ πρώτη τάξις ἦν.

LXIX. Ἐπεὶ δὲ ξυνιέναι ἔμελλον ἤδη, ἐνταῦθα
καὶ παραινέσεις καθ᾽ ἑκάστους ὑπὸ τῶν οἰκείων
στρατηγῶν τοιαίδε ἐγίγνοντο, Μαντινεῦσι μὲν ὅτι
ὑπέρ τε πατρίδος ἡ μάχη ἔσται καὶ ὑπὲρ ἀρχῆς
ἅμα καὶ δουλείας, τὴν μὲν μὴ πειρασαμένοις ἀφαι-
ρεθῆναι, τῆς δὲ μὴ αὖθις πειρᾶσθαι· Ἀργείοις δὲ
ὑπὲρ τῆς τε παλαιᾶς ἡγεμονίας καὶ τῆς ἐν Πελοποννήσῳ ποτὲ ἰσομοιρίας μὴ διὰ παντὸς στερι-
σκομένους ἀνέχεσθαι, καὶ ἄνδρας ἅμα ἐχθροὺς καὶ
ἀστυγείτονας ὑπὲρ πολλῶν ἀδικημάτων ἀμύνα-
σθαι· τοῖς δὲ Ἀθηναίοις, καλὸν εἶναι μετὰ πολλῶν
καὶ ἀγαθῶν ξυμμάχων ἀγωνιζομένους μηδενὸς
λείπεσθαι, καὶ ὅτι ἐν Πελοποννήσῳ Λακεδαιμονίους νικήσαντες τήν τε ἀρχὴν βεβαιοτέραν καὶ
μείζω ἕξουσι, καὶ οὐ μή ποτέ τις αὐτοῖς ἄλλος ἐς
2 τὴν γῆν ἔλθῃ. τοῖς μὲν Ἀργείοις καὶ ξυμμάχοις

---

[1] The sum-total of the whole army was 4,184 men
(7 × 4 × 4 × 4 = 448 × 8 = 3,584 + 600 = 4,184).

However, from the following mode of computation
it is allowable to estimate the number of the
Lacedaemonians that were then present. There
were engaged in the battle seven battalions, without
the Sciritae, who numbered six hundred, and in each
battalion were four companies of fifty, in each company four platoons. In the first rank of each
company fought four men ; in depth, however, they
were not all drawn up alike, but as each battalion-
commander preferred—on the average eight deep.
Along the whole line, then, exclusive of the Sciritae,
the first rank consisted of four hundred and forty-
eight men.[1]

LXIX. When they were on the point of engaging,
exhortations were made to the several contingents
by their own generals to the following effect : The
Mantineans were reminded that the battle would
be for fatherland, and, moreover, for dominion or
servitude—that they should not be deprived of the
one after having made trial of it, and should not
again experience the other ; the Argives, that the
contest would be both for their ancient hegemony[2]
and for their old equality of influence[3] in the Peloponnese, that they must not brook being deprived
of it forever, and at the same time must avenge
themselves for many wrongs on men who were
enemies and near neighbours at that ; the Athenians,
that it was glorious, contending along with many
and brave allies, to be inferior to none, and that if
they should conquer the Lacedaemonians in the
Peloponnese they would have a greater empire and
hold it more securely, and no one would ever invade
their country again. Such were the admonitions

[2] Under Agamemnon.   [3] Before the Persian Wars.

τοιαῦτα παρῃνέθη· Λακεδαιμόνιοι δὲ καθ' ἑκάστους τε καὶ μετὰ τῶν πολεμικῶν νόμων ἐν σφίσιν
αὐτοῖς ὧν ἠπίσταντο τὴν παρακέλευσιν τῆς μνήμης
ἀγαθοῖς οὖσιν ἐποιοῦντο, εἰδότες ἔργων ἐκ πολλοῦ
μελέτην πλείω σώζουσαν ἢ λόγων δι' ὀλίγου καλῶς
ῥηθεῖσαν παραίνεσιν.

LXX. Καὶ μετὰ ταῦτα ἡ ξύνοδος ἦν, Ἀργεῖοι
μὲν καὶ οἱ ξύμμαχοι ἐντόνως καὶ ὀργῇ χωροῦντες,
Λακεδαιμόνιοι δὲ βραδέως καὶ ὑπὸ αὐλητῶν πολλῶν νόμῳ ἐγκαθεστώτων, οὐ τοῦ θείου χάριν,
ἀλλ' ἵνα ὁμαλῶς μετὰ ῥυθμοῦ βαίνοντες προσέλ-
θοιεν[1] καὶ μὴ διασπασθείη αὐτοῖς ἡ τάξις, ὅπερ
φιλεῖ τὰ μεγάλα στρατόπεδα ἐν ταῖς προσόδοις
ποιεῖν.

LXXI. Ξυνιόντων δ' ἔτι Ἆγις ὁ βασιλεὺς τοιόνδε
ἐβουλεύσατο δρᾶσαι. τὰ στρατόπεδα ποιεῖ μὲν
καὶ ἅπαντα τοῦτο· ἐπὶ τὰ δεξιὰ κέρα τὰ αὑτῶν
ἐν ταῖς ξυνόδοις μᾶλλον ἐξωθεῖται, καὶ περιίσχουσι
κατὰ τὸ τῶν ἐναντίων εὐώνυμον ἀμφότεροι τῷ
δεξιῷ, διὰ τὸ φοβουμένους προσστέλλειν τὰ γυμνὰ
ἕκαστον ὡς μάλιστα τῇ τοῦ ἐν δεξιᾷ παρατεταγ-
μένου ἀσπίδι καὶ νομίζειν τὴν πυκνότητα τῆς
ξυγκλήσεως εὐσκεπαστότατον εἶναι· καὶ ἡγεῖται
μὲν τῆς αἰτίας ταύτης ὁ πρωτοστάτης τοῦ δεξιοῦ
κέρως, προθυμούμενος ἐξαλλάσσειν αἰεὶ τῶν ἐναντίων τὴν ἑαυτοῦ γύμνωσιν, ἕπονται δὲ διὰ τὸν
2 αὐτὸν φόβον καὶ οἱ ἄλλοι. καὶ τότε περιέσχον
μὲν οἱ Μαντινῆς πολὺ τῷ κέρᾳ τῶν Σκιριτῶν, ἔτι
δὲ πλέον οἱ Λακεδαιμόνιοι καὶ Τεγεᾶται τῶν
3 Ἀθηναίων, ὅσῳ μεῖζον τὸ στράτευμα εἶχον. δείσας δὲ Ἆγις μὴ σφῶν κυκλωθῇ τὸ εὐώνυμον, καὶ

---

[1] With Gellius and the Schol. for προέλθοιεν of the MSS.

addressed to the Argives and their allies; the Lacedaemonians, however, exhorted one another man by man, using also their war-songs—as brave men to remember what they had learned, knowing that long-continued actual practice meant more for their salvation than any brief admonition, however well spoken.

LXX. After this the conflict commenced, the Argives and their allies advancing eagerly and impetuously, but the Lacedaemonians slowly and to the music of many flute-players placed among them according to custom, not with any religious motive, but in order that they might march up with even step and keeping time without breaking their order, as large armies are apt to do in going into battle.

LXXI. But while they were still closing, King Agis resolved to make the following manœuvre. All armies are apt, on coming together, to thrust out their right wing too much; and both sides extend with their right beyond their opponents' left wing, because in their fear each man brings his uncovered side as close as possible to the shield of the man stationed on his right, thinking that the closer the shields are locked together the better is the protection. And it is the first man on the right wing who is primarily responsible for this, since he always wants to withdraw from the enemy his own uncovered side, and the rest, from a like fear, follow his example. And so on this occasion the Mantineans extended with their right wing far beyond the Sciritae; and the Lacedaemonians and Tegeates further still beyond the Athenians, inasmuch as their army was larger. So Agis, in fear that his left might be encircled, and thinking that

THUCYDIDES

νομίσας ἄγαν περιέχειν τοὺς Μαντινέας, τοῖς μὲν
Σκιρίταις καὶ Βρασιδείοις ἐσήμηνεν ἐπεξαγαγόν-
τας ἀπὸ σφῶν ἐξισῶσαι τοῖς Μαντινεῦσιν, ἐς δὲ
τὸ διάκενον τοῦτο παρήγγελλεν ἀπὸ τοῦ δεξιοῦ
κέρως δύο λόχους τῶν πολεμάρχων Ἱππονοΐδα
καὶ Ἀριστοκλεῖ ἔχουσι παρελθεῖν καὶ ἐσβαλόν-
τας πληρῶσαι, νομίζων τῷ θ' ἑαυτῶν δεξιῷ ἔτι
περιουσίαν ἔσεσθαι καὶ τὸ κατὰ τοὺς Μαντινέας
βεβαιότερον τετάξεσθαι.

LXXII. Ξυνέβη οὖν αὐτῷ ἅτε ἐν αὐτῇ τῇ ἐφόδῳ
καὶ ἐξ ὀλίγου παραγγείλαντι τόν τε Ἀριστοκλέα
καὶ τὸν Ἱππονοΐδαν μὴ 'θελῆσαι παρελθεῖν, ἀλλὰ
καὶ διὰ τοῦτο τὸ αἰτίαμα ὕστερον φεύγειν ἐκ
Σπάρτης, δόξαντας μαλακισθῆναι, καὶ τοὺς πολεμίους φθάσαι τῇ προσμείξει, καὶ κελεύσαντος
αὐτοῦ, ἐπὶ τοὺς Σκιρίτας ὡς οὐ παρῆλθον οἱ λόχοι,
πάλιν αὖ σφίσι προσμεῖξαι, μὴ δυνηθῆναι ἔτι
2 μηδὲ τούτους ξυγκλῇσαι. ἀλλὰ μάλιστα δὴ κατὰ
πάντα τῇ ἐμπειρίᾳ Λακεδαιμόνιοι ἐλασσωθέντες
τότε τῇ ἀνδρείᾳ ἔδειξαν οὐχ ἧσσον περιγενόμενοι.
3 ἐπειδὴ γὰρ ἐν χερσὶν ἐγίγνοντο τοῖς ἐναντίοις, τὸ
μὲν τῶν Μαντινέων δεξιὸν τρέπει αὐτῶν τοὺς
Σκιρίτας καὶ τοὺς Βρασιδείους, καὶ ἐσπεσόντες οἱ
Μαντινῆς καὶ οἱ ξύμμαχοι αὐτῶν καὶ τῶν Ἀργείων
οἱ χίλιοι λογάδες κατὰ τὸ διάκενον καὶ οὐ ξυγ-
κλῃσθὲν τοὺς Λακεδαιμονίους διέφθειρον καὶ κυ-
κλωσάμενοι ἔτρεψαν καὶ ἐξέωσαν ἐς τὰς ἁμάξας
καὶ τῶν πρεσβυτέρων τῶν ἐπιτεταγμένων ἀπέ-

the Mantineans were extending too far beyond it, gave orders to the Sciritae and the soldiers of Brasidas to move out, away from his main body, and make the line equal to that of the Mantineans; then he directed two polemarchs, Hipponoïdas and Aristocles, to cross over with two companies from the right wing, throw themselves in and fill up the gap thus created, thinking that his own right wing would still have more than enough men, and that the line opposed to the Mantineans would be strengthened.

LXXII. It turned out, then, as he gave this order at the very moment of the attack and on a sudden, that Aristocles and Hipponoïdas refused to move over—for which offence they were afterwards exiled from Sparta, as they were considered to have acted as cowards; and that the enemy were too quick for him in coming to close quarters; and then, when the companies did not move over to replace the Sciritae, and he gave orders to the Sciritae to join the main body again, even these were now no longer able to close up the line. Yet in the most striking way the Lacedaemonians, although they were in all respects proved inferior in point of tactical skill, did on this occasion show that they were none the less superior in courage. For when they came to close quarters with the foe, the right wing of the Mantineans routed, it is true, the Sciritae and the Brasideans, and then the Mantineans and their allies and the thousand picked men of the Argives, rushing into the gap that had not been closed, played havoc with the Lacedaemonians; for they surrounded and put them to rout, and drove them in among the wagons, slaying some of the older men

4 κτεινάν τινας. καὶ ταύτῃ μὲν ἡσσῶντο οἱ Λακε-
δαιμόνιοι· τῷ δὲ ἄλλῳ στρατοπέδῳ, καὶ μάλιστα
τῷ μέσῳ, ᾗπερ ὁ βασιλεὺς ἦν Ἆγις καὶ περὶ
αὐτὸν οἱ τριακόσιοι ἱππῆς καλούμενοι, προσπεσόντες τῶν τε Ἀργείων τοῖς πρεσβυτέροις καὶ
πεντελόχοις ὠνομασμένοις καὶ Κλεωναίοις καὶ
Ὀρνεάταις καὶ Ἀθηναίων τοῖς παρατεταγμένοις
ἔτρεψαν οὐδὲ ἐς χεῖρας τοὺς πολλοὺς ὑπομείναντας,
ἀλλ᾽ ὡς ἐπῇσαν οἱ Λακεδαιμόνιοι, εὐθὺς ἐνδόντας
καὶ ἔστιν οὓς καὶ καταπατηθέντας τοῦ μὴ φθῆναι
τὴν ἐγκατάληψιν.

LXXIII. Ὡς δὲ ταύτῃ ἐνεδεδώκει τὸ τῶν
Ἀργείων καὶ ξυμμάχων στράτευμα, παρερρή-
γνυντο ἤδη ἅμα καὶ ἐφ᾽ ἑκάτερα, καὶ ἅμα τὸ
δεξιὸν τῶν Λακεδαιμονίων καὶ Τεγεατῶν ἐκυ-
κλοῦτο τῷ περιέχοντι σφῶν τοὺς Ἀθηναίους, καὶ
ἀμφοτέρωθεν αὐτοὺς κίνδυνος περιειστήκει, τῇ
μὲν κυκλουμένους, τῇ δὲ ἤδη ἡσσημένους. καὶ
μάλιστ᾽ ἂν τοῦ στρατεύματος ἐταλαιπώρησαν, εἰ
2 μὴ οἱ ἱππῆς παρόντες αὐτοῖς ὠφέλιμοι ἦσαν. καὶ
ξυνέβη τὸν Ἆγιν, ὡς ᾔσθετο τὸ εὐώνυμον σφῶν
πονοῦν τὸ κατὰ τοὺς Μαντινέας καὶ τῶν Ἀργείων
τοὺς χιλίους, παραγγεῖλαι παντὶ τῷ στρατεύματι
3 χωρῆσαι ἐπὶ τὸ νικώμενον. καὶ γενομένου τούτου
οἱ μὲν Ἀθηναῖοι ἐν τούτῳ, ὡς παρῆλθε καὶ ἐξέ-
κλινεν ἀπὸ σφῶν τὸ στράτευμα, καθ᾽ ἡσυχίαν

stationed there. In this quarter, then, the Lacedaemonians were worsted; but in the rest of the army, and especially in the centre, where King Agis was, and about him the three hundred who were called knights,[1] they fell upon the older men of the Argives, the so-called five companies, and upon the Cleonaeans, the Orneates, and those of the Athenians that were arrayed with them, and routed them. Most of the enemy did not even wait to come to blows, but when the Lacedaemonians came on gave way at once, some of them being trodden underfoot in their effort to get out of the way before being hemmed in by the Lacedaemonians.

LXXIII. When the army of the Argives and their allies had given way in this quarter, their line was on the point of being broken in both directions; and at the same time the right wing of the Lacedaemonians and the Tegeates was beginning to encircle the Athenians with the outflanking part of their own line ; and so danger beset them on both sides, for they were being surrounded in one quarter and had been already defeated in the other. And they would have suffered more than any part of the whole army if their cavalry had not been present and proved helpful to them. It happened, too, that Agis, perceiving that the left of his own forces, which was opposed to the Mantineans and the thousand Argives, was in distress, gave orders for the whole army to go to the assistance of the part that was in danger of defeat. When this was done, the Athenians, as the enemy's force passed on and moved away from them, quietly made their escape,

[1] Chosen from the flower of the Spartan youth and serving as a royal body-guard, on foot as well as on horseback.

ἐσώθησαν καὶ τῶν Ἀργείων μετ' αὐτῶν τὸ ἡσση-
θέν. οἱ δὲ Μαντινῆς καὶ οἱ ξύμμαχοι καὶ τῶν
Ἀργείων οἱ λογάδες οὐκέτι πρὸς τὸ ἐγκεῖσθαι τοῖς
ἐναντίοις τὴν γνώμην εἶχον, ἀλλ' ὁρῶντες τούς τε
σφετέρους νενικημένους καὶ τοὺς Λακεδαιμονίους
4 ἐπιφερομένους ἐς φυγὴν ἐτράποντο. καὶ τῶν μὲν
Μαντινέων καὶ πλείους διεφθάρησαν, τῶν δὲ
Ἀργείων λογάδων τὸ πολὺ ἐσώθη. ἡ μέντοι
φυγὴ καὶ ἀποχώρησις οὐ βίαιος οὐδὲ μακρὰ ἦν·
οἱ γὰρ Λακεδαιμόνιοι μέχρι μὲν τοῦ τρέψαι χρο-
νίους τὰς μάχας καὶ βεβαίους τῷ μένειν ποιοῦνται,
τρέψαντες δὲ βραχείας καὶ οὐκ ἐπὶ πολὺ τὰς
διώξεις.

LXXIV. Καὶ ἡ μὲν μάχη τοιαύτη καὶ ὅτι
ἐγγύτατα τούτων ἐγένετο, πλείστου δὴ χρόνου
μεγίστη δὴ τῶν Ἑλληνικῶν καὶ ὑπὸ ἀξιο-
2 λογωτάτων πόλεων ξυνελθοῦσα. οἱ δὲ Λακεδαιμόνιοι προθέμενοι τῶν πολεμίων νεκρῶν τὰ
ὅπλα τροπαῖον εὐθὺς ἵστασαν καὶ τοὺς νεκροὺς
ἐσκύλευον καὶ τοὺς αὑτῶν ἀνείλοντο καὶ ἀπήγαγον ἐς Τεγέαν, οὗπερ ἐτάφησαν, καὶ τοὺς τῶν
πολεμίων ὑποσπόνδους ἀπέδοσαν. ἀπέθανον δὲ
Ἀργείων μὲν καὶ Ὀρνεατῶν καὶ Κλεωναίων
ἑπτακόσιοι, Μαντινέων δὲ διακόσιοι, καὶ Ἀθηναίων ξὺν Αἰγινήταις διακόσιοι καὶ οἱ στρατηγοὶ
ἀμφότεροι. Λακεδαιμονίων δὲ οἱ μὲν ξύμμαχοι
οὐκ ἐταλαιπώρησαν ὥστε καὶ ἀξιόλογόν τι ἀπο-
γενέσθαι· αὐτῶν δὲ χαλεπὸν μὲν ἦν τὴν ἀλήθειαν πυθέσθαι, ἐλέγοντο δὲ περὶ τριακοσίους
ἀποθανεῖν.

LXXV. Τῆς δὲ **μάχης μελλούσης ἔσεσθαι** καὶ

and with them the part of the Argives that had
been worsted. The Mantineans and their allies, on
the other hand, and the picked men of the Argives,
were no longer disposed to press home the attack on
their opponents, but seeing their own side defeated
and the Lacedaemonians bearing down upon them,
turned to flight. On the part of the Mantineans
the losses were more serious, but of the picked men
of the Argives the greater part was saved. The
flight, however, was not hotly pursued, nor did the
retreat extend to any great distance; for the
Lacedaemonians fight their battles long and
stubbornly, standing their ground until they rout
their foes, but when they have routed them their
pursuits are brief and only for a little distance.

LXXIV. Such, then, was the battle—or as like as
possible to this description—being the greatest that
had occurred within a very long time between Hellenic
forces, and fought by the most famous states. The
Lacedaemonians, halting in front of their enemies'
dead, straightway set up a trophy and stripped the
slain, then took up their own dead and withdrew to
Tegea, where they buried them, giving up under
truce those of the enemy. There were slain, of the
Argives, Orneates and Cleonaeans seven hundred, of
the Mantineans two hundred, of the Athenians,
together with the Aeginetans,[1] two hundred, and
both their generals. On the side of the Lacedaemonians, the allies did not suffer so that any number
worth mentioning was missing; about themselves it
was difficult to learn the truth, but near three
hundred were said to have been killed.

LXXV. As the battle was about to take place,

---

[1] Athenian colonists settled in Aegina; cf. II. xxvii. 1.

Πλειστοάναξ ὁ ἕτερος βασιλεὺς ἔχων τούς τε
πρεσβυτέρους καὶ νεωτέρους ἐβοήθησε, καὶ μέχρι
μὲν Τεγέας ἀφίκετο, πυθόμενος δὲ τὴν νίκην
2 ἀπεχώρησεν. καὶ τοὺς ἀπὸ Κορίνθου καὶ ἔξω
ἰσθμοῦ ξυμμάχους ἀπέτρεψαν πέμψαντες οἱ
Λακεδαιμόνιοι, καὶ αὐτοὶ ἀναχωρήσαντες καὶ
τοὺς ξυμμάχους ἀφέντες (Κάρνεια γὰρ αὐτοῖς
3 ἐτύγχανον ὄντα) τὴν ἑορτὴν ἦγον. καὶ τὴν ὑπὸ
τῶν Ἑλλήνων τότε ἐπιφερομένην αἰτίαν ἔς τε
μαλακίαν διὰ τὴν ἐν τῇ νήσῳ ξυμφορὰν καὶ ἐς
τὴν ἄλλην ἀβουλίαν τε καὶ βραδυτῆτα ἑνὶ ἔργῳ
τούτῳ ἀπελύσαντο, τύχῃ μὲν ὡς ἐδόκουν κακι-
ζόμενοι, γνώμῃ δὲ οἱ αὐτοὶ ἔτι ὄντες.

4 Τῇ δὲ προτεραίᾳ ἡμέρᾳ ξυνέβη τῆς μάχης
ταύτης καὶ τοὺς Ἐπιδαυρίους πανδημεὶ ἐσβαλεῖν
ἐς τὴν Ἀργείαν ὡς ἐρῆμον οὖσαν καὶ τοὺς
ὑπολοίπους φύλακας τῶν Ἀργείων ἐξελθόντων
5 αὐτῶν διαφθεῖραι πολλούς. καὶ Ἠλείων τρισχι-
λίων ὁπλιτῶν βοηθησάντων Μαντινεῦσιν ὕστερον
τῆς μάχης καὶ Ἀθηναίων χιλίων πρὸς τοῖς προ-
τέροις, ἐστράτευσαν ἅπαντες οἱ ξύμμαχοι οὗτοι
εὐθὺς ἐπὶ Ἐπίδαυρον, ἕως οἱ Λακεδαιμόνιοι Κάρνεια ἦγον, καὶ διελόμενοι τὴν πόλιν περιετείχιζον.
6 καὶ οἱ μὲν ἄλλοι ἐξεπαύσαντο, Ἀθηναῖοι δέ,
ὥσπερ προσετάχθησαν, τὴν ἄκραν τὸ Ἥραιον
εὐθὺς ἐξειργάσαντο. καὶ ἐν τούτῳ ξυγκαταλι-
πόντες ἅπαντες τῷ τειχίσματι φρουρὰν ἀνεχώρησαν κατὰ πόλεις ἕκαστοι. καὶ τὸ θέρος ἐτελεύτα.

---

[1] cf. ch. lxiv. 3.   [2] cf. ch. lxiv. 4.

Pleistoanax, the other king, set out with the older and younger men[1] to bring succour, and got as far as Tegea; but learning there of the victory he returned. The allies, too, from Corinth and from outside the Isthmus[2] were turned back by messengers sent by the Lacedaemonians, who then likewise withdrew and, dismissing their allies, celebrated the festival of the Carneia; for it happened to fall at that time. And the charge brought against them at that time by the Hellenes, both of cowardice because of the calamity on the island of Sphacteria, and of general bad judgment and dilatoriness, they had wiped out by this one action; they were thought to have incurred disgrace through ill-luck, but to be still the same in spirit.

Aug. 418 B.C.

The day before this battle it happened also that the Epidaurians in full force invaded the territory of Argos, thinking to find it now undefended, and slew many of those who had been left behind as guards when the main body of the Argives had taken the field. And now, since three thousand Elean hoplites had come to the aid of the Mantineans after the battle, and also one thousand Athenians in addition to their former contingent, all these allies marched at once against Epidaurus, while the Lacedaemonians were celebrating the Carneia, and proceeded to build a wall round the city, dividing up the work. The rest indeed left off, but the Athenians soon finished the fortification of the promontory on which stood the Heraeum, which was the part that had been assigned to them. In this part of the fortification they left a garrison, to which all contributed, and then withdrew to their several cities. And so the summer ended.

LXXVI. Τοῦ δ' ἐπιγιγνομένου χειμῶνος ἀρχομένου εὐθὺς οἱ Λακεδαιμόνιοι[1] ἐξεστράτευσαν, καὶ ἀφικόμενοι ἐς Τεγέαν λόγους προύπεμπον ἐς
2 τὸ Ἄργος ξυμβατηρίους. ἦσαν δὲ αὐτοῖς πρότερόν τε ἄνδρες ἐπιτήδειοι καὶ βουλόμενοι τὸν δῆμον τὸν ἐν Ἄργει καταλῦσαι, καὶ ἐπειδὴ ἡ μάχη ἐγεγένητο, πολλῷ μᾶλλον ἐδύναντο πείθειν τοὺς πολλοὺς ἐς τὴν ὁμολογίαν. ἐβούλοντο δὲ πρῶτον σπονδὰς ποιήσαντες πρὸς τοὺς Λακεδαιμονίους αὖθις ὕστερον καὶ ξυμμαχίαν, καὶ οὕτως
3 ἤδη τῷ δήμῳ ἐπιτίθεσθαι. καὶ ἀφικνεῖται πρόξενος ὢν Ἀργείων Λίχας ὁ Ἀρκεσιλάου παρὰ τῶν Λακεδαιμονίων δύο λόγω φέρων ἐς τὸ Ἄργος, τὸν μὲν καθότι εἰ βούλονται πολεμεῖν, τὸν δ' ὡς εἰ εἰρήνην ἄγειν. καὶ γενομένης πολλῆς ἀντιλογίας (ἔτυχε γὰρ καὶ ὁ Ἀλκιβιάδης παρών) οἱ ἄνδρες οἱ τοῖς Λακεδαιμονίοις πράσσοντες, ἤδη καὶ ἐκ τοῦ φανεροῦ τολμῶντες, ἔπεισαν τοὺς Ἀργείους προσδέξασθαι τὸν ξυμβατήριον λόγον. ἔστι δὲ ὅδε.

LXXVII.[2] "Καττάδε δοκεῖ τᾷ ἐκκλησίᾳ τῶν Λακεδαιμονίων ξυμβαλέσθαι ποττὼς Ἀργείως.

"Ἀποδιδόντας τὼς παῖδας τοῖς Ὀρχομενίοις καὶ τὼς ἄνδρας τοῖς Μαιναλίοις, καὶ τὼς ἄνδρας τὼς ἐν Μαντινείᾳ τοῖς Λακεδαιμονίοις ἀποδιδόντας.

2 "Καὶ ἐξ Ἐπιδαύρω ἐκβῶντας καὶ τὸ τεῖχος ἀναιροῦντας. αἰ δέ κα μὴ εἴκωντι τοὶ Ἀθηναῖοι ἐξ Ἐπιδαύρω, πολεμίως εἶμεν τοῖς Ἀργείοις καὶ

---

[1] ἐπειδὴ τὰ Κάρνεια ἤγαγον, in the MSS. after οἱ Λακεδαιμόνιοι, bracketed by Hude, following Krüger.
[2] The dialect in chs. lxxvii. and lxxix. is Doric.

LXXVI. At the very beginning of the following winter, the Lacedaemonians led out an army and came to Tegea, whence they sent on to Argos proposals for peace. There had been before this partisans of theirs at Argos who wished to put down the democracy there, and after the battle had been fought they were far better able to persuade the people to come to an agreement with Sparta. They wished, after they had first made a treaty with the Lacedaemonians, to conclude later an alliance also, and having done so to attack the democracy. And now there arrived at Argos Lichas son of Arcesilaus, proxenus of the Argives, bringing from the Lacedaemonians two proposals: the one stating on what conditions they should make war, if they wished that; the other, how they should keep the peace, if they preferred that. And after much opposition—for Alcibiades chanced to be present— the men who were working for the Lacedaemonians, venturing now to act openly, persuaded the Argives to accept the proposal for peace, which was as follows:

LXXVII. "It seems good to the assembly of the Lacedaemonians to make an agreement with the Argives on the following terms:

1. "The Argives shall restore to the Orchomenians [1] their children and to the Maenalians [2] their men, and to the Lacedaemonians [3] the men they deposited at Mantinea.

2. "They shall evacuate Epidaurus and demolish the fortification there. And if the Athenians do not withdraw from Epidaurus, they shall be enemies

---

[1] cf. ch. lxi. 5.
[2] cf. ch. lxi. 4, though the Maenalians are not expressly mentioned there. [3] cf. ch. lxi. 5.

τοῖς Λακεδαιμονίοις καὶ τοῖς τῶν Λακεδαιμονίων
ξυμμάχοις καὶ τοῖς τῶν Ἀργείων ξυμμάχοις.

3 "Καὶ αἴ τινα τοὶ Λακεδαιμόνιοι παῖδα ἔχοντι,
ἀποδόμεν ταῖς πολίεσσι πάσαις.

4 "Περὶ δὲ τῶ σιῶ σύματος, αἱ μὲν λῆν, τοῖς
Ἐπιδαυρίοις ὅρκον δόμεν, αἰ δέ, αὐτὼς ὀμόσαι.

5 "Τὰς δὲ πόλιας τὰς ἐν Πελοποννάσῳ, καὶ
μικρὰς καὶ μεγάλας, αὐτονόμως εἶμεν πάσας
καττὰ πάτρια.

6 "Αἰ δέ κα τῶν ἐκτὸς Πελοποννάσω τις ἐπὶ τὰν
Πελοπόννασον γᾶν ἴῃ ἐπὶ κακῷ, ἀλεξέμεναι
ἀμόθι βουλευσαμένως, ὅπᾳ κα δικαιότατα δοκῇ
τοῖς Πελοποννασίοις.

7 "Ὅσσοι δ' ἐκτὸς Πελοποννάσω τῶν Λακεδαιμονίων ξύμμαχοί ἐντι, ἐν τῷ αὐτῷ ἐσσοῦνται ἐν
τῷπερ καὶ τοὶ τῶν Λακεδαιμονίων καὶ τοὶ τῶν
Ἀργείων ξύμμαχοί ἐντι, τὰν αὑτῶν ἔχοντες.

8 "Ἐπιδείξαντας δὲ τοῖς ξυμμάχοις ξυμβαλέσθαι, αἴ κα αὐτοῖς δοκῇ. αἰ δέ τι δοκῇ τοῖς ξυμμάχοις, οἴκαδ' ἀπιάλλην."

LXXVIII. Τοῦτον μὲν τὸν λόγον προσεδέξαντο
πρῶτον οἱ Ἀργεῖοι, καὶ τῶν Λακεδαιμονίων τὸ
στράτευμα ἀνεχώρησεν ἐκ τῆς Τεγέας ἐπ' οἴκου·
μετὰ δὲ τοῦτο ἐπιμειξίας οὔσης ἤδη παρ' ἀλλήλους, οὐ πολλῷ ὕστερον ἔπραξαν αὖθις οἱ αὐτοὶ
ἄνδρες ὥστε τὴν Μαντινέων καὶ τὴν Ἀθηναίων καὶ
Ἠλείων ξυμμαχίαν ἀφέντας Ἀργείους σπονδὰς

to the Argives and Lacedaemonians, and to the allies of the Lacedaemonians and to the allies of the Argives.

3. "If the Lacedaemonians have in custody any children, they shall restore these in all cases to their cities.

4. "As to the offering to the god,[1] if they wish they shall impose an oath upon the Epidaurians; but if not, they shall swear it themselves.

5. "The cities in the Peloponnesus, both small and great, shall all be independent according to their hereditary usages.

6. "If anyone from outside the Peloponnesus comes against Peloponnesian territory with evil intent, they shall repel the invader, taking counsel together, in whatever way shall seem to the Peloponnesians most just.

7. "Such states as are allies of the Lacedaemonians outside of the Peloponnesus shall be on the same footing as are the other allies of the Lacedaemonians and of the Argives, all retaining their own territory.

8. "They shall communicate this agreement to their allies and make terms with them, if it seem best. But if the allies prefer, they may send the treaty home for consideration."[2]

LXXVIII. The Argives accepted this proposal at first, and the army of the Lacedaemonians returned home from Tegea. But not long after this, when there was now intercourse between them, the same men again brought it about that the Argives renounced the alliance with the Mantineans, Eleans,

---

[1] Apollo Pythaeus; cf. ch. liii.
[2] i.e. may refer it back to the states for their decision.

καὶ ξυμμαχίαν ποιήσασθαι πρὸς Λακεδαιμονίους. καὶ ἐγένοντο αἵδε.

LXXIX. "Καττάδε ἔδοξε τοῖς Λακεδαιμονίοις καὶ 'Αργείοις σπονδὰς καὶ ξυμμαχίαν εἶμεν πεντήκοντα ἔτη.

"'Επὶ τοῖς ἴσοις καὶ ὁμοίοις δίκας διδόντας καττὰ πάτρια· ταὶ δὲ ἄλλαι πόλιες ταὶ ἐν Πελοποννάσῳ κοινανεόντων τᾶν σπονδᾶν καὶ τᾶς ξυμμαχίας αὐτόνομοι καὶ αὐτόπολιες, τὰν αὐτῶν ἔχοντες, καττὰ πάτρια δίκας διδόντες τὰς ἴσας καὶ ὁμοίας.

2 "'Όσσοι δὲ ἔξω Πελοποννάσω Λακεδαιμονίοις ξύμμαχοί ἐντι, ἐν τοῖς αὐτοῖς ἐσσοῦνται τοῖσπερ καὶ τοὶ Λακεδαιμόνιοι· καὶ τοὶ τῶν 'Αργείων ξύμμαχοι ἐν τῷ αὐτῷ ἐσσοῦνται τῷπερ καὶ τοὶ 'Αργεῖοι, τὰν αὐτῶν ἔχοντες.

3 "Αἰ δέ ποι στρατείας δέῃ κοινᾶς, βουλεύεσθαι Λακεδαιμονίως καὶ 'Αργείως ὅπᾳ κα δικαιότατα κρίναντας τοῖς ξυμμάχοις.

4 "Αἰ δέ τινι τᾶν πολίων ἦ ἀμφίλογα, ἦ τᾶν ἐντὸς ἦ τᾶν ἐκτὸς Πελοποννάσω, αἴτε περὶ ὅρων αἴτε περὶ ἄλλου τινός, διακριθῆμεν. αἰ δέ τις τῶν ξυμμάχων πόλις πόλι ἐρίζοι, ἐς πόλιν ἐλθεῖν, ἅν τινα ἴσαν ἀμφοῖν ταῖς πολίεσσι δοκείοι.

"Τὼς δὲ ἔτας [1] καττὰ πάτρια δικάζεσθαι."

LXXX. Αἱ μὲν σπονδαὶ καὶ ἡ ξυμμαχία αὕτη ἐγεγένητο· καὶ ὁπόσα ἀλλήλων πολέμῳ ἦ εἴ τι ἄλλο εἶχον, διελύσαντο. κοινῇ δὲ ἤδη τὰ πράγ-

---

[1] Poppo's correction for τοῖς δὲ ἔταις of the MSS.

and Athenians and concluded a treaty and an alliance with the Lacedaemonians to this effect:

LXXIX. "It has seemed good to the Lacedaemonians and the Argives to conclude a treaty and an alliance for fifty years on the following terms:

1. "They shall offer settlements by law under conditions that are fair and impartial, according to hereditary usage. The rest of the cities in the Peloponnesus shall share in the treaty and alliance, being independent and self-governed, retaining their own territory, and offering settlements by law that are fair and impartial according to hereditary usage.

2. "Such states as are allies of the Lacedaemonians outside of the Peloponnesus shall stand upon the same footing as the Lacedaemonians; and the allies of the Argives shall be upon the same footing as the Argives, all retaining their own territory.

3. "If there be need to send a common expedition to any quarter, the Lacedaemonians and the Argives shall consult and adjudge to the allies their allotments in whatever way is fairest.

4. "If there be any dispute on the part of any one of the cities, either of those within the Peloponnesus or without, whether about boundaries or anything else, the matter shall be judicially decided. But if any city of the allies quarrel with another, they shall appeal to some city which both deem to be impartial.

5. "Individual citizens shall conduct their suits according to hereditary usage."

LXXX. Such was the treaty and alliance that was concluded; and all the places which either side had acquired from the other in war they restored, or if there was any other ground of difference between them, they came to an agreement about it. Acting

ματα τιθέμενοι ἐψηφίσαντο κήρυκα καὶ πρεσ-
βείαν παρὰ Ἀθηναίων μὴ προσδέχεσθαι, ἢν μὴ
ἐκ Πελοποννήσου ἐξίωσι τὰ τείχη ἐκλιπόντες,
καὶ μὴ ξυμβαίνειν τῷ μηδὲ πολεμεῖν ἄλλ᾽ ἢ ἅμα.
2 καὶ τά τε ἄλλα θυμῷ ἔφερον καὶ ἐς τὰ ἐπὶ
Θρᾴκης χωρία καὶ ὡς Περδίκκαν ἔπεμψαν ἀμφότεροι πρέσβεις. καὶ ἀνέπεισαν Περδίκκαν ξυνο-
μόσαι σφίσιν· οὐ μέντοι εὐθύς γε ἀπέστη τῶν
Ἀθηναίων, ἀλλὰ διενοεῖτο, ὅτι καὶ τοὺς Ἀργείους
ἑώρα· ἦν δὲ καὶ αὐτὸς τὸ ἀρχαῖον ἐξ Ἄργους.
καὶ τοῖς Χαλκιδεῦσι τούς τε παλαιοὺς ὅρκους
3 ἀνενεώσαντο καὶ ἄλλους ὤμοσαν. ἔπεμψαν δὲ
καὶ παρὰ τοὺς Ἀθηναίους οἱ Ἀργεῖοι πρέσβεις,
τὸ ἐξ Ἐπιδαύρου τεῖχος κελεύοντες ἐκλιπεῖν· οἱ
δ᾽ ὁρῶντες ὀλίγοι πρὸς πλείους ὄντες τοὺς ξυμ-
φύλακας ἔπεμψαν Δημοσθένη τοὺς σφετέρους
ἐξάξοντα. ὁ δὲ ἀφικόμενος καὶ ἀγῶνά τινα
πρόφασιν γυμνικὸν ἔξω τοῦ φρουρίου ποιήσας,
ὡς ἐξῆλθε τὸ ἄλλο φρούριον, ἀπέκλῃσε τὰς
πύλας. καὶ ὕστερον Ἐπιδαυρίοις ἀνανεωσάμενοι
τὰς σπονδὰς αὐτοὶ οἱ Ἀθηναῖοι ἀπέδοσαν τὸ
τείχισμα.

LXXXI. Μετὰ δὲ τὴν τῶν Ἀργείων ἀπόστασιν
ἐκ τῆς ξυμμαχίας καὶ οἱ Μαντινῆς, τὸ μὲν πρῶτον
ἀντέχοντες, ἔπειτ᾽ οὐ δυνάμενοι ἄνευ τῶν Ἀργείων, ξυνέβησαν καὶ αὐτοὶ τοῖς Λακεδαιμονίοις
2 καὶ τὴν ἀρχὴν ἀφεῖσαν τῶν πόλεων. καὶ Λακεδαιμόνιοι καὶ Ἀργεῖοι, χίλιοι ἑκάτεροι, ξυστρα-

---

[1] cf. II. xcix. 3.   [2] cf. ch. lxxv. 6.

now in concert in their affairs, they voted not to receive herald or embassy from the Athenians, unless they evacuated their forts and withdrew from the Peloponnesus; also not to make peace or carry on war with anyone except together. And not only did they prosecute other matters with energy, but both of them sent envoys to the places in Thrace and to Perdiccas. And they persuaded Perdiccas to swear alliance with them. He, however, did not desert the Athenians at once, but was thinking of it, because he saw the Argives had done so; for he was himself of Argive descent.[1] With the Chalcidians, too, they renewed their ancient oaths, and swore new ones. The Argives also sent envoys to the Athenians bidding them evacuate the fortress at Epidaurus;[2] and these, seeing that their contingent was small in comparison with the rest, sent Demosthenes to bring away their men. On his arrival he made a pretext of some gymnastic contest outside the fort, and when the rest of the garrison had gone out closed the gates behind them. Afterwards the Athenians renewed the treaty with the Epidaurians and of their own accord gave up the fortress.

LXXXI. After the withdrawal of the Argives from the alliance, the Mantineans also, although at first opposed to this course, afterwards, finding themselves unable to hold out without the Argives, likewise made an agreement with the Lacedaemonians and relinquished their sovereignty over the cities.[3] And now the Lacedaemonians and Argives, each a thousand strong, made a joint

[3] *i.e.* over the Parrhasians and others in Arcadia; *cf.* ch. xxix. 1; xxxiii. 1; lxii. 1.

τεύσαντες, τά τ᾽ ἐν Σικυῶνι ἐς ὀλίγους μᾶλλον
κατέστησαν αὐτοὶ οἱ Λακεδαιμόνιοι ἐλθόντες, καὶ
μετ᾽ ἐκεῖνα ξυναμφότεροι ἤδη καὶ τὸν ἐν Ἄργει
δῆμον κατέλυσαν, καὶ ὀλιγαρχία ἐπιτηδεία τοῖς
Λακεδαιμονίοις κατέστη. καὶ πρὸς ἔαρ ἤδη ταῦτα
ἦν τοῦ χειμῶνος λήγοντος, καὶ τέταρτον καὶ
δέκατον ἔτος τῷ πολέμῳ ἐτελεύτα.

LXXXII. Τοῦ δ᾽ ἐπιγιγνομένου θέρους Διῆς τε
οἱ ἐν Ἄθῳ ἀπέστησαν Ἀθηναίων πρὸς Χαλκιδέας
καὶ Λακεδαιμόνιοι τὰ ἐν Ἀχαΐᾳ οὐκ ἐπιτηδείως
2 πρότερον ἔχοντα καθίσταντο. καὶ Ἀργείων ὁ
δῆμος κατ᾽ ὀλίγον ξυνιστάμενός τε καὶ ἀναθαρσή-
σας ἐπέθεντο τοῖς ὀλίγοις, τηρήσαντες αὐτὰς τὰς
γυμνοπαιδίας τῶν Λακεδαιμονίων. καὶ μάχης
γενομένης ἐν τῇ πόλει ἐπεκράτησεν ὁ δῆμος, καὶ
3 τοὺς μὲν ἀπέκτεινε, τοὺς δὲ ἐξήλασεν. οἱ δὲ
Λακεδαιμόνιοι, ἕως μὲν αὐτοὺς μετεπέμποντο οἱ
φίλοι, οὐκ ἦλθον ἐκ πλείονος, ἀναβαλόμενοι δὲ
τὰς γυμνοπαιδίας ἐβοήθουν. καὶ ἐν Τεγέᾳ πυθόμενοι ὅτι νενίκηνται οἱ ὀλίγοι, προελθεῖν μὲν
οὐκέτι ἠθέλησαν δεομένων τῶν διαπεφευγότων,
ἀναχωρήσαντες δὲ ἐπ᾽ οἴκου τὰς γυμνοπαιδίας
4 ἦγον. καὶ ὕστερον ἐλθόντων πρέσβεων ἀπό τε
τῶν ἐν τῇ πόλει καὶ ἀγγέλων [1] τῶν ἔξω Ἀργείων,
παρόντων τε τῶν ξυμμάχων καὶ ῥηθέντων πολλῶν

---

[1] Müller-Strübing's order, for ἀγγέλων καί of the MSS.

expedition, the Lacedaemonians first going alone
and setting up a more oligarchical form of government in Sicyon, afterwards both together putting
down the democracy at Argos and establishing
an oligarchy favourable to the Lacedaemonians.
These things occurred when the winter was closing
and spring was now near at hand; and so ended the
fourteenth year of the war.

LXXXII. The next summer the people of Dium [1]   417 B.C.
on Mount Athos revolted from the Athenians and
went over to the Chalcidians; and the Lacedaemonians arranged matters in Achaea, which had
before this not been favourable to their interests.
And now the popular party at Argos, gradually
consolidating its strength and recovering boldness,
waited for the celebration of the Gymnopaediae [2]
by the Lacedaemonians and attacked the oligarchs.
A battle occurred in the city and the popular
party got the better of it, slaying some of
their enemies and expelling others. The Lacedaemonians, although their friends kept sending for
them, did not come for a long time; but at last they
put off the Gymnopaediae and went to their aid.
But hearing at Tegea that the oligarchs had been
conquered, they refused to go further, in spite of the
entreaties of the oligarchs who had escaped, and
returning home proceeded with the celebration of the
Gymnopaediae. Later, when envoys had come from
the Argives in the city and messengers from those
who had been driven out, and their allies were
present, and much had been said on either side, they

---

[1] cf. ch. xxxv. 1.
[2] A festival in which boys and men danced naked. While
it lasted the Lacedaemonians (as at the Carneia, cf. chs. liv.
and lxxv.) abstained from war.

ἀφ' ἑκατέρων ἔγνωσαν μὲν ἀδικεῖν τοὺς ἐν τῇ
πόλει καὶ ἔδοξεν αὐτοῖς στρατεύειν ἐς Ἄργος,
5 διατριβαὶ δὲ καὶ μελλήσεις ἐγίγνοντο. ὁ δὲ
δῆμος τῶν Ἀργείων ἐν τούτῳ, φοβούμενος τοὺς
Λακεδαιμονίους καὶ τὴν τῶν Ἀθηναίων ξυμμαχίαν
πάλιν προσαγόμενός τε καὶ νομίζων μέγιστον ἂν
σφᾶς ὠφελῆσαι, τειχίζει μακρὰ τείχη ἐς θάλασσαν, ὅπως, ἢν τῆς γῆς εἴργωνται, ἡ κατὰ θάλασσαν σφᾶς μετὰ τῶν Ἀθηναίων ἐπαγωγὴ τῶν
6 ἐπιτηδείων ὠφελῇ. ξυνῄδεσαν δὲ τὸν τειχισμὸν
καὶ τῶν ἐν Πελοποννήσῳ τινὲς πόλεων. καὶ οἱ
μὲν Ἀργεῖοι πανδημεί, καὶ αὐτοὶ καὶ γυναῖκες
καὶ οἰκέται, ἐτείχιζον· καὶ ἐκ τῶν Ἀθηνῶν αὐτοῖς
ἦλθον τέκτονες καὶ λιθουργοί. καὶ τὸ θέρος
ἐτελεύτα.

LXXXIII. Τοῦ δ' ἐπιγιγνομένου χειμῶνος Λακεδαιμόνιοι ὡς ᾔσθοντο τειχιζόντων, ἐστράτευσαν
ἐς τὸ Ἄργος αὐτοί τε καὶ οἱ ξύμμαχοι πλὴν
Κορινθίων· ὑπῆρχε δέ τι αὐτοῖς καὶ ἐκ τοῦ Ἄργους[1] αὐτόθεν πρασσόμενον. ἦγε δὲ τὴν στρατιὰν
Ἆγις ὁ Ἀρχιδάμου, Λακεδαιμονίων βασιλεύς.
2 καὶ τὰ μὲν ἐκ τῆς πόλεως δοκοῦντα προϋπάρχειν
οὐ προυχώρησεν ἔτι· τὰ δὲ οἰκοδομούμενα τείχη
ἑλόντες καὶ καταβαλόντες καὶ Ὑσιὰς χωρίον τῆς
Ἀργείας λαβόντες καὶ τοὺς ἐλευθέρους ἅπαντας
οὓς ἔλαβον ἀποκτείναντες ἀνεχώρησαν καὶ διε-
3 λύθησαν κατὰ πόλεις. ἐστράτευσαν δὲ μετὰ
τοῦτο καὶ Ἀργεῖοι ἐς τὴν Φλειασίαν, καὶ δῃώσαντες ἀπῆλθον, ὅτι σφῶν τοὺς φυγάδας ὑπεδέ-
χοντο· οἱ γὰρ πολλοὶ αὐτῶν ἐνταῦθα κατῴκηντο.
4 κατέκλῃσαν δὲ τοῦ αὐτοῦ χειμῶνος καὶ Μακε-

1 ἐκ τοῦ Ἄργους deleted by Huker, followed by Hude.

decided that those in the city [1] were in the wrong and determined to make an expedition to Argos; but delays and postponements occurred. Meanwhile, the democracy at Argos, fearing the Lacedaemonians and again courting the alliance of the Athenians, because they believed that it would be of the greatest benefit to themselves, proceeded to build long walls down to the sea, in order that, should they be cut off from the land, they might with the help of the Athenians have the advantage of importing supplies by sea. Some of the cities in the Peloponnesus, too, were privy to their fortifying. The whole Argive people, men, women, and slaves, set to work upon the walls; and from Athens also there came to them carpenters and stone masons. So the summer ended.

LXXXIII. The following winter, when the Lacedaemonians became aware that they were fortifying Argos, they made an expedition thither, themselves and their allies, except the Corinthians; and there was also a party in Argos itself that was working in their interest. The commander of the army was Agis son of Archidamus, king of the Lacedaemonians. The support from the city which they expected to find ready failed them, but they seized and demolished the walls that were being built; and they also seized Hysiae, a place in Argive territory, slew all the free men whom they caught, and then withdrew and dispersed to their several cities. After this the Argives in their turn invaded Phliasia and ravaged it before they returned home, because the Phliasians had received fugitives of theirs, most of whom had settled there. Also during the same winter the Athenians

[1] The popular party.

δόνας 'Αθηναῖοι, Περδίκκᾳ ἐπικαλοῦντες τήν τε πρὸς 'Αργείους καὶ Λακεδαιμονίους γενομένην ξυνωμοσίαν καὶ ὅτι παρασκευασαμένων αὐτῶν στρατιὰν ἄγειν ἐπὶ Χαλκιδέας τοὺς ἐπὶ Θράκης καὶ 'Αμφίπολιν Νικίου τοῦ Νικηράτου στρατηγοῦντος ἔψευστο τὴν ξυμμαχίαν καὶ ἡ στρατιὰ μάλιστα διελύθη ἐκείνου ἀπάραντος[1] πολέμιος οὖν ἦν· καὶ ὁ χειμὼν ἐτελεύτα οὗτος, καὶ πέμπτον καὶ δέκατον ἔτος τῷ πολέμῳ ἐτελεύτα.

LXXXIV. Τοῦ δ' ἐπιγιγνομένου θέρους 'Αλκιβιάδης τε πλεύσας ἐς "Αργος ναυσὶν εἴκοσι 'Αργείων τοὺς δοκοῦντας ἔτι ὑπόπτους εἶναι καὶ τὰ Λακεδαιμονίων φρονεῖν ἔλαβε, τριακοσίους ἄνδρας, καὶ κατέθεντο αὐτοὺς 'Αθηναῖοι ἐς τὰς ἐγγὺς νήσους ὧν ἦρχον· καὶ ἐπὶ Μῆλον τὴν νῆσον 'Αθηναῖοι ἐστράτευσαν ναυσὶν ἑαυτῶν μὲν τριάκοντα, Χίαις δὲ ἕξ, Λεσβίαιν δὲ δυοῖν, καὶ ὁπλίταις ἑαυτῶν μὲν διακοσίοις καὶ χιλίοις καὶ τοξόταις τριακοσίοις καὶ ἱπποτοξόταις εἴκοσι, τῶν δὲ ξυμμάχων καὶ νησιωτῶν ὁπλίταις μάλιστα

2 πεντακοσίοις καὶ χιλίοις. οἱ δὲ Μήλιοι Λακεδαιμονίων μέν εἰσιν ἄποικοι, τῶν δ' Ἀθηναίων οὐκ ἤθελον ὑπακούειν ὥσπερ οἱ ἄλλοι νησιῶται, ἀλλὰ τὸ μὲν πρῶτον οὐδετέρων ὄντες ἡσύχαζον, ἔπειτα ὡς αὐτοὺς ἠνάγκαζον οἱ 'Αθηναῖοι δῃοῦντες τὴν

3 γῆν, ἐς πόλεμον φανερὸν κατέστησαν. στρατοπεδευσάμενοι οὖν ἐς τὴν γῆν αὐτῶν τῇ παρασκευῇ ταύτῃ οἱ στρατηγοὶ Κλεομήδης τε ὁ Λυκομήδους καὶ Τεισίας ὁ Τεισιμάχου, πρὶν ἀδικεῖν τι τῆς γῆς, λόγους πρῶτον ποιησομένους ἔπεμψαν πρέσβεις. οὓς οἱ Μήλιοι πρὸς μὲν τὸ πλῆθος οὐκ

[1] ἀπάραντος is probably corrupt.

shut off the Macedonians from the sea, charging
Perdiccas with the league which he had made with
the Argives and the Lacedaemonians; also that
when they had prepared to lead an army against
the Chalcidians in Thrace and against Amphipolis,
under the command of Nicias son of Niceratus,
he had been false to the alliance, and the expedition had been broken up chiefly because of his de-
fection.   Accordingly, he was regarded as an enemy.
So this winter ended and with it the fifteenth year
of the war.

LXXXIV.   The next summer Alcibiades sailed to
Argos with twenty ships and seized such Argives as
seemed to be still open to suspicion and to favour
the side of the Lacedaemonians, to the number
of three hundred men; and these the Athenians deposited in the adjacent islands over which they had
sway.   The Athenians also made an expedition
against the island of Melos[1] with thirty ships of
their own, six Chian and two Lesbian, and twelve
hundred Athenian hoplites, three hundred bowmen,
and twenty mounted archers, and from their allies
and the islanders about fifteen hundred hoplites.
Now the Melians are colonists of the Lacedaemonians,
and were unwilling to obey the Athenians like the
rest of the islanders.   At first they remained quiet as
neutrals; then when the Athenians tried to force
them by ravaging their land, they went to war openly.
Accordingly, having encamped in their territory with
the forces just mentioned, the Athenian commanders,
Cleomedes son of Lycomedes and Teisias son of
Teisimachus, before doing any harm to the land, sent
envoys to make proposals to the Melians.   These
envoys the Melians did not bring before the popular

March,
416 B.C.

[1] *cf.* III. xci. 1 ; xciv. 2.

ἤγαγον, ἐν δὲ ταῖς ἀρχαῖς καὶ τοῖς ὀλίγοις λέγειν
ἐκέλευον περὶ ὧν ἥκουσιν. οἱ δὲ τῶν Ἀθηναίων
πρέσβεις ἔλεγον τοιάδε.

LXXXV. "Ἐπειδὴ οὐ πρὸς τὸ πλῆθος οἱ λόγοι
γίγνονται, ὅπως δὴ μὴ ξυνεχεῖ ῥήσει οἱ πολλοὶ
ἐπαγωγὰ καὶ ἀνέλεγκτα ἐς ἅπαξ ἀκούσαντες
ἡμῶν ἀπατηθῶσι (γιγνώσκομεν γὰρ ὅτι τοῦτο
φρονεῖ ἡμῶν ἡ ἐς τοὺς ὀλίγους ἀγωγή), ὑμεῖς οἱ
καθήμενοι ἔτι ἀσφαλέστερον ποιήσατε. καθ᾽
ἕκαστον γὰρ καὶ μηδ᾽ ὑμεῖς ἑνὶ λόγῳ, ἀλλὰ πρὸς
τὸ μὴ δοκοῦν ἐπιτηδείως λέγεσθαι εὐθὺς ὑπολαμβάνοντες κρίνετε. καὶ πρῶτον εἰ ἀρέσκει ὡς
λέγομεν εἴπατε."

LXXXVI. Οἱ δὲ τῶν Μηλίων ξύνεδροι ἀπε-
κρίναντο· "Ἡ μὲν ἐπιείκεια τοῦ διδάσκειν καθ᾽
ἡσυχίαν ἀλλήλους οὐ ψέγεται, τὰ δὲ τοῦ πολέμου, παρόντα ἤδη καὶ οὐ μέλλοντα, διαφέροντα
αὐτοῦ φαίνεται. ὁρῶμεν γὰρ αὐτούς τε κριτὰς
ἥκοντας ὑμᾶς τῶν λεχθησομένων, καὶ τὴν τελευτὴν
ἐξ αὐτοῦ κατὰ τὸ εἰκὸς περιγενομένοις μὲν τῷ
δικαίῳ καὶ δι᾽ αὐτὸ μὴ ἐνδοῦσι πόλεμον ἡμῖν
φέρουσαν, πεισθεῖσι δὲ δουλείαν."

LXXXVII. ΑΘ. Εἰ μὲν τοίνυν ὑπονοίας τῶν
μελλόντων λογιούμενοι ἢ ἄλλο τι ξυνήκετε ἢ ἐκ
τῶν παρόντων καὶ ὧν ὁρᾶτε περὶ σωτηρίας βου-
λεύσοντες τῇ πόλει, παυοίμεθ᾽ ἄν· εἰ δ᾽ ἐπὶ τοῦτο,
λέγοιμεν ἄν.

---

[1] Probably the chief governing body, a chamber of
oligarchs, to which the magistrates (αἱ ἀρχαί) belonged.

assembly, but bade them tell in the presence of the magistrates and the few [1] what they had come for. The Athenian envoys accordingly spoke as follows:

LXXXV. "Since our proposals are not to be made before the assembly, your purpose being, as it seems, that the people may not hear from us once for all, in an uninterrupted speech, arguments that are seductive and untested,[2] and so be deceived—for we see that it is with this thought that you bring us before the few—do you who sit here adopt a still safer course. Take up each point, and do not you either make a single speech, but conduct the inquiry by replying at once to any statement of ours that seems to be unsatisfactory. And first state whether our proposal suits you."

LXXXVI. The commissioners of the Melians answered: "The fairness of the proposal, that we shall at our leisure instruct one another, is not open to objection, but these acts of war, which are not in the future, but already here at hand, are manifestly at variance with your suggestion. For we see that you are come to be yourselves judges of what is to be said here, and that the outcome of the discussion will in all likelihood be, if we win the debate by the righteousness of our cause and for that very reason refuse to yield, war for us, whereas if we are persuaded, servitude."

LXXXVII. ATH. "Well, if you have met to argue from suspicions about what may happen in the future, or for any other purpose than to consult for the safety of your city in the light of what is present and before your eyes, we may as well stop; but if you have this end in view, we may speak on."

---

[2] *i.e.* not questioned or put to the proof.

LXXXVIII. ΜΗΛ. Εἰκὸς μὲν καὶ ξυγγνώμη
ἐν τῷ τοιῷδε καθεστῶτας ἐπὶ πολλὰ καὶ λέγοντας
καὶ δοκοῦντας τρέπεσθαι· ἡ μέντοι ξύνοδος καὶ
περὶ σωτηρίας ἥδε πάρεστι, καὶ ὁ λόγος ᾧ προκα-
λεῖσθε τρόπῳ, εἰ δοκεῖ, γιγνέσθω.

LXXXIX. ΑΘ. Ἡμεῖς τοίνυν οὔτε αὐτοὶ μετ᾽
ὀνομάτων καλῶν, ὡς ἢ δικαίως τὸν Μῆδον κατα-
λύσαντες ἄρχομεν ἢ ἀδικούμενοι νῦν ἐπεξερχό-
μεθα, λόγων μῆκος ἄπιστον παρέξομεν, οὔθ᾽ ὑμᾶς
ἀξιοῦμεν ἢ ὅτι Λακεδαιμονίων ἄποικοι ὄντες οὐ
ξυνεστρατεύσατε ἢ ὡς ἡμᾶς οὐδὲν ἠδικήκατε λέγοντας οἴεσθαι πείσειν, τὰ δυνατὰ δ᾽ ἐξ ὧν ἑκάτεροι
ἀληθῶς φρονοῦμεν διαπράσσεσθαι, ἐπισταμένους
πρὸς εἰδότας ὅτι δίκαια μὲν ἐν τῷ ἀνθρωπείῳ
λόγῳ ἀπὸ τῆς ἴσης ἀνάγκης κρίνεται, δυνατὰ
δὲ οἱ προύχοντες πράσσουσι καὶ οἱ ἀσθενεῖς
ξυγχωροῦσιν.

ΧϹ. ΜΗΛ. Ἦι μὲν δὴ νομίζομέν γε, χρήσιμον (ἀνάγκη γάρ, ἐπειδὴ ὑμεῖς οὕτω παρὰ τὸ δίκαιον τὸ ξυμφέρον λέγειν ὑπέθεσθε) μὴ καταλύειν
ὑμᾶς τὸ κοινὸν ἀγαθόν, ἀλλὰ τῷ αἰεὶ ἐν κινδύνῳ
γιγνομένῳ εἶναι τὰ εἰκότα καὶ δίκαια[1] καί τι καὶ
ἐντὸς τοῦ ἀκριβοῦς πείσαντά τινα ὠφεληθῆναι.
καὶ πρὸς ὑμῶν οὐχ ἧσσον τοῦτο, ὅσῳ καὶ ἐπὶ

---

[1] καὶ δίκαια deleted by Hude, after G. Hermann.

---

[1] cf. VI. lxxxiii. 2.
[2] ἐντὸς τοῦ ἀκριβοῦς, lit. "short of exactness."

LXXXVIII. MEL. "It is natural and pardonable for men in such a position as ours to resort to many arguments and many suppositions. This conference, however, is here to consider the question of our safety; so let the discussion, if it please you, proceed in the way that you propose."

LXXXIX. ATH. "Well, then, we on our part will make use of no fair phrases, saying either that we hold sway justly because we overthrew the Persians,[1] or that we now come against you because we are injured, offering in a lengthy speech arguments that would not be believed; nor, on the other hand, do we presume that you will assert, either that the reason why you did not join us in the war was because you were colonists of the Lacedaemonians, or that you have done us no wrong. Rather we presume that you aim at accomplishing what is possible in accordance with the real thoughts of both of us, since you know as well as we know that what is just is arrived at in human arguments only when the necessity on both sides is equal, and that the powerful exact what they can, while the weak yield what they must."

XC. MEL. "As we think, at any rate, it is expedient (for we are constrained to speak of expediency, since you have in this fashion, ignoring the principle of justice, suggested that we speak of what is advantageous) that you should not rule out the principle of the common good, but that for him who is at the time in peril what is equitable should also be just, and though one has not entirely[2] proved his point he should still derive some benefit therefrom. And this is not less for your interest than for our own, inasmuch as you, if you shall

μεγίστῃ τιμωρίᾳ σφαλέντες ἂν τοῖς ἄλλοις παράδειγμα γένοισθε.

XCI. ΑΘ. Ἡμεῖς δὲ τῆς ἡμετέρας ἀρχῆς, ἢν
καὶ παυσθῇ, οὐκ ἀθυμοῦμεν τὴν τελευτήν· οὐ
γὰρ οἱ ἄρχοντες ἄλλων, ὥσπερ καὶ Λακεδαιμόνιοι,
οὗτοι δεινοὶ τοῖς νικηθεῖσιν (ἔστι δὲ οὐ πρὸς Λακεδαιμονίους ἡμῖν ὁ ἀγών), ἀλλ' ἢν οἱ ὑπήκοοί που
2 τῶν ἀρξάντων αὐτοὶ ἐπιθέμενοι κρατήσωσιν. καὶ
περὶ μὲν τούτου ἡμῖν ἀφείσθω κινδυνεύεσθαι· ὡς
δὲ ἐπ' ὠφελίᾳ τε πάρεσμεν τῆς ἡμετέρας ἀρχῆς
καὶ ἐπὶ σωτηρίᾳ νῦν τοὺς λόγους ἐροῦμεν τῆς
ὑμετέρας πόλεως, ταῦτα δηλώσομεν, βουλόμενοι
ἀπόνως μὲν ὑμῶν ἄρξαι, χρησίμως δ' ὑμᾶς ἀμφοτέροις σωθῆναι.

XCII. ΜΗΛ. Καὶ πῶς χρήσιμον ἂν ξυμβαίη
ἡμῖν δουλεῦσαι, ὥσπερ καὶ ὑμῖν ἄρξαι;

XCIII. ΑΘ. Ὅτι ὑμῖν μὲν πρὸ τοῦ τὰ δεινό-
τατα παθεῖν ὑπακοῦσαι ἂν γένοιτο, ἡμεῖς δὲ μὴ
διαφθείραντες ὑμᾶς κερδαίνοιμεν ἄν.

XCIV. ΜΗΛ. Ὥστε δὲ ἡσυχίαν ἄγοντας
ἡμᾶς φίλους μὲν εἶναι ἀντὶ πολεμίων, ξυμμάχους
δὲ μηδετέρων, οὐκ ἂν δέξαισθε;

XCV. ΑΘ. Οὐ γὰρ τοσοῦτον ἡμᾶς βλάπτει
ἡ ἔχθρα ὑμῶν ὅσον ἡ φιλία μὲν ἀσθενείας, τὸ δὲ
μῖσος δυνάμεως παράδειγμα τοῖς ἀρχομένοις
δηλούμενον.

---

[1] i.e. cruel conduct on your part would justify others in
inflicting like punishment upon you should you ever be
defeated.

ever meet with a reverse, would not only incur the greatest punishment, but would also become a warning example to others." [1]

XCI. ATH. "But we on our part, so far as our empire is concerned, even if it should cease to be, do not look forward to the end with dismay. For it is not those who rule over others, as the Lacedaemonians also do—though our quarrel is not now with the Lacedaemonians—that are a terror to the vanquished, but subject peoples who may perchance themselves attack and get the better of their rulers. And as far as that is concerned, you must permit us to take the risk. But that it is for the benefit of our empire that we are here, and also the safety of your city that we now propose to speak, we shall make plain to you, since what we desire is to have dominion over you without trouble to ourselves, and that you should be saved to the advantage of both."

XCII. MEL. "And how could it prove as advantageous for us to become slaves, as it is for you to have dominion?"

XCIII. ATH. "Because it would be to your advantage to submit before suffering the most horrible fate, and we should gain by not destroying you."

XCIV. MEL. "And so, you mean, you would not consent to our remaining at peace and being friends instead of enemies, but allies of neither combatant?"

XCV. ATH. "No; for your hostility does not injure us so much as your friendship; for in the eyes of our subjects that would be a proof of our weakness, whereas your hatred is a proof of our power."

XCVI. ΜΗΛ. Σκοποῦσι δ' ὑμῶν οὕτως οἱ ὑπήκοοι τὸ εἰκός, ὥστε τούς τε μὴ προσήκοντας καὶ ὅσοι ἄποικοι ὄντες οἱ πολλοὶ καὶ ἀποστάντες τινὲς κεχείρωνται ἐς τὸ αὐτὸ τιθέασιν;

XCVII. ΑΘ. Δικαιώματι γὰρ οὐδετέρους ἐλλείπειν ἡγοῦνται, κατὰ δύναμιν δὲ τοὺς μὲν περιγίγνεσθαι, ἡμᾶς δὲ φόβῳ οὐκ ἐπιέναι· ὥστε ἔξω καὶ τοῦ πλεόνων ἄρξαι καὶ τὸ ἀσφαλὲς ἡμῖν διὰ τὸ καταστραφῆναι ἂν παράσχοιτε, ἄλλως τε καὶ νησιῶται ναυκρατόρων, καὶ ἀσθενέστεροι ἑτέρων ὄντες, εἰ μὴ περιγένοισθε.

XCVIII. ΜΗΛ. Ἐν δ' ἐκείνῳ οὐ νομίζετε ἀσφάλειαν; δεῖ γὰρ αὖ καὶ ἐνταῦθα, ὥσπερ ὑμεῖς τῶν δικαίων λόγων ἡμᾶς ἐκβιβάσαντες τῷ ὑμετέρῳ ξυμφόρῳ ὑπακούειν πείθετε, καὶ ἡμᾶς τὸ ἡμῖν χρήσιμον διδάσκοντας, εἰ τυγχάνει καὶ ὑμῖν τὸ αὐτὸ ξυμβαῖνον, πειρᾶσθαι πείθειν. ὅσοι γὰρ νῦν μηδετέροις ξυμμαχοῦσι, πῶς οὐ πολεμώσεσθε αὐτούς, ὅταν ἐς τάδε βλέψαντες ἡγήσωνταί ποτε ὑμᾶς καὶ ἐπὶ σφᾶς ἥξειν; κἂν τούτῳ τί ἄλλο ἢ τοὺς μὲν ὑπάρχοντας πολεμίους μεγαλύνετε, τοὺς δὲ μηδὲ μελλήσαντας[1] γενέσθαι ἄκοντας ἐπάγεσθε;

XCIX. ΑΘ. Οὐ γὰρ νομίζομεν ἡμῖν τούτους δεινοτέρους, ὅσοι ἠπειρῶταί που ὄντες τῶν ἐλευθέρων[2] πολλὴν τὴν διαμέλλησιν τῆς πρὸς ἡμᾶς

---

[1] Reiske's correction, for μελλήσοντας of the MSS.
[2] For τῷ ἐλευθέρῳ of the MSS., Stahl following the Schol.

XCVI. MEL. "Do your subjects regard equity in such a way as to put in the same category those that do not belong to you at all and those—your own colonists in most cases and in others revolted subjects—who have been subdued by you?"

XCVII. ATH. "As to pleas of justice, they think that neither the one nor the other lacks them, but that those who preserve their freedom owe it to their power, and that we do not attack them because we are afraid. So that, to say nothing of our enlarging our empire, you would afford us security by being subdued, especially if you, an insular power, and weaker than other islanders, should fail to show yourselves superior to a power which is master of the sea."

XCVIII. MEL. "But do you not think there is security in the other course?[1] For here also it is necessary, just as you force us to abandon all pleas of justice and seek to persuade us to give ear to what is to your own interests, that we, too, tell you what is to our advantage and try to persuade you to adopt it, if that happens to be to your advantage also. How, we say, shall you not make enemies of all who are now neutral, as soon as they look at our case and conclude that some day you will come against them also? And in this what else are you doing but strengthening the enemies you already have, and bringing upon you, against their inclination, others who would never have thought of becoming your enemies?"

XCIX. ATH. "Not so, for we do not reckon those as the more dangerous to us who, dwelling somewhere on the mainland and being free men, will defer for a

---

[1] *i.e.* in neutrality, referred to in ch. xciv.

φυλακῆς ποιήσονται, ἀλλὰ τοὺς νησιώτας τέ που
ἀνάρκτους, ὥσπερ ὑμᾶς, καὶ τοὺς ἤδη τῆς ἀρχῆς
τῷ ἀναγκαίῳ παροξυνομένους. οὗτοι γὰρ πλεῖστ᾽
ἂν τῷ ἀλογίστῳ ἐπιτρέψαντες σφᾶς τε αὐτοὺς καὶ
ἡμᾶς ἐς πρόυπτον κίνδυνον καταστήσειαν.

C. ΜΗΛ. Ἦ που ἄρα, εἰ τοσαύτην γε ὑμεῖς
τε μὴ παυσθῆναι ἀρχῆς καὶ οἱ δουλεύοντες ἤδη
ἀπαλλαγῆναι τὴν παρακινδύνευσιν ποιοῦνται,
ἡμῖν γε τοῖς ἔτι ἐλευθέροις πολλὴ κακότης καὶ
δειλία μὴ πᾶν πρὸ τοῦ δουλεῦσαι ἐπεξελθεῖν.

CI. ΑΘ. Οὔκ, ἤν γε σωφρόνως βουλεύησθε·
οὐ γὰρ περὶ ἀνδραγαθίας ὁ ἀγὼν ἀπὸ τοῦ ἴσου
ὑμῖν, μὴ αἰσχύνην ὄφλειν, περὶ δὲ σωτηρίας μᾶλλον ἡ βουλή, πρὸς τοὺς κρείσσονας πολλῷ μὴ
ἀνθίστασθαι.

CII. ΜΗΛ. Ἀλλ᾽ ἐπιστάμεθα τὰ τῶν πολέ-
μων[1] ἔστιν ὅτε κοινοτέρας τὰς τύχας λαμβάνοντα
ἢ κατὰ τὸ διαφέρον ἑκατέρων πλῆθος. καὶ ἡμῖν
τὸ μὲν εἶξαι εὐθὺς ἀνέλπιστον, μετὰ δὲ τοῦ δρωμένου ἔτι καὶ στῆναι ἐλπὶς ὀρθῶς.

CIII. ΑΘ. Ἐλπὶς δέ, κινδύνῳ παραμύθιον
οὖσα, τοὺς μὲν ἀπὸ περιουσίας χρωμένους αὐτῇ,
κἂν βλάψῃ, οὐ καθεῖλε, τοῖς δὲ ἐς ἅπαν τὸ ὑπάρχον ἀναρριπτοῦσι (δάπανος γὰρ φύσει) ἅμα τε
γιγνώσκεται σφαλέντων καὶ ἐν ὅτῳ ἔτι φυλά-

---

[1] For πολεμίων of the MSS., with Valla.

long time taking any precautions against us, but rather those who dwell in some of the islands, both those who, like you, are subject to no control, and those who are already exasperated by the necessity of submission to our rule. For it is these who are most likely to give way to recklessness and bring both themselves and us into danger which they cannot but foresee."

C. MEL. "Surely, then, if you and your subjects brave so great a risk, you in order that you may not lose your empire, and they, who are already your slaves, in order that they may be rid of it, for us surely who still have our freedom it would be the height of baseness and cowardice not to resort to every expedient before submitting to servitude."

CI. ATH. "No, not if you take a sensible view of the matter; for with you it is not a contest on equal terms to determine a point of manly honour, so as to avoid incurring disgrace; rather the question before you is one of self-preservation—to avoid offering resistance to those who are far stronger than you."

CII. MEL. "But we know that the fortune of war is sometimes impartial and not in accord with the difference in numbers. And for us, to yield is at once to give up hope; but if we make an effort, there is still hope that we may stand erect."

CIII. ATH. "Hope is indeed a solace in danger, and for those who have other resources in abundance, though she may injure, she does not ruin them; but for those who stake their all on a single throw—hope being by nature prodigal—it is only when disaster has befallen that her true nature is recognized, and when at last she is known, she leaves the victim no

ξεταί τις αὐτὴν γνωρισθεῖσαν οὐκ ἐλλείπει. ὃ
ὑμεῖς ἀσθενεῖς τε καὶ ἐπὶ ῥοπῆς μιᾶς ὄντες μὴ
βούλεσθε παθεῖν, μηδὲ ὁμοιωθῆναι τοῖς πολλοῖς,
οἷς παρὸν ἀνθρωπείως ἔτι σῴζεσθαι, ἐπειδὰν πιε-
ζομένους αὐτοὺς ἐπιλίπωσιν αἱ φανεραὶ ἐλπίδες,
ἐπὶ τὰς ἀφανεῖς καθίστανται, μαντικήν τε καὶ
χρησμοὺς καὶ ὅσα τοιαῦτα μετ' ἐλπίδων λυμαί-
νεται.

CIV. ΜΗΛ. Χαλεπὸν μὲν καὶ ἡμεῖς, εὖ ἴστε,
νομίζομεν πρὸς δύναμίν τε τὴν ὑμετέραν καὶ τὴν
τύχην, εἰ μὴ ἀπὸ τοῦ ἴσου ἔσται, ἀγωνίζεσθαι·
ὅμως δὲ πιστεύομεν τῇ μὲν τύχῃ ἐκ τοῦ θείου μὴ
ἐλασσώσεσθαι, ὅτι ὅσιοι πρὸς οὐ δικαίους ἱστά-
μεθα, τῆς δὲ δυνάμεως τῷ ἐλλείποντι τὴν Λακεδαιμονίων ἡμῖν ξυμμαχίαν προσέσεσθαι, ἀνάγκην
ἔχουσαν, καὶ εἰ μή του ἄλλου, τῆς γε ξυγγενείας
ἕνεκα καὶ αἰσχύνῃ βοηθεῖν. καὶ οὐ παντάπασιν
οὕτω ἀλόγως θρασυνόμεθα.

CV. ΑΘ. Τῆς μὲν τοίνυν πρὸς τὸ θεῖον εὐμε-
νείας οὐδ' ἡμεῖς οἰόμεθα λελείψεσθαι. οὐδὲν γὰρ
ἔξω τῆς ἀνθρωπείας τῶν μὲν ἐς τὸ θεῖον νομίσεως
τῶν δ' ἐς σφᾶς αὐτοὺς βουλήσεως δικαιοῦμεν ἢ
2 πράσσομεν. ἡγούμεθα γὰρ τό τε θεῖον δόξῃ, τὸ
ἀνθρώπειόν τε σαφῶς διὰ παντὸς ὑπὸ φύσεως
ἀναγκαίας, οὗ ἂν κρατῇ, ἄρχειν. καὶ ἡμεῖς οὔτε
θέντες τὸν νόμον οὔτε κειμένῳ πρῶτοι χρησάμενοι,
ὄντα δὲ παραλαβόντες καὶ ἐσόμενον ἐς αἰεὶ κατα-

resource wherewith to take precautions against her in future. This fate, we beg of you, weak as you are and dependent on a single turn of the scale, do not willingly incur; nor make yourselves like the common crowd who, when it is possible still to be saved by human means, as soon as distress comes and all visible grounds of hope fail them, betake themselves to those that are invisible—to divination, oracles, and the like, which, with the hopes they inspire, bring men to ruin."

CIV. MEL. "We, too, be well assured, think it difficult to contend both against your power and against fortune, unless she shall be impartial; but nevertheless we trust that, in point of fortune, we shall through the divine favour be at no disadvantage because we are god-fearing men standing our ground against men who are unjust; and as to the matter of power, that the alliance of the Lacedaemonians will supply what we lack, since that alliance must aid us, if for no other reason, because of our kinship with them and for very shame. So our confidence is not altogether so irrational as you may suppose."

CV. ATH. "Well, as to the kindness of the divine favour, neither do we expect to fall short of you therein. For in no respect are we departing from men's observances regarding that which pertains to the divine or from their desires regarding that which pertains to themselves, in aught that we demand or do. For of the gods we hold the belief, and of men we know, that by a necessity of their nature wherever they have power they always rule. And so in our case since we neither enacted this law nor when it was enacted were the first to use it, but found it in existence and expect to leave it in existence for

λείψοντες χρώμεθα αὐτῷ, εἰδότες καὶ ὑμᾶς ἂν καὶ
ἄλλους ἐν τῇ αὐτῇ δυνάμει ἡμῖν γενομένους δρῶν-
3 τας ἂν ταὐτό. καὶ πρὸς μὲν τὸ θεῖον οὕτως ἐκ
τοῦ εἰκότος οὐ φοβούμεθα ἐλασσώσεσθαι· τῆς δὲ
ἐς Λακεδαιμονίους δόξης, ἣν διὰ τὸ αἰσχρὸν δὴ
βοηθήσειν ὑμῖν πιστεύετε αὐτούς, μακαρίσαντες
ὑμῶν τὸ ἀπειρόκακον οὐ ζηλοῦμεν τὸ ἄφρον.
Λακεδαιμόνιοι γὰρ πρὸς σφᾶς μὲν αὐτοὺς καὶ τὰ
ἐπιχώρια νόμιμα πλεῖστα ἀρετῇ χρῶνται· πρὸς
δὲ τοὺς ἄλλους πολλὰ ἄν τις ἔχων εἰπεῖν ὡς
προσφέρονται, ξυνελὼν μάλιστα ἂν δηλώσειεν ὅτι
ἐπιφανέστατα ὧν ἴσμεν τὰ μὲν ἡδέα καλὰ νομίζουσι, τὰ δὲ ξυμφέροντα δίκαια. καίτοι οὐ πρὸς
τῆς ὑμετέρας νῦν ἀλόγου σωτηρίας ἡ τοιαύτη
διάνοια.

CVI. ΜΗΛ. Ἡμεῖς δὲ κατ᾽ αὐτὸ τοῦτο ἤδη
καὶ μάλιστα πιστεύομεν τῷ ξυμφέροντι αὐτῶν
Μηλίους ἀποίκους ὄντας μὴ βουλήσεσθαι προ-
δόντας τοῖς μὲν εὔνοις τῶν Ἑλλήνων ἀπίστους
καταστῆναι, τοῖς δὲ πολεμίοις ὠφελίμους.

CVII. ΑΘ. Οὔκουν οἴεσθε τὸ ξυμφέρον μὲν
μετὰ ἀσφαλείας εἶναι, τὸ δὲ δίκαιον καὶ καλὸν
μετὰ κινδύνου δρᾶσθαι· ὃ Λακεδαιμόνιοι ἥκιστα
ὡς ἐπὶ τὸ πολὺ τολμῶσιν.

CVIII. ΜΗΛ. Ἀλλὰ καὶ τοὺς κινδύνους τε
ἡμῶν ἕνεκα μᾶλλον ἡγούμεθ᾽ ἂν ἐγχειρίσασθαι

168

all time, so we make use of it, well aware that both you and others, if clothed with the same power as we are, would do the same thing. And so with regard to the divine favour, we have good reason not to be afraid that we shall be at a disadvantage. But as to your expectation regarding the Lacedaemonians, your confident trust that out of shame forsooth they will aid you—while we admire your simplicity, we do not envy you your folly. We must indeed acknowledge that with respect to themselves and the institutions of their own country, the Lacedaemonians practise virtue in a very high degree; but with respect to their conduct towards the rest of mankind, while one might speak at great length, in briefest summary one may declare that of all men with whom we are acquainted they, most conspicuously, consider what is agreeable to be honourable, and what is expedient just. And yet such an attitude is not favourable to your present unreasonable hope of deliverance."

CVI. Mel. "But we find in this very thing our strongest ground of confidence—that in their own interest the Lacedaemonians will not be willing to betray the Melians who are their colonists, and so incur, on the one hand, the distrust of all the Hellenes who are well-disposed towards them, and, on the other, give aid to their enemies."

CVII. Ath. "Do you not think, then, that self-interest goes hand in hand with security, while justice and honour are practised with danger—a danger the Lacedaemonians are in general the least disposed to risk?"

CVIII. Mel. "Nay, but even the dangers we believe they would be more ready to incur for our

αὐτοὺς καὶ βεβαιοτέρους ἢ ἐς ἄλλους νομιεῖν,
ὅσῳ πρὸς μὲν τὰ ἔργα τῆς Πελοποννήσου ἐγγὺς
κείμεθα, τῆς δὲ γνώμης τῷ ξυγγενεῖ πιστότεροι
ἑτέρων ἐσμέν.

CIX. ΑΘ. Τὸ δ' ἐχυρόν γε τοῖς ξυναγωνιου-
μένοις οὐ τὸ εὔνουν τῶν ἐπικαλεσαμένων φαίνεται,
ἀλλ' ἢν τῶν ἔργων τις δυνάμει πολὺ προύχῃ· ὃ
Λακεδαιμόνιοι καὶ πλέον τι τῶν ἄλλων σκοποῦσι
(τῆς γοῦν οἰκείας παρασκευῆς ἀπιστίᾳ καὶ μετὰ
ξυμμάχων πολλῶν τοῖς πέλας ἐπέρχονται), ὥστε
οὐκ εἰκὸς ἐς νῆσόν γε αὐτοὺς ἡμῶν ναυκρατόρων
ὄντων περαιωθῆναι.

CX. ΜΗΛ. Οἱ δὲ καὶ ἄλλους ἂν ἔχοιεν
πέμψαι· πολὺ δὲ τὸ Κρητικὸν πέλαγος, δι' οὗ
τῶν κρατούντων ἀπορώτερος ἡ λῆψις ἢ τῶν
2 λαθεῖν βουλομένων ἡ σωτηρία. καὶ εἰ τοῦδε
σφάλλοιντο, τράποιντ' ἂν καὶ ἐς τὴν γῆν ὑμῶν
καὶ ἐπὶ τοὺς λοιποὺς τῶν ξυμμάχων, ὅσους μὴ
Βρασίδας ἐπῆλθε, καὶ οὐ περὶ τῆς μὴ προσ-
ηκούσης μᾶλλον ἢ τῆς οἰκειοτέρας ξυμμαχίδος τε
καὶ γῆς ὁ πόνος ὑμῖν ἔσται.

CXI. ΑΘ. Τούτων μὲν καὶ πεπειραμένοις ἄν
τι γένοιτο, καὶ ὑμῖν [1] οὐκ ἀνεπιστήμοσιν ὅτι οὐδ'
ἀπὸ μιᾶς πώποτε πολιορκίας Ἀθηναῖοι δι' ἄλλων
2 φόβον ἀπεχώρησαν. ἐνθυμούμεθα δὲ ὅτι φή-

---

[1] καὶ in MSS. before οὐκ, deleted by Stahl.

sakes, and that they would consider them less hazardous than if incurred for others, inasmuch as we lie close to the Peloponnesus when anything is to be undertaken there and on account of affinity of sentiment are more to be trusted than any others."

CIX. ATH. "But for men who are about to take part in a struggle, that which inspires their confidence is clearly not the good will of those who call them to their aid, but such marked superiority in actual power of achievement as they may possess; and to this superiority the Lacedaemonians give heed rather more than do the rest of mankind. At any rate, they so mistrust their own resources that they always associate themselves with many allies when they attack their neighbours; so that it is not likely they will ever cross over to an island while we are masters of the sea."

CX. MEL. "But there are others whom they might send; besides, the Cretan sea is wide, so that upon it the capture of a hostile squadron by the masters of the sea will be more difficult than it would be to cross over in security for those who wish to elude them. And if they should fail in this attempt they could turn against your territory and against any of the rest of your allies whom Brasidas did not reach; and then you would have to exert yourselves, not for the acquisition of territory that never belonged to you, but for the preservation of your own confederacy, aye, and your own country."

CXI. ATH. "Of these contingencies one or another might indeed happen; but they would not be new to our experience, and you yourselves are not unaware that the Athenians have never in a single instance withdrawn from a siege through fear of any foe.

σαντες περὶ σωτηρίας βουλεύσειν οὐδὲν ἐν
τοσούτῳ λόγῳ εἰρήκατε ᾧ ἄνθρωποι ἂν πιστεύσαντες νομίσειαν σωθήσεσθαι, ἀλλ' ὑμῶν τὰ μὲν
ἰσχυρότατα ἐλπιζόμενα μέλλεται, τὰ δ' ὑπάρχοντα βραχέα πρὸς τὰ ἤδη ἀντιτεταγμένα περιγίγνεσθαι. πολλήν τε ἀλογίαν τῆς διανοίας
παρέχετε, εἰ μὴ μεταστησάμενοι ἔτι ἡμᾶς ἄλλο
3 τι τῶνδε σωφρονέστερον γνώσεσθε. οὐ γὰρ δὴ
ἐπί γε τὴν ἐν τοῖς αἰσχροῖς καὶ προύπτοις κινδύ-
νοις πλεῖστα διαφθείρουσαν ἀνθρώπους αἰσχύνην
τρέψεσθε. πολλοῖς γὰρ προορωμένοις ἔτι ἐς
οἷα φέρονται τὸ αἰσχρὸν καλούμενον ὀνόματος
ἐπαγωγοῦ δυνάμει ἐπεσπάσατο, ἡσσηθεῖσι τοῦ
ῥήματος, ἔργῳ ξυμφοραῖς ἀνηκέστοις ἑκόντας
περιπεσεῖν καὶ αἰσχύνην αἰσχίω μετὰ ἀνοίας ἢ
4 τύχης[1] προσλαβεῖν. ὃ ὑμεῖς, ἢν εὖ βουλεύσησθε,
φυλάξεσθε καὶ οὐκ ἀπρεπὲς νομιεῖτε πόλεώς τε
τῆς μεγίστης ἡσσᾶσθαι μέτρια προκαλουμένης,
ξυμμάχους γενέσθαι ἔχοντας τὴν ὑμετέραν αὐτῶν
ὑποτελεῖς, καὶ δοθείσης αἱρέσεως πολέμου πέρι
καὶ ἀσφαλείας μὴ τὰ χείρω φιλονικῆσαι· ὡς
οἵτινες τοῖς μὲν ἴσοις μὴ εἴκουσι, τοῖς δὲ κρείσ-

---

[1] Hude reads τύχῃ, after Schol.

---

[1] See chs. lxxxvii., lxxxviii.
[2] i.e. men who expect to be saved by human means, not by
divine intervention ; cf. ch. civ. f.

However, we cannot but reflect that, although you said [1] that you would take counsel concerning your deliverance, you have not in this long discussion advanced a single argument that ordinary men [2] would put their confidence in if they expected to be delivered. On the contrary, your strongest grounds for confidence are merely cherished hopes whose fulfilment is in the future, whereas your present resources are too slight, compared with those already arrayed against you, for any chance of success. And you exhibit a quite unreasonable attitude of mind if you do not even now, after permitting us to withdraw, come to some decision that is wiser than your present purpose. For surely you will not take refuge in that feeling which most often brings men to ruin when they are confronted by dangers that are clearly foreseen and therefore disgraceful—the fear of such disgrace. For many men, though they can still clearly foresee the dangers into which they are drifting, are lured on by the power of a seductive word—the thing called disgrace—until, the victims of a phrase, they are indeed plunged, of their own act, into irretrievable calamities, and thus incur in addition a disgrace that is more disgraceful, because associated with folly rather than with misfortune. Such a course you will avoid, if you take wise counsel, and you will not consider it degrading to acknowledge yourselves inferior to the most powerful state when it offers you moderate terms—to become allies, keeping your own territory but paying tribute—and, when a choice is given you of war or safety, not to hold out stubbornly for the worse alternative. Since those who, while refusing to submit to their equals, yet comport themselves wisely towards their superiors

σοσι καλῶς προσφέρονται, πρὸς δὲ τοὺς ἥσσους
5 μέτριοί εἰσι, πλεῖστ᾽ ἂν ὀρθοῖντο. σκοπεῖτε οὖν
καὶ μεταστάντων ἡμῶν καὶ ἐνθυμεῖσθε πολλάκις
ὅτι περὶ πατρίδος βουλεύεσθε, ἧς[1] μιᾶς πέρι καὶ
ἐς μίαν βουλὴν τυχοῦσάν τε καὶ μὴ κατορθώ-
σασαν ἔσται.

CXII. Καὶ οἱ μὲν Ἀθηναῖοι μετεχώρησαν ἐκ
τῶν λόγων· οἱ δὲ Μήλιοι κατὰ σφᾶς αὐτοὺς
γενόμενοι, ὡς ἔδοξεν αὐτοῖς παραπλήσια καὶ
2 ἀντέλεγον, ἀπεκρίναντο τάδε. "Οὔτε ἄλλα δοκεῖ
ἡμῖν ἢ ἅπερ καὶ τὸ πρῶτον, ὦ Ἀθηναῖοι, οὔτ᾽ ἐν
ὀλίγῳ χρόνῳ πόλεως ἑπτακόσια ἔτη ἤδη οἰκου-
μένης τὴν ἐλευθερίαν ἀφαιρησόμεθα, ἀλλὰ τῇ τε
μέχρι τοῦδε σῳζούσῃ τύχῃ ἐκ τοῦ θείου αὐτὴν
καὶ τῇ ἀπὸ τῶν ἀνθρώπων καὶ[2] Λακεδαιμονίων
τιμωρίᾳ πιστεύοντες πειρασόμεθα σῴζεσθαι.
3 προκαλούμεθα δὲ ὑμᾶς φίλοι μὲν εἶναι, πολέμιοι
δὲ μηδετέροις, καὶ ἐκ τῆς γῆς ἡμῶν ἀναχωρῆσαι
σπονδὰς ποιησαμένους αἵτινες δοκοῦσιν ἐπιτήδειοι εἶναι ἀμφοτέροις."

CXIII. Οἱ μὲν δὴ Μήλιοι τοσαῦτα ἀπεκρί-
ναντο· οἱ δὲ Ἀθηναῖοι διαλυόμενοι ἤδη ἐκ τῶν
λόγων ἔφασαν· "Ἀλλ᾽ οὖν μόνοι γε ἀπὸ τούτων
τῶν βουλευμάτων, ὡς ἡμῖν δοκεῖτε, τὰ μὲν μέλλοντα τῶν ὁρωμένων σαφέστερα κρίνετε, τὰ δὲ
ἀφανῆ τῷ βούλεσθαι ὡς γιγνόμενα ἤδη θεᾶσθε·
καὶ Λακεδαιμονίοις καὶ τύχῃ καὶ ἐλπίσι πλεῖστον

---

[1] ἧς for ἦν, as the Schol. seems to have read.
[2] καὶ Λακεδαιμονίων deleted by Hude, after Stahl.

and are moderate towards their inferiors—these, we say, are most likely to prosper. Consider, then, once more after our withdrawal, and reflect many times in your deliberations that your fatherland is at stake, your one and only fatherland, and that upon one decision only will depend her fate for weal or woe."

CXII. So the Athenians retired from the conference; and the Melians, after consulting together in private, finding themselves of much the same opinion as they had expressed before, answered as follows: "Men of Athens, our opinion is no other than it was at first, nor will we in a short moment rob of its liberty a city which has been inhabited already seven hundred years[1]; but trusting to the fortune which by divine favour has preserved her hitherto, and to such help as men, even the Lacedaemonians, can give, we shall try to win our deliverance. But we propose to you that we be your friends, but enemies to neither combatant, and that you withdraw from our territory, after making such a truce as may seem suitable for both of us."

CXIII. Such was the answer of the Melians; and the Athenians, as they were quitting the conference, said: "Then, as it seems to us, judging by the result of these deliberations of yours, you are the only men who regard future events as more certain than what lies before your eyes, and who look upon that which is out of sight, merely because you wish it, as already realized. You have staked your all, putting your trust in the Lacedaemonians, in fortune

---

[1] Evidently a merely general statement, carrying us back to the time of the Dorian invasion. Conon, *Narrat.* 36, mentions the Spartan Philonomus as founder of Melos, soon after the Dorians settled at Sparta. See Müller, *Orchomenos,* p. 317.

δὴ παραβεβλημένοι καὶ πιστεύσαντες πλεῖστον καὶ σφαλήσεσθε."

CXIV. Καὶ οἱ μὲν Ἀθηναίων πρέσβεις ἀνεχώρησαν ἐς τὸ στράτευμα· οἱ δὲ στρατηγοὶ αὐτῶν, ὡς οὐδὲν ὑπήκουον οἱ Μήλιοι, πρὸς πόλεμον εὐθὺς ἐτρέποντο καὶ διελόμενοι κατὰ πόλεις 2 περιετείχισαν κύκλῳ τοὺς Μηλίους. καὶ ὕστερον φυλακὴν σφῶν τε αὐτῶν καὶ τῶν ξυμμάχων καταλιπόντες οἱ Ἀθηναῖοι καὶ κατὰ γῆν καὶ κατὰ θάλασσαν ἀνεχώρησαν τῷ πλείονι τοῦ στρατοῦ. οἱ δὲ λειπόμενοι παραμένοντες ἐπολιόρκουν τὸ χωρίον.

CXV. Καὶ Ἀργεῖοι κατὰ τὸν χρόνον τὸν αὐτὸν ἐσβαλόντες ἐς τὴν Φλειασίαν καὶ λοχισθέντες ὑπό τε Φλειασίων καὶ τῶν σφετέρων φυγάδων 2 διεφθάρησαν ὡς ὀγδοήκοντα. καὶ οἱ ἐκ τῆς Πύλου Ἀθηναῖοι Λακεδαιμονίων πολλὴν λείαν ἔλαβον. καὶ Λακεδαιμόνιοι δι' αὐτὸ τὰς μὲν σπονδὰς οὐδ' ὣς ἀφέντες ἐπολέμουν αὐτοῖς, ἐκήρυξαν δέ, εἴ τις 3 βούλεται παρὰ σφῶν, Ἀθηναίους λήζεσθαι. καὶ Κορίνθιοι ἐπολέμησαν ἰδίων τινῶν διαφορῶν ἕνεκα τοῖς Ἀθηναίοις· οἱ δ' ἄλλοι Πελοποννήσιοι ἡσύ- 4 χαζον. εἷλον δὲ καὶ οἱ Μήλιοι τῶν Ἀθηναίων τοῦ περιτειχίσματος τὸ κατὰ τὴν ἀγορὰν προσβαλόντες νυκτός, καὶ ἄνδρας τε ἀπέκτειναν καὶ ἐσενεγκάμενοι σῖτόν τε καὶ ὅσα πλεῖστα ἐδύναντο χρήσιμα ἀναχωρήσαντες ἡσύχαζον· καὶ οἱ Ἀθηναῖοι ἄμεινον τὴν φυλακὴν τὸ ἔπειτα παρεσκευάζοντο. καὶ τὸ θέρος ἐτελεύτα.

CXVI. Τοῦ δ' ἐπιγιγνομένου χειμῶνος Λακεδαιμόνιοι μελλήσαντες ἐς τὴν Ἀργείαν στρα-

and in fond hopes ; and with your all you will come to ruin."

CXIV. So the Athenian envoys returned to the army ; and their generals, as the Melians would not yield, immediately commenced hostilities, and drew a wall round about the city of Melos, distributing the work among the several states. Afterwards, leaving some of their own troops and of their allies to keep guard both by land and by sea, they withdrew with the greater part of the army, while the rest remained behind and besieged the place.

CXV. About the same time the Argives invaded Phliasia ; but being ambushed by the Phliasians and the Argive exiles they lost about eighty men. Also the Athenians at Pylos took much booty from the Lacedaemonians; but even this did not move the Lacedaemonians to renounce the treaty and make war upon them. They made proclamation, however, that any one of their own people who wished might make reprisals upon the Athenians. The Corinthians also went to war with the Athenians on account of some private differences ; but the rest of the Peloponnesians kept quiet. The Melians, too, took the part of the Athenian wall over against the market-place by a night assault ; then having slain some of the men and brought in grain and as many other necessaries as they could, they withdrew and kept quiet. After that the Athenians maintained a better watch. So the summer ended.

CXVI. The following winter the Lacedaemonians were on the point of invading Argive territory, but

τενειν, ὡς αὐτοῖς τὰ διαβατήρια¹ οὐκ ἐγίγνετο,
ἀνεχώρησαν. καὶ ᾿Αργεῖοι διὰ τὴν ἐκείνων μέλ-
λησιν τῶν ἐν τῇ πόλει τινὰς ὑποπτεύσαντες² τοὺς
2 μὲν ξυνέλαβον, οἱ δ᾽ αὐτοὺς καὶ διέφυγον. καὶ οἱ
Μήλιοι περὶ τοὺς αὐτοὺς χρόνους αὖθις καθ᾽
ἕτερόν τι τοῦ περιτειχίσματος εἷλον τῶν ᾿Αθη-
3 ναίων, παρόντων οὐ πολλῶν τῶν φυλάκων. καὶ
ἐλθούσης στρατιᾶς ὕστερον ἐκ τῶν ᾿Αθηνῶν
ἄλλης, ὡς ταῦτα ἐγίγνετο, ἧς ἦρχε Φιλοκράτης
ὁ Δημέου, καὶ κατὰ κράτος ἤδη πολιορκούμενοι,
γενομένης καὶ προδοσίας τινὸς ἀφ᾽ ἑαυτῶν, ξυνεχώρησαν τοῖς ᾿Αθηναίοις ὥστε ἐκείνους περὶ αὐτῶν
4 βουλεῦσαι. οἱ δὲ ἀπέκτειναν Μηλίων ὅσους
ἡβῶντας ἔλαβον, παῖδας δὲ καὶ γυναῖκας ἠνδραπόδισαν. τὸ δὲ χωρίον αὐτοὶ ᾤκισαν,³ ἀποίκους
ὕστερον πεντακοσίους πέμψαντες.

---

¹ ἱερὰ ἐν τοῖς ὁρίοις, in MSS. after διαβατήρια, deleted by
Cobet as a gloss on that word. *cf.* ch. liv. 2, lv. 3.
² Meineke's conjecture for ὑποτοπήσαντες of the MSS.
³ ᾤκισαν, several good MSS. for the Vulgate ᾤκησαν.

as the sacrifices for crossing the boundaries were not favourable they returned home. On account of this intention on the part of the Lacedaemonians, the Argives, suspecting certain men in their city, seized some of them, but the rest escaped. About the same time the Melians again at another point took a part of the Athenian encompassing wall, the garrison not being numerous. But later, in consequence of these occurrences, another force came from Athens, of which Philocrates son of Demeas was commander, and the Melians, being now closely besieged—some treachery, too, having made its appearance among them—capitulated to the Athenians on the condition that these should determine their fate. The Athenians thereupon slew all the adult males whom they had taken and made slaves of the children and women. But the place they then peopled with new settlers from Athens, sending thither at a later time five hundred colonists.

BOOK VI

Ϛ

I. Τοῦ δ' αὐτοῦ χειμῶνος Ἀθηναῖοι ἐβούλοντο
αὖθις μείζονι παρασκευῇ τῆς μετὰ Λάχητος καὶ
Εὐρυμέδοντος ἐπὶ Σικελίαν πλεύσαντες κατα-
στρέψασθαι, εἰ δύναιντο, ἄπειροι οἱ πολλοὶ ὄντες
τοῦ μεγέθους τῆς νήσου καὶ τῶν ἐνοικούντων τοῦ
πλήθους καὶ Ἑλλήνων καὶ βαρβάρων, καὶ ὅτι οὐ
πολλῷ τινι ὑποδεέστερον πόλεμον ἀνῃροῦντο ἢ
τὸν πρὸς Πελοποννησίους. Σικελίας γὰρ περί-
2 πλους μέν ἐστιν ὁλκάδι οὐ πολλῷ τινι ἔλασσον ἢ
ὀκτὼ ἡμερῶν, καὶ τοσαύτη οὖσα ἐν εἰκοσισταδίῳ [1]
μάλιστα μέτρῳ [2] τῆς θαλάσσης διείργεται τὸ μὴ
ἤπειρος εἶναι.[3]

II. Ὠικίσθη δὲ ὧδε τὸ ἀρχαῖον καὶ τοσάδε
ἔθνη ἔσχε τὰ ξύμπαντα. παλαίτατοι μὲν λέγονται ἐν μέρει τινὶ τῆς χώρας Κύκλωπες καὶ Λαισ-
τρυγόνες οἰκῆσαι, ὧν ἐγὼ οὔτε γένος ἔχω εἰπεῖν
οὔτε ὁπόθεν ἐσῆλθον ἢ ὅποι ἀπεχώρησαν· ἀρκείτω δὲ ὡς ποιηταῖς τε εἴρηται καὶ ὡς ἕκαστός πη
2 γιγνώσκει περὶ αὐτῶν. Σικανοὶ δὲ μετ' αὐτοὺς

[1] For the usual εἴκοσι σταδίων (CF corrected, f₂) adopted
after M and Schol. Patm., εἴκοσι σταδίοις AB.

[2] μέτρῳ deleted by Hude as not read by Schol. Patm.

[3] εἶναι, so nearly all recent editors following H (*suprascr.
man. pr.*), Demetrius and Procopius, for οὖσα of the MSS.
Shilleto, Badham, and others prefer ἠπειροῦσθαι.

BOOK VI

I. DURING the same winter the Athenians wished to sail again to Sicily with a larger armament than that conducted by Laches and Eurymedon,[1] and subdue it, if they could, most of them being ignorant of the great size of the island and of the large number of its inhabitants, Hellenic as well as Barbarian, and that they were undertaking a war not very much inferior to that against the Peloponnesians. For the voyage round Sicily, for a merchantman, is one of not much less than eight days; and although it is so large only a distance of about twenty stadia of the sea divides the island from the mainland.

II. Sicily was settled originally in the following manner, and the whole number of the nations that occupied it were these. Most ancient of all those who are reported to have settled in any part of the island were the Cyclopes and Laestrygonians, as to whom, however, I am able to tell neither their stock nor whence they came nor whither they went; let it suffice as the story has been told by the poets,[2] and as each man has formed his opinion about them. The Sicanians appear to have been the first to settle

---

[1] Two separate earlier expeditions, one under Laches and Charoeades, 427 B.C. (III. lxxxvi. 1), the other under Pythodorus, Sophocles and Eurymedon, 424 B.C. (IV. ii.), are here comprised under the one formula.

[2] Homer, no doubt, especially, as also in I. x. 1; xi. 3; xxi. 1.

πρῶτοι φαίνονται ἐνοικισάμενοι, ὡς μὲν αὐτοὶ
φασι, καὶ πρότεροι διὰ τὸ αὐτόχθονες εἶναι, ὡς
δὲ ἡ ἀλήθεια εὑρίσκεται, Ἴβηρες ὄντες καὶ ἀπὸ
τοῦ Σικανοῦ ποταμοῦ τοῦ ἐν Ἰβηρίᾳ ὑπὸ Λιγύων
ἀναστάντες. καὶ ἀπ' αὐτῶν Σικανία τότε ἡ νῆσος
ἐκαλεῖτο, πρότερον Τρινακρία καλουμένη· οἰκοῦσι
δὲ ἔτι καὶ νῦν τὰ πρὸς ἑσπέραν τὴν Σικελίαν.

3 Ἰλίου δὲ ἁλισκομένου τῶν Τρώων τινὲς διαφυ-
γόντες Ἀχαιοὺς πλοίοις ἀφικνοῦνται πρὸς τὴν
Σικελίαν, καὶ ὅμοροι τοῖς Σικανοῖς οἰκήσαντες ξύμπαντες μὲν Ἔλυμοι ἐκλήθησαν, πόλεις δ' αὐτῶν
Ἔρυξ τε καὶ Ἔγεστα. προσξυνῴκησαν δὲ αὐτοῖς
καὶ Φωκέων τινὲς τῶν ἀπὸ Τροίας τότε χειμῶνι
ἐς Λιβύην πρῶτον, ἔπειτα ἐς Σικελίαν ἀπ' αὐτῆς

4 κατενεχθέντες. Σικελοὶ δὲ ἐξ Ἰταλίας (ἐνταῦθα
γὰρ ᾤκουν) διέβησαν ἐς Σικελίαν, φεύγοντες Ὀπι-
κούς, ὡς μὲν εἰκὸς καὶ λέγεται, ἐπὶ σχεδιῶν, τηρήσαντες τὸν πορθμὸν κατιόντος τοῦ ἀνέμου, τάχα
ἂν δὲ καὶ ἄλλως πως ἐσπλεύσαντες. εἰσὶ δὲ καὶ
νῦν ἔτι ἐν τῇ Ἰταλίᾳ Σικελοί· καὶ ἡ χώρα ἀπὸ
Ἰταλοῦ, βασιλέως τινὸς Σικελῶν, τοὔνομα τοῦτο

5 ἔχοντος, οὕτω Ἰταλία ἐπωνομάσθη. ἐλθόντες δὲ
ἐς τὴν Σικελίαν στρατὸς πολὺς τούς τε Σικανοὺς
κρατοῦντες μάχῃ ἀνέστειλαν πρὸς τὰ μεσημβρινὰ
καὶ ἑσπέρια αὐτῆς καὶ ἀντὶ Σικανίας Σικελίαν
τὴν νῆσον ἐποίησαν καλεῖσθαι, καὶ τὰ κράτιστα
τῆς γῆς ᾤκησαν ἔχοντες, ἐπεὶ διέβησαν, ἔτη ἐγγὺς
τριακόσια πρὶν Ἕλληνας ἐς Σικελίαν ἐλθεῖν· ἔτι
δὲ καὶ νῦν τὰ μέσα καὶ τὰ πρὸς βορρᾶν τῆς νήσου

6 ἔχουσιν. ᾤκουν δὲ καὶ Φοίνικες περὶ πᾶσαν μὲν
τὴν Σικελίαν ἄκρας τε ἐπὶ τῇ θαλάσσῃ ἀπολαβόντες καὶ τὰ ἐπικείμενα νησίδια ἐμπορίας ἕνεκα τῆς

there after them, indeed, as they themselves assert, even before them, as being indigenous, but as the truth is found to be, they were Iberians and were driven by the Ligurians from the River Sicanus in Iberia. From them the island was then called Sicania, having been called Trinacria before; and they still inhabit the western parts of Sicily. But on the capture of Ilium some of the Trojans, who had escaped the Achaeans, came in boats to Sicily, and settling on the borders of the Sicanians were called, as a people, Elymi, while their cities were named Eryx and Egesta. And there settled with them also some of the Phocians, who on their return at that time from Troy were driven by a storm first to Libya and thence to Sicily. The Sicels, again, crossed over from Italy, where they dwelt, to Sicily, fleeing from the Opicans—as is probable and indeed is reported— on rafts, having waited for their passage till the wind was from the shore; or perhaps they sailed thither in some other way also. Even now there are Sicels still in Italy; and the country was named Italy after Italus, a king of the Sicels who had this name. These crossed over to Sicily in a vast horde and conquering the Sicanians in battle forced them back to the southern and western parts of the island, causing it to be called Sicily instead of Sicania. They settled there after they had crossed and held the best parts of the land for nearly three hundred years before the Hellenes came to Sicily; and even now they still hold the central and northern parts of the island. Phoenicians, too, had settlements all round Sicily, on promontories along the sea coast, which they walled off, and on the adjacent islets, for the sake

πρὸς τοὺς Σικελούς· ἐπειδὴ δὲ οἱ Ἕλληνες πολλοὶ κατὰ θάλασσαν ἐπεσέπλεον, ἐκλιπόντες τὰ
πλείω Μοτύην καὶ Σολόεντα καὶ Πάνορμον ἐγγὺς
τῶν Ἐλύμων ξυνοικίσαντες ἐνέμοντο, ξυμμαχίᾳ
τε πίσυνοι τῇ τῶν Ἐλύμων καὶ ὅτι ἐντεῦθεν ἐλάχιστον πλοῦν Καρχηδὼν Σικελίας ἀπέχει. βάρ-
βαροι μὲν οὖν τοσοίδε Σικελίαν καὶ οὕτως ᾤκησαν.

III. Ἑλλήνων δὲ πρῶτοι Χαλκιδῆς ἐξ Εὐβοίας
πλεύσαντες μετὰ Θουκλέους οἰκιστοῦ Νάξον ᾤκισαν καὶ Ἀπόλλωνος Ἀρχηγέτου βωμόν, ὅστις νῦν
ἔξω τῆς πόλεώς ἐστιν, ἱδρύσαντο, ἐφ' ᾧ, ὅταν ἐκ
2 Σικελίας θεωροὶ πλέωσι, πρῶτον θύουσιν. Συρακούσας δὲ τοῦ ἐχομένου ἔτους Ἀρχίας τῶν Ἡρα-
κλειδῶν ἐκ Κορίνθου ᾤκισε, Σικελοὺς ἐξελάσας
πρῶτον ἐκ τῆς νήσου, ἐν ᾗ νῦν οὐκέτι περικλυζομένη[1] ἡ πόλις ἡ ἐντός ἐστιν· ὕστερον δὲ χρόνῳ
καὶ ἡ ἔξω προστειχισθεῖσα πολυάνθρωπος ἐγέ-
3 νετο. Θουκλῆς δὲ καὶ οἱ Χαλκιδῆς ἐκ Νάξου
ὁρμηθέντες ἔτει πέμπτῳ μετὰ Συρακούσας οἰκι-
σθείσας Λεοντίνους τε, πολέμῳ τοὺς Σικελοὺς ἐξε-
λάσαντες, οἰκίζουσι καὶ μετ' αὐτοὺς Κατάνην·
οἰκιστὴν δὲ αὐτοὶ Καταναῖοι ἐποιήσαντο Εὔαρχον·

IV. Κατὰ δὲ τὸν αὐτὸν χρόνον καὶ Λάμις ἐκ
Μεγάρων ἀποικίαν ἄγων ἐς Σικελίαν ἀφίκετο, καὶ

---

[1] With CG, the other MSS. περικλυζομένη.

---

[1] On the little island of S. Pantaleon near the promontory
of Lilybaeum.
[2] East of Palermo, now Salanto.   [3] Now Palermo.
[4] 735 B.C. The site was the best point for landing from
Hellas, near Tauromenium (Taormina).
[5] A leader appointed by a state to conduct the people sent
out to establish a colony. He probably received material

of trade with the Sicels. But when the Hellenes also began to come in by sea in large numbers, the Phoenicians left most of these places and settling together lived in Motya,[1] Soloeis[2] and Panormus[3] near the Elymi, partly because they trusted in their alliance with the Elymi and partly because from there the voyage from Sicily to Carthage is shortest. These, then, were the barbarians and such was the manner in which they settled in Sicily.

III. Of the Hellenes, on the other hand, the first to sail over were some Chalcidians from Euboea who settled Naxos[4] with Thucles as founder,[5] and built an altar in honour of Apollo Archegetes.[6] This is now outside of the city, and on it the sacred deputies,[7] when they sail from Sicily, first offer sacrifice. The following year Syracuse[8] was founded by Archias, one of the Heracleidae from Corinth, after he had first expelled the Sicels from the island, no longer surrounded by water, on which now stands the inner city; and at a later period also the outer city was connected with it by walls and became populous. In the fifth year after the settlement of Syracuse, Thucles and the Chalcidians, setting forth from Naxos, drove out the Sicels in war and settled Leontini, and after it Catana.[9] The Catanaeans, however, chose for themselves Evarchus as founder.

IV. About the same time Lamis also came to Sicily with a colony from Megara and settled in a

privileges and grants while alive, and certainly was paid divine honours—sacrifices and games—after death. If a colony afterwards founded another colony, it was customary to ask a leader from the mother city.

[6] So called as "founder" or protector of a new settlement.

[7] On missions to games or oracles.

[8] 734 B.C.   [9] 729 B.C.

ὑπὲρ Παντακύου τε ποταμοῦ Τρώτιλόν τι ὄνομα
χωρίον οἰκίσας καὶ ὕστερον αὐτόθεν τοῖς Χαλκιδεῦσιν ἐς Λεοντίνους ὀλίγον χρόνον ξυμπολιτεύσας
καὶ ὑπ᾽ αὐτῶν ἐκπεσὼν καὶ Θάψον οἰκίσας αὐτὸς
μὲν ἀποθνήσκει, οἱ δ᾽ ἄλλοι ἐκ τῆς Θάψου ἀναστάντες, Ὕβλωνος βασιλέως Σικελοῦ παραδόντος
τὴν χώραν καὶ καθηγησαμένου, Μεγαρέας ᾤκισαν
2 τοὺς Ὑβλαίους κληθέντας. καὶ ἔτη οἰκήσαντες
πέντε καὶ τεσσαράκοντα καὶ διακόσια ὑπὸ Γέλωνος
τυράννου Συρακοσίων ἀνέστησαν ἐκ τῆς πόλεως καὶ
χώρας. πρὶν δὲ ἀναστῆναι, ἔτεσιν ὕστερον ἑκατὸν
ἢ αὐτοὺς οἰκίσαι, Πάμμιλον πέμψαντες Σελινοῦντα κτίζουσι, καὶ ἐκ Μεγάρων τῆς μητροπόλεως
3 οὔσης αὐτοῖς ἐπελθὼν ξυγκατῴκισεν. Γέλαν δὲ
Ἀντίφημος ἐκ Ῥόδου καὶ Ἔντιμος ἐκ Κρήτης
ἐποίκους ἀγαγόντες κοινῇ ἔκτισαν ἔτει πέμπτῳ
καὶ τεσσαρακοστῷ μετὰ Συρακουσῶν οἴκισιν. καὶ
τῇ μὲν πόλει ἀπὸ τοῦ Γέλα ποταμοῦ τοὔνομα
ἐγένετο, τὸ δὲ χωρίον οὗ νῦν ἡ πόλις ἐστὶ καὶ ὃ
πρῶτον ἐτειχίσθη Λίνδιοι καλεῖται· νόμιμα δὲ
4 Δωρικὰ ἐτέθη αὐτοῖς. ἔτεσι δὲ ἐγγύτατα ὀκτὼ
καὶ ἑκατὸν μετὰ τὴν σφετέραν οἴκισιν Γελῷοι
Ἀκράγαντα ᾤκισαν, τὴν μὲν πόλιν ἀπὸ τοῦ Ἀκρά-
γαντος ποταμοῦ ὀνομάσαντες, οἰκιστὰς δὲ ποιήσαντες Ἀριστόνουν καὶ Πυστίλον, νόμιμα δὲ τὰ
5 Γελῴων δόντες. Ζάγκλη δὲ τὴν μὲν ἀρχὴν ἀπὸ
Κύμης τῆς ἐν Ὀπικίᾳ Χαλκιδικῆς πόλεως λῃστῶν
ἀφικομένων ᾠκίσθη, ὕστερον δὲ καὶ ἀπὸ Χαλκίδος
καὶ τῆς ἄλλης Εὐβοίας πλῆθος ἐλθὸν ξυγκατενεί-

---

[1] A peninsula just north of Syracuse (now called Isola di
Magnisi).

place called Trotilus, beyond the river Pantacyas; but afterwards, having removed from there and joined the settlement of the Chalcidians at Leontini, he was a little later driven out by them, and then after colonizing Thapsus[1] met his death. His followers were expelled from Thapsus and settled then at a place called Megara Hyblaea,[2] since Hyblon, a Sicel king, gave up the land to them and led them to the site. After dwelling there two hundred and forty-five years, they were driven out of the town and country by Gelon, tyrant of Syracuse. But before they were driven out, a hundred years after they had settled there, they founded Selinus,[3] sending thither Pammilus, who came from the mother-city Megara and joined in the settlement. In the forty-fifth year after the settlement of Syracuse Gela[4] was founded by Antiphemus from Rhodes and Entimus from Crete, who together led out the colony. The city got its name from the river Gela, but the place where the acropolis now is and which was the first to be fortified is called Lindii.[5] The institutions given it were Dorian. Just about one hundred and eight years after their own foundation, the Geloans colonized Acragas[6]; and they named the city after the river Acragas, making Aristonous and Pystilus founders, and giving it the institutions of the Geloans. Zancle was settled, in the beginning, by pirates who came from Cyme, the Chalcidian city in Opicia; but afterwards a large number of colonists came from Chalcis and the rest of Euboea and shared the land with them,

[2] 728 B.C. [3] 628 B.C. [4] 689 B.C.
[5] So called evidently from Lindus in Rhodes; cf. Hdt. VII. cliii. [6] 581 B.C.

μαντο τὴν γῆν· καὶ οἰκισταὶ Περιήρης καὶ Κρα-
ταιμένης ἐγένοντο αὐτῆς, ὁ μὲν ἀπὸ Κύμης, ὁ δὲ
ἀπὸ Χαλκίδος. ὄνομα δὲ τὸ μὲν πρῶτον Ζάγκλη
ἦν ὑπὸ τῶν Σικελῶν κληθεῖσα, ὅτι δρεπανοειδὲς
τὴν ἰδέαν τὸ χωρίον ἐστί (τὸ δὲ δρέπανον οἱ Σικελοὶ
ζάγκλον καλοῦσιν), ὕστερον δ᾽ αὐτοὶ μὲν ὑπὸ Σα-
μίων καὶ ἄλλων Ἰώνων ἐκπίπτουσιν, οἳ Μήδους
φεύγοντες προσέβαλον Σικελίᾳ, τοὺς δὲ Σαμίους
6 Ἀναξίλας Ῥηγίνων τύραννος οὐ πολλῷ ὕστερον
ἐκβαλὼν καὶ τὴν πόλιν αὐτὸς ξυμμείκτων ἀνθρώπων οἰκίσας Μεσσήνην ἀπὸ τῆς ἑαυτοῦ τὸ ἀρχαῖον
πατρίδος ἀντωνόμασεν.

V. Καὶ Ἱμέρα ἀπὸ Ζάγκλης ᾠκίσθη ὑπὸ
Εὐκλείδου καὶ Σίμου καὶ Σάκωνος, καὶ Χαλκιδῆς
μὲν οἱ πλεῖστοι ἦλθον ἐς τὴν ἀποικίαν, ξυνῴκισαν
δὲ αὐτοῖς καὶ ἐκ Συρακουσῶν φυγάδες στάσει
νικηθέντες, οἱ Μυλητίδαι καλούμενοι· καὶ φωνὴ
μὲν μεταξὺ τῆς τε Χαλκιδέων καὶ Δωρίδος
ἐκράθη, νόμιμα δὲ τὰ Χαλκιδικὰ ἐκράτησεν.
2 Ἄκραι δὲ καὶ Κασμέναι ὑπὸ Συρακοσίων ᾠκί-
σθησαν, Ἄκραι μὲν ἑβδομήκοντα ἔτεσι μετὰ
Συρακούσας, Κασμέναι δ᾽ ἐγγὺς εἴκοσι μετὰ
3 Ἄκρας. καὶ Καμάρινα τὸ πρῶτον ὑπὸ Συρακοσίων ᾠκίσθη, ἔτεσιν ἐγγύτατα πέντε καὶ τριάκοντα καὶ ἑκατὸν μετὰ Συρακουσῶν κτίσιν·
οἰκισταὶ δὲ ἐγένοντο αὐτῆς Δάσκων καὶ Μενέ-
κωλος. ἀναστάτων δὲ Καμαριναίων γενομένων
πολέμῳ ὑπὸ Συρακοσίων δι᾽ ἀπόστασιν, χρόνῳ
Ἱπποκράτης ὕστερον Γέλας τύραννος, λύτρα ἀνδρῶν Συρακοσίων αἰχμαλώτων λαβὼν τὴν γῆν τὴν
Καμαριναίων, αὐτὸς οἰκιστὴς γενόμενος κατῴκισε

the founders being Perieres and Crataemenes, the one from Cyme, the other from Chalcis. Its name at first was Zancle, and it was so called by the Sicels because the place is sickle-shaped : for the Sicels call a sickle "zanclon." Afterwards these settlers were driven out by Samians and other Ionians, who in their flight before the Persians landed in Sicily [1]; but the Samians were expelled not long afterwards by Anaxilas, tyrant of Rhegium, who colonized the place with a mixed population and changed its name to Messene [2] after his own original fatherland.

V. Himera [3] was colonized from Zancle by Eucleides, Simus and Sacon. Most of the colonists were Chalcidians; but there settled with them also fugitives from Syracuse who had been vanquished in a factional quarrel, the Myletidae as they were called. Their language was a mixture of Chalcidic and Doric, but Chalcidic institutions prevailed. Acrae and Casmenae were colonized by the Syracusans : Acrae [4] seventy years after Syracuse, Casmenae [5] nearly twenty years after Acrae. Camarina [6] was first colonized by the Syracusans, just about one hundred and thirty-five years after the foundation of Syracuse, its founders being Dascon and Menecolus. But the Camarinaeans were driven out by the Syracusans in a war which arose from a revolt, and some time later Hippocrates, tyrant of Gela,[7] receiving the territory of the Camarinaeans as ransom for some Syracusan prisoners of war, himself became founder and recolonized Camarina.

---

[1] cf. Hdt. VI. xxii., xxiii. [2] 730 B.C.
[3] 648 B.C. [4] 664 B.C. [5] 644 B.C.
[6] 599 B.C. [7] Dates 498–491.

Καμάριναν. καὶ αὖθις ὑπὸ Γέλωνος ἀνάστατος γενομένη τὸ τρίτον κατῳκίσθη ὑπὸ Γελῴων.[1]

VI. Τοσαῦτα ἔθνη Ἑλλήνων καὶ βαρβάρων Σικελίαν ᾤκει, καὶ ἐπὶ τοσήνδε οὖσαν αὐτὴν οἱ Ἀθηναῖοι στρατεύειν ὥρμηντο, ἐφιέμενοι μὲν τῇ ἀληθεστάτῃ προφάσει τῆς πάσης ἄρξαι, βοηθεῖν δὲ ἅμα εὐπρεπῶς βουλόμενοι τοῖς ἑαυτῶν ξυγγενέσι καὶ τοῖς προγεγενημένοις[2] ξυμμάχοις.

2 μάλιστα δ᾽ αὐτοὺς ἐξώρμησαν Ἐγεσταίων[3] πρέσβεις παρόντες καὶ προθυμότερον ἐπικαλούμενοι. ὅμοροι γὰρ ὄντες τοῖς Σελινουντίοις ἐς πόλεμον καθέστασαν περί τε γαμικῶν τινων καὶ περὶ γῆς ἀμφισβητήτου, καὶ οἱ Σελινούντιοι Συρακοσίους ἐπαγαγόμενοι ξυμμάχους κατεῖργον αὐτοὺς τῷ πολέμῳ καὶ κατὰ γῆν καὶ κατὰ θάλασσαν· ὥστε τὴν γενομένην ἐπὶ Λάχητος καὶ τοῦ προτέρου πολέμου Λεοντίνων[4] οἱ Ἐγεσταῖοι ξυμμαχίαν ἀναμιμνῄσκοντες τοὺς Ἀθηναίους ἐδέοντο σφίσι ναῦς πέμψαντας ἐπαμῦναι, λέγοντες ἄλλα τε πολλὰ καὶ κεφάλαιον, εἰ Συρακόσιοι Λεοντίνους τε ἀναστήσαντες ἀτιμώρητοι γενήσονται καὶ τοὺς λοιποὺς ἔτι ξυμμάχους αὐτῶν διαφθείροντες[5] αὐτοὶ τὴν ἅπασαν δύναμιν τῆς Σικελίας σχήσουσι, κίνδυνον εἶναι μή ποτε μεγάλῃ παρασκευῇ Δωριῆς τε Δωριεῦσι κατὰ τὸ ξυγγενὲς καὶ ἅμα ἄποικοι τοῖς ἐκπέμψασι Πελοποννησίοις[6] βοη-

---

[1] Dodwell's conjecture for Γέλωνος of the MSS.

[2] With EGM and Valla; Hude reads προσγεγενημένοις with the other MSS.

[3] τε after Ἐγεσταίων omitted with three inferior MSS.

[4] Λεοντίνων, Hude deletes, following Classen.

[5] διαφθείροντες, Hude reads διαφθείραντες with Cod. Clarend.

[6] Πελοποννησίοις, Hude deletes, following Cobet.

And again the place was depopulated by Gelon, and was then colonized for the third time by the Geloans.

VI. Such were the nations, Hellenic and barbarian, that inhabited Sicily; and such was the magnitude of the island which the Athenians were bent upon invading. To give the truest explanation, they were eager to attain to empire of the whole of it, but they wished at the same time to have the fair pretext of succouring their own kinsmen and their old allies.[1] But most of all they were instigated by envoys of the Egestaeans who were present and invoked their aid more earnestly than ever. For bordering as they did on the Selinuntians they had got into war with them about certain marriage rights and about disputed territory; and the Selinuntians, bringing in the Syracusans as allies, were pressing them hard in the war both by land and by sea. And so the Egestaeans, reminding the Athenians of their alliance which had been made with the Leontines in the time of Laches and the former war,[2] begged them to send ships to their relief; saying many other things but chiefly this, that if the Syracusans should go unpunished for depopulating Leontini, and by destroying those of their allies that were still left should get the whole of Sicily into their power, there was danger that some time, lending aid with a great force, both as Dorians to Dorians on account of kinship, and at the same time as colonists to the Peloponnesians that had sent them out, they might

416 B.C.

---

[1] Or, reading προσγεγενημένοις,—"the allies they had acquired besides"—the Camarinaeans and Agrigentines (v. iv. 6) and some of the Sicels (III. ciii. 1).

[2] cf. III. lxxxvi. 1.

θήσαντες καὶ τὴν ἐκείνων δύναμιν ξυγκαθέλωσιν·
σῶφρον δ᾽ εἶναι μετὰ τῶν ὑπολοίπων ἔτι ξυμμάχων ἀντέχειν τοῖς Συρακοσίοις, ἄλλως τε καὶ
χρήματα σφῶν παρεξόντων ἐς τὸν πόλεμον ἱκανά.
3 ὧν ἀκούοντες οἱ Ἀθηναῖοι ἐν ταῖς ἐκκλησίαις τῶν
τε Ἐγεσταίων πολλάκις λεγόντων καὶ τῶν ξυνα-
γορευόντων αὐτοῖς ἐψηφίσαντο πρέσβεις πέμψαι
πρῶτον ἐς τὴν Ἔγεσταν περί τε τῶν χρημάτων
σκεψομένους εἰ ὑπάρχει, ὥσπερ φασίν, ἐν τῷ
κοινῷ καὶ ἐν τοῖς ἱεροῖς, καὶ τὰ τοῦ πολέμου ἅμα
πρὸς τοὺς Σελινουντίους ἐν ὅτῳ ἐστὶν εἰσομένους.

VII. Καὶ οἱ μὲν πρέσβεις τῶν Ἀθηναίων ἀπε-
στάλησαν ἐς τὴν Σικελίαν. Λακεδαιμόνιοι δὲ
τοῦ αὐτοῦ χειμῶνος καὶ οἱ ξύμμαχοι πλὴν Κορινθίων στρατεύσαντες ἐς τὴν Ἀργείαν τῆς τε
γῆς ἔτεμον οὐ πολλὴν καὶ σῖτον ἀνεκομίσαντό
τινα ζεύγη κομίσαντες, καὶ ἐς Ὀρνεὰς κατοικί-
σαντες τοὺς Ἀργείων φυγάδας καὶ τῆς ἄλλης
στρατιᾶς παρακαταλιπόντες αὐτοῖς ὀλίγους, καὶ
σπεισάμενοί τινα χρόνον ὥστε μὴ ἀδικεῖν Ὀρνεά-
τας καὶ Ἀργείους τὴν ἀλλήλων, ἀπεχώρησαν τῷ
2 στρατῷ ἐπ᾽ οἴκου. ἐλθόντων δὲ Ἀθηναίων οὐ
πολλῷ ὕστερον ναυσὶ τριάκοντα καὶ ἑξακοσίοις
ὁπλίταις, οἱ Ἀργεῖοι μετὰ τῶν Ἀθηναίων πανστρατιᾷ ἐξελθόντες τοὺς μὲν ἐν Ὀρνεαῖς μίαν
ἡμέραν ἐπολιόρκουν· ὑπὸ δὲ νύκτα, αὐλισαμένου
τοῦ στρατεύματος ἄπωθεν, ἐκδιδράσκουσιν οἱ ἐκ
τῶν Ὀρνεῶν. καὶ τῇ ὑστεραίᾳ οἱ Ἀργεῖοι ὡς
ᾔσθοντο, κατασκάψαντες τὰς Ὀρνεὰς ἀνεχώρησαν
καὶ οἱ Ἀθηναῖοι ὕστερον ταῖς ναυσὶν ἐπ᾽ οἴκου.
3   Καὶ ἐς Μεθώνην τὴν ὅμορον Μακεδονίᾳ ἱππέας

help to pull down the power of the Athenians. It would be wise, therefore, with their allies that were still left, to oppose the Syracusans, especially as the Egestaeans would furnish money sufficient for the war. And the Athenians, hearing in their assemblies these arguments of the Egestaeans and their supporters, who constantly repeated them, voted first to send envoys to Egesta to see whether the money was on hand, as they said, in the treasury and in the temples, and at the same time to ascertain how matters stood with reference to the war with the Selinuntians.

VII. Accordingly the Athenian envoys were despatched to Sicily. But during the same winter the Lacedaemonians and their allies, except the Corinthians, invaded the Argive territory, ravaged a small part of the land and carried off some corn in wagons which they had brought with them; then having settled the Argive fugitives at Orneae, leaving with them also a small body of troops, after they had made a truce for a certain time, on condition that the Orneates and Argives were not to injure one another's land, they went home with the rest of their force. When the Athenians came not long afterwards with thirty ships and six hundred hoplites, the Argives, in company with the Athenians, went out in full force and besieged the garrison at Orneae for a single day; but under cover of night, when the besieging army had bivouacked at a distance, the garrison of Orneae escaped. The next day the Argives, on learning this, razed Orneae to the ground and withdrew, and later the Athenians also went home with their ships.

The Athenians also conveyed by sea some of their

κατὰ θάλασσαν κομίσαντες Ἀθηναῖοι σφῶν τε
αὐτῶν καὶ Μακεδόνων τοὺς παρὰ σφίσι φυγάδας
4 ἐκακούργουν τὴν Περδίκκου. Λακεδαιμόνιοι δὲ
πέμψαντες παρὰ Χαλκιδέας τοὺς ἐπὶ Θρᾴκης,
ἄγοντας πρὸς Ἀθηναίους δεχημέρους σπονδάς,
ξυμπολεμεῖν ἐκέλευον Περδίκκᾳ· οἱ δ' οὐκ ἤθελον.
καὶ ὁ χειμὼν ἐτελεύτα, καὶ ἕκτον καὶ δέκατον
ἔτος τῷ πολέμῳ ἐτελεύτα τῷδε ὃν Θουκυδίδης
ξυνέγραψεν.

VIII. Τοῦ δ' ἐπιγιγνομένου θέρους ἅμα ἦρι οἱ
τῶν Ἀθηναίων πρέσβεις ἧκον ἐκ τῆς Σικελίας
καὶ οἱ Ἐγεσταῖοι μετ' αὐτῶν ἄγοντες ἑξήκοντα
τάλαντα ἀσήμου ἀργυρίου ὡς ἐς ἑξήκοντα ναῦς
μηνὸς μισθόν, ἃς ἔμελλον δεήσεσθαι πέμπειν.
2 καὶ οἱ Ἀθηναῖοι ἐκκλησίαν ποιήσαντες καὶ ἀκούσαντες τῶν τε Ἐγεσταίων καὶ τῶν σφετέρων
πρέσβεων τά τε ἄλλα ἐπαγωγὰ καὶ οὐκ ἀληθῆ,
καὶ περὶ τῶν χρημάτων ὡς εἴη ἕτοιμα ἔν τε τοῖς
ἱεροῖς πολλὰ καὶ ἐν τῷ κοινῷ, ἐψηφίσαντο ναῦς
ἑξήκοντα πέμπειν ἐς Σικελίαν καὶ στρατηγοὺς
αὐτοκράτορας Ἀλκιβιάδην τε τὸν Κλεινίου καὶ
Νικίαν τὸν Νικηράτου καὶ Λάμαχον τὸν Ξενο-
φάνους, βοηθοὺς μὲν Ἐγεσταίοις πρὸς Σελινουντίους, ξυγκατοικίσαι δὲ καὶ Λεοντίνους, ἤν[1] τι
περιγίγνηται αὐτοῖς τοῦ πολέμου, καὶ τἆλλα τὰ
ἐν τῇ Σικελίᾳ πρᾶξαι ὅπῃ ἂν γιγνώσκωσιν ἄριστα
3 Ἀθηναίοις. μετὰ δὲ τοῦτο ἡμέρᾳ πέμπτῃ ἐκκλησία αὖθις ἐγίγνετο, καθ' ὅ τι χρὴ τὴν παρασκευὴν ταῖς ναυσὶ τάχιστα γίγνεσθαι, καὶ τοῖς
στρατηγοῖς, εἴ του προσδέοιντο, ψηφισθῆναι ἐς

---

[1] Hude inserts τε after ἤν.

own cavalry and the Macedonian exiles that were with them to Methone, which borders on Macedonia, and ravaged the country of Perdiccas. And the Lacedaemonians sent to the Chalcidians in Thrace, who were observing a truce renewable every ten days with the Athenians, and urged them to join Perdiccas in the war; but they were unwilling. So the winter ended, and with it the sixteenth year of this war of which Thucydides wrote the history.

VIII. The next year at the opening of spring the Athenian envoys returned from Sicily, and with them the Egestaeans, bringing sixty talents[1] of uncoined silver as a month's pay for sixty ships, which they were to ask the Athenians to send. And the Athenians, calling an assembly and hearing from the Egestaeans and their own envoys other things that were enticing but not true, and that the money was ready in large quantity in the temples and in the treasury, voted to send to Sicily sixty ships, with Alcibiades son of Cleinias, Nicias son of Niceratus, and Lamachus son of Xenophanes as generals with full powers, to aid the Egestaeans against the Selinuntians, and also to join in restoring Leontini, in case they should have any success in the war; and further to settle all other matters in Sicily as they might deem best for the Athenians. But on the fifth day after this a meeting of the assembly was again held, to determine in what way the ships could be equipped most speedily, and in case the generals should need anything further for the

March, 415 B.C.

[1] £12,000, $57,360.

4 τὸν ἔκπλουν. καὶ ὁ Νικίας ἀκούσιος μὲν ᾐρη-
μένος ἄρχειν, νομίζων δὲ τὴν πόλιν οὐκ ὀρθῶς
βεβουλεῦσθαι, ἀλλὰ προφάσει βραχείᾳ καὶ εὐ-
πρεπεῖ τῆς Σικελίας ἁπάσης, μεγάλου ἔργου,
ἐφίεσθαι, παρελθὼν ἀποτρέψαι ἐβούλετο καὶ
παρῄνει τοῖς Ἀθηναίοις τοιάδε.

IX. "'Η μὲν ἐκκλησία περὶ παρασκευῆς τῆς
ἡμετέρας ἥδε ξυνελέγη, καθ' ὅ τι χρὴ ἐς Σικελίαν
ἐκπλεῖν· ἐμοὶ μέντοι δοκεῖ καὶ περὶ αὐτοῦ τούτου
ἔτι χρῆναι σκέψασθαι, εἰ καὶ ἄμεινόν ἐστιν
ἐκπέμπειν τὰς ναῦς, καὶ μὴ οὕτως βραχείᾳ βουλῇ
περὶ μεγάλων πραγμάτων ἀνδράσιν ἀλλοφύλοις
πειθομένους πόλεμον οὐ προσήκοντα αἴρεσθαι.
2 καίτοι ἔγωγε καὶ τιμῶμαι ἐκ τοῦ τοιούτου καὶ
ἧσσον ἑτέρων περὶ τῷ ἐμαυτοῦ σώματι ὀρρωδῶ,
νομίζων ὁμοίως ἀγαθὸν πολίτην εἶναι ὃς ἂν καὶ
τοῦ σώματός τι καὶ τῆς οὐσίας προνοῆται· μάλιστα γὰρ ἂν ὁ τοιοῦτος καὶ τὰ τῆς πόλεως δι'
ἑαυτὸν βούλοιτο ὀρθοῦσθαι. ὅμως δὲ οὔτε ἐν τῷ
πρότερον χρόνῳ διὰ τὸ προτιμᾶσθαι εἶπον παρὰ
γνώμην οὔτε νῦν, ἀλλὰ ἧ ἂν[1] γιγνώσκω βέλτιστα
3 ἐρῶ. καὶ πρὸς μὲν τοὺς τρόπους τοὺς ὑμετέρους
ἀσθενὴς ἄν μου ὁ λόγος εἴη, εἰ τά τε ὑπάρχοντα
σῴζειν παραινοίην καὶ μὴ τοῖς ἑτοίμοις περὶ τῶν
ἀφανῶν καὶ μελλόντων κινδυνεύειν· ὡς δὲ οὔτε ἐν

---

[1] ἀλλὰ ἧ ἂν, with the MSS., Hude adopts ἀλλ' ἧ ἂν from
Reiske and Madvig.

expedition, to vote it for them. And Nicias, who had been elected to the command against his will, and thought the city had not come to a right decision, but that, with a slight and specious pretext, it was the conquest of all Sicily, a great undertaking, at which they aimed, came forward with the purpose of averting this, and advised the Athenians as follows :—

IX. "This assembly was convoked with reference to our armament, to consider in what way we should make the expedition to Sicily; to me, however, it seems that we ought to consider yet again this very question, whether it is best to send the ships at all, and that we ought not, on such slight deliberation about matters of great importance, at the instigation of men of alien race, to undertake a war that does not concern us. And yet from such an enterprise I for my part get honour, and have less dread than others about my life,[1] although I consider that he is quite as good a citizen who takes some forethought for his life and property; for such an one would, for his own sake, be most desirous that the affairs of the city should prosper. But nevertheless neither in the past have I, for the sake of being preferred in honour, spoken contrary to my judgment, nor shall I do so now, but I shall speak just as I deem best. Against tempers, indeed, like yours my words would be unavailing, if I should exhort you to preserve what you have already and not to hazard present possessions for things that are unseen and in the future; that, however, neither is your haste timely,

---

[1] He may have been suffering already from the kidney trouble of which he complained the next summer in his letter to the Athenians (VII. XV. 1).

καιρῷ σπεύδετε οὔτε ῥᾴδιά ἐστι κατασχεῖν ἐφ' ἃ
ὥρμησθε, ταῦτα διδάξω.

Χ. " Φημὶ γὰρ ὑμᾶς πολεμίους πολλοὺς ἐνθάδε
ὑπολιπόντας καὶ ἑτέρους ἐπιθυμεῖν ἐκεῖσε πλεύ-
2 σαντας δεῦρο ἐπαγαγέσθαι. καὶ οἴεσθε ἴσως τὰς
γενομένας ὑμῖν σπονδὰς ἔχειν τι βέβαιον· αἱ
ἡσυχαζόντων μὲν ὑμῶν ὀνόματι σπονδαὶ ἔσονται
(οὕτω γὰρ ἐνθένδε τε ἄνδρες ἔπραξαν αὐτὰ καὶ
ἐκ τῶν ἐναντίων), σφαλέντων δέ που ἀξιόχρεῳ
δυνάμει ταχεῖαν τὴν ἐπιχείρησιν ἡμῖν οἱ ἐχθροὶ
ποιήσονται, οἷς πρῶτον μὲν διὰ ξυμφορῶν ἡ
ξύμβασις καὶ ἐκ τοῦ αἰσχίονος ἢ ἡμῖν κατ'
ἀνάγκην ἐγένετο, ἔπειτα ἐν αὐτῇ ταύτῃ πολλὰ τὰ
3 ἀμφισβητούμενα ἔχομεν. εἰσὶ δ' οἳ οὐδὲ ταύτην
πω τὴν ὁμολογίαν ἐδέξαντο, καὶ οὐχ οἱ ἀσθενέ-
στατοι· ἀλλ' οἱ μὲν ἄντικρυς πολεμοῦσιν, οἱ δὲ
καὶ διὰ τὸ Λακεδαιμονίους ἔτι ἡσυχάζειν δεχη-
4 μέροις σπονδαῖς καὶ αὐτοὶ κατέχονται. τάχα δ'
ἂν ἴσως, εἰ δίχα ἡμῶν τὴν δύναμιν λάβοιεν, ὅπερ
νῦν σπεύδομεν, καὶ πάνυ ἂν ξυνεπίθοιντο μετὰ
Σικελιωτῶν, οὓς πρὸ πολλῶν ἂν ἐτιμήσαντο ξυμ-
5 μάχους γενέσθαι ἐν τῷ πρὶν χρόνῳ. ὥστε χρὴ
σκοπεῖν τινα αὐτὰ καὶ μὴ μετεώρῳ τῇ πόλει ἀξιοῦν
κινδυνεύειν καὶ ἀρχῆς ἄλλης ὀρέγεσθαι πρὶν ἣν
ἔχομεν βεβαιωσώμεθα, εἰ Χαλκιδῆς γε οἱ ἐπὶ
Θρᾴκης, ἔτη τοσαῦτα ἀφεστῶτες ἡμῶν, ἔτι ἀχεί-
ρωτοί εἰσι καὶ ἄλλοι τινὲς κατὰ τὰς ἠπείρους

nor is it easy to attain what you are striving for, this I shall show.

X. "I say, then, that you, leaving behind you many enemies here, are bent upon sailing there and bringing upon you here still other enemies. And you think perhaps that the treaty which has been made affords you some security—a treaty which indeed, as long as you are quiet, will be a treaty in name (for so certain men here and among our enemies have managed these matters); but should you perchance suffer defeat with a considerable force, our foes will be quick to make their attack upon us. For the compact in the first place was concluded by them under compulsion through stress of misfortune and with less credit to them than to us; and, besides, in the compact itself there are many disputed points. There are also some states which have not as yet accepted even this agreement, and these not the weakest; on the contrary, some of them are at open war with us, while others again, merely because the Lacedaemonians still keep quiet, are themselves also kept in restraint by a truce renewable every ten days. But very probably, if they should find our power divided—the very thing we are now so anxious to bring about—they would eagerly join in an attack upon us along with the Siceliots, whose alliance they would heretofore have given much to obtain. And so we must consider these matters and resolve not to run into danger while the state is still amid the waves, and reach out after another empire before we have secured that which we have, seeing that the Chalcidians in Thrace, after so many years of revolt from us, are still unsubdued, while others at various points on

ἐνδοιαστῶς ἀκροῶνται. ἡμεῖς δὲ Ἐγεσταίοις δὴ
οὖσι ξυμμάχοις ὡς ἀδικουμένοις ὀξέως βοηθοῦμεν,
ὑφ᾽ ὧν δ᾽ αὐτοὶ πάλαι ἀφεστώτων ἀδικούμεθα,
ἔτι μέλλομεν ἀμύνεσθαι.

XI. "Καίτοι τοὺς μὲν κατεργασάμενοι κἂν κατά-
σχοιμεν· τῶν δ᾽ εἰ καὶ κρατήσαιμεν, διὰ πολλοῦ γε
καὶ πολλῶν ὄντων χαλεπῶς ἂν ἄρχειν δυναίμεθα.
ἀνόητον δ᾽ ἐπὶ τοιούτους ἰέναι ὧν κρατήσας τε μὴ
κατασχήσει τις καὶ μὴ κατορθώσας μὴ ἐν τῷ ὁμοίῳ
2 καὶ πρὶν ἐπιχειρῆσαι ἔσται. Σικελιῶται δ᾽ ἄν
μοι δοκοῦσιν, ὥς γε νῦν ἔχουσι, καὶ ἔτι ἂν ἧσσον
δεινοὶ ἡμῖν γενέσθαι, εἰ ἄρξειαν αὐτῶν Συρακόσιοι,
ὅπερ οἱ Ἐγεσταῖοι μάλιστα ἡμᾶς ἐκφοβοῦσιν.
3 νῦν μὲν γὰρ κἂν ἔλθοιεν ἴσως Λακεδαιμονίων ἕκαστοι χάριτι, ἐκείνως δ᾽ οὐκ εἰκὸς ἀρχὴν ἐπὶ ἀρχὴν
στρατεῦσαι· ᾧ γὰρ ἂν τρόπῳ τὴν ἡμετέραν μετὰ
Πελοποννησίων ἀφέλωνται, εἰκὸς ὑπὸ τῶν αὐτῶν
καὶ τὴν σφετέραν διὰ τοῦ αὐτοῦ καθαιρεθῆναι.
4 ἡμᾶς δ᾽ ἂν οἱ ἐκεῖ Ἕλληνες μάλιστα μὲν ἐκπεπληγμένοι εἶεν, εἰ μὴ ἀφικοίμεθα, ἔπειτα δὲ καὶ
εἰ δείξαντες τὴν δύναμιν δι᾽ ὀλίγου ἀπέλθοιμεν
(τὰ γὰρ διὰ πλείστου πάντες ἴσμεν θαυμαζόμενα
καὶ τὰ πεῖραν ἥκιστα τῆς δόξης δόντα)· εἰ δὲ
σφαλεῖμέν τι, τάχιστ᾽ ἂν ὑπεριδόντες μετὰ τῶν

the mainland render us a dubious allegiance. But we, it seems, must rush to bring aid to Egestaeans, being, forsooth, our allies, on the ground that they are wronged, while on those by whose revolt we ourselves have long been wronged we still delay to inflict punishment.

XI. "And yet these, if once brought under control, we might also keep under control; but the Siceliots, even if we should get the better of them, we should find it hard to govern, far off as they are and formidable in numbers. But it is folly to go against men when victory will not bring control over them and failure will not leave matters in the same condition as before the attack was made. The Siceliots, moreover, it seems to me, at least as things now stand, would be even less dangerous to us if the Syracusans should acquire rule over them—that prospect with which the Egestaeans especially try to terrify us. For now they might perhaps come against us singly out of regard for the Lacedaemonians, but in the other case,[1] it is not likely that an imperial city would make war against an imperial city; for by whatsoever means they, in concert with the Peloponnesians, might despoil us of our sway, by the same means very likely would their own empire be pulled down by these same Peloponnesians. And as to us, the Hellenes there would be most in awe, first, if we should not come at all; next, if after showing our power we should after a brief interval depart. For it is, as we all know, things that are farthest off and least allow a test of their reputation which excite wonder; but if we should suffer a defeat, they would very quickly

---

[1] i.e. in case the Syracusans acquired sway over them.

5 ἐνθάδε ἐπίθοιντο. ὅπερ νῦν ὑμεῖς, ὦ Ἀθηναῖοι, ἐς
Λακεδαιμονίους καὶ τοὺς ξυμμάχους πεπόνθατε,
διὰ τὸ παρὰ γνώμην αὐτῶν πρὸς ἃ ἐφοβεῖσθε τὸ
πρῶτον περιγεγενῆσθαι καταφρονήσαντες ἤδη καὶ
6 Σικελίας ἐφίεσθε.¹ χρὴ δὲ μὴ πρὸς τὰς τύχας
τῶν ἐναντίων ἐπαίρεσθαι, ἀλλὰ τὰς διανοίας
κρατήσαντας θαρσεῖν, μηδὲ Λακεδαιμονίους ἄλλο
τι ἡγήσασθαι ἢ διὰ τὸ αἰσχρὸν σκοπεῖν ὅτῳ
τρόπῳ ἔτι καὶ νῦν, ἢν δύνωνται, σφήλαντες ἡμᾶς
τὸ σφέτερον ἀπρεπὲς εὖ θήσονται, ὅσῳ καὶ περὶ
πλείστου καὶ διὰ πλείστου δόξαν ἀρετῆς μελε-
7 τῶσιν. ὥστε οὐ περὶ τῶν ἐν Σικελίᾳ Ἐγεσταίων
ἡμῖν, ἀνδρῶν βαρβάρων, ὁ ἀγών, εἰ σωφρονοῦμεν,
ἀλλ᾽ ὅπως πόλιν δι᾽ ὀλιγαρχίας ἐπιβουλεύουσαν
ὀξέως φυλαξόμεθα.

XII. "Καὶ μεμνῆσθαι χρὴ ἡμᾶς ὅτι νεωστὶ
ἀπὸ νόσου μεγάλης καὶ πολέμου βραχύ τι λε-
λωφήκαμεν, ὥστε καὶ χρήμασι καὶ τοῖς σώμασιν
ηὐξῆσθαι· καὶ ταῦτα ὑπὲρ ἡμῶν δίκαιον ἐνθάδε
ἀναλοῦν, καὶ μὴ ὑπὲρ ἀνδρῶν φυγάδων τῶνδε
ἐπικουρίας δεομένων, οἷς τό τε ψεύσασθαι καλῶς
χρήσιμον, καὶ τῷ τοῦ πέλας κινδύνῳ, αὐτοὺς
λόγους μόνον παρασχομένους, ἢ κατορθώσαντας
χάριν μὴ ἀξίαν εἰδέναι ἢ πταίσαντάς που τοὺς
2 φίλους ξυναπολέσαι.² εἴ τέ τις ἄρχειν ἄσμενος
αἱρεθεὶς παραινεῖ ὑμῖν ἐκπλεῖν, τὸ ἑαυτοῦ μόνον

¹ For ἐφίεσθαι of the MSS., after Schol.
² For ξυναπολέσθαι of the MSS., Reiske's correction.

despise us and join our enemies here in attacking us. And just this has been your experience, men of Athens, with regard to the Lacedaemonians and their allies : because you have got the better of them beyond your expectation—in comparison with what you feared at first—you despise them now and aim even at the conquest of Sicily. You have no right, however, to be elated at the misfortunes of your opponents, but only when you have mastered their spirits should you feel confidence ; nor must you believe that the Lacedaemonians, on account of their humiliation, have anything else in view than to discover in what way they may even yet defeat us and retrieve their own dishonour—the more so as they have been in the highest degree and for the longest time courting a reputation for valour. And so the issue before us, if we are prudent, is not the fate of the Egestaeans, a barbaric people in Sicily, but how we shall keep a sharp watch upon a state which is intriguing against us with the devices of oligarchy.

XII. "And we should remember that we have but lately recovered somewhat from a great pestilence and war, so as to recruit our strength both in money and in men ; and these resources it is but right to expend for ourselves here, and not for these fugitives that are begging our aid, whose interest it is to lie cleverly, and, at their neighbour's cost, supplying nothing but words themselves, either, in case of success, to show no proper gratitude, or, in the event of failure, to involve their friends in ruin. And if there be anyone here who, elated at being chosen to command, exhorts you to sail, considering—especially as he is too

σκοπῶν, ἄλλως τε καὶ νεώτερος ὢν ἔτι ἐς τὸ
ἄρχειν, ὅπως θαυμασθῇ μὲν ἀπὸ τῆς ἱπποτροφίας,
διὰ δὲ πολυτέλειαν καὶ ὠφεληθῇ τι ἐκ τῆς ἀρχῆς,
μηδὲ τούτῳ ἐμπαράσχητε τῷ τῆς πόλεως κινδύνῳ
ἰδίᾳ ἐλλαμπρύνεσθαι, νομίσατε δὲ τοὺς τοιούτους
τὰ μὲν δημόσια ἀδικεῖν, τὰ δὲ ἴδια ἀναλοῦν, καὶ
τὸ πρᾶγμα μέγα εἶναι καὶ μὴ οἷον νεωτέρῳ [1]
βουλεύσασθαί τε καὶ ὀξέως μεταχειρίσαι.

XIII. "Οὓς ἐγὼ ὁρῶν νῦν ἐνθάδε τῷ αὐτῷ ἀνδρὶ
παρακελευστοὺς καθημένους φοβοῦμαι, καὶ τοῖς
πρεσβυτέροις ἀντιπαρακελεύομαι μὴ καταισχυν-
θῆναι, εἴ τῳ τις παρακάθηται τῶνδε, ὅπως μὴ
δόξει, ἂν μὴ ψηφίζηται πολεμεῖν, μαλακὸς εἶναι,
μηδ᾽, ὅπερ ἂν αὐτοὶ πάθοιεν, δυσέρωτας εἶναι τῶν
ἀπόντων, γνόντας ὅτι ἐπιθυμίᾳ μὲν ἐλάχιστα
κατορθοῦνται,[2] προνοίᾳ δὲ πλεῖστα, ἀλλ᾽ ὑπὲρ
τῆς πατρίδος, ὡς μέγιστον δὴ τῶν πρὶν κίνδυνον
ἀναρριπτούσης, ἀντιχειροτονεῖν καὶ ψηφίζεσθαι
τοὺς μὲν Σικελιώτας οἷσπερ νῦν ὅροις χρωμένους
πρὸς ἡμᾶς, οὐ μεμπτοῖς, τῷ τε Ἰονίῳ κόλπῳ,
παρὰ γῆν ἤν τις πλέῃ, καὶ τῷ Σικελικῷ, διὰ
πελάγους, τὰ αὑτῶν νεμομένους καθ᾽ αὑτοὺς καὶ
2 ξυμφέρεσθαι· τοῖς δὲ Ἐγεσταίοις ἰδίᾳ εἰπεῖν,
ἐπειδὴ ἄνευ Ἀθηναίων καὶ ξυνῆψαν πρὸς Σελινουντίους τὸ πρῶτον πόλεμον, μετὰ σφῶν αὐτῶν
καὶ καταλύεσθαι· καὶ τὸ λοιπὸν ξυμμάχους μὴ
ποιεῖσθαι, ὥσπερ εἰώθαμεν, οἷς κακῶς μὲν πρά-

---

[1] MSS.; Hude adopts Pluygers' correction, νεωτέρους.
[2] κατορθοῦνται MSS., κατορθοῦται Goeller's conjecture.

young to command—only his own interest, how he
may get admiration for his raising of fine horses,
and then, because that is very expensive, how he
may also get some profit from his command, do not
afford this man, at the cost of the state, opportunity
to make a personal display, but rather consider
that such men damage the public interest while
they waste their own property, and that the matter
is one of great seriousness, and not such as a youth
may decide and rashly take in hand.

XIII. "It is of such youths, when I see them
sitting here in answer to the appeal of this same
man, that I am afraid; and I make a counter-
appeal to the older men, if any of you sit by
one of these, not to be shamed into fear lest
he may seem to be a coward if he do not vote for
war, and not, though that may be *their* feeling, to
have a morbid craving for what is out of reach,
knowing that few successes are won by greed, but
very many by foresight; on the contrary, on behalf
of our country, which is now running the greatest
risk it has ever run, hold up your hands in opposition
and vote that the Siceliots, keeping the same boundaries with respect to us as at present—boundaries
no one can find fault with—namely, the Ionian Sea,
if one sail along the coast, and the Sicilian, if one
cross the open deep—shall enjoy their own possessions and settle their own quarrels among themselves. But tell the Egestaeans in particular that,
as they went to war with the Selinuntians in the
first place without the Athenians, so they must bring
it to an end by themselves; and for the future let
us not make allies, as we are wont to do, whom
we must assist when they fare ill, but from whom

ξασιν ἀμυνοῦμεν, ὠφελίας δ' αὐτοὶ δεηθέντες οὐ τευξόμεθα.

XIV. " Καὶ σύ, ὦ πρύτανι, ταῦτα, εἴπερ ἡγεῖ σοι προσήκειν κήδεσθαί τε τῆς πόλεως καὶ βούλει γενέσθαι πολίτης ἀγαθός, ἐπιψήφιζε καὶ γνώμας προτίθει αὖθις Ἀθηναίοις, νομίσας, εἰ ὀρρωδεῖς τὸ ἀναψηφίσαι, τὸ¹ μὲν λύειν τοὺς νόμους μὴ μετὰ τοσῶνδ' ἂν μαρτύρων αἰτίαν σχεῖν, τῆς δὲ πόλεως βουλευσαμένης² ἰατρὸς ἂν γενέσθαι, καὶ τὸ καλῶς ἄρξαι τοῦτ' εἶναι, ὃς ἂν τὴν πατρίδα ὠφελήσῃ ὡς πλεῖστα ἢ ἑκὼν εἶναι μηδὲν βλάψῃ."

XV. Ὁ μὲν Νικίας τοιαῦτα εἶπεν· τῶν δὲ Ἀθηναίων παριόντες οἱ μὲν πλεῖστοι στρατεύειν παρῄνουν καὶ τὰ ἐψηφισμένα μὴ λύειν, οἱ δέ τινες 2 καὶ ἀντέλεγον. ἐνῆγε δὲ προθυμότατα τὴν στρατείαν Ἀλκιβιάδης ὁ Κλεινίου, βουλόμενος τῷ τε Νικίᾳ ἐναντιοῦσθαι, ὢν καὶ ἐς τὰ ἄλλα διάφορος τὰ πολιτικὰ καὶ ὅτι αὐτοῦ διαβόλως ἐμνήσθη, καὶ μάλιστα στρατηγῆσαί τε ἐπιθυμῶν καὶ ἐλπίζων Σικελίαν τε δι' αὐτοῦ καὶ Καρχηδόνα λήψεσθαι καὶ τὰ ἴδια ἅμα εὐτυχήσας χρήμασί τε καὶ δόξῃ 3 ὠφελήσειν. ὢν γὰρ ἐν ἀξιώματι ὑπὸ τῶν ἀστῶν, ταῖς ἐπιθυμίαις μείζοσιν ἢ κατὰ τὴν ὑπάρχουσαν οὐσίαν ἐχρῆτο ἔς τε τὰς ἱπποτροφίας καὶ τὰς ἄλλας δαπάνας· ὅπερ καὶ καθεῖλεν ὕστερον τὴν 4 τῶν Ἀθηναίων πόλιν οὐχ ἥκιστα. φοβηθέντες γὰρ οἱ πολλοὶ τὸ μέγεθος τῆς τε κατὰ τὸ ἑαυτοῦ σῶμα παρανομίας ἐς τὴν δίαιταν καὶ τῆς διανοίας

¹ τὸ μὲν λύειν, Hude substitutes τοῦ, following van Herwerden.
² βουλευσαμένης, inferior MSS. and the Scholiast κακῶς βουλευσαμένης.

we shall get no help when we are ourselves in need.

XIV. "And do you, Mr. President, if you think it your duty to care for the state and you wish to prove yourself a good citizen, bring these matters again to a vote and lay the question once more before the Athenians. If you fear to put the issue to vote again, reflect that it would involve no guilt to break the law in the presence of so many witnesses, but that you would thus become a physician for the state when it has taken evil counsel; and remember that this is the part of a good governor—to benefit his country as much as possible, or willingly at least to do it no harm."

XV. Thus Nicias spoke. Most of the Athenians that came forward advised the people to make the expedition and not to rescind the vote, while some spoke against it. But most zealous in urging the expedition was Alcibiades son of Cleinias, wishing as he did to oppose Nicias, because, along with their general political disagreement, Nicias had made invidious reference to him,[1] and above all he was eager to be made general and hoped thereby to subdue both Sicily and Carthage, and in case of success to promote at the same time his private interests in wealth as well as in glory. For being held in high esteem by his townsmen, he indulged desires beyond his actual means, in keeping horses as well as in his other expenses. And it was precisely this sort of thing that most of all later destroyed the Athenian state. For the masses, afraid of the greatness of his lawless and sensual self-indulgence in his manner of living, as also of his

[1] cf. ch. xii. 2.

ὧν καθ᾽ ἓν ἕκαστον ἐν ὅτῳ γίγνοιτο ἔπρασσεν, ὡς
τυραννίδος ἐπιθυμοῦντι πολέμιοι καθέστασαν, καὶ
δημοσίᾳ κράτιστα διαθέντι τὰ τοῦ πολέμου ἰδίᾳ
ἕκαστοι τοῖς ἐπιτηδεύμασιν αὐτοῦ ἀχθεσθέντες
καὶ ἄλλοις ἐπιτρέψαντες οὐ διὰ μακροῦ ἔσφηλαν
τὴν πόλιν. τότε δ᾽ οὖν παρελθὼν τοῖς Ἀθηναίοις
παρῄνει τοιάδε.

XVI. "Καὶ προσήκει μοι μᾶλλον ἑτέρων, ὦ
Ἀθηναῖοι, ἄρχειν (ἀνάγκη γὰρ ἐντεῦθεν ἄρξασθαι,
ἐπειδή μου Νικίας καθήψατο), καὶ ἄξιος ἅμα
νομίζω εἶναι. ὧν γὰρ πέρι ἐπιβόητός εἰμι, τοῖς
μὲν προγόνοις μου καὶ ἐμοὶ δόξαν φέρει ταῦτα, τῇ
2 δὲ πατρίδι καὶ ὠφελίαν. οἱ γὰρ Ἕλληνες καὶ
ὑπὲρ δύναμιν μείζω ἡμῶν τὴν πόλιν ἐνόμισαν τῷ
ἐμῷ διαπρεπεῖ τῆς Ὀλυμπίαζε θεωρίας, πρότερον
ἐλπίζοντες αὐτὴν καταπεπολεμῆσθαι, διότι ἅρμα-
τα μὲν ἑπτὰ καθῆκα, ὅσα οὐδείς πω ἰδιώτης πρότερον, ἐνίκησα δὲ καὶ δεύτερος καὶ τέταρτος ἐγε-
νόμην καὶ τἆλλα ἀξίως τῆς νίκης παρεσκευασάμην.
νόμῳ μὲν γὰρ τιμὴ τὰ τοιαῦτα, ἐκ δὲ τοῦ δρωμένου
3 καὶ δύναμις ἅμα ὑπονοεῖται. καὶ ὅσα αὖ ἐν τῇ
πόλει χορηγίαις ἢ ἄλλῳ τῳ λαμπρύνομαι, τοῖς μὲν
ἀστοῖς φθονεῖται φύσει, πρὸς δὲ τοὺς ξένους καὶ

---

[1] Probably 416 B.C.; though Thirlwall assumes 424,
Grote 420.

[2] *i.e.* at the public festivals and especially at dramatic
exhibitions. Choruses were provided by well-to-do public-
spirited citizens, called Choregi, appointed to this duty by
the state, these securing the choristers and their trainers

designs as revealed in every single intrigue in which he was involved, became hostile to him on the ground that he was aiming at a tyranny; and, though publicly he managed the affairs of the war most excellently, in his private life every man had been offended at his practices, and so entrusting the city to other hands after no long time they brought it to ruin. He now came forward and advised the Athenians as follows:—

XVI. "It belongs to me more than to others, Athenians, to have command—for I must needs begin with this, since Nicias has attacked me—and I think, too, that I am worthy to command. For those things for which I am railed at bring glory to my ancestors and myself, as well as advantage to my country. For the Hellenes, who had previously hoped that our state had been exhausted by the war, conceived an idea of its greatness that even transcended its actual power by reason of the magnificence of my display as sacred deputy at Olympia,[1] because I entered seven chariots, a number that no private citizen had ever entered before, and won the first prize and the second and the fourth, and provided everything else in a style worthy of my victory. For by general custom such things do indeed mean honour, and from what is done men also infer power. And again, although whatever display I made in the city, by providing choruses[2] or in any other way, naturally causes jealousy among my townsmen, yet in the eyes of strangers this too gives an impression of

and defraying all their expenses for dress, maintenance and training. As choregi generally vied with each other in bringing out choruses with all possible splendour, such service was costly, sometimes exhausting a man's whole patrimony.

αὕτη ἰσχὺς φαίνεται. καὶ οὐκ ἄχρηστος ἥδ᾽ ἡ
ἄνοια, ὃς ἂν τοῖς ἰδίοις τέλεσι μὴ ἑαυτὸν μόνον,
4 ἀλλὰ καὶ τὴν πόλιν ὠφελῇ, οὐδέ γε ἄδικον ἐφ᾽
ἑαυτῷ μέγα φρονοῦντα μὴ ἴσον εἶναι, ἐπεὶ καὶ ὁ
κακῶς πράσσων πρὸς οὐδένα τῆς ξυμφορᾶς ἰσο-
μοιρεῖ· ἀλλ᾽ ὥσπερ δυστυχοῦντες οὐ προσαγο-
ρευόμεθα, ἐν τῷ ὁμοίῳ τις ἀνεχέσθω καὶ ὑπὸ τῶν
εὐπραγούντων ὑπερφρονούμενος, ἢ τὰ ἴσα νέμων
5 τὰ ὁμοῖα ἀνταξιούτω. οἶδα δὲ τοὺς τοιούτους, καὶ
ὅσοι ἔν τινος λαμπρότητι προέσχον, ἐν μὲν τῷ
κατ᾽ αὐτοὺς βίῳ λυπηροὺς ὄντας, τοῖς ὁμοίοις μὲν
μάλιστα, ἔπειτα δὲ καὶ τοῖς ἄλλοις ξυνόντας, τῶν
δὲ ἔπειτα ἀνθρώπων προσποίησίν τε ξυγγενείας
τισὶ καὶ μὴ οὖσαν καταλιπόντας, καὶ ἧς ἂν ὦσι
πατρίδος, ταύτῃ αὔχησιν, ὡς οὐ περὶ ἀλλοτρίων
οὐδ᾽ ἁμαρτόντων, ἀλλ᾽ ὡς περὶ σφετέρων τε καὶ
6 καλὰ πραξάντων. ὧν ἐγὼ ὀρεγόμενος καὶ διὰ
ταῦτα τὰ ἴδια ἐπιβοώμενος τὰ δημόσια σκοπεῖτε
εἴ του χεῖρον μεταχειρίζω. Πελοποννήσου γὰρ
τὰ δυνατώτατα ξυστήσας ἄνευ μεγάλου ὑμῖν
κινδύνου καὶ δαπάνης Λακεδαιμονίους ἐς μίαν
ἡμέραν κατέστησα ἐν Μαντινείᾳ περὶ τῶν ἁπάντων ἀγωνίσασθαι· ἐξ οὗ καὶ περιγενόμενοι τῇ
μάχῃ οὐδέπω καὶ νῦν βεβαίως θαρσοῦσιν.

XVII. "Καὶ ταῦτα ἡ ἐμὴ νεότης καὶ ἄνοια
παρὰ φύσιν δοκοῦσα εἶναι ἐς τὴν Πελοποννησίων
δύναμιν λόγοις τε πρέπουσιν ὡμίλησε καὶ ὀργῇ

strength. And that is no useless folly, when a man by his private expenditures benefits not himself only but also his state. Nor is it unfair, either, that one who has a high opinion of himself should refuse to be on an equality with others, since he who fares ill finds no one to be an equal participator in his evil plight. On the contrary, just as in misfortune we receive no greetings, in like manner let a man submit even though despised by those who prosper; or else, let him mete out equal measure to all, and then claim the like in turn. I know, however, that men of this stamp, and all others who have in any way stood out as illustrious, are indeed in their own lifetime an offence, most of all to their equals, then also to others, while still among them, but that they leave behind to those who come after the claiming of kinship even where there is none; and, whatever their fatherland, to it they leave exultant pride in them, as men who are not aliens or offenders, but who are their own and have done well. And such being my ambition and these the grounds on which I am decried in my private life, look at my public acts and see whether I execute them worse than another. I brought together the greatest powers[1] of the Peloponnesus without great danger to you or expense and forced the Lacedaemonians to stake all upon a single day at Mantinea[2]; and in consequence of this, though victorious in the field, even yet they have not firm confidence.

XVII. "Thus did my youthfulness and my seemingly abnormal folly cope with the power of the Peloponnesians in fitting words and with a spirit that

[1] Argos, Mantinea and Elis; *cf.* v. xlvi., lii.
[2] *cf.* v. lxvi. ff.

πίστιν παρασχομένη ἔπεισε· καὶ νῦν μὴ πεφό-
βησθε αὐτήν, ἀλλ' ἕως ἐγώ τε ἔτι ἀκμάζω μετ'
αὐτῆς καὶ ὁ Νικίας εὐτυχὴς δοκεῖ εἶναι, ἀποχρή-
2 σασθε τῇ ἑκατέρου ἡμῶν ὠφελίᾳ. καὶ τὸν ἐς τὴν
Σικελίαν πλοῦν μὴ μεταγιγνώσκετε ὡς ἐπὶ μεγάλην δύναμιν ἐσόμενον. ὄχλοις τε γὰρ ξυμμείκτοις
πολυανδροῦσιν αἱ πόλεις καὶ ῥᾳδίας ἔχουσι τῶν
3 πολιτῶν¹ τὰς μεταβολὰς καὶ ἐπιδοχάς· καὶ οὐδεὶς
δι' αὐτὸ ὡς περὶ οἰκείας πατρίδος οὔτε τὰ περὶ τὸ
σῶμα ὅπλοις ἐξήρτυται οὔτε τὰ ἐν τῇ χώρᾳ μονί-
μοις² κατασκευαῖς, ὅ τι δὲ ἕκαστος ἢ ἐκ τοῦ
λέγων πείθειν οἴεται ἢ στασιάζων ἀπὸ τοῦ κοινοῦ
λαβὼν ἄλλην γῆν, μὴ κατορθώσας, οἰκήσειν, ταῦτα
4 ἑτοιμάζεται. καὶ οὐκ εἰκὸς τὸν τοιοῦτον ὅμιλον
οὔτε λόγου μιᾷ γνώμῃ ἀκροᾶσθαι οὔτε ἐς τὰ ἔργα
κοινῶς τρέπεσθαι· ταχὺ δ' ἂν ὡς ἕκαστοι, εἴ τι
καθ' ἡδονὴν λέγοιτο, προσχωροῖεν, ἄλλως τε καὶ
5 εἰ στασιάζουσιν, ὥσπερ πυνθανόμεθα. καὶ μὴν
οὐδ' ὁπλῖται οὔτ' ἐκείνοις ὅσοιπερ κομποῦνται,
οὔτε οἱ ἄλλοι Ἕλληνες διεφάνησαν τοσοῦτοι ὄντες
ὅσους ἕκαστοι σφᾶς αὐτοὺς ἠρίθμουν, ἀλλὰ μέγιστον δὴ αὐτοὺς ἐψευσμένη ἡ Ἑλλὰς μόλις ἐν
6 τῷδε τῷ πολέμῳ ἱκανῶς ὡπλίσθη. τά τε οὖν ἐκεῖ
ἐξ ὧν ἐγὼ ἀκοῇ αἰσθάνομαι τοιαῦτα καὶ ἔτι εὐπο-

¹ With E, the rest of the MSS. πολιτειῶν.
² Hude adopts νομίμοις, Dukas' conjecture, which is supported by the Schol., who explains νομίμοις by οὐ ταῖς
νομιζομέναις, ἀλλὰ ταῖς ἱκαναῖς· οὕτω καὶ νόμιμον ῥήτορα τὸν
ἱκανὸν καὶ νόμιμον ἀθλητὴν φαμεν.

inspired faith win assent. And now be not afraid of
it, but while I am still in the flower of youth, and
Nicias has the reputation of good luck, make the
most of the services of us both. And as to the
voyage to Sicily, do not change your minds on
the ground that you are going against a formidable
power. For it is only with a mixed rabble that the
cities there [1] are populous, and changes and acces-
sions in the body of their citizens [2] are easy. And
for this reason no one is equipped, as he would be
in behalf of his own country, either with arms for
personal protection or with permanent improvements
for the cultivation of his land; but whatever each
one thinks he can obtain from the common stock by
persuasive oratory or by sedition, in the expectation
that if he fails he will settle in some other land, this
he provides himself with. And it is not likely that a
rabble of this kind would either listen to counsel with
one mind or turn to action with a common purpose;
but quickly, if anything were said to please them, [3]
they would each for himself come over to our side,
especially if they are in a state of revolution as we
hear. Further, as regards hoplites neither have
they as many as they boast; nor have the rest of the
Hellenes proved to have such numbers as they each
reckon; on the contrary, Hellas has been very
greatly deceived in its estimates of hoplites and in this
war has with difficulty been adequately equipped with
them. Such, then, is the situation in Sicily, to judge
from what I learn by report, and it is likely to be

[1] Referring to Syracuse and its dependencies.
[2] Or, reading πολιτειῶν, "changes in old forms of government and adoption of new."
[3] *i.e.* by Athenian representatives.

ρώτερα ἔσται (βαρβάρους [1] γὰρ πολλοὺς ἕξομεν
οἳ Συρακοσίων μίσει ξυνεπιθήσονται αὐτοῖς), καὶ
τὰ ἐνθάδε οὐκ ἐπικωλύσει, ἢν ὑμεῖς ὀρθῶς βουλεύ-
7 ησθε. οἱ γὰρ πατέρες ἡμῶν τοὺς αὐτοὺς τούτους
οὕσπερ νῦν φασι πολεμίους ὑπολιπόντας ἂν ἡμᾶς
πλεῖν καὶ προσέτι τὸν Μῆδον ἐχθρὸν ἔχοντες τὴν
ἀρχὴν ἐκτήσαντο, οὐκ ἄλλῳ τινὶ ἢ τῇ περιουσίᾳ
8 τοῦ ναυτικοῦ ἰσχύοντες. καὶ νῦν οὔτε ἀνέλπιστοί
πω μᾶλλον Πελοποννήσιοι ἐς ἡμᾶς ἐγένοντο, εἴ
τε καὶ πάνυ ἔρρωνται, τὸ μὲν ἐς τὴν γῆν ἡμῶν
ἐσβάλλειν, κἂν μὴ ἐκπλεύσωμεν, ἱκανοί εἰσι, τῷ
δὲ ναυτικῷ οὐκ ἂν δύναιντο βλάπτειν· ὑπόλοιπον
γὰρ ἡμῖν ἐστιν ἀντίπαλον ναυτικόν.

XVIII. "Ὥστε τί ἂν λέγοντες εἰκὸς ἢ αὐτοὶ
ἀποκνοῖμεν ἢ πρὸς τοὺς ἐκεῖ ξυμμάχους σκηπτό-
μενοι μὴ βοηθοῖμεν; οἷς χρεών, ἐπειδή γε καὶ
ξυνωμόσαμεν, ἐπαμύνειν καὶ μὴ ἀντιτιθέναι ὅτι
οὐδὲ ἐκεῖνοι ἡμῖν. οὐ γὰρ ἵνα δεῦρο ἀντιβοηθῶσι
προσεθέμεθα αὐτούς, ἀλλ' ἵνα τοῖς ἐκεῖ ἐχθροῖς
ἡμῶν λυπηροὶ ὄντες δεῦρο κωλύωσιν αὐτοὺς ἐπ-
2 ιέναι. τήν τε ἀρχὴν οὕτως ἐκτησάμεθα καὶ ἡμεῖς
καὶ ὅσοι δὴ ἄλλοι ἦρξαν, παραγιγνόμενοι προθύμως
τοῖς αἰεὶ ἢ βαρβάροις ἢ Ἕλλησιν ἐπικαλουμένοις,
ἐπεί, εἴ γε ἡσυχάζοιμεν πάντες [2] ἢ φυλοκρινοῖμεν
οἷς χρεὼν βοηθεῖν, βραχὺ ἄν τι προσκτώμενοι
αὐτῇ περὶ αὐτῆς ἂν ταύτης μᾶλλον κινδυνεύοιμεν.
τὸν γὰρ προύχοντα οὐ μόνον ἐπιόντα τις ἀμύνεται,
ἀλλὰ καὶ ὅπως μὴ [3] ἔπεισι προκαταλαμβάνει.

---

[1] τε of the MSS. after βαρβάρους bracketed by Haacke.
[2] πάντες, Hude emends the MSS. reading to πάντως.
[3] Transposing μὴ ὅπως of the MSS., after Krüger.

still more easy to deal with—for we shall have many
barbarians, who from hatred of the Syracusans will
join us in attacking them; and matters here will be
no actual hindrance, if you are rightly advised. For
our fathers had as enemies these same men whom,
as they say, you would be leaving behind if you
should sail thither, and the Persian besides as a foe,
yet acquired their empire without being strong in
anything else than in the superiority of their fleet.
As for the present, never were the Peloponnesians
more hopeless against us; and let them be never so
confident, they can invade us only by land—and that
they can do even if we do not make this expedition;
but with their fleet they cannot hurt us, for we have
in reserve a fleet that is a match for them.

XVIII. "On what reasonable plea, then, can we
hold back ourselves, or make excuse to our allies
there for refusing to aid them ? We ought to assist
them, especially as we have actually sworn to do so,
and may not object that they did not help us, either.
For we took them into our alliance, not that they
might bring aid here, but in order that by annoying
our enemies there they might hinder them from
coming hither against us. It was in this way that
we acquired our empire—both we and all others that
have ever won empire—by coming zealously to the
aid of those, whether barbarians or Hellenes, who
have at any time appealed to us; whereas, if we
should all keep quiet or draw distinctions of race as
to whom we ought to assist, we should add but little
to our empire and should rather run a risk of losing
that empire itself. For against a superior one does
not merely defend oneself when he attacks, but even
takes precaution that he shall not attack at all.

3 καὶ οὐκ ἔστιν ἡμῖν ταμιεύεσθαι ἐς ὅσον βουλόμεθα
ἄρχειν, ἀλλὰ ἀνάγκη, ἐπειδήπερ ἐν τῷδε καθέ-
σταμεν, τοῖς μὲν ἐπιβουλεύειν, τοὺς δὲ μὴ ἀνιέναι,
διὰ τὸ ἀρχθῆναι ἂν ὑφ' ἑτέρων αὐτοῖς κίνδυνον
εἶναι, εἰ μὴ αὐτοὶ ἄλλων ἄρχοιμεν. καὶ οὐκ ἐκ
τοῦ αὐτοῦ ἐπισκεπτέον ὑμῖν τοῖς ἄλλοις τὸ ἥσυχον,
εἰ μὴ καὶ τὰ ἐπιτηδεύματα ἐς τὸ ὁμοῖον μεταλή-
ψεσθε.

4 "Λογισάμενοι οὖν τάδε μᾶλλον αὐξήσειν, ἐπ'
ἐκεῖνα ἢν ἴωμεν, ποιώμεθα τὸν πλοῦν, ἵνα Πελοποννησίων τε στορέσωμεν τὸ φρόνημα, εἰ δόξομεν
ὑπεριδόντες τὴν ἐν τῷ παρόντι ἡσυχίαν καὶ ἐπὶ
Σικελίαν πλεῦσαι, καὶ ἅμα ἢ τῆς Ἑλλάδος, τῶν
ἐκεῖ προσγενομένων, πάσης τῷ εἰκότι ἄρξωμεν, ἢ
κακώσωμέν γε Συρακοσίους, ἐν ᾧ καὶ αὐτοὶ καὶ
5 οἱ ξύμμαχοι ὠφελησόμεθα. τὸ δὲ ἀσφαλές, καὶ
μένειν, ἤν τι προχωρῇ, καὶ ἀπελθεῖν, αἱ νῆες παρέ-
ξουσιν· ναυκράτορες γὰρ ἐσόμεθα καὶ ξυμπάντων
6 Σικελιωτῶν. καὶ μὴ ὑμᾶς ἡ Νικίου τῶν λόγων
ἀπραγμοσύνη καὶ διάστασις τοῖς νέοις ἐς τοὺς
πρεσβυτέρους ἀποτρέψῃ, τῷ δὲ εἰωθότι κόσμῳ,
ὥσπερ καὶ οἱ πατέρες ἡμῶν ἅμα νέοι γεραιτέροις
βουλεύοντες ἐς τάδε ἦραν αὐτά, καὶ νῦν τῷ αὐτῷ
τρόπῳ πειρᾶσθε προαγαγεῖν τὴν πόλιν, καὶ νομί-

---

[1] The other Hellenic states, it would seem, were preaching
the doctrine of non-interference or self-determination;
Athens, according to Alcibiades, cannot accept this doctrine

And it is not possible for us to exercise a careful
stewardship of the limits we would set to our empire;
but, since we are placed in this position, it is necessary to plot against some and not let go our hold
upon others, because there is a danger of coming
ourselves under the empire of others, should we not
ourselves hold empire over other peoples. And you
cannot regard a pacific policy in the same light as
other states might, unless you will change your practices also to correspond with theirs.[1]

"Calculating, then, that we shall rather strengthen
our power here if we go over there, let us make the
voyage, that we may lay low the haughty spirit of the
Peloponnesians, as we shall if we let men see that in
contempt of our present peaceful condition[2] we even
sail against Sicily; and that we may, at the same
time, either acquire empire over all Hellas, as in all
probability we shall, when the Hellenes there have
been added to us, or may at least cripple the Syracusans, whereby both ourselves and our allies will
be benefited. And as to safety—both to remain,
if things go well, and to come away—our ships will
provide that; for we shall be masters of the sea even
against all the Siceliots combined. And let not the
policy of inaction that Nicias proposes, or his putting
the younger at variance with the older men, divert
you from your purpose; but in our usual good order,
just as our fathers, young men taking counsel
with older men, raised our power to its present
height, do you now also in the same way strive to

without accepting the consequences and relinquishing her
empire.

[2] Which was in reality an armed truce renewable every
ten days.

σατε νεότητα μὲν καὶ γῆρας ἄνευ ἀλλήλων μηδὲν
δύνασθαι, ὁμοῦ δὲ τό τε φαῦλον καὶ τὸ μέσον καὶ
τὸ πάνυ ἀκριβὲς ἂν ξυγκραθὲν μάλιστ᾽ ἂν ἰσχύειν,
καὶ τὴν πόλιν, ἂν μὲν ἡσυχάζῃ, τρίψεσθαί τε
αὐτὴν περὶ αὑτὴν ὥσπερ καὶ ἄλλο τι, καὶ πάντων
τὴν ἐπιστήμην ἐγγηράσεσθαι, ἀγωνιζομένην δὲ
αἰεὶ προσλήψεσθαί τε τὴν ἐμπειρίαν καὶ τὸ ἀμύνεσθαι οὐ λόγῳ ἀλλ᾽ ἔργῳ μᾶλλον ξύνηθες ἕξειν.
7 παράπαν τε γιγνώσκω πόλιν μὴ ἀπράγμονα τά-
χιστ᾽ ἄν μοι δοκεῖν ἀπραγμοσύνης μεταβολῇ
διαφθαρῆναι, καὶ τῶν ἀνθρώπων ἀσφαλέστατα
τούτους οἰκεῖν οἳ ἂν τοῖς παροῦσιν ἤθεσι καὶ
νόμοις, ἢν καὶ χείρω ᾖ, ἥκιστα διαφόρως πολι-
τεύωσιν."

XIX. Τοιαῦτα δὲ ὁ Ἀλκιβιάδης εἶπεν. οἱ δ᾽
Ἀθηναῖοι ἀκούσαντες ἐκείνου τε καὶ τῶν Ἐγεσταίων καὶ Λεοντίνων φυγάδων, οἳ παρελθόντες ἐδέ-
οντό τε καὶ τῶν ὁρκίων ὑπομιμνήσκοντες ἱκέτευον
βοηθῆσαι σφίσι, πολλῷ μᾶλλον ἢ πρότερον ὥρ-
2 μηντο στρατεύειν. καὶ ὁ Νικίας γνοὺς ὅτι ἀπὸ μὲν
τῶν αὐτῶν λόγων οὐκ ἂν ἔτι ἀποτρέψειε, παρασκευῆς δὲ πλήθει, εἰ πολλὴν ἐπιτάξειε, τάχ᾽ ἂν
μεταστήσειεν αὐτούς, παρελθὼν αὐτοῖς αὖθις ἔλεγε
τοιάδε.

XX. "Ἐπειδὴ πάντως ὁρῶ ὑμᾶς, ὦ Ἀθηναῖοι,
ὡρμημένους στρατεύειν, ξυνενέγκοι μὲν ταῦτα ὡς
βουλόμεθα, ἐπὶ δὲ τῷ παρόντι ἃ γιγνώσκω σημανῶ.
2 ἐπὶ γὰρ πόλεις, ὡς ἐγὼ ἀκοῇ αἰσθάνομαι, μέλλομεν ἰέναι μεγάλας καὶ οὔθ᾽ ὑπηκόους ἀλλήλων
οὐδὲ δεομένας μεταβολῆς, ᾗ ἂν ἐκ βιαίου τις δουλείας ἄσμενος ἐς ῥᾴω μετάστασιν χωροίη, οὔτ᾽ ἂν
τὴν ἀρχὴν τὴν ἡμετέραν εἰκότως ἀντ᾽ ἐλευθερίας

advance the state. And consider that youth and age without one another avail nothing, but that the simple, the mediocre, and the very subtle tempered together will have most strength; and that the state, if she remain at peace, will, like anything else, wear herself out upon herself, and her skill in all pursuits will grow old; whereas, if she is continually at conflict, she will always be adding to her experience, and will acquire more, not in word but in deed, the habit of defending herself. In short, I declare that a state which is accustomed to activity would very quickly be ruined by a change to inactivity; and that those men live most securely whose political action is least at variance with existing habits and institutions, even when these are not the best."

XIX. Thus Alcibiades spoke. After hearing him and the Egestaeans and some Leontine exiles, who coming forward, besought them and implored them for succour, reminding them of their oaths, the Athenians were far more eager for the expedition than before. And Nicias, seeing that he could no longer deter them with the same arguments, but thinking that by the magnitude of the armament, if he insisted upon a large one, he might possibly change their minds, came forward and spoke as follows:

XX. "Since I see, men of Athens, that you are wholly bent upon the expedition, I pray that these matters may turn out as we wish; for the present juncture, however, I will show what my judgment is. The cities we are about to attack are, as I learn by report, large, and neither subject to one another nor in need of any such change as a person might be happy to accept in order to escape from enforced servitude to an easier condition, nor likely to accept our rule in

προσδεξαμένας, τό τε πλῆθος, ὡς ἐν μιᾷ νήσῳ,
3 πολλὰς τὰς Ἑλληνίδας. πλὴν γὰρ Νάξου καὶ
Κατάνης, ἃς ἐλπίζω ἡμῖν κατὰ τὸ Λεοντίνων ξυγγενὲς προσέσεσθαι, ἄλλαι εἰσὶν ἑπτά, καὶ παρε-
σκευασμέναι τοῖς πᾶσιν ὁμοιοτρόπως μάλιστα τῇ
ἡμετέρᾳ δυνάμει, καὶ οὐχ ἥκιστα ἐπὶ ἃς μᾶλλον
4 πλέομεν, Σελινοῦς καὶ Συράκουσαι. πολλοὶ μὲν
γὰρ ὁπλῖται ἔνεισι καὶ τοξόται καὶ ἀκοντισταί,
πολλαὶ δὲ τριήρεις καὶ ὄχλος ὁ πληρώσων αὐτάς.
χρήματά τ᾽ ἔχουσι, τὰ μὲν ἴδια, τὰ δὲ καὶ ἐν τοῖς
ἱεροῖς ἔστι Σελινουντίοις· Συρακοσίοις δὲ καὶ ἀπὸ
βαρβάρων τινῶν ἀπ᾽ ἀρχῆς φέρεται.[1] ᾧ δὲ μάλιστα
ἡμῶν προύχουσιν, ἵππους τε πολλοὺς κέκτηνται
καὶ σίτῳ οἰκείῳ καὶ οὐκ ἐπακτῷ χρῶνται.

XXI. "Πρὸς οὖν τοιαύτην δύναμιν οὐ ναυ-
τικῆς καὶ φαύλου στρατιᾶς μόνον δεῖ, ἀλλὰ καὶ
πεζὸν πολὺν ξυμπλεῖν, εἴπερ βουλόμεθα ἄξιον τῆς
διανοίας δρᾶν καὶ μὴ ὑπὸ ἱππέων πολλῶν εἴργε-
σθαι τῆς γῆς, ἄλλως τε καὶ εἰ ξυστῶσιν αἱ πόλεις
φοβηθεῖσαι καὶ μὴ ἀντιπαράσχωσιν ἡμῖν φίλοι
τινὲς γενόμενοι ἄλλοι ἢ Ἐγεσταῖοι ᾧ ἀμυνούμεθα
2 ἱππικόν· αἰσχρὸν δὲ βιασθέντας ἀπελθεῖν ἢ ὕστερον ἐπιμεταπέμπεσθαι τὸ πρῶτον ἀσκέπτως βου-
λευσαμένους. αὐτόθεν δὲ [2] παρασκευῇ ἀξιόχρεῳ
ἐπιέναι, γνόντας ὅτι πολύ τε ἀπὸ τῆς ἡμετέρας

---

[1] ἀπ᾽ ἀρχῆς φέρεται, the reading of G (adopted by some of
the best editors), for ἀπαρχῆς φέρεται ABCEFM, ἀπαρχὴ
ἐσφέρεται vulg.

[2] Understanding δεῖ from § 1, which Hude inserts with
van Herwerden and Madvig.

place of liberty; and the number is large, for a single island, of cities of Hellenic origin. For except Naxos and Catana, which I expect will side with us on account of their kinship to the Leontines, there are seven others;[1] and these are equipped with everything in a style very like to our own armament, and not least those against which our expedition is more immediately directed, Selinus and Syracuse. For they can supply many hoplites, archers and javelin-men, and possess many triremes and a multitude of men to man them. They have wealth, too, partly in private possession and partly in the temples at Selinus; and to the Syracusans tribute has come in from time immemorial from certain barbarians also; but their chief advantage over us is in the fact that they have many horses, and use grain that is home-grown and not imported.

XXI. "To cope with such a power we need not only a naval armament of such insignificant size, but also that a large force for use on land should accompany the expedition, if we would accomplish anything worthy of our design and not be shut out from the land by their numerous cavalry; especially if the cities become terrified and stand together, and some of the others, besides Egesta, do not become our friends and supply us cavalry with which to defend ourselves against that of the enemy. And it would be shameful to be forced to return home, or later to send for fresh supplies, because we had made our plans at first without due consideration. So we must start from home with an adequate armament, realizing that we are about to sail, not only far from our

[1] Syracuse, Selinus, Gela, Agrigentum, Messene, Himera, Camarina (Schol.).

αὐτῶν μέλλομεν πλεῖν καὶ οὐκ ἐν τῷ ὁμοίῳ στρα
τευσόμενοι καὶ ¹ εἰ τοῖς τῇδε ὑπηκόοις ξύμμαχοι
ἤλθετε ἐπί τινα, ὅθεν ῥᾴδιαι αἱ κομιδαὶ ἐκ τῆς
φιλίας ὧν προσέδει, ἀλλὰ ἐς ἀλλοτρίαν πᾶσαν
ἀπαρτήσαντες,² ἐξ ἧς μηνῶν οὐδὲ τεσσάρων τῶν
χειμερινῶν ἄγγελον ῥᾴδιον ἐλθεῖν.

XXII. "Ὁπλίτας τε οὖν πολλούς μοι δοκεῖ
χρῆναι ἡμᾶς ἄγειν καὶ ἡμῶν αὐτῶν καὶ τῶν
ξυμμάχων, τῶν τε ὑπηκόων καὶ ἤν τινα ἐκ Πελο
ποννήσου δυνώμεθα ἢ πεῖσαι ἢ μισθῷ προσαγα
γέσθαι, καὶ τοξότας πολλοὺς καὶ σφενδονήτας,
ὅπως πρὸς τὸ ἐκείνων ἱππικὸν ἀντέχωσι, ναυσί
τε καὶ πολὺ περιεῖναι, ἵνα καὶ τὰ ἐπιτήδεια ῥᾶον
ἐσκομιζώμεθα, τὸν δὲ καὶ αὐτόθεν σῖτον ἐν ὁλκάσι,
πυροὺς καὶ πεφρυγμένας κριθάς, ἄγειν καὶ σιτο
ποιοὺς ἐκ τῶν μυλώνων πρὸς μέρος ἠναγκασμένους
ἐμμίσθους, ἵνα, ἤν που ὑπὸ ἀπλοίας ἀπολαμ
βανώμεθα, ἔχῃ ἡ στρατιὰ τὰ ἐπιτήδεια (πολλὴ
γὰρ οὖσα οὐ πάσης ἔσται πόλεως ὑποδέξασθαι),
τά τε ἄλλα ὅσον δυνατὸν ἑτοιμάσασθαι καὶ μὴ
ἐπὶ ἑτέροις γίγνεσθαι, μάλιστα δὲ χρήματα αὐτό
θεν ὡς πλεῖστα ἔχειν. τὰ δὲ παρ' Ἐγεσταίων,
ἃ λέγεται ἐκεῖ ἕτοιμα, νομίσατε καὶ λόγῳ ἂν
μάλιστα ἕτοιμα εἶναι.

XXIII. "Ἢν γὰρ αὐτοὶ ἔλθωμεν ἐνθένδε μὴ
ἀντίπαλον μόνον παρασκευασάμενοι, πλήν γε πρὸς
τὸ μάχιμον αὐτῶν τὸ ὁπλιτικόν, ἀλλὰ καὶ ὑπερ-

---

¹ καὶ εἰ for καὶ οὐκ ἐν of the MSS., with Classen.
² ἀπαρτήσαντες, with ABF and Schol. (ἀντὶ τοῦ ἀπαρτηθέντες,
ἀπελθόντες), ἀπαρτήσοντες CEM.

224

own land, but also on a campaign that will be carried on under no such conditions as if you had gone against an enemy as allies of your subject-states over here, where it would be easy to get whatever further supplies you needed from the friendly territory; nay, you will have removed into an utterly alien land, from which during the winter it is not easy for a messenger to come even in four months.

XXII. "And so it seems to me that we ought to take hoplites in large numbers, both of our own and of our allies, and from our subjects, as well as any from the Peloponnesus that we can attract by pay or persuade; many bowmen, and also slingers, in order that they may withstand the cavalry of the enemy. And in ships we must have a decided superiority, in order that we may bring in our supplies more easily. And we must also take with us in merchantmen the grain in our stores here, wheat and parched barley, together with bakers requisitioned for pay from the mills in proportion to their size, in order that, if perchance we be detained by stress of weather, the army may have supplies. For the force will be large, and it will not be every city that can receive it. And all other things so far as possible we must get ready for ourselves, and not come to be at the mercy of the Siceliots; but we must especially have from here as much money as possible; for as to that of the Egestaeans, which is reported to be ready there, you may assume that it is indeed chiefly by report that it will ever be ready.

XXIII. "For if we go from here provided with an equipment of our own that is not only equal to theirs —except indeed as regards their fighting troops of heavy-armed men—but that even surpasses it in all

THUCYDIDES

βάλλοντες τοῖς πᾶσι, μόλις οὕτως οἷοί τε ἐσόμεθα
2 τῶν μὲν κρατεῖν, τὰ δὲ καὶ διασῶσαι. πόλιν τε
νομίσαι χρὴ ἐν ἀλλοφύλοις καὶ πολεμίοις οἰκι-
οῦντας ἰέναι, οὓς πρέπει τῇ πρώτῃ ἡμέρᾳ ᾗ ἂν
κατάσχωσιν εὐθὺς κρατεῖν τῆς γῆς ἢ εἰδέναι ὅτι,
3 ἢν σφάλλωνται, πάντα πολέμια ἕξουσιν. ὅπερ
ἐγὼ φοβούμενος καὶ εἰδὼς πολλὰ μὲν ἡμᾶς δέον εὖ
βουλεύσασθαι, ἔτι δὲ πλείω εὐτυχῆσαι, χαλεπὸν
δὲ ἀνθρώπους ὄντας, ὅτι ἐλάχιστα τῇ τύχῃ παρα-
δοὺς ἐμαυτὸν βούλομαι ἐκπλεῖν, παρασκευῇ δὲ
4 ἀπὸ τῶν εἰκότων ἀσφαλής.[1] ταῦτα γὰρ τῇ τε
ξυμπάσῃ πόλει βεβαιότατα ἡγοῦμαι καὶ ἡμῖν τοῖς
στρατευσομένοις σωτήρια. εἰ δέ τῳ ἄλλως δοκεῖ,
παρίημι αὐτῷ τὴν ἀρχήν."

XXIV. Ὁ μὲν Νικίας τοσαῦτα εἶπε, νομίζων
τοὺς Ἀθηναίους τῷ πλήθει τῶν πραγμάτων ἢ
ἀποτρέψειν ἤ, εἰ ἀναγκάζοιτο στρατεύεσθαι, μά-
2 λιστ' ἂν οὕτως ἀσφαλῶς ἐκπλεῦσαι. οἱ δὲ τὸ μὲν
ἐπιθυμοῦν τοῦ πλοῦ οὐκ ἐξῃρέθησαν ὑπὸ τοῦ
ὀχλώδους τῆς παρασκευῆς, πολὺ δὲ μᾶλλον ὥρμηντο καὶ τοὐναντίον περιέστη αὐτῷ· εὖ τε γὰρ
παραινέσαι ἔδοξε καὶ ἀσφάλεια νῦν δὴ καὶ πολλὴ
3 ἔσεσθαι. καὶ ἔρως ἐνέπεσε τοῖς πᾶσιν ὁμοίως
ἐκπλεῦσαι, τοῖς μὲν γὰρ πρεσβυτέροις ὡς ἢ κατα-
στρεψομένοις ἐφ' ἃ ἔπλεον ἢ οὐδὲν ἂν σφαλεῖσαν
μεγάλην δύναμιν, τοῖς δ' ἐν τῇ ἡλικίᾳ τῆς τε ἀπού-

---

[1] ἐκπλεῦσαι of the MSS., after ἀσφαλής, deleted by
Krüger.

226

respects, scarcely even so shall we be able to conquer
Sicily or indeed to preserve our own army. It is, in
fact, as you must believe, a city that we are going
forth to found amid alien and hostile peoples, and it
behooves men in such an enterprise to be at once,
on the very day they land, masters of the soil, or
at least to know that, if they fail in this, everything
will be hostile to them. Fearing, then, this very
result, and knowing that to succeed we must have
been wise in planning to a large extent, but to a
still larger extent must have good fortune—a difficult
thing, as we are but men—I wish, when I set sail,
to have committed myself as little as possible to
fortune, but so far as preparation is concerned to be,
in all human probability, safe. For these precautions
I regard as not only surest for the whole state but
also as safeguards for us who are to go on the
expedition. But if it seem otherwise to anyone, I
yield the command to him."

XXIV. So much Nicias said, thinking that he
would deter the Athenians by the multitude of his
requirements, or, if he should be forced to make the
expedition, he would in this way set out most safely.
They, however, were not diverted from their eagerness for the voyage by reason of the burdensomeness
of the equipment, but were far more bent upon it;
and the result was just the opposite of what he had
expected; for it seemed to them that he had given
good advice, and that now certainly there would be
abundant security. And upon all alike there fell an
eager desire to sail—upon the elders, from a belief
that they would either subdue the places they were
sailing against, or that at any rate a great force could
suffer no disaster; upon those in the flower of their

σης πόθῳ ὄψεως καὶ θεωρίας, καὶ εὐέλπιδες ὄντες
σωθήσεσθαι, ὁ δὲ πολὺς ὅμιλος καὶ στρατιώτης
ἔν τε τῷ παρόντι ἀργύριον οἴσειν καὶ προσκτήσε-
σθαι δύναμιν ὅθεν ἀίδιον μισθοφορὰν ὑπάρξειν.
4 ὥστε διὰ τὴν ἄγαν τῶν πλειόνων ἐπιθυμίαν, εἴ τῳ
ἄρα καὶ μὴ ἤρεσκε, δεδιὼς μὴ ἀντιχειροτονῶν
κακόνους δόξειεν εἶναι τῇ πόλει ἡσυχίαν ἦγεν.

XXV. Καὶ τέλος παρελθών τις τῶν Ἀθηναίων
καὶ παρακαλέσας τὸν Νικίαν οὐκ ἔφη χρῆναι
προφασίζεσθαι οὐδὲ διαμέλλειν, ἀλλ᾽ ἐναντίον
ἁπάντων ἤδη λέγειν ἥντινα αὐτῷ παρασκευὴν
2 Ἀθηναῖοι ψηφίσωνται. ὁ δὲ ἄκων μὲν εἶπεν ὅτι
καὶ μετὰ τῶν ξυναρχόντων καθ᾽ ἡσυχίαν μᾶλλον
βουλεύσοιτο, ὅσα μέντοι ἤδη δοκεῖν αὐτῷ, τριήρεσι μὲν οὐκ ἔλασσον ἢ[1] ἑκατὸν πλευστέα εἶναι
(αὐτῶν δ᾽[2] Ἀθηναίων ἔσεσθαι ὁπλιταγωγοὺς ὅσαι
ἂν δοκῶσι, καὶ ἄλλας ἐκ τῶν ξυμμάχων μετα-
πεμπτέας εἶναι), ὁπλίταις δὲ τοῖς ξύμπασιν Ἀθηναίων καὶ τῶν ξυμμάχων πεντακισχιλίων μὲν οὐκ
ἐλάσσοσιν, ἢν δέ τι δύνωνται, καὶ πλείοσιν· τὴν
δὲ ἄλλην παρασκευὴν ὡς κατὰ λόγον καὶ τοξοτῶν
τῶν αὐτόθεν καὶ ἐκ Κρήτης καὶ σφενδονητῶν καὶ
ἤν τι ἄλλο πρέπον δοκῇ εἶναι ἑτοιμασάμενοι ἄξειν.

XXVI. Ἀκούσαντες δ᾽ οἱ Ἀθηναῖοι ἐψηφίσαντο
εὐθὺς αὐτοκράτορας εἶναι καὶ περὶ στρατιᾶς πλήθους καὶ περὶ τοῦ παντὸς πλοῦ τοὺς στρατηγοὺς

---

[1] ἢ Hude omits with E.
[2] δ᾽ Hude brackets and inserts ὧν after Ἀθηναίων, on
Krüger's suggestion.

age, through a longing for far-off sights and scenes, in good hopes as they were of a safe return; and upon the great multitude—that is, the soldiers [1]—who hoped not only to get money for the present, but also to acquire additional dominion which would always be an inexhaustible source of pay. And so, on account of the exceeding eagerness of the majority, even if anyone was not satisfied, he held his peace, in the fear that if he voted in opposition he might seem to be disloyal to the state.

XXV. Finally a certain Athenian came forward and, calling upon Nicias, said he ought not to be making excuses and causing delays, but should say at once before them all what force the Athenians should vote him. He then, though reluctantly, said that he would prefer to deliberate with his colleagues more at their leisure; so far, however, as he could see at present, they must sail with not fewer than one hundred triremes—there would also have to be as many transports as should be determined upon, furnished by the Athenians themselves and others they must call upon their allies to supply—and with hoplites, both of the Athenians and their allies, in all not fewer than five thousand, and more if possible; and the rest of the armament which they must get ready and take with them must be in proportion—bowmen from home and from Crete, and slingers, and whatever else should be determined upon.

XXVI. Upon hearing this, the Athenians straightway voted that the generals should have full powers, with regard both to the size of the armament

---

[1] Taking στρατιώτης as predicate; or, "the great multitude and the soldiery were hoping to get money for the present," etc.

πράσσειν ᾗ ἂν αὐτοῖς δοκῇ ἄριστα εἶναι Ἀθηναί-
2 οις. καὶ μετὰ ταῦτα ἡ παρασκευὴ ἐγίγνετο, καὶ
ἔς τε τοὺς ξυμμάχους ἔπεμπον καὶ αὐτόθεν κατα-
λόγους ἐποιοῦντο. ἄρτι δ᾽ ἀνειλήφει ἡ πόλις
ἑαυτὴν ἀπὸ τῆς νόσου καὶ τοῦ ξυνεχοῦς πολέμου
ἔς τε ἡλικίας πλῆθος ἐπιγεγενημένης καὶ ἐς χρημάτων ἄθροισιν διὰ τὴν ἐκεχειρίαν, ὥστε ῥᾷον πάντα
ἐπορίζετο. καὶ οἱ μὲν ἐν παρασκευῇ ἦσαν.

XXVII. Ἐν δὲ τούτῳ, ὅσοι Ἑρμαῖ ἦσαν λίθινοι
ἐν τῇ πόλει τῇ Ἀθηναίων (εἰσὶ δὲ κατὰ τὸ ἐπιχώριον ἡ τετράγωνος ἐργασία [1] πολλοὶ καὶ ἐν ἰδίοις
προθύροις καὶ ἐν ἱεροῖς) μιᾷ νυκτὶ οἱ πλεῖστοι
2 περιεκόπησαν τὰ πρόσωπα. καὶ τοὺς δράσαντας
ᾔδει οὐδείς, ἀλλὰ μεγάλοις μηνύτροις δημοσίᾳ
οὗτοί τε ἐζητοῦντο καὶ προσέτι ἐψηφίσαντο, καὶ
εἴ τις ἄλλο τι οἶδεν ἀσέβημα γεγενημένον, μηνύειν
ἀδεῶς τὸν βουλόμενον καὶ ἀστῶν καὶ ξένων καὶ
3 δούλων. καὶ τὸ πρᾶγμα μειζόνως ἐλάμβανον· τοῦ
τε γὰρ ἔκπλου οἰωνὸς ἐδόκει εἶναι, καὶ ἐπὶ ξυνωμοσίᾳ ἅμα νεωτέρων πραγμάτων καὶ δήμου κατα-
λύσεως γεγενῆσθαι. XXVIII. μηνύεται οὖν ἀπὸ
μετοίκων τέ τινων καὶ ἀκολούθων περὶ μὲν τῶν
Ἑρμῶν οὐδέν, ἄλλων δὲ ἀγαλμάτων περικοπαί
τινες πρότερον ὑπὸ νεωτέρων μετὰ παιδιᾶς καὶ
οἴνου γεγενημέναι, καὶ τὰ μυστήρια ἅμα ὡς ποιεῖται ἐν οἰκίαις ἐφ᾽ ὕβρει· ὧν καὶ τὸν Ἀλκιβιάδην
2 ἐπῃτιῶντο. καὶ αὐτὰ ὑπολαμβάνοντες οἱ μάλιστα

---

[1] ἡ τετράγωνος ἐργασία, deleted by Hude, as not read by
Schol. Patm.

230

and to the whole expedition, to act in whatever way might seem to them best for Athens. After this the preparation was begun; and they sent notice to their allies and made levies at home. Now the city had just recovered from the plague and from the continuous war, both in point of the multitude of young men who had grown up and of the money that had accumulated in consequence of the truce, so that everything was provided more easily. So the Athenians were engaged in preparation.

XXVII. But in the meantime the stone statues of Hermes in the city of Athens—they are the pillars of square construction which according to local custom stand in great numbers both in the doorways of private houses and in sacred places—nearly all had their faces mutilated on the same night. No one knew the perpetrators, but great rewards were publicly offered for their detection; and it was voted, besides, that if anyone, citizen or stranger or slave, knew of any other profanation that had been done, whoever would might fearlessly give information. The matter was taken very seriously; for it seemed to be ominous for the expedition and to have been done withal in furtherance of a conspiracy with a view to a revolution and the overthrow of the democracy. XXVIII. Accordingly, information was given by certain metics and serving-men, not indeed about the statues of Hermes, but to the effect that before this there had been certain mutilations of other statues perpetrated by younger men in drunken sport, and also that the mysteries were being performed in private houses in mockery; and Alcibiades, among others, was implicated in the charges. They

τῷ ᾿Αλκιβιάδῃ ἀχθόμενοι ἐμποδὼν ὄντι σφίσι μὴ
αὐτοῖς τοῦ δήμου βεβαίως προεστάναι, καὶ νομίσαντες, εἰ αὐτὸν ἐξελάσειαν, πρῶτοι ἂν εἶναι, ἐμεγά-
λυννον καὶ ἐβόων ὡς ἐπὶ δήμου καταλύσει τά τε
μυστικὰ καὶ ἡ τῶν Ἑρμῶν περικοπὴ γένοιτο καὶ
οὐδὲν εἴη αὐτῶν ὅ τι οὐ μετ᾿ ἐκείνου ἐπράχθη,
ἐπιλέγοντες τεκμήρια τὴν ἄλλην αὐτοῦ ἐς τὰ ἐπιτηδεύματα οὐ δημοτικὴν παρανομίαν.

XXIX. Ὁ δ᾿ ἔν τε τῷ παρόντι πρὸς τὰ μηνύ-
ματα ἀπελογεῖτο καὶ ἕτοιμος ἦν πρὶν ἐκπλεῖν
κρίνεσθαι, εἴ τι τούτων εἰργασμένος ἦν (ἤδη γὰρ
καὶ τὰ τῆς παρασκευῆς ἐπεπόριστο), καὶ εἰ μὲν
τούτων τι εἴργαστο, δίκην δοῦναι, εἰ δ᾿ ἀπολυθείη,
2 ἄρχειν. καὶ ἐπεμαρτύρετο μὴ ἀπόντος περὶ αὐτοῦ
διαβολὰς ἀποδέχεσθαι, ἀλλ᾿ ἤδη ἀποκτείνειν, εἰ
ἀδικεῖ, καὶ ὅτι σωφρονέστερον εἴη μὴ μετὰ τοιαύτης αἰτίας, πρὶν διαγνῶσι, πέμπειν αὐτὸν ἐπὶ
3 τοσούτῳ στρατεύματι. οἱ δ᾿ ἐχθροὶ δεδιότες τό
τε στράτευμα μὴ εὔνουν ἔχῃ, ἢν ἤδη ἀγωνίζηται,
ὅ τε δῆμος μὴ μαλακίζηται, θεραπεύων ὅτι δι᾿
ἐκεῖνον οἵ τ᾿ Ἀργεῖοι ξυνεστράτευον καὶ τῶν Μαντινέων τινές, ἀπέτρεπον καὶ ἀπέσπευδον, ἄλλους
ῥήτορας ἐνιέντες οἳ ἔλεγον νῦν μὲν πλεῖν αὐτὸν
καὶ μὴ κατασχεῖν τὴν ἀναγωγήν, ἐλθόντα δὲ
κρίνεσθαι ἐν ἡμέραις ῥηταῖς, βουλόμενοι ἐκ μεί-

---

[1] Notably a certain Androcles (VIII. lxv. 2); cf. Plut.
Alcib. 19.

were taken up by those who were most jealous of him [1] as an obstacle in the way of their secure preeminence among the people ; and these men, thinking that if they could get rid of him they would have first place, magnified the matter and shouted that both the mockery of the mysteries and the mutilation of the Hermae had been committed with a view to the overthrow of the democracy, and that there was none of these things but had been done in collusion with him, citing as further proofs other instances of his undemocratic lawlessness of conduct.

XXIX. He defended himself at the time against the informers' charges, and was ready before sailing —for already the preparations had been completed— to be tried on the question of his having done any of these things, and if he had been guilty of any of them to pay the penalty, but demanded that if he were acquitted he should keep his command. And he protested that they should not accept slanderous charges against him in his absence, but should put him to death at once if he were guilty, and that it was wiser not to send him at the head of so great an army, under such an imputation, until they had decided the question. But his enemies, fearing that the army might be favourable to him if he were brought to trial at once and that the populace might be lenient, inasmuch as it favoured him because it was through his influence that the Argives and some of the Mantineans were taking part in the campaign, were eager to postpone the trial, suborning other orators who insisted that he should sail now and not delay the departure of the expedition, but that he should come back and be tried at an appointed time. Their purpose was to have a more slanderous charge

ζονος διαβολῆς, ἣν ἔμελλον ῥᾷον αὐτοῦ ἀπόντος
ποριεῖν, μετάπεμπτον κομισθέντα αὐτὸν ἀγωνί-
σασθαι. καὶ ἔδοξε πλεῖν τὸν Ἀλκιβιάδην.

XXX. Μετὰ δὲ ταῦτα θέρους μεσοῦντος ἤδη ἡ
ἀναγωγὴ ἐγίγνετο ἐς τὴν Σικελίαν. τῶν μὲν οὖν
ξυμμάχων τοῖς πλείστοις καὶ ταῖς σιταγωγοῖς
ὁλκάσι καὶ τοῖς πλοίοις καὶ ὅση ἄλλη παρασκευὴ
ξυνείπετο πρότερον εἴρητο ἐς Κέρκυραν ξυλλέ-
γεσθαι, ὡς ἐκεῖθεν ἁθρόοις ἐπὶ ἄκραν Ἰαπυγίαν
τὸν Ἰόνιον διαβαλοῦσιν· αὐτοὶ δ' Ἀθηναῖοι καὶ
εἴ τινες τῶν ξυμμάχων παρῆσαν ἐς τὸν Πειραιᾶ
καταβάντες ἐν ἡμέρᾳ ῥητῇ ἅμα ἕῳ ἐπλήρουν τὰς
2 ναῦς ὡς ἀναξόμενοι. ξυγκατέβη δὲ καὶ ὁ ἄλλος
ὅμιλος ἅπας ὡς εἰπεῖν ὁ ἐν τῇ πόλει καὶ ἀστῶν
καὶ ξένων, οἱ μὲν ἐπιχώριοι τοὺς σφετέρους αὐτῶν
ἕκαστοι προπέμποντες, οἱ μὲν ἑταίρους, οἱ δὲ
ξυγγενεῖς, οἱ δὲ υἱεῖς, καὶ μετ' ἐλπίδος τε ἅμα
ἰόντες καὶ ὀλοφυρμῶν, τὰ μὲν ὡς κτήσοιντο, τοὺς
δ' εἴ ποτε ὄψοιντο, ἐνθυμούμενοι ὅσον πλοῦν ἐκ
τῆς σφετέρας ἀπεστέλλοντο. καὶ ἐν τῷ παρόντι
καιρῷ, ὡς ἤδη ἔμελλον μετὰ κινδύνων ἀλλήλους
ἀπολιπεῖν, μᾶλλον αὐτοὺς ἐσῄει τὰ δεινὰ ἢ ὅτε
ἐψηφίζοντο πλεῖν· ὅμως δὲ τῇ παρούσῃ ῥώμῃ διὰ
τὸ πλῆθος ἑκάστων ὧν ἑώρων τῇ ὄψει[1] ἀνεθάρσουν. οἱ δὲ ξένοι καὶ ὁ ἄλλος ὄχλος κατὰ θέαν
ἧκεν ὡς ἐπὶ ἀξιόχρεων καὶ ἄπιστον διάνοιαν.

---

[1] τῇ ὄψει, Hude inserts ἐν.

—and this they would find it easier to procure in his absence—and then to have him recalled and brought home for trial. So it was determined that Alcibiades should sail.

XXX. After that, when it was already midsummer, the departure for Sicily was made. Orders had been given beforehand for most of the allies, as well as for the provision-ships and smaller boats and all the rest of the armament that went with them, to assemble at Corcyra, with the intention that from there they should all cross the Ionian Gulf to the promontory of Iapygia in one body. But the Athenians themselves and the allies that were present went down to the Peiraeus at dawn on a day appointed and proceeded to man the ships for the purpose of putting to sea. And with them went down also all the general throng, everyone, we may almost say, that was in the city, both citizens and strangers, the natives to send off each their own, whether friends or kinsmen or sons, going at once in hope and with lamentations —hope that they would make conquests in Sicily, lamentations that they might never see their friends again, considering how long was the voyage from their own land on which they were being sent. And at this crisis, when under impending dangers they were now about to take leave of one another, the risks came home to them more than when they were voting for the expedition ; but still their courage revived at the sight of their present strength because of the abundance of everything they saw before their eyes. The strangers on the other hand and the rest of the multitude had come for a spectacle, in the feeling that the enterprise was noteworthy and surpassing belief.

XXXI. Παρασκευὴ γὰρ αὕτη ἡ[1] πρώτη ἐκ-
πλεύσασα μιᾶς πόλεως δυνάμει Ἑλληνικῇ[2]
πολυτελεστάτη δὴ καὶ εὐπρεπεστάτη τῶν ἐς
2 ἐκεῖνον τὸν χρόνον ἐγένετο. ἀριθμῷ δὲ νεῶν
καὶ ὁπλιτῶν καὶ ἡ ἐς Ἐπίδαυρον μετὰ Περι-
κλέους καὶ ἡ αὐτὴ ἐς Ποτείδαιαν μετὰ Ἅγνωνος
οὐκ ἐλάσσων ἦν· τετράκις γὰρ χίλιοι ὁπλῖται αὐτῶν Ἀθηναίων καὶ τριακόσιοι ἱππῆς καὶ
τριήρεις ἑκατὸν καὶ Λεσβίων καὶ Χίων πεντήκοντα καὶ ξύμμαχοι ἔτι πολλοὶ ξυνέπλευσαν·
3 ἀλλὰ ἐπί τε βραχεῖ πλῷ ὡρμήθησαν καὶ παρασκευῇ φαύλῃ, οὗτος δὲ ὁ στόλος ὡς χρόνιός τε
ἐσόμενος καὶ κατ᾽ ἀμφότερα, οὗ ἂν δέῃ, καὶ ναυσὶ
καὶ πεζῷ ἅμα ἐξαρτυθείς, τὸ μὲν ναυτικὸν μεγά-
λαις δαπάναις τῶν τε τριηράρχων καὶ τῆς πόλεως
ἐκπονηθέν, τοῦ μὲν δημοσίου δραχμὴν τῆς ἡμέρας
τῷ ναύτῃ ἑκάστῳ διδόντος καὶ ναῦς παρασχόντος
κενὰς ἑξήκοντα μὲν ταχείας, τεσσαράκοντα δὲ
ὁπλιταγωγοὺς καὶ ὑπηρεσίας ταύταις τὰς κρατί-
στας, τῶν δὲ[3] τριηράρχων ἐπιφοράς τε πρὸς
τῷ ἐκ δημοσίου μισθῷ διδόντων τοῖς θρα-
νίταις τῶν ναυτῶν[4] καὶ τἆλλα σημείοις καὶ
κατασκευαῖς πολυτελέσι χρησαμένων, καὶ ἐς τὰ
μακρότατα προθυμηθέντος ἑνὸς ἑκάστου ὅπως
αὐτῷ τινι εὐπρεπείᾳ τε ἡ ναῦς μάλιστα προέξει
καὶ τῷ ταχυναυτεῖν, τὸ δὲ πεζὸν καταλόγοις τε
χρηστοῖς ἐκκριθὲν καὶ ὅπλων καὶ τῶν περὶ τὸ
σῶμα σκευῶν μεγάλῃ σπουδῇ πρὸς ἀλλήλους

---

[1] ἡ added by Dobree.
[2] Ἑλληνικῇ, Hude writes Ἑλληνικῆς, after Haacke.
[3] δὲ adopted from Schol. Patm.
[4] καὶ ταῖς ὑπηρεσίαις after τῶν ναυτῶν is deleted as not read
by the Scholiast.

XXXI. For this first armament that sailed for
Sicily was the costliest and most splendid, belonging
to a single city and with a purely Hellenic force,
that had ever up to that time set sail. In number
of ships, however, and of hoplites the expedition
against Epidaurus under Pericles, and the same one
afterwards under Hagnon against Potidaea, was not
inferior; for in that voyage four thousand Athenian
hoplites and three hundred knights and one hundred
triremes had participated, and from Lesbos and Chios
fifty triremes, and allied troops besides in large numbers. But they had set off for a short voyage with
a poor equipment; whereas this expedition, as one
likely to be of long duration, was fitted out for both
kinds of service, according as there might be need
of either, with ships and also with land-forces.
The fleet was built up at great expense on the part
both of the trierarchs and of the city: the state giving
a drachma per day for each sailor and furnishing sixty
empty [1] warships and forty transports, with crews to
man them of the very best; the trierarchs giving
bounties to the thranitae [2] or uppermost bench of the
sailors in addition to the pay from the state, and
using, besides, figure-heads and equipments that
were very expensive; for each one strove to the
utmost that his own ship should excel all others
both in fine appearance and in swiftness of sailing.
The land-forces were picked out of the best lists,
and there was keen rivalry among the men in the

[1] *i.e.* empty hulls without equipment, which the trierarch
was to furnish.

[2] In the trireme there were three ranks of oars: the
thranites rowed with the longest oars; the zygites occupied
the middle row; the thalamites the lowest row, using the
shortest oars and drawing least pay.

4 ἀμιλληθέν. ξυνέβη δὲ πρός τε σφᾶς αὐτοὺς ἅμα
ἔριν γενέσθαι, ᾧ τις ἕκαστος προσετάχθη, καὶ ἐς
τοὺς ἄλλους Ἕλληνας ἐπίδειξιν μᾶλλον εἰκα-
σθῆναι τῆς δυνάμεως καὶ ἐξουσίας ἢ ἐπὶ πολεμίους
5 παρασκευήν. εἰ γάρ τις ἐλογίσατο τήν τε τῆς
πόλεως ἀνάλωσιν δημοσίαν καὶ τῶν στρατευο-
μένων τὴν ἰδίαν, τῆς μὲν πόλεως ὅσα τε ἤδη
προυτετελέκει καὶ ἃ ἔχοντας τοὺς στρατηγοὺς
ἀπέστελλε, τῶν δὲ ἰδιωτῶν ἅ τε περὶ τὸ σῶμά τις
καὶ τριήραρχος ἐς τὴν ναῦν ἀνηλώκει καὶ ὅσα ἔτι
ἔμελλεν ἀναλώσειν, χωρὶς δ' ἃ εἰκὸς ἦν καὶ ἄνευ
τοῦ ἐκ δημοσίου μισθοῦ πάντα τινὰ παρασκευά-
σασθαι ἐφόδιον ὡς ἐπὶ χρόνιον στρατείαν, καὶ ὅσα
ἐπὶ μεταβολῇ τις ἢ στρατιώτης ἢ ἔμπορος ἔχων
ἔπλει, πολλὰ ἂν τάλαντα ηὑρέθη ἐκ τῆς πόλεως
6 τὰ πάντα ἐξαγόμενα. καὶ ὁ στόλος οὐχ ἧσσον
τόλμης τε θάμβει καὶ ὄψεως λαμπρότητι περι-
βόητος ἐγένετο ἢ στρατιᾶς πρὸς οὓς ἐπῇσαν
ὑπερβολῇ, καὶ ὅτι μέγιστος ἤδη διάπλους ἀπὸ
τῆς οἰκείας καὶ ἐπὶ μεγίστῃ ἐλπίδι τῶν μελλόντων πρὸς τὰ ὑπάρχοντα ἐπεχειρήθη.

XXXII. Ἐπειδὴ δὲ αἱ νῆες πλήρεις ἦσαν καὶ
ἐσέκειτο πάντα ἤδη ὅσα ἔχοντες ἔμελλον ἀνά-
ξεσθαι, τῇ μὲν σάλπιγγι σιωπὴ ὑπεσημάνθη,
εὐχὰς δὲ τὰς νομιζομένας πρὸ τῆς ἀναγωγῆς οὐ

matter of arms and personal equipment. And so it came about that among themselves there was emulation, wherever each was assigned to duty, and the whole thing seemed more like a display of wealth and power before the rest of the Hellenes than an undertaking against enemies. For if one had reckoned the public expenditure on the part of the state and the private outlay of those who made the expedition—on the part of the city, both what it had already advanced and what it was sending in the hands of the generals, and on the part of private individuals whatever a man had expended on his own person or, if trierarch, on his ship, and what they were going to spend still, and, besides, the money we may suppose that everyone, even apart from the pay he received from the state, provided for himself as travelling expenses, counting upon an expedition of long duration, and all the articles for barter and sale merchant or soldier took with him on the voyage—it would have been found that many talents in all were taken from the city. And the fame of the armament was noised abroad, not less because of amazement at its boldness and the splendour of the spectacle than on account of its overwhelming force as compared with those whom they were going against; and also because it was the longest voyage from home as yet attempted and undertaken with the highest hopes for the future as compared with their present resources.

XXXII. When the ships had been manned and everything had at last been put aboard which they were to take with them on the voyage, the trumpeter proclaimed silence, and they offered the prayers that were customary before putting out to sea, not

κατὰ ναῦν ἑκάστην, ξύμπαντες δὲ ὑπὸ κήρυκος
ἐποιοῦντο, κρατῆράς τε κεράσαντες παρ' ἅπαν τὸ
στράτευμα καὶ ἐκπώμασι χρυσοῖς τε καὶ ἀργυ-
ροῖς οἵ τε ἐπιβάται καὶ οἱ ἄρχοντες σπένδοντες.
2 ξυνεπηύχοντο δὲ καὶ ὁ ἄλλος ὅμιλος ὁ ἐκ τῆς γῆς
τῶν τε πολιτῶν καὶ εἴ τις ἄλλος εὔνους παρῆν
σφίσιν. παιανίσαντες δὲ καὶ τελεώσαντες τὰς
σπονδὰς ἀνήγοντο, καὶ ἐπὶ κέρως τὸ πρῶτον
ἐκπλεύσαντες ἅμιλλαν ἤδη μέχρι Αἰγίνης ἐποιοῦντο. καὶ οἱ μὲν ἐς τὴν Κέρκυραν, ἔνθαπερ καὶ
τὸ ἄλλο στράτευμα τῶν ξυμμάχων ξυνελέγετο,
ἠπείγοντο ἀφικέσθαι.

3 Ἐς δὲ τὰς Συρακούσας ἠγγέλλετο μὲν πολλα-
χόθεν τὰ περὶ τοῦ ἐπίπλου, οὐ μέντοι ἐπιστεύετο
ἐπὶ πολὺν χρόνον οὐδέν, ἀλλὰ καὶ γενομένης
ἐκκλησίας ἐλέχθησαν τοιοίδε λόγοι ἀπό τε ἄλλων,
τῶν μὲν πιστευόντων τὰ περὶ τῆς στρατείας τῆς
τῶν Ἀθηναίων, τῶν δὲ τὰ ἐναντία λεγόντων, καὶ
Ἑρμοκράτης ὁ Ἕρμωνος παρελθὼν αὐτοῖς ὡς
σαφῶς οἰόμενος εἰδέναι τὰ περὶ αὐτῶν, ἔλεγε καὶ
παρῄνει τοιάδε.

XXXIII. "Ἄπιστα μὲν ἴσως, ὥσπερ καὶ ἄλλοι
τινές, δόξω ὑμῖν περὶ τοῦ ἐπίπλου τῆς ἀληθείας
λέγειν, καὶ γιγνώσκω ὅτι οἱ τὰ μὴ πιστὰ δοκοῦντα
εἶναι ἢ λέγοντες ἢ ἀπαγγέλλοντες οὐ μόνον οὐ
πείθουσιν, ἀλλὰ καὶ ἄφρονες δοκοῦσιν εἶναι·
ὅμως δὲ οὐ καταφοβηθεὶς ἐπισχήσω κινδυνευούσης
τῆς πόλεως, πείθων γε ἐμαυτὸν σαφέστερόν τι
2 ἑτέρου εἰδὼς λέγειν. Ἀθηναῖοι γὰρ ἐφ' ὑμᾶς, ὃ

ship by ship but all together, led by a herald, the mariners as well as the officers throughout the whole army making libations with golden and silver cups from wine they had mixed. And the rest of the throng of people on the shore, both the citizens and all others present who wished the Athenians well, also joined in the prayers. And when they had sung the paean and had finished the libations, they put off, and sailing out at first in single column they then raced as far as Aegina. The Athenian fleet, then, was pressing on to reach Corcyra, where the rest of the armament of the allies was assembling.

But meanwhile reports of the expedition were coming to Syracuse from many quarters, but were not believed at all for a long time. Nay, even when an assembly was held speeches to the following effect [1] were made on the part of others, some crediting the reports about the expedition of the Athenians, others contradicting them, and Hermocrates son of Hermon came forward, in the conviction that he knew the truth of the matter, and spoke, exhorting them as follows:

XXXIII. "Possibly it will seem to you that what I and certain others say about the reality of the expedition against us is incredible, and I am aware that those who either make or repeat statements that seem not credible not only do not carry conviction but are also regarded as foolish; but nevertheless I will not be frightened into holding my tongue when the state is in danger, persuaded as I am that I speak with more certain knowledge than my opponents. For it is indeed against you, much

---

[1] *i.e.* like those of Hermocrates and Athenagoras.

πάνυ θαυμάζετε, πολλῇ στρατιᾷ ὥρμηνται καὶ
ναυτικῇ καὶ πεζικῇ, πρόφασιν μὲν Ἐγεσταίων
ξυμμαχίᾳ καὶ Λεοντίνων κατοικίσει, τὸ δὲ ἀληθὲς
Σικελίας ἐπιθυμίᾳ, μάλιστα δὲ τῆς ἡμετέρας
πόλεως, ἡγούμενοι, εἰ ταύτην σχοῖεν, ῥᾳδίως καὶ
3 τἆλλα ἕξειν. ὡς οὖν ἐν τάχει παρεσομένων, ὁρᾶτε
ἀπὸ τῶν ὑπαρχόντων ὅτῳ τρόπῳ κάλλιστα
ἀμυνεῖσθε αὐτοὺς καὶ μήτε καταφρονήσαντες
ἄφαρκτοι ληφθήσεσθε μήτε ἀπιστήσαντες τοῦ
4 ξύμπαντος ἀμελήσετε. εἰ δέ τῳ καὶ πιστά, τὴν
τόλμαν αὐτῶν καὶ δύναμιν μὴ ἐκπλαγῇ. οὔτε γὰρ
βλάπτειν ἡμᾶς πλείω οἷοί τ᾽ ἔσονται ἢ πάσχειν,
οὔθ᾽ ὅτι μεγάλῳ στόλῳ ἐπέρχονται, ἀνωφελές,[1]
ἀλλὰ πρός τε τοὺς ἄλλους Σικελιώτας πολὺ
ἄμεινον (μᾶλλον γὰρ ἐθελήσουσιν ἐκπλαγέντες
ἡμῖν ξυμμαχεῖν), καὶ ἢν ἄρα ἢ κατεργασώμεθα
αὐτοὺς ἢ ἀπράκτους ὧν ἐφίενται ἀπώσωμεν (οὐ
γὰρ δὴ μὴ τύχωσί γε ὧν προσδέχονται φοβοῦμαι),
κάλλιστον δὴ ἔργων ἡμῖν ξυμβήσεται καὶ οὐκ
5 ἀνέλπιστον ἔμοιγε. ὀλίγοι γὰρ δὴ στόλοι μεγάλοι
ἢ Ἑλλήνων ἢ βαρβάρων πολὺ ἀπὸ τῆς ἑαυτῶν
ἀπάραντες κατώρθωσαν. οὔτε γὰρ πλείους τῶν
ἐνοικούντων καὶ ἀστυγειτόνων ἔρχονται (πάντα
γὰρ ὑπὸ δέους ξυνίσταται), ἤν τε δι᾽ ἀπορίαν τῶν
ἐπιτηδείων ἐν ἀλλοτρίᾳ γῇ σφαλῶσι, τοῖς ἐπι-
βουλευθεῖσιν ὄνομα, κἂν περὶ σφίσιν αὐτοῖς τὰ

---

[1] ἀνωφέλες, Dobree's correction, for ἀνωφελεῖς of the MSS.,
which Hude retains.

as you wonder at it, that the Athenians have
set out with a large armament for use on land
as well as on the sea, on the pretext of an
alliance with the Egestaeans and the restoration
of the Leontines, but in truth with a covetous desire
for Sicily, and above all for our city, thinking that
once in possession of it they would easily get possession of the rest also. With the certainty, then,
that they will soon be here, consider in what way
with your present resources you can best ward them
off, and may neither by despising them be caught off
your guard nor through incredulity neglect the whole
matter. If, however, anyone does find my words
credible, let him not be dismayed at their daring and
power. For neither will they be able to inflict more injury upon us than they will suffer, nor is it without
advantage for us that they are coming with a great
armament; on the contrary, it is far better so as
regards the rest of the Siceliots, for in their consternation they will be more inclined to join our alliance;
and if in the end we either overpower them or drive
them off baffled in their designs—for I certainly have
no fear as to their attaining the success they anticipate
—it will prove the most glorious of achievements
for us, and one which I at least do not despair of.
For few great armaments, whether of Hellenes or of
barbarians, when sent far from their own land, have
been successful. The reason is that they are not, in
the first place, superior in numbers to the people
against whom they go and the neighbours of these—
for fear always brings about union; and if, in the
second place, they fail on account of lack of supplies
in a foreign land, they leave a proud name to those
whom they plotted against, even though their failure

6 πλείω πταίσωσιν, ὅμως καταλείπουσιν. ὅπερ
καὶ Ἀθηναῖοι [1] αὐτοὶ οὗτοι, τοῦ Μήδου παρὰ λόγον
πολλὰ σφαλέντος, ἐπὶ τῷ ὀνόματι ὡς ἐπὶ Ἀθήνας
ᾔει ηὐξήθησαν, καὶ ἡμῖν οὐκ ἀνέλπιστον τὸ τοιοῦτον ξυμβῆναι.

XXXIV. "Θαρσοῦντες οὖν τά τε αὑτοῦ παρα-
σκευαζώμεθα καὶ ἐς τοὺς Σικελοὺς πέμποντες
τοὺς μὲν μᾶλλον βεβαιωσώμεθα, τοῖς δὲ φιλίαν
καὶ ξυμμαχίαν πειρώμεθα ποιεῖσθαι, ἔς τε τὴν
ἄλλην Σικελίαν πέμπωμεν πρέσβεις, δηλοῦντες
ὡς κοινὸς ὁ κίνδυνος, καὶ ἐς τὴν Ἰταλίαν, ὅπως
ἢ ξυμμαχίδα ποιώμεθα ἡμῖν ἢ μὴ δέχωνται
2 Ἀθηναίους. δοκεῖ δέ μοι καὶ ἐς Καρχηδόνα ἄμεινον εἶναι πέμψαι. οὐ γὰρ ἀνέλπιστον αὐτοῖς,
ἀλλ᾽ αἰεὶ διὰ φόβου εἰσὶ μή ποτε Ἀθηναῖοι αὐτοῖς
ἐπὶ τὴν πόλιν ἔλθωσιν, ὥστε τάχ᾽ ἂν ἴσως νομίσαντες, εἰ τάδε προήσονται, καὶ ἂν σφεῖς ἐν πόνῳ
εἶναι, ἐθελήσειαν ἡμῖν ἤτοι κρύφα γε ἢ φανερῶς
ἢ ἐξ ἑνός γέ του τρόπου ἀμῦναι. δυνατοὶ δέ εἰσι
μάλιστα τῶν νῦν, βουληθέντες· χρυσὸν γὰρ καὶ
ἄργυρον πλεῖστον κέκτηνται, ὅθεν ὅ τε πόλεμος
3 καὶ τἆλλα εὐπορεῖ. πέμπωμεν δὲ καὶ ἐς τὴν
Λακεδαίμονα καὶ ἐς Κόρινθον, δεόμενοι δεῦρο
κατὰ τάχος βοηθεῖν καὶ τὸν ἐκεῖ πόλεμον κινεῖν.
4 ὃ δὲ μάλιστα ἐγώ τε νομίζω ἐπίκαιρον ὑμεῖς τε
διὰ τὸ ξύνηθες ἥσυχον ἥκιστ᾽ ἂν ὀξέως πείθοισθε,
ὅμως εἰρήσεται. Σικελιῶται γὰρ εἰ ἐθέλοιμεν ξύμπαντες, εἰ δὲ μή, ὅτι πλεῖστοι μεθ᾽ ἡμῶν,

---

[1] Ἀθηναῖοι, Hude deletes with Badham.

be due chiefly to themselves. These very Athenians, for example, when the Persians contrary to expectation signally failed, grew great on the repute that it was Athens they went against; so in our case a like issue is not beyond hope.

XXXIV. "With confidence, then, let us make our preparations here, but also send envoys to the Sicels, to confirm the allegiance of some and to endeavour to make friendship and alliance with others; and let us despatch envoys to the rest of Sicily, to show that the danger is a common one, and to Italy, that we may either secure their alliance for ourselves or else prevent their receiving the Athenians. And to me it seems best to send also to Carthage. For the Carthaginians are not without expectation, or rather they are always in fear, that some time the Athenians may come against their city; and so they will probably feel that if they shall leave things here to their fate, they may be in trouble themselves, and therefore will be inclined to assist us, secretly perhaps, or openly, or by some means or other. And they, of all men of the present day, are the most able to do so, if they will; for they have an abundance of gold and silver, by which war and everything else is expedited. And let us send also to Lacedaemon and to Corinth, begging them to bring aid here with all speed, and to stir up the war over there. And now the measure which I think would be most opportune, but which you on account of your habitual love of ease would be least likely to adopt promptly, shall nevertheless be proposed If we Siceliots—all together, or, in default of this, as many as will join us—were willing to launch all our

καθελκύσαντες ἅπαν τὸ ὑπάρχον ναυτικὸν μετὰ
δυοῖν μηνοῖν τροφῆς ἀπαντῆσαι ᾿Αθηναίοις ἐς
Τάραντα καὶ ἄκραν ᾿Ιαπυγίαν, καὶ δῆλον ποιῆσαι
αὐτοῖς ὅτι οὐ περὶ τῆς Σικελίας[1] πρότερον ἔσται
ὁ ἀγὼν ἢ τοῦ ἐκείνους περαιωθῆναι τὸν ᾿Ιόνιον,
μάλιστ᾿ ἂν αὐτοὺς ἐκπλήξαιμεν καὶ ἐς λογισμὸν
καταστήσαιμεν ὅτι ὁρμώμεθα μὲν ἐκ φιλίας
χώρας φύλακες (ὑποδέχεται γὰρ ἡμᾶς Τάρας), τὸ
δὲ πέλαγος αὐτοῖς πολὺ περαιοῦσθαι μετὰ πάσης
τῆς παρασκευῆς, χαλεπὸν δὲ διὰ πλοῦ μῆκος ἐν
τάξει μεῖναι, καὶ ἡμῖν ἂν εὐεπίθετος εἴη, βραδεῖά
5 τε καὶ κατ᾿ ὀλίγον προσπίπτουσα. εἰ δ᾿ αὖ τῷ
ταχυναυτοῦντι ἀθροωτέρῳ κουφίσαντες προσβά-
λοιεν, εἰ μὲν κώπαις χρήσαιντο, ἐπιθοίμεθ᾿ ἂν
κεκμηκόσιν, εἰ δὲ μὴ δοκοίη, ἔστι καὶ ὑποχωρῆσαι
ἡμῖν ἐς Τάραντα· οἱ δὲ μετ᾿ ὀλίγων ἐφοδίων ὡς
ἐπὶ ναυμαχίᾳ περαιωθέντες ἀποροῖεν ἂν κατὰ
χωρία ἐρῆμα, καὶ ἢ μένοντες πολιορκοῖντο ἂν ἢ
πειρώμενοι παραπλεῖν τήν τε ἄλλην παρασκευὴν
ἀπολείποιεν ἂν καὶ τὰ τῶν πόλεων οὐκ ἂν βέβαια
6 ἔχοντες, εἰ ὑποδέξοιντο, ἀθυμοῖεν. ὥστ᾿ ἔγωγε
τούτῳ τῷ λογισμῷ ἡγοῦμαι ἀποκληομένους αὐτοὺς
οὐδ᾿ ἂν ἀπᾶραι ἀπὸ Κερκύρας, ἀλλ᾿ ἢ διαβουλευ-
σαμένους καὶ κατασκοπαῖς χρωμένους ὁπόσοι τ᾿
ἐσμὲν καὶ ἐν ᾧ χωρίῳ, ἐξωσθῆναι ἂν τῇ ὥρᾳ ἐς

---

[1] περὶ τῆς Σικελίας, Duker's correction for περὶ τῇ Σικελίᾳ
of the MSS.

---

[1] The Athenians would naturally expect to cross from
Corcyra to Tarentum, then follow the coast to Messene. By

available naval force and with two months' provisions
go to meet the Athenians at Tarentum and the
promontory of Iapygia, and make plain to them that
the contest will not be first for Sicily, but before
that for their passage across the Ionian Sea, we
should mightily astound them and force them to
reflect that we have as our base a friendly country
from which to keep watch and ward—for Tarentum
is ready to receive us—whereas for them the open
sea is a wide one to cross with all their armament,[1]
and it is difficult on account of the length of the
voyage to keep in formation; consequently, coming
up slowly and few at a time, they would be at the
mercy of our attack. But if on the other hand they
should lighten their ships and attack with the
swift-sailing part of their fleet in a more compact
body, then, in case they used their oars, we should
set upon them when weary with rowing; or if it
did not seem wise to attack them, we could retire to
Tarentum again. They, however, having crossed
with slender supplies in the prospect of a naval en-
gagement, would be in distress in uninhabited
regions, and either would remain and be blockaded,
or trying to sail along the coast would leave behind
the rest of their equipment, and, having no certainty
as to the temper of the cities, whether they would
receive them or not, would be discouraged. And
so I for my part am of opinion that, deterred by
this consideration, they would not even put out
from Corcyra, but either, after taking time for
deliberation and spying out how many we are and in
what position, would be driven into winter-quarters

making Tarentum their base the Siceliots would force the
Athenians to cross the open sea—a hazardous undertaking.

χειμῶνα, ἢ καταπλαγέντας τῷ ἀδοκήτῳ καταλῦσαι ἂν τὸν πλοῦν, ἄλλως τε καὶ τοῦ ἐμ-
πειροτάτου τῶν στρατηγῶν, ὡς ἐγὼ ἀκούω,
ἄκοντος ἡγουμένου καὶ ἀσμένου ἂν πρόφασιν
λαβόντος, εἴ τι ἀξιόχρεων ἀφ' ἡμῶν ὀφθείη.
7 ἀγγελλοίμεθα δ' ἂν εὖ οἶδ' ὅτι ἐπὶ τὸ πλέον· τῶν
δ' ἀνθρώπων πρὸς τὰ λεγόμενα καὶ αἱ γνῶμαι
ἵστανται, καὶ τοὺς προεπιχειροῦντας ἢ τοῖς γε
ἐπιχειροῦσι προδηλοῦντας ὅτι ἀμυνοῦνται μᾶλλον
πεφόβηνται, ἰσοκινδύνους ἡγούμενοι. ὅπερ ἂν νῦν
8 Ἀθηναῖοι πάθοιεν. ἐπέρχονται γὰρ ἡμῖν ὡς οὐκ
ἀμυνουμένοις, δικαίως κατεγνωκότες ὅτι αὐτοὺς οὐ
μετὰ Λακεδαιμονίων ἐφθείρομεν· εἰ δ' ἴδοιεν παρὰ
γνώμην τολμήσαντας, τῷ ἀδοκήτῳ μᾶλλον ἂν
καταπλαγεῖεν ἢ τῇ ἀπὸ τοῦ ἀληθοῦς δυνάμει.

9   "Πείθεσθε οὖν, μάλιστα μὲν ταῦτα τολμή-
σαντες, εἰ δὲ μή, ὅτι τάχιστα τἆλλα ἐς τὸν
πόλεμον ἑτοιμάζειν, καὶ παραστῆναι παντὶ τὸ
μὲν καταφρονεῖν τοὺς ἐπιόντας ἐν τῶν ἔργων τῇ
ἀλκῇ δείκνυσθαι, τὸ δ' ἤδη τὰς μετὰ φόβου
παρασκευὰς ἀσφαλεστάτας νομίσαντας ὡς ἐπὶ
κινδύνου πράσσειν χρησιμώτατον ἂν ξυμβῆναι.
οἱ δὲ ἄνδρες καὶ ἐπέρχονται καὶ ἐν πλῷ εὖ οἶδ'
ὅτι ἤδη εἰσὶ καὶ ὅσον οὔπω πάρεισιν."

by the lateness of the season, or in dismay at the unexpected turn of events would abandon the expedition, especially as the most experienced of their generals takes command, as I hear, against his will, and would gladly seize upon an excuse to abandon it if any considerable opposition on our part were observed. And reports of our strength would, I am convinced, be exaggerated; the opinions of men are apt to veer according to what they are told; and those who are first to attack, or those at any rate who in advance make it clear to the aggressors that they will defend themselves, inspire the greater fear in the foe, who thinks them equal to the emergency. And precisely this would be the effect at this time upon the Athenians. For they are coming against us in the belief that we shall not defend ourselves, rightly contemning us because we did not join the Lacedaemonians in the effort to destroy them. But if they should see us unexpectedly displaying courage, they would be more dismayed by this unlooked for resistance than by our real power.

"Be persuaded, then, as best of all to take this bold step, but if not that, to make all other preparations for the war with all speed; and let it come home to everyone that contempt of invaders is shown by valour in actual conflict,[1] but that at this present time, realizing that preparations made with fear are safest, it would prove most advantageous so to act as though in imminent danger. For the Athenians are surely coming against us; they are, I am quite certain, already under sail, and all but here."

---

[1] Or, "by an energetic defence."

XXXV. Καὶ ὁ μὲν Ἑρμοκράτης τοσαῦτα εἶπεν. τῶν δὲ Συρακοσίων ὁ δῆμος ἐν πολλῇ πρὸς ἀλλήλους ἔριδι ἦσαν, οἱ μὲν ὡς οὐδενὶ ἂν τρόπῳ ἔλθοιεν οἱ Ἀθηναῖοι οὐδ' ἀληθῆ ἐστιν ἃ λέγεται, οἱ δέ, εἰ καὶ ἔλθοιεν, τί ἂν δράσειαν αὐτοὺς ὅ τι οὐκ ἂν μεῖζον ἀντιπάθοιεν; ἄλλοι δὲ καὶ πάνυ καταφρονοῦντες ἐς γέλωτα ἔτρεπον τὸ πρᾶγμα. ὀλίγον δ' ἦν τὸ πιστεῦον τῷ Ἑρμοκράτει καὶ 2 φοβούμενον τὸ μέλλον. παρελθὼν δ' αὐτοῖς Ἀθηναγόρας, ὃς δήμου τε προστάτης ἦν καὶ ἐν τῷ παρόντι πιθανώτατος τοῖς πολλοῖς, ἔλεγε τοιάδε.

XXXVI. "Τοὺς μὲν Ἀθηναίους ὅστις μὴ βούλεται οὕτως κακῶς φρονῆσαι καὶ ὑποχειρίους ἡμῖν γενέσθαι ἐνθάδε ἐλθόντας, ἢ δειλός ἐστιν ἢ τῇ πόλει οὐκ εὔνους· τοὺς δὲ ἀγγέλλοντας τὰ τοιαῦτα καὶ περιφόβους ὑμᾶς ποιοῦντας τῆς μὲν τόλμης οὐ θαυμάζω, τῆς δὲ ἀξυνεσίας, εἰ μὴ 2 οἴονται ἔνδηλοι εἶναι. οἱ γὰρ δεδιότες ἰδίᾳ τι βούλονται τὴν πόλιν ἐς ἔκπληξιν καθιστάναι, ὅπως τῷ κοινῷ φόβῳ τὸ σφέτερον ἐπηλυγάζωνται. καὶ νῦν αὗται αἱ ἀγγελίαι τοῦτο δύνανται, αἱ[1] οὐκ ἀπὸ ταὐτομάτου, ἐκ δὲ ἀνδρῶν οἵπερ αἰεὶ 3 τάδε κινοῦσι ξύγκεινται. ὑμεῖς δὲ ἢν εὖ βουλεύησθε, οὐκ ἐξ ὧν οὗτοι ἀγγέλλουσι σκοποῦντες λογιεῖσθε τὰ εἰκότα, ἀλλ' ἐξ ὧν ἂν ἄνθρωποι δεινοὶ καὶ πολλῶν ἔμπειροι, ὥσπερ ἐγὼ Ἀθηναίους 4 ἀξιῶ, δράσειαν. οὐ γὰρ αὐτοὺς εἰκὸς Πελοποννησίους τε ὑπολιπόντας καὶ τὸν ἐκεῖ πόλεμον μήπω βεβαίως καταλελυμένους ἐπ' ἄλλον πόλεμον οὐκ ἐλάσσω ἑκόντας ἐλθεῖν, ἐπεὶ ἔγωγε

[1] αἱ added by Classen.

XXXV. Such was the speech of Hermocrates. But the Syracusan people were at great strife among themselves: some maintained that the Athenians would not come at all and that the reports were not true; others asked, even if they did come, what could they do to them that they would not themselves suffer still more; others quite contemptuously turned the matter into ridicule. There were, however, a few who believed Hermocrates and feared what was coming. But Athenagoras, who was a popular leader and at the present time most influential with the masses, came forward and addressed them as follows :—

XXXVI. "As to the Athenians, whoever does not wish them to be so ill witted as to come here and fall into our hands, is either a coward or not loyal to the state; as to the men, however, who tell such stories and fill you with fear, I do not wonder at their audacity so much as at their simplicity, if they fancy we do not see through them. For men who have some private grounds of fear wish to plunge the city into consternation, in order that in the common fear their own may be overshadowed. So now this is the meaning of these reports, which are not spontaneous, but have been concocted by men who are always stirring up trouble here. But you, if you are well advised, will examine and form your estimate of what is probable, not from what these men report, but from what shrewd men of much experience, such as I deem the Athenians to be, would be likely to do. For it is not probable that they would leave the Peloponnesians behind them before they have yet brought the war there surely to an end, and voluntarily come here to prosecute

ἀγαπᾶν οἴομαι αὐτοὺς ὅτι οὐχ ἡμεῖς ἐπ᾽ ἐκείνους
ἐρχόμεθα, πόλεις τοσαῦται καὶ οὕτω μεγάλαι.

XXXVII. " Εἰ δὲ δή, ὥσπερ λέγονται, ἔλθοιεν,
ἱκανωτέραν ἡγοῦμαι Σικελίαν Πελοποννήσου δια-
πολεμῆσαι ὅσῳ κατὰ πάντα ἄμεινον ἐξήρτυται,
τὴν δὲ ἡμετέραν πόλιν αὐτὴν τῆς νῦν στρατιᾶς,
ὥς φασιν, ἐπιούσης, καὶ εἰ δὶς τοσαύτη ἔλθοι,
πολὺ κρείσσω εἶναι· οἷς γ᾽ ἐπίσταμαι οὔθ᾽ ἵππους
ἀκολουθήσοντας οὐδ᾽ αὐτόθεν πορισθησομένους εἰ
μὴ ὀλίγους τινὰς παρὰ Ἐγεσταίων, οὔθ᾽ ὁπλίτας
ἰσοπληθεῖς τοῖς ἡμετέροις ἐπὶ νεῶν γε ἐλθόντας
(μέγα γὰρ τὸ καὶ αὐταῖς ταῖς ναυσὶ κούφαις
τοσοῦτον πλοῦν δεῦρο κομισθῆναι), τήν τε ἄλλην
παρασκευήν, ὅσην δεῖ ἐπὶ πόλιν τοσήνδε πορι-
2 σθῆναι, οὐκ ὀλίγην οὖσαν. ὥστε (παρὰ τοσοῦτον
γιγνώσκω) μόλις ἄν μοι δοκοῦσιν, εἰ πόλιν ἑτέραν
τοσαύτην ὅσαι Συράκουσαί εἰσιν ἔλθοιεν ἔχοντες
καὶ ὅμοροι οἰκήσαντες τὸν πόλεμον ποιοῖντο, οὐκ
ἂν παντάπασι διαφθαρῆναι, ἦ πού γε δὴ ἐν πάσῃ
πολεμίᾳ Σικελίᾳ (ξυστήσεται γάρ) στρατοπέδῳ
τε ἐκ νεῶν ἱδρυθέντι καὶ ἐκ σκηνιδίων καὶ
ἀναγκαίας παρασκευῆς, οὐκ ἐπὶ πολὺ ὑπὸ τῶν
ἡμετέρων ἱππέων ἐξιόντες. τό τε ξύμπαν οὐδ᾽ ἂν
κρατῆσαι αὐτοὺς τῆς γῆς ἡγοῦμαι· τοσούτῳ τὴν
ἡμετέραν παρασκευὴν κρείσσω νομίζω.

XXXVIII. "Ἀλλὰ ταῦτα, ὥσπερ ἐγὼ λέγω, οἵ
τε Ἀθηναῖοι γιγνώσκοντες τὰ σφέτερα αὐτῶν εὖ
οἶδ᾽ ὅτι σῴζουσι, καὶ ἐνθένδε ἄνδρες οὔτε ὄντα οὔτε
ἂν γενόμενα λογοποιοῦσιν, οὓς ἐγὼ οὐ νῦν πρῶτον,

another war quite as great; for I myself think that they are content that we do not come against them, being so numerous and so powerful.

XXXVII. " If, however, they should come, as it is reported, I think Sicily more competent to carry the war through than the Peloponnesus, inasmuch as it is better provided in all respects, and that our city by itself is much stronger than this army which now, as they say, is coming on—aye, even if it should come in twice the number. For I know that neither horses will accompany them—and from here also none will be provided, except a few from Egesta—nor hoplites equal in number to ours, since they have to come on ships; for it is a great thing to make the long voyage to Sicily even with their ships alone, lightly laden. And the rest of the equipment which must be provided against so large a city as ours is not small. So much, then, do I differ in my judgment from these men that it seems to me, if they brought with them another city as large as Syracuse and settling here on our borders should wage the war, they would hardly fail to be utterly destroyed; much less, then, when all Sicily is hostile—for it will be united—and they are in a camp pitched just after landing from the ships and cannot venture far from their wretched tents and meagre supplies by reason of our cavalry. In short, I think they would not even get a foothold on the land; so much do I judge our forces to be superior.

XXXVIII. " But of these things, as I maintain, the Athenians are aware and they are, I am quite sure, taking care of their own interests, and men from here are fabricating stories neither true nor possible, men whom not now for the first time but always I have

2 ἀλλ' αἰεὶ ἐπίσταμαι ἤτοι λόγοις γε τοιοῖσδε καὶ
ἔτι τούτων κακουργοτέροις ἢ ἔργοις βουλομένους
καταπλήξαντας τὸ ὑμέτερον πλῆθος αὐτοὺς τῆς
πόλεως ἄρχειν. καὶ δέδοικα μέντοι μή ποτε πολλὰ
πειρῶντες καὶ κατορθώσωσιν· ἡμεῖς δὲ κακοί,
πρὶν ἐν τῷ παθεῖν ὦμεν, προφυλάξασθαί τε καὶ
3 αἰσθόμενοι ἐπεξελθεῖν. τοιγάρτοι δι' αὐτὰ ἡ πόλις
ἡμῶν ὀλιγάκις μὲν ἡσυχάζει, στάσεις δὲ πολλὰς
καὶ ἀγῶνας οὐ πρὸς τοὺς πολεμίους πλείονας ἢ
πρὸς αὑτὴν ἀναιρεῖται, τυραννίδας δὲ ἔστιν ὅτε καὶ
4 δυναστείας ἀδίκους. ὧν ἐγὼ πειράσομαι, ἤν γε
ὑμεῖς ἐθέλητε ἕπεσθαι, μήποτε ἐφ' ἡμῶν τι περι-
ιδεῖν γενέσθαι, ὑμᾶς μὲν τοὺς πολλοὺς πείθων
τοὺς δὲ [1] τὰ τοιαῦτα μηχανωμένους κολάζων, μὴ
μόνον αὐτοφώρους (χαλεπὸν γὰρ ἐπιτυγχάνειν),
ἀλλὰ καὶ ὧν βούλονται μὲν δύνανται δ' οὔ (τὸν
γὰρ ἐχθρὸν οὐχ ὧν δρᾷ μόνον, ἀλλὰ καὶ τῆς
διανοίας προαμύνεσθαι χρή, εἴπερ καὶ μὴ προφυ-
λαξάμενός τις προπείσεται), τοὺς δ' αὖ ὀλίγους
τὰ μὲν ἐλέγχων, τὰ δὲ φυλάσσων, τὰ δὲ καὶ διδά-
σκων· μάλιστα γὰρ δοκῶ ἄν μοι οὕτως ἀπο-
5 τρέπειν τῆς κακουργίας. καὶ δῆτα, ὃ πολλάκις
ἐσκεψάμην, τί καὶ βούλεσθε, ὦ νεώτεροι; πότερον
ἄρχειν ἤδη; ἀλλ' οὐκ ἔννομον. ὁ δὲ νόμος ἐκ τοῦ
μὴ δύνασθαι ὑμᾶς μᾶλλον ἢ δυναμένους ἐτέθη
ἀτιμάζειν. ἀλλὰ δὴ μὴ μετὰ τῶν [2] πολλῶν ἰσο-

---

[1] Hude follows Weil in bracketing δέ and changing κολάζων to κολάζειν.
[2] τῶν added by Hude as probably read by the Scholiast.

known to be wishing, either by reports such as these
and still more mischievous than these, or by overt
acts, to frighten the mass of you and themselves
dominate the city. And I fear, moreover, that some
day, by dint of repeated attempts, they may actually
succeed ; for we are poor hands at taking precautions
before we are at their mercy, and, if we have discovered their plots, at dealing conclusively with the
plotters. Therefore it is on this very account that
our city is seldom quiet, but is subject to frequent
feuds and conflicts—not so much with the enemy
as with itself—and sometimes to tyrannies and
wicked oligarchies. But if you will only follow me,
I will try to see to it that never in our time shall
any of these things come to pass, persuading you
who are the mass of the people, but chastising the
men who devise such things, not only when they
are caught in the act—as it is difficult to come upon
them—but even for what they would but cannot do.
For an enemy one must forestall, not only in what
he does, but even in his designs, since indeed a
man who is not first to safeguard himself will be
first to suffer. As to the oligarchs, on the other
hand, I shall sometimes expose them, and sometimes
watch them, but sometimes also I shall instruct them,
for in this way I think I could best deter them from
evil-doing. And now—a question which I have often
asked myself—what do you want, you young men ?
To hold office already ? But that is not lawful ; and
the law was enacted in consequence of your incompe-
tency, rather than to keep you from office when
competent. Well, then, you do not want to be on an

νομεῖσθαι; καὶ πῶς δίκαιον τοὺς αὐτοὺς μὴ τῶν
αὐτῶν ἀξιοῦσθαι;

XXXIX. " Φήσει τις δημοκρατίαν οὔτε ξυνετὸν
οὔτ᾽ ἴσον εἶναι, τοὺς δὲ ἔχοντας τὰ χρήματα καὶ
ἄρχειν ἄριστα βελτίους. ἐγὼ δέ φημι πρῶτα μὲν
δῆμον ξύμπαν ὠνομάσθαι, ὀλιγαρχίαν δὲ μέρος,
ἔπειτα φύλακας μὲν ἀρίστους εἶναι χρημάτων τοὺς
πλουσίους, βουλεῦσαι δ᾽ ἂν βέλτιστα τοὺς ξυνε-
τούς, κρῖναι δ᾽ ἂν ἀκούσαντας ἄριστα τοὺς πολλούς,
καὶ ταῦτα ὁμοίως καὶ κατὰ μέρη καὶ ξύμπαντα
2 ἐν δημοκρατίᾳ ἰσομοιρεῖν. ὀλιγαρχία δὲ τῶν μὲν
κινδύνων τοῖς πολλοῖς μεταδίδωσι, τῶν δ᾽ ὠφε-
λίμων οὐ πλεονεκτεῖ μόνον, ἀλλὰ καὶ ξύμπαντ᾽
ἀφελομένη ἔχει· ἃ ὑμῶν οἵ τε δυνάμενοι καὶ οἱ
νέοι προθυμοῦνται, ἀδύνατα ἐν μεγάλῃ πόλει
κατασχεῖν.

XL. "᾽Αλλ᾽ ἔτι καὶ νῦν, ὦ πάντων ἀξυνετώ-
τατοι, ὧν ἐγὼ οἶδα Ἑλλήνων, εἰ μὴ μανθάνετε
κακὰ σπεύδοντες,[1] ἢ ἀδικώτατοι, εἰ εἰδότες τολ-
μᾶτε, ἀλλ᾽ ἤτοι μαθόντες γε ἢ μεταγνόντες τὸ τῆς
πόλεως ξύμπασι κοινὸν αὔξετε, ἡγησάμενοι τοῦτο
μὲν ἂν καὶ ἴσον καὶ πλέον οἱ ἀγαθοὶ ὑμῶν ἤπερ
τὸ τῆς πόλεως πλῆθος[2] μετασχεῖν, εἰ δ᾽ ἄλλα
βουλήσεσθε, κἂν τοῦ παντὸς κινδυνεῦσαι στερη-
θῆναι· καὶ τῶν τοιῶνδε ἀγγελιῶν ὡς πρὸς αἰσθα-
2 νομένους καὶ μὴ ἐπιτρέψοντας ἀπαλλάγητε. ἡ
γὰρ πόλις ἥδε, καὶ εἰ ἔρχονται Ἀθηναῖοι, ἀμυνεῖται
αὐτοὺς ἀξίως αὑτῆς, καὶ στρατηγοί εἰσιν ἡμῖν οἳ

---

[1] ἢ ἀμαθέστατοί ἐστε, before ἢ ἀδικώτατοι in the MSS.,
deleted by Dobree and Madvig.
[2] ἤπερ τὸ τῆς πόλεως πλῆθος, Hude deletes, following
Krüger.

equality with the many? And how is it right that the same folk should not be deemed worthy of the same privileges?

XXXIX. "Some will say that a democracy is neither wise nor equitable, and that those that have property are more competent to rule best. But I say, first, that democracy is a name for all, oligarchy for only a part; next, that while the wealthy are the best guardians of property, the wise would be the best counsellors, and the many, after hearing matters discussed, would be the best judges; and that these classes, whether severally or collectively, enjoy a like equality in a democracy. An oligarchy, on the other hand, gives the many a share of the dangers, but of the advantages it not merely claims the lion's share, but even takes and keeps all. And this is what the powerful among you and the young men are bent upon—a thing impossible to attain in a great city.

XL. "Still, even now, O ye most senseless of all Hellenes that I know, if you do not see that your designs are wicked, or most criminal, if you know and yet dare to persist in them,—even now, I say, either learn wisdom or repent of your folly and strive to advance the common interests of the state for the good of all, reflecting that the good among you would share this in equal or larger measure than the mass of the people, whereas if you have other aims you will run the risk of losing all. So have done with such reports, understanding that you are dealing with men who are aware of your designs and will not put up with them. For this city, even if the Athenians come, will ward them off in a manner worthy of herself; and we have generals who will

σκέψονται αὐτά. καὶ εἰ μή τι αὐτῶν ἀληθές
ἐστιν, ὥσπερ οὐκ οἴομαι, οὐ πρὸς τὰς ὑμετέρας
ἀγγελίας καταπλαγεῖσα καὶ ἑλομένη ὑμᾶς ἄρχον-
τας αὐθαίρετον δουλείαν ἐπιβαλεῖται, αὐτὴ δ' ἐφ'
αὑτῆς σκοποῦσα τούς τε λόγους ἀφ' ὑμῶν ὡς ἔργα
βουλομένους κρινεῖ καὶ τὴν ὑπάρχουσαν ἐλευθερίαν οὐχὶ ἐκ τοῦ ἀκούειν ἀφαιρεθήσεται, ἐκ δὲ
τοῦ ἔργῳ φυλασσομένη μὴ ἐπιτρέπειν πειράσεται
σῴζειν.''

XLI. Τοιαῦτα δὲ 'Αθηναγόρας εἶπεν. τῶν δὲ
στρατηγῶν εἷς ἀναστὰς ἄλλον μὲν οὐδένα ἔτι
εἴασε παρελθεῖν, αὐτὸς δὲ πρὸς τὰ παρόντα ἔλεξε
2 τοιάδε. ''Διαβολὰς μὲν οὐ σῶφρον οὔτε λέγειν
τινὰς ἐς ἀλλήλους οὔτε τοὺς ἀκούοντας ἀποδέχεσθαι, πρὸς δὲ τὰ ἐσαγγελλόμενα μᾶλλον ὁρᾶν,
ὅπως εἷς τε ἕκαστος καὶ ἡ ξύμπασα πόλις καλῶς
3 τοὺς ἐπιόντας παρασκευασόμεθα ἀμύνεσθαι. καὶ
ἢν ἄρα μηδὲν δεήσῃ, οὐδεμία βλάβη τοῦ τε τὸ
κοινὸν κοσμηθῆναι καὶ ἵπποις καὶ ὅπλοις καὶ τοῖς
ἄλλοις οἷς ὁ πόλεμος ἀγάλλεται (τὴν δ' ἐπιμέ-
λειαν καὶ ἐξέτασιν αὐτῶν ἡμεῖς ἕξομεν) καὶ τῶν
πρὸς τὰς πόλεις διαπομπῶν ἅμα ἔς τε κατασκοπὴν
καὶ ἤν τι ἄλλο φαίνηται ἐπιτήδειον. τὰ δὲ καὶ
ἐπιμεμελήμεθα ἤδη καὶ ὅ τι ἂν αἰσθώμεθα ἐς ὑμᾶς
οἴσομεν.''

Καὶ οἱ μὲν Συρακόσιοι τοσαῦτα εἰπόντος τοῦ
στρατηγοῦ διελύθησαν ἐκ τοῦ ξυλλόγου.

XLII. Οἱ δ' 'Αθηναῖοι ἤδη ἐν τῇ Κερκύρᾳ αὐτοί
τε καὶ οἱ ξύμμαχοι ἅπαντες ἦσαν· καὶ πρῶτον

look after these matters. And if none of these things be true—as indeed I think they are not—the state will not, through terror at your reports and by choosing you as rulers, place on her neck, of her own choice, the yoke of slavery, but looking at the matter for herself she will pass judgment on your words as if they were deeds ; and will not by listening to such reports be deprived of her present liberty, but will try to preserve it by taking active precautions so as to frustrate your designs."

XLI. Such was the speech of Athenagoras. Whereupon one of the generals rose up and forbade any one else to come forward, but himself spoke as follows with reference to the matter in hand : " Personal imputations it is not wise either for any speaker to utter against another or for those who hear to tolerate; but in view of the reports that are coming in, we should rather see how we, each person and the city as a whole, shall prepare to defend ourselves effectively against the invaders. And if after all there shall be no need of it, there is no harm in the commonwealth being equipped with horses and arms and all other things wherein war takes pride—the provision and inspection of such equipment we shall have in charge—and in sending men round to the cities for observation as well as for any other purpose that may seem expedient. These provisions we have in part already made, and whatever we find out we will bring before you."

And the Syracusans, when the general had said thus much, dispersed from the assembly.

XLII. Meanwhile the Athenians themselves and all their allies also were already at Corcyra. And

μὲν ἐπεξέτασιν τοῦ στρατεύματος καὶ ξύνταξιν
ὥσπερ ἔμελλον ὁρμιεῖσθαί τε καὶ στρατοπεδεύ-
σεσθαι οἱ στρατηγοὶ ἐποιήσαντο, καὶ τρία μέρη
νείμαντες ἐν ἑκάστῳ ἐκλήρωσαν, ἵνα μήτε ἅμα
πλέοντες ἀπορῶσιν ὕδατος καὶ λιμένων καὶ τῶν
ἐπιτηδείων ἐν ταῖς καταγωγαῖς, πρός τε τἆλλα
εὐκοσμότεροι καὶ ῥᾴους ἄρχειν ὦσι, κατὰ τέλη
2 στρατηγῷ προστεταγμένοι· ἔπειτα δὲ προύπεμψαν καὶ ἐς τὴν Ἰταλίαν καὶ Σικελίαν τρεῖς ναῦς
εἰσομένας αἵτινες σφᾶς τῶν πόλεων δέξονται.
καὶ εἴρητο αὐταῖς προαπαντᾶν, ὅπως ἐπιστάμενοι
καταπλέωσιν.

XLIII. Μετὰ δὲ ταῦτα τοσῇδε ἤδη τῇ παρασκευῇ Ἀθηναῖοι ἄραντες ἐκ τῆς Κερκύρας ἐς
τὴν Σικελίαν ἐπεραιοῦντο, τριήρεσι μὲν ταῖς
πάσαις τέσσαρσι καὶ τριάκοντα καὶ ἑκατὸν καὶ
δυοῖν Ῥοδίοιν πεντηκοντέροιν (τούτων Ἀττικαὶ
μὲν ἦσαν ἑκατόν, ὧν αἱ μὲν ἑξήκοντα ταχεῖαι,
αἱ δ᾽ ἄλλαι στρατιώτιδες, τὸ δὲ ἄλλο ναυτικὸν
Χίων καὶ τῶν ἄλλων ξυμμάχων), ὁπλίταις δὲ τοῖς
ξύμπασιν ἑκατὸν καὶ πεντακισχιλίοις (καὶ τούτων
Ἀθηναίων μὲν αὐτῶν ἦσαν πεντακόσιοι μὲν καὶ
χίλιοι ἐκ καταλόγου, ἑπτακόσιοι δὲ θῆτες ἐπιβάται τῶν νεῶν, ξύμμαχοι δὲ οἱ ἄλλοι ξυνεστράτευον, οἱ μὲν τῶν ὑπηκόων, οἱ δ᾽ Ἀργείων
πεντακόσιοι καὶ Μαντινέων καὶ μισθοφόρων πεντήκοντα καὶ διακόσιοι), τοξόταις δὲ τοῖς πᾶσιν
ὀγδοήκοντα καὶ τετρακοσίοις (καὶ τούτων Κρῆτες
οἱ ὀγδοήκοντα ἦσαν), καὶ σφενδονήταις Ῥοδίων

first the generals held a final review of the armament and made disposition in what order the forces were to anchor and to encamp. Making three divisions they allotted one to each general, in order that they might not, by sailing together, be at a loss for water and ports and provisions when they put in to shore, and that they might in general be more orderly and easy to control, being thus assigned in divisions to separate commanders. And next they sent forward to Italy and Sicily three ships, to ascertain which of the cities would receive them. And orders were given to these ships to come back to meet them, that they might know before putting to shore.

XLIII. After this the Athenians weighed anchor and crossed over from Corcyra to Sicily with a force that was now of this strength: Of triremes there were in all one hundred and thirty-four, and two Rhodian fifty-oared galleys—one hundred of these Attic, sixty of which were swift vessels, the others transports for soldiers, the rest of the fleet being furnished by the Chians and the other allies. Of hoplites there were all together five thousand one hundred—and of these, fifteen hundred were Athenians from the muster-roll and seven hundred Thetes[1] serving as marines on the ships, and the rest allies who shared in the expedition, some from the subject-states, others from the Argives to the number of five hundred, and of Mantineans and other mercenaries two hundred and fifty. Of bowmen there were in all four hundred and eighty, and eighty of these were Cretans; of slingers, seven hundred Rhodians; one

---

[1] Citizens of the lowest property-class, who served usually as oarsmen, but in extraordinary cases, as here, served as marines with hoplite armour.

ἑπτακοσίοις, καὶ Μεγαρεῦσι ψιλοῖς φυγάσιν εἴκοσι καὶ ἑκατόν, καὶ ἱππαγωγῷ μιᾷ τριάκοντα ἀγούσῃ ἱππέας.

XLIV. Τοσαύτη ἡ πρώτη παρασκευὴ πρὸς τὸν πόλεμον διέπλει, τούτοις δὲ τὰ ἐπιτήδεια ἄγουσαι ὁλκάδες μὲν τριάκοντα σιταγωγοί, καὶ τοὺς σιτοποιοὺς ἔχουσαι καὶ λιθολόγους καὶ τέκτονας καὶ ὅσα ἐς τειχισμὸν ἐργαλεῖα, πλοῖα δὲ ἑκατόν, ἃ ἐξ ἀνάγκης μετὰ τῶν ὁλκάδων ξυνέπλει· πολλὰ δὲ καὶ ἄλλα πλοῖα καὶ ὁλκάδες ἑκούσιοι ξυνηκολούθουν τῇ στρατιᾷ ἐμπορίας ἕνεκα· ἃ τότε πάντα ἐκ τῆς Κερκύρας ξυν-
2 διέβαλλε τὸν Ἰόνιον κόλπον. καὶ προσβαλοῦσα ἡ πᾶσα παρασκευὴ πρός τε ἄκραν Ἰαπυγίαν καὶ πρὸς Τάραντα καὶ ὡς ἕκαστοι ηὐπόρησαν, παρεκομίζοντο τὴν Ἰταλίαν, τῶν μὲν πόλεων οὐ δεχομένων αὐτοὺς ἀγορᾷ οὐδὲ ἄστει, ὕδατι δὲ καὶ ὅρμῳ, Τάραντος δὲ καὶ Λοκρῶν οὐδὲ τούτοις, ἕως
3 ἀφίκοντο ἐς Ῥήγιον τῆς Ἰταλίας ἀκρωτήριον. καὶ ἐνταῦθα ἤδη ἠθροίζοντο, καὶ ἔξω τῆς πόλεως, ὡς αὐτοὺς ἔσω οὐκ ἐδέχοντο, στρατόπεδόν τε κατεσκευάσαντο ἐν τῷ τῆς Ἀρτέμιδος ἱερῷ, οὗ αὐτοῖς καὶ ἀγορὰν παρεῖχον, καὶ ναῦς ἀνελκύσαντες ἡσύχασαν. καὶ πρὸς [1] τοὺς Ῥηγίνους λόγους ἐποιήσαντο, ἀξιοῦντες Χαλκιδέας ὄντας Χαλκιδεῦσιν οὖσι Λεοντίνοις βοηθεῖν· οἱ δὲ οὐδὲ μεθ' ἑτέρων ἔφασαν ἔσεσθαι, ἀλλ' ὅ τι ἂν καὶ τοῖς
4 ἄλλοις Ἰταλιώταις ξυνδοκῇ, τοῦτο ποιήσειν. οἱ δὲ πρὸς τὰ ἐν τῇ Σικελίᾳ πράγματα ἐσκόπουν ὅτῳ τρόπῳ ἄριστα προσοίσονται· καὶ τὰς πρό-

---

[1] τε of the MSS., after πρὸς, deleted by Krüger.

hundred and twenty light-armed Megarian exiles; and one horse-transport carrying thirty cavalry.

XLIV. Such was the strength of the first armament that sailed over for the war.[1] And for these, thirty food-bearing transports brought supplies, having also bakers, stone-masons, carpenters, and all tools for wall-building; and there sailed also one hundred boats that were pressed into service, along with the transports. But many boats besides, as well as transports, voluntarily accompanied the expedition, for the sake of trade. All these, at that time, sailed together from Corcyra across the Ionian Gulf. And when the whole armament reached the Iapygian promontory, or Tarentum, or wherever they severally found opportunity to make land, they sailed along the coast of Italy—some of the cities not receiving them with a market nor into the town, though furnishing them with water and anchorage, and Tarentum and Locri not even with these—until they came to Rhegium, a promontory of Italy. There they now assembled, and, as the Rhegians did not admit them within the walls, they pitched a camp outside of the town in the precinct of Artemis, where a market also was provided for them; and so drawing up their ships on shore they took a rest. And they also held a conference with the Rhegians, claiming that they as Chalcidians[2] should aid the Leontines who were Chalcidians. They, however, said that they would be neutral, but would do whatever the rest of the Italiots should decide. The Athenians now considered what would be the best course to take with reference to affairs in Sicily; and at the same time

---

[1] cf. ch. xxxi. 1.
[2] cf. Strabo vi. 257 a, κτίσμα ἐστὶ τὸ Ῥήγιον Χαλκιδέων.

πλους ναῦς ἐκ τῆς Ἐγέστης ἅμα προσέμενον, βουλόμενοι εἰδέναι περὶ τῶν χρημάτων εἰ ἔστιν ἃ
ἔλεγον ἐν ταῖς Ἀθήναις οἱ ἄγγελοι.

XLV. Τοῖς δὲ Συρακοσίοις ἐν τούτῳ πολλα-
χόθεν τε ἤδη καὶ ἀπὸ τῶν κατασκόπων σαφῆ
ἠγγέλλετο ὅτι ἐν Ῥηγίῳ αἱ νῆές εἰσι, καὶ ὡς ἐπὶ
τούτοις παρεσκευάζοντο πάσῃ τῇ γνώμῃ καὶ
οὐκέτι ἠπίστουν. καὶ ἔς τε τοὺς Σικελοὺς περι-
έπεμπον, ἔνθα μὲν φύλακας, πρὸς δὲ τοὺς πρέσβεις, καὶ ἐς τὰ περιπόλια τὰ ἐν τῇ χώρᾳ φρουρὰς
ἐσεκόμιζον, τά τε ἐν τῇ πόλει ὅπλων ἐξετάσει καὶ
ἵππων ἐσκόπουν εἰ ἐντελῆ ἐστι, καὶ τἆλλα ὡς
ἐπὶ ταχεῖ πολέμῳ καὶ ὅσον οὐ παρόντι καθίσταντο.

XLVI. Αἱ δ' ἐκ τῆς Ἐγέστης τρεῖς νῆες αἱ
πρόπλοι παραγίγνονται τοῖς Ἀθηναίοις ἐς τὸ
Ῥήγιον, ἀγγέλλουσαι ὅτι τἆλλα μὲν οὐκ ἔστι
χρήματα ἃ ὑπέσχοντο, τριάκοντα δὲ τάλαντα
2 μόνα φαίνεται. καὶ οἱ στρατηγοὶ εὐθὺς ἐν ἀθυμίᾳ
ἦσαν ὅτι αὐτοῖς τοῦτό τε πρῶτον ἀντεκεκρούκει
καὶ οἱ Ῥηγῖνοι οὐκ ἐθελήσαντες ξυστρατεύειν,
οὓς πρῶτον ἤρξαντο πείθειν καὶ εἰκὸς ἦν μάλιστα,
Λεοντίνων τε ξυγγενεῖς ὄντας καὶ σφίσιν αἰεὶ ἐπι-
τηδείους. καὶ τῷ μὲν Νικίᾳ προσδεχομένῳ ἦν τὰ
παρὰ τῶν Ἐγεσταίων, τοῖν δὲ ἑτέροιν καὶ ἀλογώ-
3 τερα. οἱ δὲ Ἐγεσταῖοι τοιόνδε τι ἐξετεχνήσαντο
τότε ὅτε οἱ πρῶτοι πρέσβεις τῶν Ἀθηναίων ἦλθον

they were awaiting the arrival from Egesta of the ships that had been sent ahead, wishing to know about the money, whether there actually was what the messengers had reported at Athens.

XLV. Meanwhile, through spies, as well as from many other sources, positive information was already coming in to the Syracusans that the Athenian fleet was at Rhegium; and under these conditions they began to make preparations with all zeal, and were no longer incredulous. They sent around also to the Sicels, to some places guards, to others envoys; they brought garrisons into the forts in the outlying districts; as to affairs in the city, they made an inspection of arms and of horses, to see whether everything was up to full strength; and all other matters they were arranging with a view to a war that was imminent and all but upon them.

XLVI. The three ships that had gone ahead to Egesta met the Athenians at Rhegium, announcing that the rest of the money which the Egestaeans had promised was not there, but only thirty talents were to be found. And the generals were at once out of spirits, both because this had turned out contrary at the start, and because the Rhegians, the first people whom they had tried to persuade to join the expedition and with whom it was most likely they should succeed, seeing that they were kinsmen of the Leontines and always friendly to the Athenians, refused their consent. Nicias, indeed, was expecting this news from the Egestaeans, but for the other two it was actually somewhat of a surprise. The fact was that the Egestaeans had resorted to the following device at the time when the first envoys of the Athenians came to them to see about

αὐτοῖς ἐς τὴν κατασκοπὴν τῶν χρημάτων. ἔς τε
τὸ ἐν Ἔρυκι ἱερὸν τῆς Ἀφροδίτης ἀγαγόντες
αὐτοὺς ἐπέδειξαν τὰ ἀναθήματα, φιάλας τε
καὶ οἰνοχόας καὶ θυμιατήρια καὶ ἄλλην κατα-
σκευὴν οὐκ ὀλίγην, ἃ ὄντα ἀργυρᾶ πολλῷ πλείω
τὴν ὄψιν ἀπ᾽ ὀλίγης δυνάμεως χρημάτων παρεί-
χετο, καὶ ἰδίᾳ ξενίσεις ποιούμενοι τῶν τριηριτῶν
τά τε ἐξ αὐτῆς Ἐγέστης ἐκπώματα καὶ χρυσᾶ
καὶ ἀργυρᾶ ξυλλέξαντες καὶ τὰ ἐκ τῶν ἐγγὺς
πόλεων καὶ Φοινικικῶν καὶ Ἑλληνίδων αἰτη-
σάμενοι ἐσέφερον ἐς τὰς ἑστιάσεις ὡς οἰκεῖα
4 ἕκαστοι. καὶ πάντων ὡς ἐπὶ τὸ πολὺ τοῖς αὐτοῖς
χρωμένων καὶ πανταχοῦ πολλῶν φαινομένων
μεγάλην τὴν ἔκπληξιν τοῖς ἐκ τῶν τριήρων Ἀθηναίοις παρεῖχε, καὶ ἀφικόμενοι ἐς τὰς Ἀθήνας
5 διεθρόησαν ὡς χρήματα πολλὰ ἴδοιεν. καὶ οἱ μὲν
αὐτοί τε ἀπατηθέντες καὶ τοὺς ἄλλους τότε πείσαντες, ἐπειδὴ διῆλθεν ὁ λόγος ὅτι οὐκ εἴη ἐν τῇ
Ἐγέστῃ τὰ χρήματα, πολλὴν τὴν αἰτίαν εἶχον ὑπὸ
τῶν στρατιωτῶν· οἱ δὲ στρατηγοὶ πρὸς τὰ παρόντα ἐβουλεύοντο.

XLVII. Καὶ Νικίου μὲν ἦν γνώμη πλεῖν ἐπὶ
Σελινοῦντα πάσῃ τῇ στρατιᾷ, ἐφ᾽ ὅπερ μάλιστα
ἐπέμφθησαν, καὶ ἢν μὲν παρέχωσι χρήματα
παντὶ τῷ στρατεύματι Ἐγεσταῖοι, πρὸς ταῦτα
βουλεύεσθαι, εἰ δὲ μή, ταῖς ἑξήκοντα ναυσίν,
ὅσασπερ ᾐτήσαντο, ἀξιοῦν διδόναι αὐτοὺς τροφὴν
καὶ παραμείναντας Σελινουντίους ἢ βίᾳ ἢ ξυμ-
βάσει διαλλάξαι αὐτοῖς, καὶ οὕτω, παραπλεύ-
σαντας τὰς ἄλλας πόλεις καὶ ἐπιδείξαντας μὲν
τὴν δύναμιν τῆς Ἀθηναίων πόλεως, δηλώσαντας

the money : they brought them into the temple of Aphrodite at Eryx and showed them the dedicatory offerings—bowls, wine-ladles, censers, and not a little other table-furniture, which being of silver made, though of small value in money, a much greater display. And in giving private entertainments for the crews of the triremes, they not only collected the gold and silver drinking-cups from Egesta itself, but borrowed those from the neighbouring cities, both Phoenician and Hellenic, and brought them each to the banquets as though they were their own. And as all used for the most part the same vessels and there was a great display of them everywhere, it caused great astonishment to the Athenians from the triremes, and they on returning to Athens spread the report of how much treasure they had seen. And these men who had been themselves deceived and had at the time persuaded the rest, later, when the story got out that the money was not at Egesta, were much blamed by the soldiers. The generals, however, took counsel in view of the present situation.

XLVII. It was the judgment of Nicias that they should sail with their whole armament against Selinus, which was the object for which they had chiefly been sent out, and if the Egestaeans should furnish money for the whole army, they should then determine accordingly; otherwise, they should demand that they give maintenance for sixty ships, the number they had asked for, and remaining there they should reconcile the Selinuntians to the Egestaeans, either by force or by agreement. This being accomplished, the Athenians should sail along by the other cities, displaying the power of the city of Athens and making manifest their zeal towards their

δὲ τὴν ἐς τοὺς φίλους καὶ ξυμμάχους προθυμίαν,
ἀποπλεῖν οἴκαδε, ἢν μή τι δι' ὀλίγου καὶ ἀπὸ τοῦ
ἀδοκήτου ἢ Λεοντίνους οἷοί τε ὦσιν ὠφελῆσαι ἢ
τῶν ἄλλων τινὰ πόλεων προσαγαγέσθαι, καὶ τῇ
πόλει δαπανῶντας τὰ οἰκεῖα μὴ κινδυνεύειν.

XLVIII. Ἀλκιβιάδης δὲ οὐκ ἔφη χρῆναι τοσ-
αύτῃ δυνάμει ἐκπλεύσαντας αἰσχρῶς καὶ ἀπράκτους ἀπελθεῖν, ἀλλ' ἔς τε τὰς πόλεις ἐπικη-
ρυκεύεσθαι πλὴν Σελινοῦντος καὶ Συρακουσῶν
τὰς ἄλλας, καὶ πειρᾶσθαι καὶ τοὺς Σικελοὺς τοὺς
μὲν ἀφιστάναι ἀπὸ τῶν Συρακοσίων, τοὺς δὲ
φίλους ποιεῖσθαι, ἵνα σῖτον καὶ στρατιὰν παρέχωσι, πρῶτον δὲ πείθειν Μεσσηνίους (ἐν πόρῳ
γὰρ μάλιστα καὶ προσβολῇ εἶναι αὐτοὺς τῆς
Σικελίας, καὶ λιμένα καὶ ἐφόρμησιν τῇ στρατιᾷ
ἱκανωτάτην ἔσεσθαι), προσαγαγομένους δὲ τὰς
πόλεις, εἰδότας μεθ' ὧν τις πολεμήσει, οὕτως ἤδη
Συρακούσαις καὶ Σελινοῦντι ἐπιχειρεῖν, ἢν μὴ οἱ
μὲν Ἐγεσταίοις ξυμβαίνωσιν, οἱ δὲ Λεοντίνους
ἐῶσι κατοικίζειν.

XLIX. Λάμαχος δὲ ἄντικρυς ἔφη χρῆναι πλεῖν
ἐπὶ Συρακούσας καὶ πρὸς τῇ πόλει ὡς τάχιστα
τὴν μάχην ποιεῖσθαι, ἕως ἔτι ἀπαράσκευοί τέ
2 εἰσι καὶ μάλιστα ἐκπεπληγμένοι. τὸ γὰρ πρῶτον πᾶν στράτευμα δεινότατον εἶναι· ἢν δὲ χρο-
νίσῃ πρὶν ἐς ὄψιν ἐλθεῖν, τῇ γνώμῃ ἀναθαρσοῦντας
ἀνθρώπους καὶ[1] τῇ ὄψει καταφρονεῖν μᾶλλον.

----

[1] καί, Hude reads κἂν after van Herwerden.

friends and allies, and then should sail back home—
unless perchance they should be able quickly and
unexpectedly either to aid the Leontines, or to bring
over some of the other cities—and not imperil the
safety of the state at the expense of their own
resources.[1]

XLVIII. Alcibiades insisted that they ought not,
after sailing out with so great an armament, to go
back in disgrace without effecting anything; but urged
rather that they send heralds to the other cities, except
Selinus and Syracuse, and try to detach some of the
Sicels from the Syracusans, and to make friends of
others, in order that these might furnish grain and
troops, but first of all that they try to persuade the
Messenians; for their city, he urged, was most con-
veniently situated on a line of traffic [2] and at the
approach to Sicily and would be a harbour and a
most suitable watch-station for the armament. Then,
after they had brought over these cities and knew
with whose assistance they would carry on the war,
they should proceed to attack Syracuse and Selinus,
unless the latter came to terms with the Egestaeans,
and the former permitted them to restore the
Leontines.

XLIX. Lamachus maintained that they ought to
sail direct for Syracuse and as soon as possible make
the fight near the city, while the Syracusans were still
unprepared and their consternation was at its height.
For every army, he argued, is always most formidable at first, but if it delay before coming into sight,
men recover their spirit and even at the sight of it
are more inclined to despise than to fear it. But

---

[1] As opposed to those of the Egestaeans.
[2] ἐν πόρῳ is used of the position of Corinth, I. cxx. 2.

αἰφνίδιοι δὲ ἢν προσπέσωσιν, ἕως ἔτι περιδεεῖς
προσδέχονται, μάλιστ' ἂν σφεῖς περιγενέσθαι καὶ
κατὰ πάντα ἂν αὐτοὺς ἐκφοβῆσαι, τῇ τε ὄψει
(πλεῖστοι γὰρ ἂν νῦν φανῆναι) καὶ τῇ προσδοκίᾳ
ὧν πείσονται, μάλιστα δ' ἂν τῷ αὐτίκα κινδύνῳ
3 τῆς μάχης. εἰκὸς δὲ εἶναι καὶ ἐν τοῖς ἀγροῖς
πολλοὺς ἀποληφθῆναι ἔξω διὰ τὸ ἀπιστεῖν σφᾶς
μὴ ἥξειν, καὶ ἐσκομιζομένων αὐτῶν τὴν στρατιὰν
οὐκ ἀπορήσειν χρημάτων, ἢν πρὸς τῇ πόλει
κρατοῦσα καθέζηται. τούς τε ἄλλους Σικελιώτας
οὕτως ἤδη μᾶλλον καὶ ἐκείνοις οὐ ξυμμαχήσειν
καὶ σφίσι προσιέναι καὶ οὐ διαμελλήσειν περι-
4 σκοποῦντας ὁπότεροι κρατήσουσιν. ναύσταθμον δὲ
ἐπαναχωρήσαντας καὶ ἐφόρμησιν τὰ [1] Μέγαρα
ἔφη χρῆναι ποιεῖσθαι, ἃ ἦν ἐρῆμα, ἀπέχοντα
Συρακουσῶν οὔτε πλοῦν πολὺν οὔτε ὁδόν.

L. Λάμαχος μὲν ταῦτα εἰπὼν ὅμως προσέθετο
αὐτὸς τῇ Ἀλκιβιάδου γνώμῃ. μετὰ δὲ τοῦτο
Ἀλκιβιάδης τῇ αὑτοῦ νηὶ διαπλεύσας ἐς Μεσσήνην καὶ λόγους ποιησάμενος περὶ ξυμμαχίας
πρὸς αὐτούς, ὡς οὐκ ἔπειθεν, ἀλλ' ἀπεκρίναντο
πόλει μὲν ἂν οὐ δέξασθαι, ἀγορὰν δ' ἔξω παρέξειν,
2 ἀπέπλει ἐς τὸ Ῥήγιον. καὶ εὐθὺς ξυμπληρώσαν-
τες ἑξήκοντα ναῦς ἐκ πασῶν οἱ στρατηγοὶ καὶ τὰ
ἐπιτήδεια λαβόντες παρέπλεον ἐς Νάξον, τὴν
ἄλλην στρατιὰν ἐν Ῥηγίῳ καταλιπόντες καὶ ἕνα
3 σφῶν αὐτῶν. Ναξίων δὲ δεξαμένων τῇ πόλει
παρέπλεον ἐς Κατάνην. καὶ ὡς αὐτοὺς οἱ Κατα-

---

[1] ἐφόρμησιν τά, Boehme's correction for ἐφορμηθέντας of the
MSS. Schaefer's conjecture, ἐφορμισθέντας, gives the same
sense.

if it attack suddenly, while the enemy are still in terror of its coming, it will have the best chance for victory and in every way will strike fear into them, both by the sight of it—for at this moment it would appear most numerous—and by the expectation of the fate in store for them, but most of all by the immediate peril of the battle. And, he added, probably many people have been left behind on their farms outside the city on account of the disbelief that the Athenians will come, and while they are bringing in their property the army will not lack supplies, if it once controls the land and invests the city. And as for the rest of the Siceliots, if we follow this course they will at once be more likely, not to make an alliance with the enemy, but to come over to us, and not to make delays, looking about to see which side will be the stronger. And he said, finally, that they should return and make a naval base and a watch-station at Megara, since it was uninhabited, and not far from Syracuse either by sea or by land.

L. Lamachus, though speaking to this effect, nevertheless gave his support to the opinion of Alcibiades. After this Alcibiades sailed in his own ship over to Messene and made proposals to the Messenians for an alliance ; but as they could not be persuaded, answering that they would not receive him within the city, but would furnish a market outside, he sailed back to Rhegium. Then the generals straightway manned sixty ships out of their whole number, and taking provisions sailed along the coast to Naxos, leaving at Rhegium the rest of the army and one of the generals. The Naxians received them into their city, and they sailed on then to Catana. When

ναῖοι οὐκ ἐδέχοντο (ἐνῆσαν γὰρ αὐτόθι ἄνδρες τὰ
Συρακοσίων βουλόμενοι), ἐκομίσθησαν ἐπὶ τὸν
Τηρίαν ποταμόν, καὶ αὐλισάμενοι τῇ ὑστεραίᾳ
ἐπὶ Συρακούσας ἔπλεον, ἐπὶ κέρως ἔχοντες τὰς
4 ἄλλας ναῦς· δέκα δὲ τῶν νεῶν προύπεμψαν ἐς
τὸν μέγαν λιμένα πλεῦσαί τε καὶ κατασκέψασθαι
εἴ τι ναυτικόν ἐστι καθειλκυσμένον, καὶ κηρῦξαι
ἀπὸ τῶν νεῶν προσπλεύσαντας ὅτι Ἀθηναῖοι
ἥκουσι Λεοντίνους ἐς τὴν ἑαυτῶν κατοικιοῦντες
κατὰ ξυμμαχίαν καὶ ξυγγένειαν· τοὺς οὖν ὄντας
ἐν Συρακούσαις Λεοντίνων ὡς παρὰ φίλους καὶ
5 εὐεργέτας Ἀθηναίους ἀδεῶς ἀπιέναι. ἐπεὶ δ᾽ ἐκη-
ρύχθη καὶ κατεσκέψαντο τήν τε πόλιν καὶ τοὺς
λιμένας καὶ τὰ περὶ τὴν χώραν, ἐξ ἧς αὐτοῖς
ὁρμωμένοις πολεμητέα ἦν, ἀπέπλευσαν πάλιν ἐς
Κατάνην.

LI. Καὶ ἐκκλησίας γενομένης τὴν μὲν στρατιὰν
οὐκ ἐδέχοντο οἱ Καταναῖοι, τοὺς δὲ στρατηγοὺς
ἐσελθόντας ἐκέλευον, εἴ τι βούλονται, εἰπεῖν. καὶ
λέγοντος τοῦ Ἀλκιβιάδου καὶ τῶν ἐν τῇ πόλει
πρὸς τὴν ἐκκλησίαν τετραμμένων οἱ στρατιῶται
πυλίδα τινὰ ἐνῳκοδομημένην κακῶς ἔλαθον διε-
2 λόντες καὶ ἐσελθόντες ἠγόραζον.[1] τῶν δὲ Καταναίων οἱ μὲν τὰ τῶν Συρακοσίων φρονοῦντες ὡς
εἶδον τὸ στράτευμα ἔνδον, εὐθὺς περιδεεῖς γενόμενοι
ὑπεξῆλθον οὐ πολλοί τινες, οἱ δὲ ἄλλοι ἐψηφίσαντό τε ξυμμαχίαν τοῖς Ἀθηναίοις καὶ τὸ ἄλλο
3 στράτευμα ἐκέλευον ἐκ Ῥηγίου κομίζειν. μετὰ δὲ
τοῦτο πλεύσαντες οἱ Ἀθηναῖοι ἐς τὸ Ῥήγιον, πάσῃ

---

[1] ἐς τὴν πόλιν, after ἠγόραζον in the MSS., deleted by van
Herwerden.

the Catanaeans would not receive them—for there
were in that place men who favoured the cause of the
Syracusans—they moved on to the river Terias, and
having bivouacked there sailed next day to Syracuse
with all their ships in single file, except ten, for this
number they had sent forward to sail into the Great
Harbour and observe whether any fleet was launched.
After sailing up the commanders of these were to
proclaim from the ships that the Athenians had come
to reinstate the Leontines in their own country on
the ground of alliance and kinship; any Leontines
therefore who were in Syracuse should come over
without fear to the Athenians as friends and bene-
factors.   When this proclamation had been made
and they had observed the city and the harbours and
the features of the country which they would have
to make their base for warlike operations, they sailed
back to Catana.

LI. An assembly being held there, the Catanaeans
would not receive the army but bade the generals
come in and say what they wanted.   While, then,
Alcibiades was speaking, and the attention of the
people in the city was wholly directed to the assembly,
the soldiers, breaking unobserved through a postern-
gate that had been badly built into the wall, entered
and were walking about in the market-place.   Those
Catanaeans who were partisans of the Syracusans,
seeing the soldiers inside, at once became much
frightened and slipped away, not in any large numbers;
the others voted alliance with the Athenians and
bade them bring the rest of their army from Rhegium.
After this the Athenians sailed back to Rhegium,
then putting out from there with their whole

ἤδη τῇ στρατιᾷ ἄραντες ἐς τὴν Κατάνην, ἐπειδὴ ἀφίκοντο, κατεσκευάζοντο τὸ στρατόπεδον.

LII. Ἐσηγγέλλετο δὲ αὐτοῖς ἔκ τε Καμαρίνης ὡς, εἰ ἔλθοιεν, προσχωροῖεν ἂν καὶ ὅτι Συρακόσιοι πληροῦσι ναυτικόν. ἁπάσῃ οὖν τῇ στρατιᾷ παρέπλευσαν πρῶτον μὲν ἐπὶ Συρακούσας· καὶ ὡς οὐδὲν ηὗρον ναυτικὸν πληρούμενον, παρεκο-μίζοντο αὖθις ἐπὶ Καμαρίνης καὶ σχόντες ἐς τὸν αἰγιαλὸν ἐπεκηρυκεύοντο. οἱ δ' οὐκ ἐδέχοντο, λέγοντες σφίσι τὰ ὅρκια εἶναι μιᾷ νηὶ καταπλεόν-των Ἀθηναίων δέχεσθαι, ἢν μὴ αὐτοὶ πλείους 2 μεταπέμπωσιν. ἄπρακτοι δὲ γενόμενοι ἀπέπλεον· καὶ ἀποβάντες κατά τι τῆς Συρακοσίας καὶ ἁρπαγὴν ποιησάμενοι καὶ τῶν Συρακοσίων ἱππέων βοηθησάντων καὶ τῶν ψιλῶν τινὰς ἐσκεδασμένους διαφθειράντων ἀπεκομίσθησαν ἐς Κατάνην.

LIII. Καὶ καταλαμβάνουσι τὴν Σαλαμινίαν ναῦν ἐκ τῶν Ἀθηνῶν ἥκουσαν ἐπί τε Ἀλκιβιάδην, ὡς κελεύσοντας ἀποπλεῖν ἐς ἀπολογίαν ὧν ἡ πόλις ἐνεκάλει, καὶ ἐπ' ἄλλους τινὰς τῶν στρα-τιωτῶν, τῶν μὲν[1] μετ' αὐτοῦ μεμηνυμένων περὶ τῶν μυστηρίων ὡς ἀσεβούντων, τῶν δὲ καὶ περὶ 2 τῶν Ἑρμῶν. οἱ γὰρ Ἀθηναῖοι, ἐπειδὴ ἡ στρατιὰ ἀπέπλευσεν, οὐδὲν ἧσσον ζήτησιν ἐποιοῦντο τῶν περὶ τὰ μυστήρια καὶ τῶν περὶ τοὺς Ἑρμᾶς δρασθέντων, καὶ οὐ δοκιμάζοντες τοὺς μηνυτάς,

---

[1] μὲν added by Hude.

armament for Catana, on their arrival they set about arranging their camp.

LII. Meanwhile news came from Camarina that if the Athenians would go thither the Camarinaeans would join them, and also that the Syracusans were manning a fleet. Accordingly they proceeded with their whole army along the coast, first to Syracuse; and when they found no fleet was being manned, they again continued along the coast to Camarina and putting to shore sent forward a herald. The Camarinaeans, however, would not receive them, saying that the terms of their oath were to receive the Athenians only if they put in with a single ship, unless they themselves sent for more. So the Athenians sailed away without accomplishing anything; and after landing at a point in Syracusan territory and making raids, when the Syracusan cavalry had come to the rescue and killed some of their light-armed troops that were straggling they went back to Catana.

LIII. There they found that the galley Salaminia[1] had come from Athens for Alcibiades—to order him to come home and make his defence against the charges which the city was bringing—and for certain of the soldiers also, some of them having been denounced with him as guilty of profanation with regard to the mysteries, and some also with regard to the Hermae. For after the armament sailed, the Athenians had been pursuing with no less zeal than before their investigation of what had been done in the matter of the mysteries as well as the Hermae; and as they did not test the witnesses, but in their

---

[1] One of the two swift Athenian state triremes kept always manned ready for extraordinary occasions and purposes.

ἀλλὰ πάντα ὑπόπτως ἀποδεχόμενοι, διὰ πονηρῶν
ἀνθρώπων πίστιν πάνυ χρηστοὺς τῶν πολιτῶν
ξυλλαμβάνοντες κατέδουν, χρησιμώτερον ἡγούμενοι εἶναι βασανίσαι τὸ πρᾶγμα καὶ εὑρεῖν ἢ διὰ
μηνυτοῦ πονηρίαν τινὰ καὶ χρηστὸν δοκοῦντα
3 εἶναι αἰτιαθέντα ἀνέλεγκτον διαφυγεῖν. ἐπιστάμενος γὰρ ὁ δῆμος ἀκοῇ τὴν Πεισιστράτου καὶ τῶν
παίδων τυραννίδα χαλεπὴν τελευτῶσαν γενομένην καὶ προσέτι οὐδ' ὑφ' ἑαυτῶν καὶ Ἁρμοδίου
καταλυθεῖσαν, ἀλλ' ὑπὸ τῶν Λακεδαιμονίων,
ἐφοβεῖτο αἰεὶ καὶ πάντα ὑπόπτως ἐλάμβανεν.

LIV. Τὸ γὰρ Ἀριστογείτονος καὶ Ἁρμοδίου
τόλμημα δι' ἐρωτικὴν ξυντυχίαν ἐπεχειρήθη, ἣν
ἐγὼ ἐπὶ πλέον διηγησάμενος ἀποφανῶ οὔτε τοὺς
ἄλλους οὔτε αὐτοὺς Ἀθηναίους περὶ τῶν σφετέρων τυράννων οὐδὲ περὶ τοῦ γενομένου ἀκριβὲς
2 οὐδὲν λέγοντας. Πεισιστράτου γὰρ γηραιοῦ τελευ-
τήσαντος ἐν τῇ τυραννίδι οὐχ Ἵππαρχος, ὥσπερ
οἱ πολλοὶ οἴονται, ἀλλὰ Ἱππίας πρεσβύτατος ὢν
ἔσχε τὴν ἀρχήν. γενομένου δὲ Ἁρμοδίου ὥρᾳ
ἡλικίας λαμπροῦ Ἀριστογείτων, ἀνὴρ τῶν ἀστῶν,
3 μέσος πολίτης, ἐραστὴς ὢν εἶχεν αὐτόν. πειραθεὶς
δὲ ὁ Ἁρμόδιος ὑπὸ Ἱππάρχου τοῦ Πεισιστράτου
καὶ οὐ πεισθεὶς καταγορεύει τῷ Ἀριστογείτονι. ὁ
δὲ ἐρωτικῶς περιαλγήσας καὶ φοβηθεὶς τὴν
Ἱππάρχου δύναμιν μὴ βίᾳ προσαγάγηται αὐτόν,
ἐπιβουλεύει εὐθὺς ὡς ἀπὸ τῆς ὑπαρχούσης ἀξιώ-
4 σεως κατάλυσιν τῇ τυραννίδι. καὶ ἐν τούτῳ ὁ

state of suspicion accepted everything, on the credit of bad men they arrested and threw into prison very excellent citizens, thinking it more expedient to sift the matter to the bottom and find out the truth, than that anybody, even one reputed to be good and accused only through the villainy of an informer, should escape without close investigation. For the people, knowing by tradition that the tyranny of Peisistratus and his sons had become galling at the last, and moreover had been put down, not by themselves and Harmodius, but by the Lacedaemonians,[1] were in constant fear and regarded everything with suspicion.

LIV. Now the daring deed of Aristogeiton[2] and Harmodius was undertaken on account of a love affair, and by relating this at some length I shall prove that neither the Hellenes at large nor even the Athenians themselves give an accurate account about their own tyrants or about this incident. For when Peisistratus died,[3] as an old man, in possession of the tyranny, it was not Hipparchus, as most suppose, but Hippias, as eldest son, that succeeded to the sovereignty. And Harmodius, being then in the flower of youthful beauty, had as his lover Aristogeiton, a citizen of the middle class. An attempt to seduce him having been made by Hipparchus son of Peisistratus without success, Harmodius denounced him to Aristogeiton. And he, lover-like, deeply resented it, and fearing the power of Hipparchus, lest he might take Harmodius by force, at once plotted, with such influence as he possessed, to overthrow the tyranny. Meanwhile Hipparchus,

---

[1] Under Cleomenes, 510 B.C.
[2] 514 B.C.   [3] Probably 527 B.C.

Ἵππαρχος ὡς αὖθις πειράσας οὐδὲν μᾶλλον ἔπειθε
τὸν Ἁρμόδιον, βίαιον μὲν οὐδὲν ἐβούλετο δρᾶν, ἐν
τρόπῳ¹ δέ τινι ἀφανεῖ ὡς οὐ διὰ τοῦτο δὴ παρε-
5 σκευάζετο προπηλακιῶν αὐτόν. οὐδὲ γὰρ τὴν
ἄλλην ἀρχὴν ἐπαχθὴς ἦν ἐς τοὺς πολλούς, ἀλλ'
ἀνεπιφθόνως κατεστήσατο· καὶ ἐπετήδευσαν ἐπὶ
πλεῖστον δὴ τύραννοι οὗτοι ἀρετὴν καὶ ξύνεσιν,
καὶ Ἀθηναίους εἰκοστὴν μόνον πρασσόμενοι τῶν
γιγνομένων τήν τε πόλιν αὐτῶν καλῶς διεκόσμη-
σαν καὶ τοὺς πολέμους διέφερον καὶ ἐς τὰ ἱερὰ
6 ἔθυον. τὰ δὲ ἄλλα αὐτὴ ἡ πόλις τοῖς πρὶν κειμένοις
νόμοις ἐχρῆτο, πλὴν καθ' ὅσον αἰεί τινα ἐπεμέλοντο
σφῶν αὐτῶν ἐν ταῖς ἀρχαῖς εἶναι.   καὶ ἄλλοι τε
αὐτῶν ἦρξαν τὴν ἐνιαύσιον Ἀθηναίοις ἀρχὴν καὶ
Πεισίστρατος ὁ Ἱππίου τοῦ τυραννεύσαντος υἱός,
τοῦ πάππου ἔχων τοὔνομα, ὃς τῶν δώδεκα θεῶν
βωμὸν τὸν ἐν τῇ ἀγορᾷ ἄρχων ἀνέθηκε καὶ τὸν
7 τοῦ Ἀπόλλωνος ἐν Πυθίου. καὶ τῷ μὲν ἐν τῇ
ἀγορᾷ προσοικοδομήσας ὕστερον ὁ δῆμος Ἀθηναίων μεῖζον μῆκος² ἠφάνισε τοὐπίγραμμα· τοῦ
δὲ ἐν Πυθίου ἔτι καὶ νῦν δῆλόν ἐστιν ἀμυδροῖς
γράμμασι λέγον τάδε·

μνῆμα τόδ' ἧς ἀρχῆς Πεισίστρατος Ἱππίου υἱὸς
θῆκεν Ἀπόλλωνος Πυθίου ἐν τεμένει.

LV. Ὅτι δὲ πρεσβύτατος ὢν Ἱππίας ἦρξεν, εἰδὼς
μὲν καὶ ἀκοῇ ἀκριβέστερον ἄλλων ἰσχυρίζομαι,

---

¹ Levesque's correction for τόπῳ of the MSS.
² τοῦ βωμοῦ, in the MSS. after μῆκος, deleted by Krüger.

---

¹ This seems to point to a near relationship of the his-
torian with the family of the Peisistratidae, so that more

having in a second attempt met with no better success in persuading Harmodius, although he had no intention of offering violence, yet laid a plan to insult him in some covert way, as though it were not for this reason. For he did not generally so exercise his authority as to be oppressive to the mass of the people, but maintained it without giving offence. And indeed the Peisistratidae carried the practice of virtue and discretion to a very high degree, considering that they were tyrants, and although they exacted from the Athenians only five per cent. of their incomes, not only had they embellished their city, but they also carried on its wars and provided sacrifices for the temples. In other respects the city itself enjoyed the laws before established, except in so far that the tyrants took precaution that one of their own family should always be in office. Amongst others of them who held the annual archonship at Athens was Peisistratus, a son of the Hippias who had been tyrant. He was named after his grandfather and, when he was archon, dedicated the altar of the twelve gods in the Agora and that of Apollo in the Pythian precinct. The people of Athens afterwards, in extending the length of the altar in the Agora, effaced the inscription; but that on the altar of the Pythian Apollo can still be seen in indistinct letters, reading as follows:

"This memorial of his office Peisistratus son of
    Hippias
Set up in the precinct of Pythian Apollo."

LV. That it was Hippias who, as eldest son, succeeded to the sovereignty I positively affirm because I know it even by tradition more accurately than others,[1]

exact knowledge had come to him by word of mouth (καὶ ἀκοῇ); cf. Marcellinus, § 18, and Schol. on I. xx. 2.

γνοίη δ' ἄν τις καὶ αὐτῷ τούτῳ· παῖδες γὰρ αὐτῷ
μόνον φαίνονται τῶν γνησίων ἀδελφῶν γενόμενοι,
ὡς ὅ τε βωμὸς σημαίνει καὶ ἡ στήλη περὶ τῆς
τῶν τυράννων ἀδικίας, ἡ ἐν τῇ Ἀθηναίων ἀκρο-
πόλει σταθεῖσα, ἐν ᾗ Θεσσαλοῦ μὲν οὐδ' Ἱππάρχου οὐδεὶς παῖς γέγραπται, Ἱππίου δὲ πέντε,
οἳ αὐτῷ ἐκ Μυρσίνης τῆς Καλλίου τοῦ Ὑπερο-
χίδου θυγατρὸς ἐγένοντο· εἰκὸς γὰρ ἦν τὸν
2 πρεσβύτατον πρῶτον γῆμαι. καὶ ἐν τῇ αὐτῇ
στήλῃ πρῶτος γέγραπται μετὰ τὸν πατέρα, οὐδὲ
τοῦτο ἀπεικότως διὰ τὸ πρεσβεύειν τε ἀπ' αὐτοῦ
3 καὶ τυραννεῦσαι. οὐ μὴν οὐδ' ἂν κατασχεῖν μοι
δοκεῖ ποτε Ἱππίας τὸ παραχρῆμα ῥᾳδίως τὴν
τυραννίδα, εἰ Ἵππαρχος μὲν ἐν τῇ ἀρχῇ ὢν ἀπέ-
θανεν, αὐτὸς δὲ αὐθημερὸν καθίστατο· ἀλλὰ διὰ
τὸ πρότερον ξύνηθες τοῖς μὲν πολίταις φοβερόν,
ἐς δὲ τοὺς ἐπικούρους ἀκριβές, πολλῷ τῷ περιόντι
τοῦ ἀσφαλοῦς κατεκράτησε, καὶ οὐχ ὡς ἀδελφὸς
νεώτερος ὢν ἠπόρησεν, ἐν ᾧ οὐ πρότερον ξυνεχῶς
4 ὡμιλήκει τῇ ἀρχῇ. Ἱππάρχῳ δὲ ξυνέβη τοῦ πά-
θους τῇ δυστυχίᾳ ὀνομασθέντα καὶ τὴν δόξαν τῆς
τυραννίδος ἐς τὰ ἔπειτα προσλαβεῖν.

LVI. Τὸν δ' οὖν Ἁρμόδιον ἀπαρνηθέντα τὴν
πείρασιν, ὥσπερ διενοεῖτο, προυπηλάκισεν· ἀδελ-
φὴν γὰρ αὐτοῦ κόρην ἐπαγγείλαντες ἥκειν κανοῦν
οἴσουσαν ἐν πομπῇ τινι, ἀπήλασαν λέγοντες οὐδὲ
2 ἐπαγγεῖλαι τὴν ἀρχὴν διὰ τὸ μὴ ἀξίαν εἶναι. χαλεπῶς δὲ ἐνεγκόντος τοῦ Ἁρμοδίου πολλῷ δὴ μᾶλλον

and anyone might be convinced of it also by this simple
fact—he alone of the legitimate brothers appears to
have had children, as not only the altar signifies, but
also the column commemorating the wrong-doing of
the tyrants that was set up on the acropolis of Athens,
on which no child of Thessalus or of Hipparchus is
inscribed, but of Hippias five, who were borne to him
by Myrrhine daughter of Callias son of Hyperochi-
das; for it was natural for the eldest to marry first.
And on this same column his name is written first
after his father's, this also not unnaturally, as he was
the eldest after him and had been tyrant. Nor yet
again would Hippias, as it seems to me, have obtained
the tyranny at once with ease, if Hipparchus had been
in power when killed, and had had to establish himself therein on the same day. Nay, it was owing to
the habitual fear which before that he had inspired
in the citizens, and the strict discipline he had maintained in the bodyguard, that he got the upper hand
with superabundant security and was at no loss, as a
younger brother would have been, since in that case
he would not previously have been regularly used to
power. Hipparchus, however, as it fell out, having
become famous by his tragic fate, obtained in after-
time the credit also of having been tyrant.

LVI. So, then, when Harmodius had repulsed his
suit, Hipparchus insulted him, as he intended. For
after summoning a maiden-sister of his to serve as a
basket-bearer [1] in some procession, they rejected her,
declaring they had never summoned her at all, because
she was unworthy. As Harmodius was indignant at

---

[1] This service of carrying at festivals baskets containing
the requisites for religious ceremonies was a great distinction,
so that the rejection of the maiden was regarded as a bitter
insult to the family.

δι' ἐκεῖνον καὶ ὁ Ἀριστογείτων παρωξύνετο. καὶ
αὐτοῖς τὰ μὲν ἄλλα πρὸς τοὺς ξυνεπιθησομένους
τῷ ἔργῳ ἐπέπρακτο, περιέμενον δὲ Παναθήναια τὰ
μεγάλα, ἐν ᾗ μόνον ἡμέρᾳ οὐχ ὕποπτον ἐγίγνετο ἐν
ὅπλοις τῶν πολιτῶν τοὺς τὴν πομπὴν πέμψοντας
ἀθρόους γενέσθαι· καὶ ἔδει ἄρξαι μὲν αὐτούς, ξυνε-
παμύνειν δὲ εὐθὺς τὰ πρὸς τοὺς δορυφόρους ἐκεί-
3 νους. ἦσαν δὲ οὐ πολλοὶ οἱ ξυνομωμοκότες ἀσφαλείας ἕνεκα· ἤλπιζον γὰρ καὶ τοὺς μὴ προει-
δότας, εἰ καὶ ὁποσοιοῦν τολμήσειαν, ἐκ τοῦ
παραχρῆμα, ἔχοντάς γε ὅπλα, ἐθελήσειν σφᾶς
αὐτοὺς ξυνελευθεροῦν.

LVII. Καὶ ὡς ἐπῆλθεν ἡ ἑορτή, Ἱππίας μὲν
ἔξω ἐν τῷ Κεραμεικῷ καλουμένῳ μετὰ τῶν δο-
ρυφόρων διεκόσμει ὡς ἕκαστα ἐχρῆν τῆς πομπῆς
προϊέναι· ὁ δὲ Ἁρμόδιος καὶ ὁ Ἀριστογείτων
ἔχοντες ἤδη τὰ ἐγχειρίδια ἐς τὸ ἔργον προῆσαν.
2 καὶ ὡς εἶδόν τινα τῶν ξυνωμοτῶν σφίσι διαλεγό-
μενον οἰκείως τῷ Ἱππίᾳ (ἦν δὲ πᾶσιν εὐπρόσοδος
ὁ Ἱππίας), ἔδεισαν καὶ ἐνόμισαν μεμηνῦσθαί τε
3 καὶ ὅσον οὐκ ἤδη ξυλληφθήσεσθαι. τὸν λυπή-
σαντα οὖν σφᾶς καὶ δι' ὅνπερ πάντα ἐκινδύνευον
ἐβούλοντο πρότερον, εἰ δύναιντο, προτιμωρή-
σασθαι, καὶ ὥσπερ εἶχον ὥρμησαν ἔσω τῶν
πυλῶν, καὶ περιέτυχον τῷ Ἱππάρχῳ παρὰ τὸ
Λεωκόρειον καλούμενον. εὐθὺς δ'[1] ἀπερισκέπτως
προσπεσόντες καὶ ὡς ἂν μάλιστα δι' ὀργῆς, ὁ μὲν

---

[1] δ' added by Pontus.

this, Aristogeiton for his sake was far more exasperated. And now the details had been arranged by them with those who were to take part in the execution of their scheme; but they were waiting for the great Panathenaea, for on that day only it excited no suspicion for the citizens who were to take part in the procession to be assembled in arms. They were themselves to begin the attack, but the others were to join them at once in dealing with the bodyguard. The conspirators were not many, for better security; for they hoped that, if ever so few made the bold attempt, at once even those who were not before privy to it, having arms in their hands, would be inclined to bear a part in winning their own freedom.

LVII. And when the festival came on, Hippias with his bodyguard was outside the walls, in the place called the Cerameicus, arranging the order in which the several parts of the procession were to go forward; and Harmodius and Aristogeiton, who were ready with their daggers, stepped forward to put their scheme in effect. But when they saw one of their accomplices talking familiarly with Hippias, who was accessible to all, they took fright, thinking that they had been informed upon and would in a moment be arrested. So wishing first to take vengeance, if they could, upon the one who had aggrieved them and because of whom they were risking all, they rushed, just as they were, within the gates and came upon Hipparchus at the place called Leocorium.[1] And at once falling upon him recklessly and as men will in extreme wrath, the one

---

[1] The sanctuary of the daughters of Leos, an ancient Attic king, who in a famine were sacrificed for the state. It was in the Inner Cerameicus, near the temple of Apollo Patrous.

ἐρωτικῆς, ὁ δὲ ὑβρισμένος, ἔτυπτον καὶ ἀποκτεί-
4 νουσιν αὐτόν. καὶ ὁ μὲν τοὺς δορυφόρους τὸ
αὐτίκα διαφεύγει, ὁ Ἀριστογείτων, ξυνδραμόντος
τοῦ ὄχλου, καὶ ὕστερον ληφθεὶς οὐ ῥᾳδίως διετέθη·
Ἁρμόδιος δὲ αὐτοῦ παραχρῆμα ἀπόλλυται.

LVIII. Ἀγγελθέντος δὲ Ἱππίᾳ ἐς τὸν Κερα-
μεικόν, οὐκ ἐπὶ τὸ γενόμενον ἀλλ' ἐπὶ τοὺς
πομπέας τοὺς ὁπλίτας, πρότερον ἢ αἰσθέσθαι
αὐτοὺς ἄπωθεν ὄντας, εὐθὺς ἐχώρησε, καὶ ἀδήλως
τῇ ὄψει πλασάμενος πρὸς τὴν ξυμφορὰν ἐκέλευσεν αὐτούς, δείξας τι χωρίον, ἀπελθεῖν ἐς
2 αὐτὸ ἄνευ τῶν ὅπλων. καὶ οἱ μὲν ἀπεχώρησαν
οἰόμενοί τι ἐρεῖν αὐτόν, ὁ δὲ τοῖς ἐπικούροις
φράσας τὰ ὅπλα ὑπολαβεῖν ἐξελέγετο εὐθὺς οὓς
ἐπῃτιᾶτο καὶ εἴ τις ηὑρέθη ἐγχειρίδιον ἔχων·
μετὰ γὰρ ἀσπίδος καὶ δόρατος εἰώθεσαν τὰς
πομπὰς ποιεῖν.

LIX. Τοιούτῳ μὲν τρόπῳ δι' ἐρωτικὴν λύπην
ἥ τε ἀρχὴ τῆς ἐπιβουλῆς καὶ ἡ ἀλόγιστος
τόλμα ἐκ τοῦ παραχρῆμα περιδεοῦς Ἁρμοδίῳ
2 καὶ Ἀριστογείτονι ἐγένετο. τοῖς δ' Ἀθηναίοις
χαλεπωτέρα μετὰ τοῦτο ἡ τυραννὶς κατέστη,
καὶ ὁ Ἱππίας διὰ φόβου ἤδη μᾶλλον ὢν τῶν
τε πολιτῶν πολλοὺς ἔκτεινε καὶ πρὸς τὰ
ἔξω ἅμα διεσκοπεῖτο, εἴ ποθεν ἀσφάλειάν τινα
3 ὁρῴη μεταβολῆς γενομένης ὑπάρχουσάν οἱ. Ἱπ-
πόκλου γοῦν τοῦ Λαμψακηνοῦ τυράννου Αἰαν-
τίδῃ τῷ παιδὶ θυγατέρα ἑαυτοῦ μετὰ ταῦτα
Ἀρχεδίκην, Ἀθηναῖος ὢν Λαμψακηνῷ, ἔδωκεν,

inflamed by jealousy, the other by insult, they smote and slew him. Aristogeiton, indeed, escaped the guards for the moment, as the crowd ran together, but afterwards was caught and handled in no gentle manner; but Harmodius perished on the spot.

LVIII. When the news was brought to Hippias in the Cerameicus, he went at once, not to the scene of action, but to the hoplites in the procession, before they, being some distance away, had become aware of what had happened, and, disguising his looks so as to betray nothing in regard to the calamity, pointed to a certain place and ordered them to go thither without their arms. So they withdrew, thinking that he had something to say to them; while he, ordering the mercenaries to take up the arms of the others, immediately picked out those whom he held guilty, and anyone besides who was found with a dagger; for it was customary to march in the processions armed with shield and spear only.

LIX. It was in such wise, for an affront in love, that the plot of Harmodius and Aristogeiton was first conceived and their reckless attempt made under the influence of their momentary alarm. After this the tyranny became harsher for the Athenians, and Hippias, being now in greater apprehension, not only put to death many of the citizens, but also began to look abroad, to see if in any quarter he might find any door of safety open to him in case of a revolution. At any rate after this he gave his own daughter Archedice in marriage to Aeantides son of Hippocles, tyrant of Lampsacus—an Athenian to a Lampsacene!—perceiving that this family had

αἰσθανόμενος αὐτοὺς μέγα παρὰ βασιλεῖ Δαρείῳ
δύνασθαι. καὶ αὐτῆς σῆμα ἐν Λαμψάκῳ ἐστὶν
ἐπίγραμμα ἔχον τόδε·

ἀνδρὸς ἀριστεύσαντος ἐν Ἑλλάδι τῶν ἐφ᾽ ἑαυτοῦ
Ἱππίου Ἀρχεδίκην ἥδε κέκευθε κόνις·
ἣ πατρός τε καὶ ἀνδρὸς ἀδελφῶν τ᾽ οὖσα τυράννων
παίδων τ᾽ οὐκ ἤρθη νοῦν ἐς ἀτασθαλίην.

4 τυραννεύσας δὲ ἔτη τρία Ἱππίας ἔτι Ἀθηναίων
καὶ παυσθεὶς ἐν τῷ τετάρτῳ ὑπὸ Λακεδαιμονίων
καὶ Ἀλκμεωνιδῶν τῶν φευγόντων ἐχώρει ὑπόσπονδος ἔς τε Σίγειον καὶ παρ᾽ Αἰαντίδην ἐς
Λάμψακον, ἐκεῖθεν δὲ ὡς βασιλέα Δαρεῖον, ὅθεν
καὶ ὁρμώμενος ἐς Μαραθῶνα ὕστερον ἔτει εἰκοστῷ
ἤδη γέρων ὢν μετὰ Μήδων ἐστράτευσεν.

LX. Ὧν ἐνθυμούμενος ὁ δῆμος ὁ τῶν Ἀθηναίων
καὶ μιμνησκόμενος ὅσα ἀκοῇ περὶ αὐτῶν ἠπίστατο,
χαλεπὸς ἦν τότε καὶ ὕποπτης ἐς τοὺς περὶ τῶν
μυστικῶν τὴν αἰτίαν λαβόντας, καὶ πάντα αὐτοῖς
ἐδόκει ἐπὶ ξυνωμοσίᾳ ὀλιγαρχικῇ καὶ τυραννικῇ
2 πεπρᾶχθαι. καὶ ὡς αὐτῶν διὰ τὸ τοιοῦτον ὀργιζο-
μένων πολλοί τε καὶ ἀξιόλογοι ἄνθρωποι ἤδη ἐν
τῷ δεσμωτηρίῳ ἦσαν καὶ οὐκ ἐν παύλῃ ἐφαίνετο,
ἀλλὰ καθ᾽ ἡμέραν ἐπεδίδοσαν μᾶλλον ἐς τὸ
ἀγριώτερόν τε καὶ πλείους ἔτι ξυλλαμβάνειν,
ἐνταῦθα ἀναπείθεται εἷς τῶν δεδεμένων, ὅσπερ

---

[1] Ascribed to Simonides of Ceos (Aristotle, *Rhet.* i. 9).
[2] 510 B.C.

great influence with King Darius. And there is
at Lampsacus a monument of her bearing this inscription : [1]

"This dust covers Archedice daughter of Hippias,
    Who was foremost in Hellas among the men of his
        time :
Her father and husband, her brothers and children
    were tyrants,
Yet was not her mind lifted up to vainglory."

Hippias, however, after being tyrant for three years
more at Athens, was then deposed [2] in the fourth
year by the Lacedaemonians and the exiled Alcmae-
onidae, and retired under truce to Sigeium, from
there to Aeantides at Lampsacus, and thence to the
court of King Darius ; whence twenty years later,
being already an old man, he went with the Persians
on the expedition to Marathon.

LX. With these events in mind and recalling all
that they knew of them by report, the Athenian
people were in an ugly temper at this time and
suspicious towards those who had incurred blame in
the matter of the mysteries ; and the whole thing
seemed to them to have been done in connection
with a conspiracy that aimed at an oligarchy or a
tyranny. So when, in consequence of their anger
on this account, many noteworthy men were already
imprisoned and there seemed to be no end of the
matter, but day by day they were growing more savage
and still more men were being arrested, then at last
one of the men in confinement,[3] the one in fact who

[3] The orator Andocides, who gives his account of the
matter in his speech *De Mysteriis*. The man who persuaded
him was, according to Andocides, his cousin Charmides ;
according to Plutarch (*Alcib*. ii.), it was Timaeus.

ἐδόκει αἰτιώτατος εἶναι, ὑπὸ τῶν ξυνδεσμωτῶι
τινος εἴτε ἄρα καὶ τὰ ὄντα μηνῦσαι εἴτε καὶ οὔ·
ἐπ᾽ ἀμφότερα γὰρ εἰκάζεται, τὸ δὲ σαφὲς οὐδεὶς
οὔτε τότε οὔτε ὕστερον ἔχει εἰπεῖν περὶ τῶν
3 δρασάντων τὸ ἔργον. λέγων δὲ ἔπεισεν αὐτὸν
ὡς χρή, εἰ μὴ καὶ δέδρακεν, αὑτόν τε ἄδειαν
ποιησάμενον σῶσαι καὶ τὴν πόλιν τῆς παρούσης
ὑποψίας παῦσαι· βεβαιοτέραν γὰρ αὐτῷ σωτηρίαν εἶναι ὁμολογήσαντι μετ᾽ ἀδείας ἢ ἀρνηθέντι
4 διὰ δίκης ἐλθεῖν. καὶ ὁ μὲν αὐτός τε καθ᾽ ἑαυτοῦ
καὶ κατ᾽ ἄλλων μηνύει τὸ τῶν Ἑρμῶν· ὁ δὲ δῆμος
ὁ τῶν Ἀθηναίων[1] ἄσμενος λαβών, ὡς ᾤετο, τὸ
σαφὲς καὶ δεινὸν ποιούμενοι πρότερον, εἰ τοὺς
ἐπιβουλεύοντας σφῶν τῷ πλήθει μὴ εἴσονται,
τὸν μὲν μηνυτὴν εὐθὺς καὶ τοὺς ἄλλους μετ᾽
αὐτοῦ ὅσων μὴ κατηγορήκει ἔλυσαν, τοὺς δὲ
καταιτιαθέντας κρίσεις ποιήσαντες τοὺς μὲν
ἀπέκτειναν, ὅσοι ξυνελήφθησαν, τῶν δὲ διαφυ-
γόντων θάνατον καταγνόντες ἐπανεῖπον ἀργύριον
5 τῷ ἀποκτείναντι. κἀν τούτῳ οἱ μὲν παθόντες
ἄδηλον ἦν εἰ ἀδίκως ἐτετιμώρηντο, ἡ μέντοι ἄλλη
πόλις ἐν τῷ παρόντι περιφανῶς ὠφέλητο.

LXI. Περὶ δὲ τοῦ Ἀλκιβιάδου ἐναγόντων τῶν
ἐχθρῶν, οἵπερ καὶ πρὶν ἐκπλεῖν αὐτὸν ἐπέθεντο,
χαλεπῶς οἱ Ἀθηναῖοι ἐλάμβανον· καὶ ἐπειδὴ τὸ
τῶν Ἑρμῶν ᾤοντο σαφὲς ἔχειν, πολὺ δὴ μᾶλλον
καὶ τὰ μυστικά, ὧν ἐπαίτιος ἦν, μετὰ τοῦ αὐτοῦ

---

[1] ὁ τῶν Ἀθηναίων Krüger deletes, followed by Hude.

was regarded as the most guilty, was persuaded by
one of his fellow-prisoners to make a confession,
which may have been true or not; for there are
conjectures both ways, but no one has been able,
either then or afterwards, to tell the truth with
reference to those who did the deed. At any rate,
the other prisoner persuaded this man that, even
if he had not done the deed, he ought, having first
secured immunity,[1] to save himself and free the state
from the prevailing suspicion; for, he said, he had
a surer chance of saving his life by confessing, with
the promise of immunity, than by denying the
charge and undergoing trial. Accordingly he informed against himself and others in the affair of
the Hermae; and the people, delighted at getting
the truth, as they thought, and already making
much ado that they should not discover those who
were plotting against the democracy, at once set free
the informer and with him all the rest whom he had
not denounced; but with regard to those who were
accused they instituted trials and put to death all
who had been arrested, while on those who had fled
they passed sentence of death, offering a reward in
money to anyone who killed them. And in all this
it was uncertain whether those who suffered had not
been punished unjustly; the city at large, however,
at the time was clearly benefited.

LXI. With regard to Alcibiades, the Athenians took
the matter seriously, being urged on by his enemies,
the men who had attacked him before he sailed. And
thinking now that they had the truth about the
Hermae, they were far more convinced that the profanation of the mysteries also, in which he was implicated,

---

[1] *i.e.* promise of a free pardon.

λόγου καὶ τῆς ξυνωμοσίας ἐπὶ τῷ δήμῳ ἀπ'
2 ἐκείνου ἐδόκει πραχθῆναι. καὶ γάρ τις καὶ
στρατιὰ Λακεδαιμονίων οὐ πολλὴ ἔτυχε κατὰ
τὸν καιρὸν τοῦτον ἐν ᾧ περὶ ταῦτα ἐθορυβοῦντο
μέχρι ἰσθμοῦ προελθοῦσα πρὸς Βοιωτούς, τι
πράσσοντες. ἐδόκει οὖν ἐκείνου πράξαντος καὶ
οὐ Βοιωτῶν ἕνεκα ἀπὸ ξυνθήματος ἥκειν, καὶ εἰ
μὴ ἔφθασαν δὴ αὐτοὶ κατὰ τὸ μήνυμα ξυλλα-
βόντες τοὺς ἄνδρας, προδοθῆναι ἂν ἡ πόλις. καί
τινα μίαν νύκτα καὶ κατέδαρθον ἐν Θησείῳ τῷ ἐν
3 πόλει ἐν ὅπλοις. οἵ τε ξένοι τοῦ Ἀλκιβιάδου οἱ
ἐν Ἄργει κατὰ τὸν αὐτὸν χρόνον ὑπωπτεύθησαν
τῷ δήμῳ ἐπιτίθεσθαι· καὶ τοὺς ὁμήρους τῶν Ἀργείων τοὺς ἐν ταῖς νήσοις κειμένους οἱ Ἀθηναῖοι
τότε παρέδοσαν τῷ Ἀργείων δήμῳ διὰ ταῦτα δια-
4 χρήσασθαι. πανταχόθεν τε περιειστήκει ὑποψία
ἐς τὸν Ἀλκιβιάδην. ὥστε βουλόμενοι αὐτὸν ἐς
κρίσιν ἀγαγόντες ἀποκτεῖναι, πέμπουσιν οὕτω
τὴν Σαλαμινίαν ναῦν ἐς τὴν Σικελίαν ἐπί τε
5 ἐκεῖνον καὶ ὧν πέρι ἄλλων ἐμεμήνυτο. εἴρητο δὲ
προειπεῖν αὐτῷ ἀπολογησομένῳ ἀκολουθεῖν, ξυλλαμβάνειν δὲ μή, θεραπεύοντες τό τε πρὸς τοὺς
ἐν τῇ Σικελίᾳ στρατιώτας τε σφετέρους καὶ πολεμίους μὴ θορυβεῖν, καὶ οὐχ ἥκιστα τοὺς Μαντινέας καὶ Ἀργείους βουλόμενοι παραμεῖναι, δι'
ἐκείνου νομίζοντες πεισθῆναι σφίσι ξυστρατεύειν.
6 καὶ ὁ μὲν ἔχων τὴν ἑαυτοῦ ναῦν καὶ οἱ ξυνδια-

had been committed by him with the same intent, that
is of conspiring against the people. For it so happened
that a small Lacedaemonian force, at the moment
when they were in commotion about these matters,
had come as far as the Isthmus in pursuance of some
arrangement with the Boeotians. The opinion prevailed, therefore, that it had come on agreement at
his instigation, and not in the interest of the Boeotians; and that, if they had not themselves been
beforehand in arresting the men on the strength
of the information given, the city would have been
betrayed. And once for a whole night they lay
under arms in the precinct of Theseus within the
walls. Furthermore, the friends of Alcibiades at
Argos were at the same time suspected of a design
to attack the people; and on this account the
Argive hostages who had been deposited in the
islands[1] were at that time delivered by the Athenians
to the Argive people to be put to death. Thus from
all sides suspicion had gathered about Alcibiades.
And so, wishing to bring him to trial and put him
to death, they had sent the Salaminia to Sicily for
him and for the others who had been informed upon.
And the orders were to give him formal summons
to follow, that he might make his defence, but
not to arrest him; for they were solicitous about
both their own soldiers in Sicily and the enemy,
not wishing to stir up excitement among them, and
they were especially desirous that the Mantineans
and Argives should remain with them, thinking that
it was through him that they had been persuaded
to join in the expedition. So he, in his own ship,
and those who were accused with him, sailed off in

[1] *cf.* v. lxxxiv. 1.

βεβλημένοι ἀπέπλεον μετὰ τῆς Σαλαμινίας ἐκ
τῆς Σικελίας ὡς ἐς τὰς Ἀθήνας· καὶ ἐπειδὴ
ἐγένοντο ἐν Θουρίοις, οὐκέτι ξυνείποντο, ἀλλ᾽
ἀπελθόντες ἀπὸ τῆς νεὼς οὐ φανεροὶ ἦσαν, δείσαντες τὸ ἐπὶ διαβολῇ ἐς δίκην καταπλεῦσαι.
7 οἱ δ᾽ ἐκ τῆς Σαλαμινίας τέως μὲν ἐζήτουν τὸν
Ἀλκιβιάδην καὶ τοὺς μετ᾽ αὐτοῦ· ὡς δ᾽ οὐδαμοῦ
φανεροὶ ἦσαν, ᾤχοντο ἀποπλέοντες. ὁ δὲ Ἀλκιβιάδης ἤδη φυγὰς ὢν οὐ πολὺ ὕστερον ἐπὶ
πλοίου ἐπεραιώθη ἐς Πελοπόννησον ἐκ τῆς Θου-
ρίας· οἱ δ᾽ Ἀθηναῖοι ἐρήμῃ δίκῃ θάνατον κατέ-
γνωσαν αὐτοῦ τε καὶ τῶν μετ᾽ ἐκείνου.

LXII. Μετὰ δὲ ταῦτα οἱ λοιποὶ τῶν Ἀθηναίων
στρατηγοὶ ἐν τῇ Σικελίᾳ, δύο μέρη ποιήσαντες
τοῦ στρατεύματος καὶ λαχὼν ἑκάτερος, ἔπλεον
ξύμπαντι ἐπὶ Σελινοῦντος καὶ Ἐγέστης, βουλόμενοι μὲν εἰδέναι τὰ χρήματα εἰ δώσουσιν οἱ
Ἐγεσταῖοι, κατασκέψασθαι δὲ καὶ τῶν Σελινουν-
τίων τὰ πράγματα καὶ τὰ διάφορα μαθεῖν τὰ
2 πρὸς Ἐγεσταίους. παραπλέοντες δ᾽ ἐν ἀριστερᾷ
τὴν Σικελίαν, τὸ μέρος τὸ πρὸς τὸν Τυρσηνικὸν
κόλπον, ἔσχον ἐς Ἱμέραν, ἥπερ μόνη ἐν τούτῳ τῷ
μέρει τῆς Σικελίας Ἑλλὰς πόλις ἐστίν· καὶ ὡς
3 οὐκ ἐδέχοντο αὐτούς, παρεκομίζοντο. καὶ ἐν τῷ
παράπλῳ αἱροῦσιν Ὕκκαρα, πόλισμα Σικανικὸν
μέν, Ἐγεσταίοις δὲ πολέμιον· ἦν δὲ παραθαλασ-
σίδιον. καὶ ἀνδραποδίσαντες τὴν πόλιν παρέδοσαν
Ἐγεσταίοις (παρεγένοντο γὰρ αὐτῶν ἱππῆς), αὐτοὶ
δὲ πάλιν τῷ μὲν πεζῷ ἐχώρουν διὰ τῶν Σικελῶν,

company with the Salaminia from Sicily, as if for Athens. When, however, they reached the territory of the Thurians, they followed no further, but left their ship and disappeared, being afraid to sail home for trial in the face of the existing prejudice. The crew of the Salaminia sought for Alcibiades and his companions for some time; but when these were nowhere to be found, they sailed home. Alcibiades, however, being now an outlaw, not long afterwards crossed over by boat from Thurii to the Peloponnesus; and the Athenians through a judgment by default[1] sentenced him and his companions to death.

LXII. After this the two generals who were left in Sicily, making two divisions of the army and each taking one by lot, sailed with the whole force for Selinus and Egesta, wishing to know whether the Egestaeans would give the promised money, and to look into the affairs of the Selinuntians and learn their points of contention with the Egestaeans. So sailing along the coast, with Sicily—that is, the part of it which faces the Tyrrhenian gulf—on their left hand, they put into Himera, which is the only Hellenic city in that part of Sicily; and as Himera would not receive them, they proceeded along the coast. On their passage they took Hyccara, a petty town by the seaside, which, though Sicanian, was yet hostile to the Egestaeans. They enslaved the inhabitants, and turned the town over to the Egestaeans, some of whose cavalry had joined them, but themselves went back with their land-force through the territory of the Sicels until they came to Catana,

[1] Given in cases where the person indicted failed to appear for trial.

ἕως ἀφίκοντο ἐς Κατάνην, αἱ δὲ νῆες περιέπλευσαν
4 τὰ ἀνδράποδα ἄγουσαι. Νικίας δὲ εὐθὺς ἐξ
Ὑκκάρων ἐπὶ Ἐγέστης παραπλεύσας καὶ τἆλλα
χρηματίσας καὶ λαβὼν τάλαντα τριάκοντα παρῆν
ἐς τὸ στράτευμα· καὶ τἀνδράποδα ἀπέδοσαν, καὶ
ἐγένοντο ἐξ αὐτῶν εἴκοσι καὶ ἑκατὸν τάλαντα.
5 καὶ ἐς τῶν Σικελῶν τοὺς ξυμμάχους περιέπλευσαν,
στρατιὰν κελεύοντες πέμπειν· τῇ τε ἡμισείᾳ τῆς
ἑαυτῶν ἦλθον ἐπὶ Ὕβλαν τὴν Γελεᾶτιν πολεμίαν
οὖσαν καὶ οὐχ εἷλον. καὶ τὸ θέρος ἐτελεύτα.

LXIII. Τοῦ δ' ἐπιγιγνομένου χειμῶνος εὐθὺς
τὴν ἔφοδον οἱ Ἀθηναῖοι ἐπὶ Συρακούσας παρεσκευάζοντο, οἱ δὲ Συρακόσιοι καὶ αὐτοὶ ὡς ἐπ'
2 ἐκείνους ἰόντες. ἐπειδὴ γὰρ αὐτοῖς πρὸς τὸν
πρῶτον φόβον καὶ τὴν [1] προσδοκίαν οἱ Ἀθηναῖοι
οὐκ εὐθὺς ἐπέκειντο, κατά τε τὴν ἡμέραν ἑκάστην
προϊοῦσαν ἀνεθάρσουν μᾶλλον, καὶ ἐπειδὴ πλέ-
οντές τε τὰ ἐπ' ἐκεῖνα τῆς Σικελίας πολὺ ἀπὸ
σφῶν ἐφαίνοντο καὶ πρὸς τὴν Ὕβλαν ἐλθόντες
καὶ πειράσαντες οὐχ εἷλον βίᾳ, ἔτι πλέον κατε-
φρόνησαν καὶ ἠξίουν τοὺς στρατηγούς, οἷον δὴ
ὄχλος φιλεῖ θαρσήσας ποιεῖν, ἄγειν σφᾶς ἐπὶ
Κατάνην, ἐπειδὴ οὐκ ἐκεῖνοι ἐφ' ἑαυτοὺς ἔρχονται.
3 ἱππῆς τε [2] προσελαύνοντες αἰεὶ κατάσκοποι τῶν
Συρακοσίων πρὸς τὸ στράτευμα τῶν Ἀθηναίων
ἐφύβριζον ἄλλα τε καὶ εἰ ξυνοικήσοντες σφίσιν
αὐτοὶ μᾶλλον ἥκοιεν ἐν τῇ ἀλλοτρίᾳ ἢ Λεοντίνους
ἐς τὴν οἰκείαν κατοικιοῦντες.

LXIV. Ἃ γιγνώσκοντες οἱ στρατηγοὶ τῶν
Ἀθηναίων καὶ βουλόμενοι αὐτοὺς ἄγειν πανδημεὶ

[1] τὴν, Hude deletes with E.
[2] τε is indispensable, but omitted in all MSS.

while the ships sailed round to Catana with the captives. Nicias, however, had sailed at once [1] from Hyccara for Egesta, and after transacting his other business and receiving thirty talents had rejoined the army. Their slaves they sold, receiving for them one hundred and twenty talents. They sent round also to their allies among the Sicels, bidding them send troops; and with half of their own force went against Hybla Geleatis, a hostile town, but failed to take it. And so the summer ended.

LXIII. The following winter the Athenians began at once to prepare for the advance upon Syracuse, and the Syracusans also, on their side, to go against them. For when the Athenians did not, in accordance with their first alarm and expectation, at once attack them, with each successive day their courage revived; and when the Athenians sailed along the opposite coast of Sicily and showed themselves only at a distance from Syracuse, and going against Hybla failed in the attempt to take it by storm, the Syracusans had still greater contempt for them, and, as a crowd is wont to do when it has become elated, demanded that their generals should lead them against Catana, since the Athenians would not come against them. Moreover, mounted Syracusan scouts constantly rode up to the Athenian army and amongst other insults asked them: "Are you come to settle yourselves here with us, on land which belongs to other people, instead of resettling the Leontines on their own?"

LXIV. The Athenian generals were aware of all this and purposed to draw the whole of the Syra-

---

[1] *i.e.* without waiting for Hyccara to be reduced and its inhabitants disposed of.

THUCYDIDES

ἐκ τῆς πόλεως ὅτι πλεῖστον, αὐτοὶ δὲ ταῖς ναυσὶν
ἐν τοσούτῳ ὑπὸ νύκτα παραπλεύσαντες στρατόπεδον καταλαμβάνειν ἐν ἐπιτηδείῳ καθ᾽ ἡσυχίαν,
εἰδότες οὐκ ἂν ὁμοίως δυνηθέντες,¹ εἰ ἐκ τῶν νεῶν
πρὸς παρεσκευασμένους ἐκβιβάζοιεν ἢ κατὰ γῆν
ἰόντες γνωσθεῖεν (τοὺς γὰρ ἂν ψιλοὺς τοὺς σφῶν
καὶ τὸν ὄχλον τῶν Συρακοσίων τοὺς ἱππέας
πολλοὺς ὄντας, σφίσι δ᾽ οὐ παρόντων ἱππέων,
βλάπτειν ἂν μεγάλα· οὕτω δὲ λήψεσθαι χωρίον
ὅθεν ὑπὸ τῶν ἱππέων οὐ βλάψονται ἄξια λόγου·
ἐδίδασκον δ᾽ αὐτοὺς περὶ τοῦ πρὸς τῷ Ὀλυμπιείῳ
χωρίου, ὅπερ καὶ κατέλαβον, Συρακοσίων φυγάδες
οἳ ξυνείποντο), τοιόνδε τι οὖν πρὸς ἃ ἐβούλοντο οἱ
2 στρατηγοὶ μηχανῶνται. πέμπουσιν ἄνδρα σφίσι
μὲν πιστόν, τοῖς δὲ τῶν Συρακοσίων στρατηγοῖς
τῇ δοκήσει οὐχ ἧσσον ἐπιτήδειον. ἦν δὲ Κατα-
ναῖος ὁ ἀνήρ, καὶ ἀπ᾽ ἀνδρῶν ἐκ τῆς Κατάνης
ἥκειν ἔφη ὧν ἐκεῖνοι τὰ ὀνόματα ἐγίγνωσκον καὶ
ἠπίσταντο ἐν τῇ πόλει ἔτι ὑπολοίπους ὄντας τῶν
3 σφίσιν εὔνων. ἔλεγε δὲ τοὺς Ἀθηναίους αὐλί-
ζεσθαι ἀπὸ τῶν ὅπλων ἐν τῇ πόλει, καὶ εἰ βούλονται ἐκεῖνοι πανδημεὶ ἐν ἡμέρᾳ ῥητῇ ἅμα ἕῳ
ἐπὶ τὸ στράτευμα ἐλθεῖν, αὐτοὶ μὲν ἀποκλήσειν
τοὺς παρὰ σφίσι καὶ τὰς ναῦς ἐμπρήσειν, ἐκείνους
δὲ ῥᾳδίως τὸ στράτευμα προσβαλόντας τῷ σταυρώματι αἱρήσειν· εἶναι δὲ ταῦτα τοὺς ξυνδρά-
σοντας πολλοὺς Καταναίων καὶ ἡτοιμάσθαι ἤδη,
ἀφ᾽ ὧν αὐτὸς ἥκειν.

¹ καὶ, before εἰ in MSS., ignored by Valla and the Scholiast.

cusan force as far as possible away from the city, and themselves meanwhile to sail down under cover of night and undisturbed to occupy a camp at a suitable place, knowing that they would not be able to do this so well if they should disembark from their ships in the face of an enemy prepared to meet them, or should be detected going by land. For being without horsemen themselves, their own light-armed troops and their mob of camp-followers would, they thought, suffer great harm at the hands of the numerous Syracusan cavalry; but in the way proposed they would take a position where they would not suffer any harm worth mentioning from the cavalry; and certain Syracusan exiles who were with them gave them information as to the position close to the Olympieium, which in fact they subsequently occupied. So then, in furtherance of their plan, the generals devised some such scheme as this: They sent a man loyal to themselves, but in the opinion of the Syracusan generals no less a friend of theirs. The man was a Catanaean, and said that he had come from men at Catana whose names they recognized and whom they knew to be the remnant of those who were still loyal to them in the city. He said that the Athenians were in the habit of passing the night in the city away from their arms, and if the Syracusans would come in full force at dawn on an appointed day against their army, they would close the gates on the Athenians in their city and set fire to the ships, and the Syracusans could attack the stockade and easily take the whole army; for there were many Catanaeans who would help them in this undertaking, and the men from whom he himself had come were ready now.

LXV. Οἱ δὲ στρατηγοὶ τῶν Συρακοσίων, μετὰ τοῦ καὶ ἐς τὰ ἄλλα θαρσεῖν καὶ εἶναι ἐν διανοίᾳ καὶ ἄνευ τούτων ἰέναι[1] ἐπὶ Κατάνην, ἐπίστευσάν τε τῷ ἀνθρώπῳ πολλῷ ἀπερισκεπτότερον καὶ εὐθὺς ἡμέραν ξυνθέμενοι ᾗ παρέσονται ἀπέστειλαν αὐτόν, καὶ αὐτοὶ (ἤδη γὰρ καὶ τῶν ξυμμάχων Σελινούντιοι καὶ ἄλλοι τινὲς παρῆσαν) προεῖπον πανδημεὶ πᾶσιν ἐξιέναι Συρακοσίοις. ἐπεὶ δὲ ἔτοιμα αὐτοῖς καὶ τὰ τῆς παρασκευῆς ἦν καὶ αἱ ἡμέραι ἐν αἷς ξυνέθεντο ἥξειν ἐγγὺς ἦσαν, πορευόμενοι ἐπὶ Κατάνης ηὐλίσαντο ἐπὶ τῷ Συμαίθῳ ποταμῷ ἐν 2 τῇ Λεοντίνῃ. οἱ δ᾽ Ἀθηναῖοι ὡς ᾔσθοντο αὐτοὺς προσιόντας, ἀναλαβόντες τό τε στράτευμα ἅπαν τὸ ἑαυτῶν καὶ ὅσοι Σικελῶν αὐτοῖς ἢ ἄλλος τις προσεληλύθει καὶ ἐπιβιβάσαντες ἐπὶ τὰς ναῦς καὶ τὰ πλοῖα, ὑπὸ νύκτα ἔπλεον ἐπὶ τὰς Συρα- 3 κούσας. καὶ οἵ τε Ἀθηναῖοι ἅμα ἕῳ ἐξέβαινον ἐς τὸ[2] κατὰ τὸ Ὀλυμπιεῖον ὡς στρατόπεδον καταληψόμενοι, καὶ οἱ ἱππῆς οἱ Συρακοσίων πρῶτοι προσελάσαντες ἐς τὴν Κατάνην[3] καὶ αἰσθόμενοι ὅτι τὸ στράτευμα ἅπαν ἀνῆκται, ἀποστρέψαντες ἀγγέλλουσι τοῖς πεζοῖς, καὶ ξύμπαντες ἤδη ἀποτρεπόμενοι ἐβοήθουν ἐπὶ τὴν πόλιν.

LXVI. Ἐν τούτῳ δ᾽ οἱ Ἀθηναῖοι, μακρᾶς οὔσης τῆς ὁδοῦ αὐτοῖς, καθ᾽ ἡσυχίαν καθίσαν τὸ στράτευμα ἐς χωρίον ἐπιτήδειον καὶ ἐν ᾧ μάχης τε ἄρξειν ἔμελλον ὁπότε βούλοιντο καὶ οἱ ἱππῆς τῶν Συρακοσίων ἥκιστ᾽[4] αὐτοὺς καὶ ἐν τῷ ἔργῳ καὶ

---

[1] παρεσκευάσθαι, in MSS. after ἰέναι, deleted by Dobree.
[2] With E, all other MSS. τὸν.
[3] ἐς τὴν Κατάνην, Hude corrects to τῇ Κατάνῃ.
[4] ἂν, after ἥκιστ᾽ in MSS., deleted by Stahl.

LXV. And the Syracusan generals, who were
already confident as to the general situation, and
intended even without this help to go against
Catana, trusted the fellow much too incautiously, and
at once, agreeing upon a day on which they would
be there, sent him back; and themselves—the
Selinuntians and some others of their allies being
already present—made proclamation for the whole
force of the Syracusans to take the field. And when
their preparations were made and the days were
near on which they had agreed to come, they proceeded towards Catana and bivouacked at the River
Simaethus in the territory of Leontini. But the
Athenians, when they learned of their approach,
took all their own army and such of the Sicels or
others as had joined them, and embarking on their
ships and boats sailed under cover of night against
Syracuse. And they disembarked at daybreak at a
point opposite the Olympieium, where they proposed to occupy a camping-place; but the Syracusan
horsemen, who were the first to reach Catana and
found there that the whole army was gone, turned
about and announced this to the infantry, and all
then turned back at once and hastened to bring aid
to the city.

LXVI. Meanwhile the Athenians, undisturbed, as
the Syracusans had a long way to go, settled their
army in a suitable position, where they could begin
a battle whenever they wished and the Syracusan
horsemen would annoy them the least either in the

πρὸ αὐτοῦ λυπήσειν· τῇ μὲν γὰρ τειχία τε καὶ
οἰκίαι εἶργον καὶ δένδρα καὶ λίμνη, παρὰ δὲ τὸ
2 κρημνοί. καὶ τὰ ἐγγὺς δένδρα κόψαντες καὶ
κατενεγκόντες ἐπὶ τὴν θάλασσαν παρά τε τὰς
ναῦς σταύρωμα ἔπηξαν καὶ ἐπὶ τῷ Δάσκωνι ἔρυμά
τε, ἢ εὐεφοδώτατον ἦν τοῖς πολεμίοις, λίθοις
λογάδην καὶ ξύλοις διὰ ταχέων ὤρθωσαν καὶ τὴν
3 τοῦ Ἀνάπου γέφυραν ἔλυσαν. παρασκευαζομένων
δὲ ἐκ μὲν τῆς πόλεως οὐδεὶς ἐξιὼν ἐκώλυε, πρῶτοι
δὲ οἱ ἱππῆς τῶν Συρακοσίων προσεβοήθησαν,
ἔπειτα δὲ ὕστερον καὶ τὸ πεζὸν ἅπαν ξυνελέγη.
καὶ προσῆλθον μὲν ἐγγὺς τοῦ στρατεύματος τῶν
Ἀθηναίων τὸ πρῶτον, ἔπειτα δέ, ὡς οὐκ ἀντι-
προῇσαν αὐτοῖς, ἀναχωρήσαντες καὶ διαβάντες
τὴν Ἑλωρίνην ὁδὸν ηὐλίσαντο.

LXVII. Τῇ δ' ὑστεραίᾳ οἱ Ἀθηναῖοι καὶ οἱ
ξύμμαχοι παρεσκευάζοντο ὡς ἐς μάχην καὶ ξυνετάξαντο ὧδε. δεξιὸν μὲν κέρας Ἀργεῖοι εἶχον καὶ
Μαντινῆς, Ἀθηναῖοι δὲ τὸ μέσον, τὸ δὲ ἄλλο οἱ
ξύμμαχοι οἱ ἄλλοι. καὶ τὸ μὲν ἥμισυ αὐτοῖς τοῦ
στρατεύματος ἐν τῷ πρόσθεν ἦν, τεταγμένον ἐπὶ
ὀκτώ, τὸ δὲ ἥμισυ ἐπὶ ταῖς εὐναῖς ἐν πλαισίῳ,
ἐπὶ ὀκτὼ καὶ τοῦτο τεταγμένον· οἷς εἴρητο, ᾗ ἂν
τοῦ στρατεύματός τι πονῇ μάλιστα, ἐφορῶντας
παραγίγνεσθαι. καὶ τοὺς σκευοφόρους ἐντὸς τού-
2 των τῶν ἐπιτάκτων ἐποιήσαντο. οἱ δὲ Συρακόσιοι
ἔταξαν τοὺς μὲν ὁπλίτας πάντας ἐφ' ἑκκαίδεκα,
ὄντας πανδημεὶ Συρακοσίους καὶ ὅσοι ξύμμαχοι
παρῆσαν (ἐβοήθησαν δὲ αὐτοῖς Σελινούντιοι μὲν

actual fighting or before; for on one side walls and
houses and trees and a swamp furnished a barrier,
on the other side a line of cliffs. They also cut
down the trees near at hand and bringing them
down to the sea built a stockade by the ships;
and at Dascon, where the place was most accessible
to the enemy, they quickly erected a bulwark of
stones picked up in the fields and of timbers, and
pulled down the bridge over the Anapus. While
they were making these preparations nobody came
out from the city to hinder them; the first that
came against them were the horsemen of the Syracusans, but afterwards the infantry also gathered in
full force. And at first they drew near the Athenian
camp, but later, when these did not come out against
them, they withdrew across the Elorine road and
spent the night.

LXVII. On the next day the Athenians and their
allies made preparations for battle, and were drawn
up in the following order: On the right were the
Argives and Mantineans, the Athenians had the
centre, the other allies the rest of the line. Half of
their army was in the van, arrayed eight deep; the
other half near their sleeping-places, formed in a
hollow square, these too arrayed eight deep; and
the orders of the latter were, to be on the alert to
support any part of the army that was most in distress. And the baggage-carriers they put inside
the body of reserves. The Syracusans, on the other
hand, arranged all their hoplites sixteen deep, that
is, the whole force of the Syracusans and as many
of their allies as were present; for they had received
some reinforcements, chiefly from the Selinuntians,

μάλιστα, ἔπειτα δὲ καὶ Γελῴων ἱππῆς, τὸ ξύμπαν
ἐς διακοσίους, καὶ Καμαριναίων ἱππῆς ὅσον εἴκοσι
καὶ τοξόται ὡς πεντήκοντα), τοὺς δὲ ἱππέας ἐπε-
τάξαντο ἐπὶ τῷ δεξιῷ, οὐκ ἔλασσον ὄντας ἢ
διακοσίους καὶ χιλίους, παρὰ δ' αὐτοὺς καὶ τοὺς
3 ἀκοντιστάς. μέλλουσι δὲ τοῖς Ἀθηναίοις προ-
τέροις ἐπιχειρήσειν ὁ Νικίας κατά τε ἔθνη
ἐπιπαριὼν ἕκαστα καὶ ξύμπασι τοιάδε παρεκε-
λεύετο.

LXVIII. "Πολλῇ μὲν παραινέσει, ὦ ἄνδρες, τί
δεῖ χρῆσθαι, οἳ πάρεσμεν ἐπὶ τὸν αὐτὸν [1] ἀγῶνα;
αὐτὴ γὰρ ἡ παρασκευὴ ἱκανωτέρα μοι δοκεῖ εἶναι
θάρσος παρασχεῖν ἢ καλῶς λεχθέντες λόγοι μετὰ
2 ἀσθενοῦς στρατοπέδου. ὅπου γὰρ Ἀργεῖοι καὶ
Μαντινῆς καὶ Ἀθηναῖοι καὶ νησιωτῶν οἱ πρῶτοί
ἐσμεν, πῶς οὐ χρὴ μετὰ τοιῶνδε καὶ τοσῶνδε
ξυμμάχων πάντα τινὰ μεγάλην τὴν ἐλπίδα τῆς
νίκης ἔχειν, ἄλλως τε καὶ πρὸς ἄνδρας πανδημεί
τε ἀμυνομένους καὶ οὐκ ἀπολέκτους ὥσπερ καὶ
ἡμᾶς, καὶ προσέτι Σικελιώτας, οἳ ὑπερφρονοῦσι
μὲν ἡμᾶς, ὑπομενοῦσι δὲ οὔ, διὰ τὸ τὴν ἐπιστήμην
3 τῆς τόλμης ἥσσω ἔχειν. παραστήτω δέ τινι καὶ
τόδε, πολύ τε ἀπὸ τῆς ἡμετέρας αὐτῶν εἶναι καὶ
πρὸς γῇ οὐδεμιᾷ φιλίᾳ, ἥντινα μὴ αὐτοὶ μαχόμενοι
κτήσεσθε. καὶ τοὐναντίον ὑπομιμνήσκω ὑμᾶς ἢ
οἱ πολέμιοι σφίσιν αὐτοῖς εὖ οἶδ' ὅτι παρακελεύ-
ονται· οἱ μὲν γὰρ ὅτι περὶ πατρίδος ἔσται ὁ ἀγών,
ἐγὼ δὲ ὅτι οὐκ ἐν πατρίδι, ἐξ ἧς κρατεῖν δεῖ ἢ μὴ
ῥᾳδίως ἀποχωρεῖν· οἱ γὰρ ἱππῆς πολλοὶ ἐπικεί-
4 σονται. τῆς τε οὖν ὑμετέρας αὐτῶν ἀξίας μνη-

---

[1] τὸν αὐτὸν, Hude changes to τοιοῦτον.

but next to them some cavalry from the Geloans, about two hundred in all, and also from the Camarinaeans about twenty horsemen and fifty bowmen. Their cavalry, which was not less than twelve hundred in number, they placed on the right, and on its flank the javelin-men. As the Athenians were on the point of beginning the attack, Nicias went along the line and exhorted them, nation by nation as well as all together, in the following manner:

LXVIII. "What need is there, soldiers, of long exhortation, when we are all here for one and the same contest? Our array of itself seems to me more calculated to inspire confidence than well chosen words with a weak army. For where are Argives and Mantineans and Athenians and the best of the islanders, why should not everyone, in company with allies so brave and so numerous, have great hope of victory, especially against men that meet us in a mob and are not picked men as we ourselves are, and against Siceliots, moreover, who scorn us, indeed, but do not stand their ground against us, because the skill they have is not equal to their daring. This, too, must be fixed in the mind of everyone, that we are far from our own land and not near to any friendly country, unless you shall win such by your own swords. And my admonition is the opposite of the exhortation which, I am sure, the enemy is addressing to his troops; for they urge that the contest will be for fatherland, but I remind you that it will be, not in our fatherland, but where you either must win victory or may not easily get away; for their cavalry will be upon us in great numbers. Be mindful, therefore, of your own repu-

σθέντες ἐπέλθετε τοῖς ἐναντίοις προθύμως καὶ τὴν
παροῦσαν ἀνάγκην καὶ ἀπορίαν φοβερωτέραν
ἡγησάμενοι τῶν πολεμίων."

LXIX. Ὁ μὲν Νικίας τοιαῦτα παρακελευσά-
μενος ἐπῆγε τὸ στρατόπεδον εὐθύς. οἱ δὲ Συρακόσιοι ἀπροσδόκητοι μὲν ἐν τῷ καιρῷ τούτῳ ἦσαν
ὡς ἤδη μαχούμενοι, καί τινες αὐτοῖς ἐγγὺς τῆς
πόλεως οὔσης καὶ ἀπεληλύθεσαν· οἱ δὲ καὶ διὰ
σπουδῆς προσβοηθοῦντες δρόμῳ ὑστέριζον μέν,
ὡς δὲ ἕκαστός πῃ τοῖς πλείοσι προσμείξειε καθίσταντο. οὐ γὰρ δὴ προθυμίᾳ ἐλλιπεῖς ἦσαν οὐδὲ
τόλμῃ οὔτ' ἐν ταύτῃ τῇ μάχῃ οὔτ' ἐν ταῖς ἄλλαις,
ἀλλὰ τῇ μὲν ἀνδρείᾳ οὐχ ἥσσους ἐς ὅσον ἡ
ἐπιστήμη ἀντέχοι, τῷ δὲ ἐλλείποντι αὐτῆς καὶ
τὴν βούλησιν ἄκοντες προυδίδοσαν· ὅμως δὲ
οὐκ ἂν οἰόμενοι σφίσι τοὺς Ἀθηναίους προτέρους
ἐπελθεῖν καὶ διὰ τάχους ἀναγκαζόμενοι ἀμύνασθαι
2 ἀναλαβόντες τὰ ὅπλα εὐθὺς ἀντεπῇσαν. καὶ
πρῶτον μὲν αὐτῶν ἑκατέρων οἵ τε λιθοβόλοι καὶ
σφενδονῆται καὶ τοξόται προυμάχοντο καὶ τροπάς,
οἵας εἰκὸς ψιλούς, ἀλλήλων ἐποίουν· ἔπειτα δὲ
μάντεις τε σφάγια προύφερον τὰ νομιζόμενα καὶ
σαλπικταὶ ξύνοδον ἐπώτρυνον τοῖς ὁπλίταις, οἱ
3 δ' ἐχώρουν, Συρακόσιοι μὲν περί τε πατρίδος
μαχούμενοι καὶ τῆς ἰδίας ἕκαστος τὸ μὲν αὐτίκα
σωτηρίας, τὸ δὲ μέλλον ἐλευθερίας, τῶν δ' ἐναντίων Ἀθηναῖοι μὲν περί τε τῆς ἀλλοτρίας οἰκείαν
σχεῖν καὶ τὴν οἰκείαν μὴ βλάψαι ἡσσώμενοι,
Ἀργεῖοι δὲ καὶ τῶν ξυμμάχων οἱ αὐτόνομοι

tation, and attack the enemy with spirit and with the thought that our present necessity and the straits in which we stand are more to be feared than our foes."

LXIX. After such an exhortation Nicias straightway led on his army; but the Syracusans were not expecting to fight at just that moment, and some of them, as the city was near them, had even gone home; and these, though they came running to the lines as fast as they could, were late, and had to fall in wherever each one happened to reach the main body. For they were not lacking in zeal nor in daring either in this battle or in those which followed; nay, in bravery they were not inferior to their enemies, so far as they had experience, but through their lack of experience in spite of themselves they failed to do justice to their good intentions. Nevertheless, though they did not expect the Athenians to be the first to attack, and though they were forced to defend themselves in haste, they took up their arms at once and went against them. And at first the stone-throwers and slingers and bowmen skirmished, driving each other back, first one side and then the other, as light-armed troops would be likely to do. Afterwards the soothsayers brought forward the customary sacrifices and trumpeters stirred the hoplites to the charge. So they advanced—the Syracusans, to fight for fatherland and every man for his own present safety and future freedom; on the other side the Athenians, to fight for an alien land in order to win it for their own and to save their own land from the disaster of defeat; the Argives and those of the allies that were independent, to help the Athenians in securing

ξυγκτήσασθαί τε ἐκείνοις ἐφ᾽ ἃ ἦλθον καὶ τὴν
ὑπάρχουσαν σφίσι πατρίδα νικήσαντες πάλιν
ἐπιδεῖν· τὸ δ᾽ ὑπήκοον τῶν ξυμμάχων μέγιστον
μὲν περὶ τῆς αὐτίκα ἀνελπίστου σωτηρίας, ἢν μὴ
κρατῶσι, τὸ πρόθυμον εἶχον, ἔπειτα δὲ ἐν παρέργῳ
καὶ εἴ τι ἄλλο ξυγκαταστρεψάμενον ῥᾷον αὐτοῖς
ὑπακούσεται.

LXX. Γενομένης δ᾽ ἐν χερσὶ τῆς μάχης ἐπὶ
πολὺ ἀντεῖχον ἀλλήλοις, καὶ ξυνέβη βροντάς
τε ἅμα τινὰς γενέσθαι καὶ ἀστραπὰς καὶ ὕδωρ
πολύ, ὥστε τοῖς μὲν πρῶτον μαχομένοις καὶ
ἐλάχιστα πολέμῳ ὡμιληκόσι καὶ τοῦτο ξυν-
επιλαβέσθαι τοῦ φόβου, τοῖς δ᾽ ἐμπειροτέροις τὰ
μὲν γιγνόμενα καὶ ὥρᾳ ἔτους περαίνεσθαι δοκεῖν,
τοὺς δὲ ἀνθεστῶτας πολὺ μείζω ἔκπληξιν μὴ
2 νικωμένους παρέχειν. ὠσαμένων δὲ τῶν Ἀργείων
πρῶτον τὸ εὐώνυμον κέρας τῶν Συρακοσίων καὶ
μετ᾽ αὐτοὺς τῶν Ἀθηναίων τὸ κατὰ σφᾶς αὐτούς,
παρερρήγνυτο ἤδη καὶ τὸ ἄλλο στράτευμα τῶν
3 Συρακοσίων καὶ ἐς φυγὴν κατέστη. καὶ ἐπὶ πολὺ
μὲν οὐκ ἐδίωξαν οἱ Ἀθηναῖοι (οἱ γὰρ ἱππῆς τῶν
Συρακοσίων πολλοὶ ὄντες καὶ ἀήσσητοι εἶργον
καὶ ἐσβαλόντες ἐς τοὺς ὁπλίτας αὐτῶν, εἴ τινας
προδιώκοντας ἴδοιεν, ἀνέστελλον), ἐπακολουθή-
σαντες δὲ ἀθρόοι ὅσον ἀσφαλῶς εἶχε πάλιν
4 ἐπανεχώρουν καὶ τροπαῖον ἵστασαν. οἱ δὲ Συρακόσιοι ἀθροισθέντες ἐς τὴν Ἐλωρίνην ὁδὸν καὶ ὡς
ἐκ τῶν παρόντων ξυνταξάμενοι ἔς τε τὸ Ὀλυμ-

the objects for which they had come, and having won victory to see again their own fatherland; the subject-allies, above all zealous for their own immediate safety, for which there was no hope unless they conquered, then also with the secondary motive that having helped the Athenians to overthrow another power they might find the terms of their own subjection milder.

LXX. When they had come to close combat, they held out for a long time against one another; and there chanced to occur at the same time some claps of thunder and flashes of lightning and much rain, so that this too contributed to the fear of those who were fighting for the first time and were but little conversant with war, whereas to those who were more experienced[1] the storm seemed of course to be due merely to the season of the year, but the fact that their antagonists were not overcome caused them far greater alarm. When, however, the Argives had first driven back the left wing of the Syracusans, and after them the Athenians had repulsed their own opponents, then the rest also of the Syracusan line began to break and was reduced to flight. But the Athenians did not pursue far; for the Syracusan cavalry, being numerous and undefeated, held them in check, and falling upon their hoplites, if they saw any ahead in pursuit, drove them back. They only followed up in a body as far as it was safe, and then drew back and set up a trophy. The Syracusans, on the other hand, collecting on the Elorine road and drawing up as well as possible under the circumstances, in spite of their defeat sent some of their

---

[1] *i.e.* the Athenians.

πιεῖον ὅμως σφῶν αὐτῶν παρέπεμψαν φυλακήν,
δείσαντες μὴ οἱ Ἀθηναῖοι τῶν χρημάτων ἃ ἦν
αὐτόθι κινήσωσι, καὶ οἱ λοιποὶ ἐπανεχώρησαν ἐς
τὴν πόλιν.

LXXI. Οἱ δὲ Ἀθηναῖοι πρὸς μὲν τὸ ἱερὸν οὐκ
ἦλθον, ξυγκομίσαντες δὲ τοὺς ἑαυτῶν νεκροὺς καὶ
ἐπὶ πυρὰν ἐπιθέντες ηὐλίσαντο αὐτοῦ. τῇ δ᾽
ὑστεραίᾳ τοῖς μὲν Συρακοσίοις ἀπέδοσαν ὑποσπόνδους τοὺς νεκρούς (ἀπέθανον δὲ αὐτῶν καὶ τῶν
ξυμμάχων περὶ ἑξήκοντα καὶ διακοσίους), τῶν δὲ
σφετέρων τὰ ὀστᾶ ἀνέλεξαν (ἀπέθανον δὲ αὐτῶν
καὶ τῶν ξυμμάχων ὡς πεντήκοντα), καὶ τὰ τῶν
πολεμίων σκῦλα ἔχοντες ἀπέπλευσαν ἐς Κατάνην.
2 χειμών τε γὰρ ἦν καὶ τὸν πόλεμον αὐτόθεν ποιεῖσθαι οὔπω ἐδόκει δυνατὸν εἶναι, πρὶν ἂν ἱππέας
τε μεταπέμψωσιν ἐκ τῶν Ἀθηνῶν καὶ ἐκ τῶν
αὐτόθεν ξυμμάχων ἀγείρωσιν, ὅπως μὴ παντάπασιν ἱπποκρατῶνται, καὶ χρήματα δὲ ἅμα αὐτόθεν τε ξυλλέξωνται καὶ παρ᾽ Ἀθηναίων ἔλθῃ,
τῶν τε πόλεών τινας προσαγάγωνται, ἃς ἤλπιζον
μετὰ τὴν μάχην μᾶλλον σφῶν ὑπακούσεσθαι, τά
τε ἄλλα, καὶ σῖτον καὶ ὅσων δέοι, παρασκευά-
σωνται, ὡς ἐς τὸ ἔαρ ἐπιχειρήσοντες ταῖς Συρακούσαις.

LXXII. Καὶ οἱ μὲν ταύτῃ τῇ γνώμῃ ἀπέπλευσαν
ἐς τὴν Νάξον καὶ Κατάνην διαχειμάσοντες· Συρακόσιοι δὲ τοὺς σφετέρους αὐτῶν νεκροὺς θάψαντες
2 ἐκκλησίαν ἐποίουν. καὶ παρελθὼν αὐτοῖς Ἑρμοκράτης ὁ Ἕρμωνος, ἀνὴρ καὶ ἐς τἆλλα ξύνεσιν
οὐδενὸς λειπόμενος καὶ κατὰ τὸν πόλεμον ἐμπειρίᾳ
τε ἱκανὸς γενόμενος καὶ ἀνδρείᾳ ἐπιφανής, ἐθάρ-

own men to the Olympieium as a guard, fearing that the Athenians might disturb some of the treasures which were there; and the rest withdrew to the city.

LXXI. The Athenians, however, did not go to the temple, but collecting their own dead and placing them on a pyre they passed the night where they were. But on the next day they gave back under truce the Syracusan dead, of whom and of their allies about two hundred and sixty were slain; then gathering up the bones of their own dead—of themselves and their allies about fifty—and taking with them the spoils of the enemy, they sailed back to Catana. For it was winter, and it seemed as yet impossible to carry on the war from this base until they should send to Athens for horsemen, besides collecting them from their allies in Sicily, that they might not be altogether at the mercy of the enemy's cavalry. And they wanted at the same time to collect money from the island itself, and to have a supply come from Athens; also to bring over some of the cities, which they hoped would be more ready to listen to them since the battle; and to prepare other things, both food and whatever was needed, with a view to attacking Syracuse the next spring.

LXXII. With this purpose they sailed away to Naxos and Catana to spend the winter. The Syracusans, on the other hand, after burying their own dead, called an assembly. And there came before them Hermocrates son of Hermon,[1] a man who was in general second to none in point of intelligence, and had shown himself in this war both competent by reason of experience and conspicuous for courage.

---

[1] cf. IV. lviii.; VI. xxxiii.

σ με τε καὶ οὐκ εἴα τῷ γεγενημένῳ ἐνδιδόναι·
3 τὴν μὲν γὰρ γνώμην αὐτῶν οὐχ ἡσσῆσθαι, τὴν
δὲ ἀταξίαν βλάψαι. οὐ μέντοι τοσοῦτόν γε
λειφθῆναι ὅσον εἰκὸς εἶναι, ἄλλως τε τοῖς πρώτοις
τῶν Ἑλλήνων ἐμπειρίᾳ, ἰδιώτας ὡς εἰπεῖν χειρο-
4 τέχναις, ἀνταγωνισαμένους. μέγα δὲ βλάψαι καὶ
τὸ πλῆθος τῶν στρατηγῶν καὶ [1] τὴν πολυαρχίαν
(ἦσαν γὰρ πέντε καὶ δέκα οἱ στρατηγοὶ αὐτοῖς),
τῶν τε πολλῶν τὴν ἀξύντακτον ἀναρχίαν. ἢν δὲ
ὀλίγοι τε στρατηγοὶ γένωνται ἔμπειροι καὶ ἐν τῷ
χειμῶνι τούτῳ παρασκευάσωσι τὸ ὁπλιτικόν, οἷς
τε ὅπλα μὴ ἔστιν ἐκπορίζοντες, ὅπως ὡς πλεῖστοι
ἔσονται, καὶ τῇ ἄλλῃ μελέτῃ προσαναγκάζοντες,
ἔφη κατὰ τὸ εἰκὸς κρατήσειν σφᾶς τῶν ἐναντίων,
ἀνδρείας μὲν σφίσιν ὑπαρχούσης, εὐταξίας δ' ἐς
τὰ ἔργα προσγενομένης· ἐπιδώσειν γὰρ ἀμφότερα
αὐτά, τὴν μὲν μετὰ κινδύνων μελετωμένην, τὴν
δ' εὐψυχίαν αὐτὴν ἑαυτῆς μετὰ τοῦ πιστοῦ τῆς
5 ἐπιστήμης θαρσαλεωτέραν ἔσεσθαι. τούς τε στρατηγοὺς καὶ ὀλίγους καὶ αὐτοκράτορας χρῆναι
ἑλέσθαι καὶ ὀμόσαι αὐτοῖς τὸ ὅρκιον ἦ μὴν ἐάσειν
ἄρχειν ὅπῃ ἂν ἐπίστωνται· οὕτω γὰρ ἅ τε κρύπ-
τεσθαι δεῖ μᾶλλον ἂν στέγεσθαι καὶ τἆλλα κατὰ
κόσμον καὶ ἀπροφασίστως παρασκευασθῆναι.

---

[1] τὸ πλῆθος τῶν στρατηγῶν καὶ deleted by van Herwerden,
followed by Hude.

He encouraged them and protested against their giving way because of what had happened: their spirit, he told them, was not defeated; it was their lack of discipline that had done mischief. They had not, however, been so much inferior as might have been expected, especially as they had been pitted against troops who were the foremost among the Hellenes in experience, mere tiros so to speak against skilled craftsmen. Much mischief had also been caused by the large number of the generals and the division of command—for they had fifteen generals—and the disorder and anarchy among the troops. If only a few men of experience should be chosen as generals, and during this winter they should get the hoplite-force ready, providing arms for those who had none, in order that the number might be as large as possible, and enforcing the general training, in all likelihood, he said, they would get the better of the enemy, if to courage, which they had already, discipline were added when it came to action. For both these things would improve of themselves; their discipline would be practised in the midst of dangers, and their courage, in proportion as their confidence in their skill increased, would prove more self-reliant than ever. The generals, then, whom they should elect ought to be few in number and clothed with full powers and they should give them their oath that they would in very truth allow them to command according to their judgment; for in this way whatever ought to be kept secret would be better concealed, and their preparations in general would be made in an orderly way and without evasions.

THUCYDIDES

LXXIII. Καὶ οἱ Συρακόσιοι αὐτοῦ ἀκούσαντες
ἐψηφίσαντό τε πάντα ὡς ἐκέλευε καὶ στρατηγὸν
αὑτόν τε εἵλοντο τὸν Ἑρμοκράτη καὶ Ἡρακλείδην
τὸν Λυσιμάχου καὶ Σικανὸν τὸν Ἐξηκέστου,
2 τούτους τρεῖς, καὶ ἐς τὴν Κόρινθον καὶ ἐς τὴν
Λακεδαίμονα πρέσβεις ἀπέστειλαν, ὅπως ξυμμαχία τε αὐτοῖς παραγένηται καὶ τὸν πρὸς Ἀθηναίους
πόλεμον βεβαιότερον πείθωσι ποιεῖσθαι ἐκ τοῦ
προφανοῦς ὑπὲρ σφῶν τοὺς Λακεδαιμονίους, ἵνα
ἢ ἀπὸ τῆς Σικελίας ἀπαγάγωσιν αὐτοὺς ἢ πρὸς
τὸ ἐν Σικελίᾳ στράτευμα ἧσσον ὠφελίαν ἄλλην
ἐπιπέμπωσιν.

LXXIV. Τὸ δ' ἐν τῇ Κατάνῃ στράτευμα τῶν
Ἀθηναίων ἔπλευσεν εὐθὺς ἐπὶ Μεσσήνην ὡς προ-
δοθησομένην. καὶ ἃ μὲν ἐπράσσετο οὐκ ἐγένετο·
Ἀλκιβιάδης γὰρ ὅτ' ἀπῄει ἐκ τῆς ἀρχῆς ἤδη
μετάπεμπτος, ἐπιστάμενος ὅτι φεύξοιτο, μηνύει
τοῖς τῶν Συρακοσίων φίλοις τοῖς ἐν τῇ Μεσσήνῃ
ξυνειδὼς τὸ μέλλον· οἱ δὲ τούς τε ἄνδρας διέφθει-
ραν πρότερον καὶ τότε στασιάζοντες καὶ ἐν ὅπλοις
ὄντες ἐπεκράτουν μὴ δέχεσθαι τοὺς Ἀθηναίους
2 οἱ ταῦτα βουλόμενοι. ἡμέρας δὲ μείναντες περὶ
τρεῖς καὶ δέκα οἱ Ἀθηναῖοι ὡς ἐχειμάζοντο καὶ
τὰ ἐπιτήδεια οὐκ εἶχον καὶ προυχώρει οὐδέν,
ἀπελθόντες ἐς Νάξον καὶ ὅρια καὶ σταυρώματα
περὶ τὸ στρατόπεδον ποιησάμενοι αὐτοῦ διεχεί-
μαζον· καὶ τριήρη ἀπέστειλαν ἐς τὰς Ἀθήνας
ἐπί τε χρήματα καὶ ἱππέας, ὅπως ἅμα τῷ ἦρι
παραγένωνται.

LXXV. Ἐτείχιζον δὲ καὶ οἱ Συρακόσιοι ἐν τῷ
χειμῶνι πρός τε τῇ πόλει, τὸν Τεμενίτην ἐντὸς

LXXIII. The Syracusans, when they had heard him, voted everything as he advised, and chose three generals, Hermocrates himself, Heracleides son of Lysimachus, and Sicanus son of Execestus. They also sent envoys to Corinth and Lacedaemon to induce an allied force to join them, and to persuade the Lacedaemonians to prosecute the war with the Athenians openly in their behalf and more persistently, in order that they might either draw them away from Sicily, or else to some extent prevent their sending reinforcements to their army in Sicily.

LXXIV. The Athenian army at Catana, directly after its return,[1] sailed to Messene, in the hope that it would be betrayed to them. But the negotiations were not successful. For as soon as Alcibiades left his command under summons from home, knowing that he would be an exile, he gave information of the plot, of which he was cognizant, to the friends of the Syracusans at Messene; these had previously put the conspirators to death, and at this time, when the Athenians arrived, those who were of this faction, being already in revolt and under arms, were strong enough to prevent their admission. So the Athenians stayed there about thirteen days, and as they were vexed by storms and without provisions and were making no progress at all, they retired to Naxos, and constructing dock-yards and building stockades round their camp, went into winter-quarters there. They also sent a trireme to Athens for money and cavalry, that these might be on hand at the opening of spring.

LXXV. During this winter the Syracusans also proceeded to build a wall next to the city, along

[1] *cf.* ch. lxxii. 1.

THUCYDIDES

ποιησάμενοι, τεῖχος παρὰ πᾶν τὸ πρὸς τὰς Ἐπιπολὰς ὁρῶν, ὅπως μὴ δι᾽ ἐλάσσονος εὐαποτείχιστοι
ὦσιν, ἢν ἄρα σφάλλωνται, καὶ τὰ Μέγαρα φρούριον καὶ ἐν τῷ Ὀλυμπιείῳ ἄλλο· καὶ τὴν θάλασσαν
2 προυσταύρωσαν πανταχῇ ᾗ ἀποβάσεις ἦσαν. καὶ
τοὺς Ἀθηναίους εἰδότες ἐν τῇ Νάξῳ χειμάζοντας
ἐστράτευσαν πανδημεὶ ἐπὶ τὴν Κατάνην, καὶ τῆς
τε γῆς αὐτῶν ἔτεμον καὶ τὰς τῶν Ἀθηναίων
σκηνὰς καὶ τὸ στρατόπεδον ἐμπρήσαντες ἀνεχώ-
3 ρησαν ἐπ᾽ οἴκου. καὶ πυνθανόμενοι τοὺς Ἀθηναίους ἐς τὴν Καμάριναν κατὰ τὴν ἐπὶ Λάχητος
γενομένην ξυμμαχίαν πρεσβεύεσθαι, εἴ πως προσ-
αγάγοιντο αὐτούς, ἀντεπρεσβεύοντο καὶ αὐτοί·
ἦσαν γὰρ ὕποπτοι αὐτοῖς οἱ Καμαριναῖοι μὴ προθύμως σφίσι μήτ᾽ ἐπὶ τὴν πρώτην μάχην πέμψαι
ἃ ἔπεμψαν, ἔς τε τὸ λοιπὸν μὴ οὐκέτι βούλωνται
ἀμύνειν, ὁρῶντες τοὺς Ἀθηναίους ἐν τῇ μάχῃ εὖ
πράξαντας, προσχωρῶσι δ᾽ αὐτοῖς κατὰ τὴν προ-
4 τέραν φιλίαν πεισθέντες. ἀφικομένων οὖν ἐκ μὲν
Συρακουσῶν Ἑρμοκράτους καὶ ἄλλων ἐς τὴν
Καμάριναν, ἀπὸ δὲ τῶν Ἀθηναίων Εὐφήμου μεθ᾽
ἑτέρων, ὁ Ἑρμοκράτης ξυλλόγου γενομένου τῶν
Καμαριναίων βουλόμενος προδιαβάλλειν τοὺς
Ἀθηναίους ἔλεγε τοιάδε.

LXXVI. "Οὐ τὴν παροῦσαν δύναμιν τῶν
Ἀθηναίων, ὦ Καμαριναῖοι, μὴ αὐτὴν καταπλα-

the entire extent that faces Epipolae, taking in the Temenites precinct,[1] in order that, in case of a possible reverse, they might not be so easily shut in as if the circuit of the town were smaller; and they also put a garrison at Megara and another at the Olympieium, and fixed palisades on the sea-shore at all points where landings were possible. And knowing that the Athenians were wintering at Naxos, they went out with all their forces against Catana and ravaged some of its territory, then having set fire to the tents and the camp of the Athenians they returned home. Moreover, on learning that the Athenians had, in accordance with an alliance concluded with the Camarinaeans in the time of Laches,[2] sent envoys to these, in the hope that they might win them to their side, they themselves sent a counter-embassy; for they had suspicions that the Camarinaeans had not been zealous in sending such help as they had sent for the first battle, and might not wish to aid them in future, seeing that the Athenians had fared well in the fight, but might rather be induced, on the plea of their former friendship, to go over to the Athenians. Accordingly, when Hermocrates and others had arrived at Camarina from Syracuse, and from the Athenians Euphemus and the rest, an assembly of the Camarinaeans was held and Hermocrates, wishing to prejudice them against the Athenians, spoke as follows:

LXXVI. "We have come on this embassy, men of Camarina, not because we feared that you will be

---

[1] The temple of Apollo Temenites and the suburb which had grown up about it, the later Neapolis.

[2] 427 B.C.; cf. III. lxxxvi. 2.

γῆτε δείσαντες ἐπρεσβευσάμεθα, ἀλλὰ μᾶλλον
τοὺς μέλλοντας ἀπ' αὐτῶν λόγους, πρίν τι καὶ
2 ἡμῶν ἀκοῦσαι, μὴ ὑμᾶς πείσωσιν. ἥκουσι γὰρ
ἐς τὴν Σικελίαν προφάσει μὲν ᾗ πυνθάνεσθε,
διανοίᾳ δὲ ἦν πάντες ὑπονοοῦμεν· καί μοι δοκοῦσιν
οὐ Λεοντίνους βούλεσθαι κατοικίσαι, ἀλλ' ἡμᾶς
μᾶλλον ἐξοικίσαι. οὐ γὰρ δὴ εὔλογον τὰς μὲν
ἐκεῖ πόλεις ἀναστάτους ποιεῖν, τὰς δὲ ἐνθάδε
κατοικίζειν, καὶ Λεοντίνων μὲν Χαλκιδέων ὄντων
κατὰ τὸ ξυγγενὲς κήδεσθαι, Χαλκιδέας δὲ τοὺς
ἐν Εὐβοίᾳ, ὧν οἵδε ἄποικοί εἰσι, δουλωσαμένους
3 ἔχειν. τῇ δὲ αὐτῇ ἰδέᾳ ἐκεῖνά τε ἔσχον καὶ τὰ
ἐνθάδε νῦν πειρῶνται· ἡγεμόνες γὰρ γενόμενοι
ἑκόντων τῶν τε Ἰώνων καὶ ὅσοι ἀπὸ σφῶν ἦσαν
ξύμμαχοι ὡς ἐπὶ τοῦ Μήδου τιμωρίᾳ, τοὺς μὲν
λιποστρατίαν, τοὺς δὲ ἐπ' ἀλλήλους στρατεύειν,
τοῖς δ' ὡς ἑκάστοις τινὰ εἶχον αἰτίαν εὐπρεπῆ
4 ἐπενεγκόντες κατεστρέψαντο. καὶ οὐ περὶ τῆς
ἐλευθερίας ἄρα οὔτε οὗτοι τῶν Ἑλλήνων οὔθ' οἱ
Ἕλληνες τῆς ἑαυτῶν τῷ Μήδῳ ἀντέστησαν, περὶ
δὲ οἱ μὲν σφίσιν ἀλλὰ μὴ ἐκείνῳ καταδουλώσεως,
οἱ δ' ἐπὶ δεσπότου μεταβολῇ οὐκ ἀξυνετωτέρου,
κακοξυνετωτέρου δέ.

LXXVII. "'Ἀλλ' οὐ γὰρ δὴ τὴν τῶν Ἀθηναίων
εὐκατηγόρητον οὖσαν πόλιν νῦν ἥκομεν ἀποφα-

dismayed by the presence of the Athenian force, but rather through fear of the words that are going to be said on their part, lest these persuade you before you hear anything from us. For they are come to Sicily on the pretext that you hear, but with the design that we all suspect; and to me they seem to wish, not to resettle the Leontines, but rather to unsettle us. For surely it is not reasonable to suppose that, while desolating the cities in their own country, they are resettling the cities of Sicily, and that they care for the Leontines, on the score of kinship, as being Chalcidians, while holding in slavery the Chalcidians in Euboea, of whom these are colonists. Nay, one and the same design has guided them in acquiring their possessions over there and is now guiding them in their endeavour to acquire possessions here: after they had become leaders, by the free choice of their associates, both of the Ionians and of all those, descendants of the Ionians, who were members of the alliance that was concluded, avowedly, for revenge upon the Persians, they charged some with refusal to serve, others with warring upon one another, others with whatever specious charge they had at hand, and so reduced them to subjection. And so, after all, it was not for 'freedom' that they withstood the Persians, neither the Athenians to win it for the Hellenes nor the Hellenes to win it for themselves, but they fought for the enslavement of the rest to themselves, and the Hellenes for a change of master, not to one more unwise, but more wickedly wise.

LXXVII. "But we are not come now, easy though it be to denounce the Athenian state, to declare before those who know already how many are its mis-

νοῦντες ἐν εἰδόσιν ὅσα ἀδικεῖ, πολὺ δὲ μᾶλλον ἡμᾶς
αὐτοὺς αἰτιασόμενοι ὅτι ἔχοντες παραδείγματα
τῶν τ' ἐκεῖ Ἑλλήνων ὡς ἐδουλώθησαν, οὐκ ἀμύ-
νοντες σφίσιν αὐτοῖς, καὶ νῦν ἐφ' ἡμᾶς ταὐτὰ
παρόντα σοφίσματα, Λεοντίνων τε ξυγγενῶν
κατοικίσεις καὶ Ἐγεσταίων ξυμμάχων ἐπικουρίας,
οὐ ξυστραφέντες βουλόμεθα προθυμότερον δεῖξαι
αὐτοῖς ὅτι οὐκ Ἴωνες τάδε εἰσὶν οὐδ' Ἑλλησπόν-
τιοι καὶ νησιῶται, οἳ δεσπότην ἢ Μῆδον ἢ ἕνα
γέ τινα αἰεὶ μεταβάλλοντες δουλοῦνται, ἀλλὰ
Δωριῆς, ἐλεύθεροι ἀπ' αὐτονόμου τῆς Πελοπον-
2 νήσου τὴν Σικελίαν οἰκοῦντες. ἢ μένομεν ἕως ἂν
ἕκαστοι κατὰ πόλεις ληφθῶμεν, εἰδότες ὅτι ταύτῃ
μόνον ἁλωτοί ἐσμεν καὶ ὁρῶντες αὐτοὺς ἐπὶ τοῦτο
τὸ εἶδος τρεπομένους ὥστε τοὺς μὲν λόγοις ἡμῶν
διιστάναι, τοὺς δὲ ξυμμάχων ἐλπίδι ἐκπολεμοῦν
πρὸς ἀλλήλους, τοὺς δὲ ὡς ἑκάστοις τι προσηνὲς
λέγοντες δύνανται κακουργεῖν; καὶ οἰόμεθα τοῦ
ἄπωθεν ξυνοίκου προαπολλυμένου οὐ καὶ ἐς αὐτόν
τινα ἥξειν τὸ δεινόν, πρὸ δὲ αὐτοῦ μᾶλλον τὸν
πάσχοντα καθ' ἑαυτὸν δυστυχεῖν;

LXXVIII. "Καὶ εἴ τῳ ἄρα παρέστηκε τὸν μὲν
Συρακόσιον, ἑαυτὸν δ' οὐ πολέμιον εἶναι τῷ Ἀθη-
ναίῳ, καὶ δεινὸν ἡγεῖται ὑπέρ γε τῆς ἐμῆς κινδυνεύειν, ἐνθυμηθήτω οὐ περὶ τῆς ἐμῆς μᾶλλον, ἐν
ἴσῳ δὲ καὶ τῆς ἑαυτοῦ ἅμα ἐν τῇ ἐμῇ μαχούμενος,
τοσούτῳ δὲ καὶ ἀσφαλέστερον ὅσῳ οὐ προδιεφθαρ-

deeds ; but much more to blame ourselves, because, though we have warning examples in the way that the Hellenes over there have been enslaved because they would not defend one another, and though the same sophisms are now practised upon us—restorings of Leontine kinsmen and succourings of Egestaean allies !—we are unwilling to combine together and with more spirit show them that here are not Ionians nor yet Hellespontines and islanders, who are always taking some new master, Persian or whoever it may be, and continue in a state of slavery, but Dorians, free men sprung from independent Peloponnesus, and now dwelling in Sicily. Or are we waiting until we shall be taken one at a time, city by city, when we know that in this way only can we be conquered, and when we see them resorting to this policy, endeavouring to cause division among some of us by means of cunning words, to set others at war one with another by the hope of obtaining allies, and to ruin others in whatever way they can by saying something alluring to each ? And do we think that, when a distant compatriot perishes before us, the same danger will not come also to ourselves, but rather that whoever before us meets with disaster merely incurs misfortune by himself alone ?

LXXVIII. "And if the thought has occurred to anyone that it is the Syracusans, not himself, who are enemies to the Athenians, and thinks it preposterous that he should incur danger for our country, let him reflect that it will not be chiefly for our country, but equally for his own at the same time that he will fight in our land, and with the greater safety, too, inasmuch as he will enter the contest, not when we have already been ruined,

μένου ἐμοῦ, ἔχων δὲ ξύμμαχον ἐμὲ καὶ οὐκ ἐρῆμος[1]
ἀγωνιεῖται, τόν τε Ἀθηναῖον μὴ τὴν τοῦ Συρακοσίου ἔχθραν κολάσασθαι, τῇ δ' ἐμῇ προφάσει
τὴν ἐκείνου φιλίαν οὐχ ἦσσον βεβαιώσασθαι
2 βούλεσθαι. εἴ τέ τις φθονεῖ μὲν ἢ καὶ φοβεῖται
(ἀμφότερα γὰρ τάδε πάσχει τὰ μείζω), διὰ δὲ
αὐτὰ τὰς Συρακούσας κακωθῆναι μέν, ἵνα σωφρο-
νισθῶμεν, βούλεται, περιγενέσθαι δὲ ἕνεκα τῆς
αὐτοῦ ἀσφαλείας, οὐκ ἀνθρωπίνης δυνάμεως βούλησιν ἐλπίζει. οὐ γὰρ οἷόν τε ἅμα τῆς τε ἐπιθυ-
μίας καὶ τῆς τύχης τὸν αὐτὸν ὁμοίως ταμίαν
3 γενέσθαι. καὶ εἰ γνώμῃ ἁμάρτοι, τοῖς αὑτοῦ
κακοῖς ὀλοφυρθεὶς τάχ' ἂν ἴσως καὶ τοῖς ἐμοῖς
ἀγαθοῖς ποτε βουληθείη αὖθις φθονῆσαι. ἀδύ-
νατον δὲ προεμένῳ καὶ μὴ τοὺς αὐτοὺς κινδύνους,
οὐ περὶ τῶν ὀνομάτων ἀλλὰ περὶ τῶν ἔργων,
ἐθελήσαντι προσλαβεῖν· λόγῳ μὲν γὰρ τὴν ἡμετέραν δύναμιν σῴζοι ἄν τις, ἔργῳ δὲ τὴν αὐτοῦ
4 σωτηρίαν. καὶ μάλιστα εἰκὸς ἦν ὑμᾶς, ὦ Καμαριναῖοι, ὁμόρους ὄντας καὶ τὰ δεύτερα κινδυνεύ-
σοντας, προορᾶσθαι αὐτὰ καὶ μὴ μαλακῶς ὥσπερ
νῦν ξυμμαχεῖν, αὐτοὺς δὲ πρὸς ἡμᾶς μᾶλλον
ἰόντας, ἅπερ, εἰ ἐς τὴν Καμαριναίαν πρῶτον
ἀφίκοντο οἱ Ἀθηναῖοι, δεόμενοι ἂν ἐπεκαλεῖσθε,
ταῦτα ἐκ τοῦ ὁμοίου καὶ νῦν παρακελευομένους,
ὅπως μηδὲν ἐνδώσομεν, φαίνεσθαι. ἀλλ' οὔθ'
ὑμεῖς νῦν γέ πω οὔθ' οἱ ἄλλοι ἐπὶ ταῦτα ὡρμήσατε.

LXXIX. "Δειλίᾳ δὲ ἴσως τὸ δίκαιον πρός τε
ἡμᾶς καὶ πρὸς τοὺς ἐπιόντας θεραπεύσετε, λέγοντες

---

[1] ἐρῆμος, the reading of some inferior MSS., seems to be
rightly preferred by Bekker, Stahl, and Hude to ἐρῆμον of
all the better MSS.

and not isolated himself, but having us as allies; and that the object of the Athenians is not to punish the enmity of the Syracusans, but having us as a pretext to make your 'friendship' still more secure. If, moreover, anyone is envious, or even afraid of us—for greater states are exposed to both these passions—and for this reason wishes that the Syracusans shall be humbled, indeed, in order that we may be sobered, but shall survive for the sake of his own safety, he indulges a wish that is not within human power to attain. For it is not possible for the same person to be in like measure the controller of his own desires and of Fortune; and if he should err in judgment, when he has to lament his own ills he may perhaps some day wish once more to become envious of our good fortune. But that will be impossible, if he abandons us and does not consent to incur the same dangers, which are not about names but about facts; for though nominally a man would be preserving our power, in fact he would be securing his own safety. And most of all it were fitting that you, men of Camarina, who are on our borders and will incur danger next, should have foreseen these things and not be, as now, slack in your alliance, but rather should have come to us of yourselves, and just as you, in case the Athenians had come against Camarina first, would be calling upon us and begging us not to yield an inch, so should you be seen in like manner now also using the same exhortation. But neither you, so far at least, nor the rest have bestirred yourselves for this.

LXXIX. "But through timidity, perhaps, you will make much of the point of right as between us and

ξυμμαχίαν εἶναι ὑμῖν πρὸς Ἀθηναίους· ἤν γε οὐκ
ἐπὶ τοῖς φίλοις ἐποιήσασθε, τῶν δὲ ἐχθρῶν ἤν τις
ἐφ' ὑμᾶς ἴῃ, καὶ τοῖς γε Ἀθηναίοις βοηθεῖν, ὅταν
ὑπ' ἄλλων, καὶ μὴ αὐτοὶ ὥσπερ νῦν τοὺς πέλας
ἀδικῶσιν, ἐπεὶ οὐδ' οἱ Ῥηγῖνοι ὄντες Χαλκιδῆς
Χαλκιδέας ὄντας Λεοντίνους ἐθέλουσι ξυγκατοικί-
2 ζειν. καὶ δεινὸν εἰ ἐκεῖνοι μὲν τὸ ἔργον τοῦ καλοῦ
δικαιώματος ὑποπτεύοντες ἀλόγως σωφρονοῦσιν,
ὑμεῖς δ' εὐλόγῳ προφάσει τοὺς μὲν φύσει πολεμίους βούλεσθε ὠφελεῖν, τοὺς δὲ ἔτι μᾶλλον φύσει
3 ξυγγενεῖς μετὰ τῶν ἐχθίστων διαφθεῖραι. ἀλλ'
οὐ δίκαιον, ἀμύνειν δὲ καὶ μὴ φοβεῖσθαι τὴν
παρασκευὴν αὐτῶν· οὐ γάρ, ἢν ἡμεῖς ξυστῶμεν
πάντες, δεινή ἐστιν, ἀλλ' ἤν, ὅπερ οὗτοι σπεύ-
δουσι, τἀναντία διαστῶμεν, ἐπεὶ οὐδὲ πρὸς ἡμᾶς
μόνους ἐλθόντες καὶ μάχῃ περιγενόμενοι ἔπραξαν
ἃ ἐβούλοντο, ἀπῆλθον δὲ διὰ τάχους.

LXXX. "Ὥστε οὐχ ἀθρόους γε ὄντας εἰκὸς
ἀθυμεῖν, ἰέναι δὲ ἐς τὴν ξυμμαχίαν προθυμότερον,
ἄλλως τε καὶ ἀπὸ Πελοποννήσου παρεσομένης
ὠφελίας, οἳ τῶνδε κρείσσους εἰσὶ τὸ παράπαν τὰ
πολέμια· καὶ μὴ ἐκείνην τὴν προμηθίαν δοκεῖν
τῳ ἡμῖν μὲν ἴσην εἶναι, ὑμῖν δὲ ἀσφαλῆ, τὸ
μηδετέροις δὴ ὡς καὶ ἀμφοτέρων ὄντας ξυμμάχους
2 βοηθεῖν. οὐ γὰρ ἔργῳ ἴσον ὥσπερ τῷ δικαιώματί

---

¹ ἀδικῶνται is to be understood. For similar ellipses, *cf.*
I. lxxviii. 10; II. xi. 34; VII. lxix. 3.

the invaders, alleging that you have an alliance with
the Athenians. That alliance, however, you made,
not against your friends, but in the event of any of
your enemies attacking you; and you were to aid
the Athenians only when they were wronged [1] by
others, and not when, as now, they are themselves
wronging their neighbours. Why, not even the
Rhegians, themselves Chalcidians, are willing to
help to restore the Leontines who are Chalcidians.
And it is monstrous if they, suspicious of what this
fine plea of right really means in practice, are un-
reasonably prudent,[2] while you, on a speciously
reasonable pretext, desire to aid those who by nature
are your enemies, and in concert with your bitterest
foes to ruin those who by a still closer tie of nature
are your kinsmen.[3] Nay, that is not right; but
it is right to aid us and not be afraid of their
armament. For if we all stand together, it is
not formidable. The only danger is—and this is
just what they are eager for—that we may stand
opposed to each other; for not even when they came
against us alone and proved superior in battle did
they effect what they wished, but quickly went away.

LXXX. "So then, if only we be united, we have
reason not to be disheartened, but rather to enter into
the proposed alliance more heartily, especially as aid
is sure to come from the Peloponnesians, who are
altogether superior to these people in matters of
war. And no one should regard as fair to us, while
safe for you, that prudent course of yours—to aid
neither, forsooth, as being allies of both. Indeed
it is not as fair in fact, as when urged to justify

[2] *i.e.* discard logic and obey policy.
[3] As Dorians and Sicilians.

ἐστιν. εἰ γὰρ δι' ὑμᾶς μὴ ξυμμαχήσαντας ὅ τε
παθὼν σφαλήσεται καὶ ὁ κρατῶν περιέσται, τί
ἄλλο ἢ τῇ αὐτῇ ἀπουσίᾳ τοῖς μὲν οὐκ ἠμύνατε
σωθῆναι, τοὺς δὲ οὐκ ἐκωλύσατε κακοὺς γενέσθαι;
καίτοι κάλλιον τοῖς ἀδικουμένοις καὶ ἅμα ξυγγενέσι προσθεμένους τήν τε κοινὴν ὠφελίαν τῇ
Σικελίᾳ φυλάξαι καὶ τοὺς Ἀθηναίους φίλους δὴ
ὄντας μὴ ἐᾶσαι ἁμαρτεῖν.

3 " Ξυνελόντες τε λέγομεν οἱ Συρακόσιοι ἐκδιδά-
σκειν μὲν οὐδὲν ἔργον εἶναι σαφῶς οὔτε ὑμᾶς οὔτε
τοὺς ἄλλους περὶ ὧν αὐτοὶ οὐδὲν χεῖρον γιγνώ-
σκετε· δεόμεθα δὲ καὶ μαρτυρόμεθα ἅμα, εἰ μὴ
πείσομεν, ὅτι ἐπιβουλευόμεθα μὲν ὑπὸ Ἰώνων
αἰεὶ πολεμίων, προδιδόμεθα δὲ ὑπὸ ὑμῶν Δωριῆς
4 Δωριῶν. καὶ εἰ καταστρέψονται ἡμᾶς Ἀθηναῖοι,
ταῖς μὲν ὑμετέραις γνώμαις κρατήσουσι, τῷ δ'
αὑτῶν ὀνόματι τιμηθήσονται, καὶ τῆς νίκης οὐκ
ἄλλον τινὰ ἆθλον ἢ τὸν τὴν νίκην παρασχόντα
λήψονται· καὶ εἰ αὖ ἡμεῖς περιεσόμεθα, τῆς
αἰτίας τῶν κινδύνων οἱ αὐτοὶ τὴν τιμωρίαν ὑφέ-
5 ξετε. σκοπεῖτε οὖν καὶ αἱρεῖσθε ἤδη ἢ τὴν
αὐτίκα ἀκινδύνως δουλείαν ἢ κἂν περιγενόμενοι
μεθ' ἡμῶν τούσδε τε μὴ αἰσχρῶς δεσπότας λαβεῖν
καὶ τὴν πρὸς ἡμᾶς ἔχθραν μὴ ἂν βραχεῖαν γενομένην διαφυγεῖν."

LXXXI. Τοιαῦτα μὲν ὁ Ἑρμοκράτης εἶπεν, ὁ

you.[1] For if through your failure to take sides as allies the sufferer shall be defeated and the conqueror shall prevail, what else have you done by this selfsame standing aloof but refused to aid the one to secure his salvation and to prevent the other from incurring guilt? And yet it were more honourable for you, by siding with those who are being wronged[2] and are at the same time your kinsmen, at once to guard the common interest of Sicily and not suffer the Athenians, seeing that they are your ' good friends,' to make a serious mistake.

"Summing up, then, we Syracusans say that it is no hard matter to demonstrate, either to you or to others, what you yourselves know as well as we; but we do entreat you, and at the same time we protest, if we fail to persuade you, that while we are plotted against by Ionians,[3] our inveterate enemies, we are betrayed by you, Dorians by Dorians. And if the Athenians shall subdue us, it is by your decisions that they will prevail, but it is in their own name that they will be honoured, and the prize of victory they will take will be none other than those who procured them the victory; if, on the other hand, we shall conquer, you also will have to pay the penalty of being the cause of our perils. Reflect, therefore, and choose here and now, either immediate slavery with no danger or, if you join us and prevail, the chance of not having to take, with disgrace, these men as masters, and also, as regards us, of escaping an enmity that would not be transitory."

LXXXI. Such was the speech of Hermocrates;

---

[1] Or, "as the plea of right represents it."
[2] The Syracusans.　　[3] The Athenians.

δ' Εὔφημος ὁ τῶν Ἀθηναίων πρεσβευτὴς μετ'
αὐτὸν τοιάδε.

LXXXII. " Ἀφικόμεθα μὲν ἐπὶ τῆς πρότερον
οὔσης ξυμμαχίας ἀνανεώσει, τοῦ δὲ Συρακοσίου
καθαψαμένου ἀνάγκη καὶ περὶ τῆς ἀρχῆς εἰπεῖν
2 ὡς εἰκότως ἔχομεν. τὸ μὲν οὖν μέγιστον μαρτύ-
ριον αὐτὸς εἶπεν, ὅτι οἱ Ἴωνες αἰεί ποτε πολέμιοι
τοῖς Δωριεῦσίν εἰσιν. ἔχει δὲ καὶ οὕτως. ἡμεῖς
γὰρ Ἴωνες ὄντες Πελοποννησίοις Δωριεῦσι, καὶ
πλείοσιν οὖσι καὶ παροικοῦσιν, ἐσκεψάμεθα ὅτῳ
3 τρόπῳ ἥκιστα¹ ὑπακουσόμεθα· καὶ μετὰ τὰ
Μηδικὰ ναῦς κτησάμενοι τῆς μὲν Λακεδαιμονίων
ἀρχῆς καὶ ἡγεμονίας ἀπηλλάγημεν, οὐδὲν προσῆ-
κον μᾶλλόν τι ἐκείνους ἡμῖν ἢ καὶ ἡμᾶς ἐκείνοις
ἐπιτάσσειν, πλὴν καθ' ὅσον ἐν τῷ παρόντι μεῖζον
ἴσχυον, αὐτοὶ² δὲ τῶν ὑπὸ βασιλεῖ πρότερον ὄντων ἡγεμόνες καταστάντες οἰκοῦμεν, νομίσαντες
ἥκιστ' ἂν ὑπὸ Πελοποννησίοις οὕτως εἶναι, δύναμιν
ἔχοντες ᾗ ἀμυνούμεθα, καὶ ὡς τὸ ἀκριβὲς εἰπεῖν
οὐδὲ ἀδίκως καταστρεψάμενοι τούς τε Ἴωνας καὶ
νησιώτας, οὓς ξυγγενεῖς φασιν ὄντας ἡμᾶς Συρα-
4 κόσιοι δεδουλῶσθαι. ἦλθον γὰρ ἐπὶ τὴν μητρό-
πολιν ἐφ' ἡμᾶς μετὰ τοῦ Μήδου καὶ οὐκ ἐτόλμη-
σαν ἀποστάντες τὰ οἰκεῖα φθεῖραι, ὥσπερ ἡμεῖς
ἐκλιπόντες τὴν πόλιν, δουλείαν δὲ αὐτοί τε ἐβούλοντο καὶ ἡμῖν τὸ αὐτὸ ἐπενεγκεῖν.

¹ αὐτῶν, in MSS. before ἥκιστα, deleted by van Herwerden,
followed by Hude.
² αὐτοὶ, Hude emends to αὐτόνομοι.

after him Euphemus, the envoy of the Athenians, spoke as follows :—

LXXXII. "We had come here for the renewal of the alliance [1] which formerly existed, but as the Syracusan has attacked us it is necessary to speak also about our empire, showing how rightly we hold it. Now the strongest proof of this the speaker himself stated—that Ionians have always been enemies to the Dorians. It is even so. Accordingly, we, being Ionians, considered in what way we should be least subject to the Peloponnesians who are Dorians and not only more numerous than we but our near neighbours.[2] And after the Persian wars we acquired a fleet and rid ourselves of the rule and supremacy of the Lacedaemonians, it being not in any way more fitting that they give orders to us than we to them, except in so far as they at the time were stronger. Having, then, ourselves become leaders of those who were before subject to the King, we so continue, thinking that we should in this way be least subject to the Peloponnesians, because we have power with which to defend ourselves. And to say the exact truth, not unjustly, either, did we subdue both the Ionians and the islanders, whom the Syracusans say we have enslaved though they are our kinsmen. For they came against us, their mother-city, along with the Persians, and had not the courage to revolt and sacrifice their homes, as we did when we abandoned our city, but chose slavery for themselves and wished to impose the same condition upon us.

[1] cf. ch. lxxv. 3.
[2] Or, retaining αὐτῶν, "For we, being Ionians in the eyes of Peloponnesians who are Dorians, not only more numerous than we but also our near neighbours, considered in what way we should be least subject to them."

LXXXIII. "'Ανθ' ὧν ἄξιοί τε ὄντες ἅμα ἄρχομεν,
ὅτι τε ναυτικὸν πλεῖστόν τε καὶ προθυμίαν ἀπρο-
φάσιστον παρεσχόμεθα ἐς τοὺς Ἕλληνας, καὶ
διότι καὶ τῷ Μήδῳ ἑτοίμως τοῦτο δρῶντες οὗτοι
ἡμᾶς ἔβλαπτον, ἅμα δὲ τῆς πρὸς Πελοποννησίους
2 ἰσχύος ὀρεγόμενοι. καὶ οὐ καλλιεπούμεθα ὡς ἢ
τὸν βάρβαρον μόνοι καθελόντες εἰκότως ἄρχομεν
ἢ ἐπ' ἐλευθερίᾳ τῇ τῶνδε μᾶλλον ἢ τῶν ξυμπάντων τε καὶ τῇ ἡμετέρᾳ αὐτῶν κινδυνεύσαντες.
πᾶσι δὲ ἀνεπίφθονον τὴν προσήκουσαν σωτηρίαν
ἐκπορίζεσθαι. καὶ νῦν τῆς ἡμετέρας ἀσφαλείας
ἕνεκα καὶ ἐνθάδε παρόντες ὁρῶμεν καὶ ὑμῖν ταὐτὰ
3 ξυμφέροντα· ἀποφαίνομεν δὲ ἐξ ὧν οἵδε τε δια-
βάλλουσι καὶ ὑμεῖς μάλιστα ἐπὶ τὸ φοβερώτερον
ὑπονοεῖτε, εἰδότες τοὺς περιδεῶς ὑποπτεύοντάς τι
λόγου μὲν ἡδονῇ τὸ παραυτίκα τερπομένους, τῇ
δ' ἐγχειρήσει ὕστερον τὰ ξυμφέροντα πράσσοντας.
4 τήν τε γὰρ ἐκεῖ ἀρχὴν εἰρήκαμεν διὰ δέος ἔχειν
καὶ τὰ ἐνθάδε διὰ τὸ αὐτὸ ἥκειν μετὰ τῶν φίλων
ἀσφαλῶς καταστησόμενοι, καὶ οὐ δουλωσόμενοι,
μὴ παθεῖν δὲ μᾶλλον τοῦτο κωλύσοντες.

LXXXIV. "Ὑπολάβῃ δὲ μηδεὶς ὡς οὐδὲν προσ-
ῆκον ὑμῶν κηδόμεθα, γνοὺς ὅτι σῳζομένων ὑμῶν
καὶ διὰ τὸ μὴ ἀσθενεῖς ὑμᾶς ὄντας ἀντέχειν
Συρακοσίοις ἧσσον ἂν τούτων πεμψάντων τινὰ
δύναμιν Πελοποννησίοις ἡμεῖς βλαπτοίμεθα. καὶ
2 ἐν τούτῳ προσήκετε ἤδη ἡμῖν τὰ μέγιστα. δι'

LXXXIII. "We have dominion, therefore, both because we are worthy of it—seeing that we furnished the largest fleet and unhesitating zeal toward the Hellenes, and that they, readily taking the course they did in the interest of the Persians, were doing us harm—and at the same time because we aimed at strength with which to resist the Peloponnesians. And we do not say in fine phrases that we deserve to rule either because we alone overthrew the Barbarian or because we incurred danger for the liberty of these men more than for that of all the Hellenes, including our own. But no one can be reproached because he makes provision for his proper safety. And now when for the sake of our own security we have come here also, we see that your interests also are the same as ours. And this we prove to you both from these men's calumnies and from those suspicions of yours which most tend to undue alarm, because we know that those who are suspicious through excessive fear may indeed take delight for the moment in seductive speech, but afterwards when it comes to action consult their own interests. For just as we have said that we hold our dominion over there because of fear, so we say that for the same reason we have come here with the help of our friends to place your affairs on a footing of safety for us, and not to enslave you, but rather to prevent your being enslaved.

LXXXIV. "And let no one object that we are solicitous for you when it does not concern us; let him reflect that, if you are preserved and by not being weak are able to offer resistance to the Syracusans, we should be less liable to injury through their sending a force to aid the Peloponnesians. And herein you become at once our chief concern

ὅπερ καὶ τοὺς Λεοντίνους εὔλογον κατοικίζειν, μὴ
ὑπηκόους ὥσπερ τοὺς ξυγγενεῖς αὐτῶν τοὺς ἐν
Εὐβοίᾳ, ἀλλ' ὡς δυνατωτάτους, ἵνα ἐκ τῆς σφετέρας ὅμοροι ὄντες τοῖσδε ὑπὲρ ἡμῶν λυπηροὶ
3 ὦσιν. τὰ μὲν γὰρ ἐκεῖ καὶ αὐτοὶ ἀρκοῦμεν πρὸς
τοὺς πολεμίους, καὶ ὁ Χαλκιδεύς, ὃν ἀλόγως ἡμᾶς
φησι δουλωσαμένους τοὺς ἐνθάδε ἐλευθεροῦν,
ξύμφορος ἡμῖν ἀπαράσκευος ὢν καὶ χρήματα
μόνον φέρων, τὰ δὲ ἐνθάδε καὶ Λεοντῖνοι καὶ
οἱ ἄλλοι φίλοι ὅτι μάλιστα αὐτονομούμενοι.

LXXXV. "'Ανδρὶ δὲ τυράννῳ ἢ πόλει ἀρχὴν
ἐχούσῃ οὐδὲν ἄλογον ὅ τι ξυμφέρον οὐδ' οἰκεῖον
ὅ τι μὴ πιστόν· πρὸς ἕκαστα δὲ δεῖ ἢ ἐχθρὸν ἢ
φίλον μετὰ καιροῦ γίγνεσθαι, καὶ ἡμᾶς τοῦτο
ὠφελεῖ ἐνθάδε, οὐκ ἢν τοὺς φίλους κακώσωμεν,
ἀλλ' ἢν οἱ ἐχθροὶ διὰ τὴν τῶν φίλων ῥώμην
2 ἀδύνατοι ὦσιν. ἀπιστεῖν δὲ οὐ χρή· καὶ γὰρ
τοὺς ἐκεῖ ξυμμάχους ὡς ἕκαστοι χρήσιμοι ἐξηγού-
μεθα, Χίους μὲν καὶ Μηθυμναίους νεῶν παροκωχῇ
αὐτονόμους, τοὺς δὲ πολλοὺς χρημάτων βιαιό-
τερον φορᾷ, ἄλλους δὲ καὶ πάνυ ἐλευθέρως ξυμ-
μαχοῦντας, καίπερ νησιώτας ὄντας καὶ εὐλήπτους,
διότι ἐν χωρίοις ἐπικαίροις εἰσὶ περὶ τὴν Πελο-
3 πόννησον. ὥστε καὶ τἀνθάδε εἰκὸς πρὸς τὸ
λυσιτελοῦν καί, ὃ λέγομεν, ἐς Συρακοσίους δέος
καθίστασθαι. ἀρχῆς γὰρ ἐφίενται ὑμῶν καὶ

For this very cause, too, it is reasonable that we should restore the Leontines, so that they shall not be subjects like their kinsmen in Euboea, but shall be as powerful as possible, in order that, bordering as they do on the Syracusans, they may from their own territory be troublesome to these in our behalf. For as to matters in Hellas, we by ourselves are a match for our enemies, and in regard to the Chalcidians, whom he says we are inconsistent in freeing here after enslaving them at home, it is to our interest that they should possess no armament and should contribute money only; but as to matters here, it is to our interest that both the Leontines and our other friends should enjoy the fullest measure of independence.

LXXXV. "To an autocrat or an imperial city nothing is inconsistent which is to its interest, nor is anyone a kinsman who cannot be trusted; in every case one must be enemy or friend according to circumstances. And in Sicily it is to our advantage, not that we should weaken our friends, but that our enemies should be powerless because of the strength of our friends. And you must not mistrust us; for we lead our allies in Hellas as they are each useful to us: the Chians and Methymnaeans as independent, on the condition of furnishing ships; the majority on more compulsory terms, with payment of tribute in money; others, though islanders and easy to be reduced, on terms of absolute freedom as our allies, because they occupy strategic positions along the coast of the Peloponnese. So that it is natural that matters here also should be ordered with an eye to our advantage, and, as we say, with reference to our fear of the Syracusans. For they aim at

βούλονται ἐπὶ τῷ ἡμετέρῳ ξυστήσαντες ὑμᾶς
ὑπόπτῳ, βίᾳ ἢ καὶ κατ' ἐρημίαν, ἀπράκτων ἡμῶν
ἀπελθόντων, αὐτοὶ ἄρξαι τῆς Σικελίας. ἀνάγκη
δέ, ἢν ξυστῆτε πρὸς αὐτούς· οὔτε γὰρ ἡμῖν ἔτι
ἔσται ἰσχὺς τοσαύτη ἐς ἓν ξυστᾶσα εὐμεταχεί-
ριστος, οὔθ' οἶδ' ἀσθενεῖς ἂν ἡμῶν μὴ παρόντων
πρὸς ὑμᾶς εἶεν.

LXXXVI. "Καὶ ὅτῳ ταῦτα μὴ δοκεῖ, αὐτὸ
τὸ ἔργον ἐλέγχει. τὸ γὰρ πρότερον ἡμᾶς ἐπ-
ηγάγεσθε οὐκ ἄλλον τινὰ προσείοντες φόβον ἤ,
εἰ περιοψόμεθα ὑμᾶς ὑπὸ Συρακοσίοις γενέ-
2 σθαι, ὅτι καὶ αὐτοὶ κινδυνεύσομεν. καὶ νῦν
οὐ δίκαιον, ᾧπερ καὶ ἡμᾶς ἠξιοῦτε λόγῳ πείθειν,
τῷ αὐτῷ ἀπιστεῖν, οὐδ' ὅτι δυνάμει μείζονι πρὸς
τὴν τῶνδε ἰσχὺν πάρεσμεν ὑποπτεύεσθαι, πολὺ
3 δὲ μᾶλλον τοῖσδε ἀπιστεῖν. ἡμεῖς μέν γε οὔτε
ἐμμεῖναι δυνατοὶ μὴ μεθ' ὑμῶν, εἴ τε καὶ γενόμενοι κακοὶ κατεργασαίμεθα, ἀδύνατοι κατασχεῖν
διὰ μῆκός τε πλοῦ καὶ ἀπορίᾳ φυλακῆς πόλεων
μεγάλων καὶ τῇ παρασκευῇ ἠπειρωτίδων· οἵδε δὲ
οὐ στρατοπέδῳ, πόλει δὲ μείζονι τῆς ἡμετέρας
παρουσίας ἐποικοῦντες ὑμῖν αἰεί τε ἐπιβουλεύουσι
καί, ὅταν καιρὸν λάβωσιν ἑκάστου, οὐκ ἀνιᾶσιν
(ἔδειξαν δὲ καὶ ἄλλα ἤδη καὶ τὰ ἐς Λεοντίνους),
4 καὶ νῦν τολμῶσιν ἐπὶ τοὺς ταῦτα κωλύοντας καὶ

---

[1] In 427 B.C., when Camarina stood with the Leontines and
other Chalcidians against Syracuse ; cf. III. lxxxvi. 2.

[2] i.e. with infantry and cavalry, our forces being purely
naval.

dominion over you, and wish, after uniting you with themselves on the ground of your suspicion of us, then by force, or because of your isolation when we shall have gone away unsuccessful, themselves to rule Sicily. And that is sure to happen if you unite with them; for neither will so great a force, if once combined, be any longer easy for us to handle, nor would the Syracusans lack strength to deal with you if we should not be present.

LXXXVI. "And if there be anyone who does not accept this view, that which has taken place will itself prove his error. For you brought us over before,[1] flaunting in our faces no other terror but this, that we ourselves should be in danger if we should permit you to come under the power of the Syracusans. And it is not right for you now to distrust the very argument by which you thought it right to persuade us then, nor to be suspicious because we are present with a force out of all proportion to the strength of the Syracusans; far more should you distrust them. We certainly are not able to maintain ourselves in Sicily without you; and even if we should prove false and subdue Sicily, we should be unable to hold it on account of the length of the voyage and the difficulty of guarding cities that are as large and well equipped as continental cities[2]; whereas these Syracusans, in hostile proximity to you, not with a mere army in the field, but a city greater than our present force, are always plotting against you, and whenever they get an opportunity against you singly, do not let it slip, as they have shown several times already and especially in their dealings with the Leontines; and now they make bold to urge you to oppose those who seek to

ἀνέχοντας τὴν Σικελίαν μέχρι τοῦδε μὴ ὑπ'
αὐτοὺς εἶναι παρακαλεῖν ὑμᾶς ὡς ἀναισθήτους.
5 πολὺ δὲ ἐπὶ ἀληθεστέραν γε σωτηρίαν ἡμεῖς
ἀντιπαρακαλοῦμεν, δεόμενοι τὴν ὑπάρχουσαν ἀπ'
ἀλλήλων ἀμφοτέροις μὴ προδιδόναι, νομίσαι τε [1]
τοῖσδε μὲν καὶ ἄνευ ξυμμάχων αἰεὶ ἐφ' ὑμᾶς
ἑτοίμην διὰ τὸ πλῆθος εἶναι ὁδόν, ὑμῖν δ' οὐ
πολλάκις παρασχήσειν μετὰ τοσῆσδε ἐπικουρίας
ἀμύνασθαι· ἣν εἰ τῷ ὑπόπτῳ ἢ ἄπρακτον ἐάσετε
ἀπελθεῖν ἢ καὶ σφαλεῖσαν, ἔτι βουλήσεσθε καὶ
πολλοστὸν μόριον αὐτῆς ἰδεῖν, ὅτε οὐδὲν ἔτι πε-
ρανεῖ παραγενόμενον ὑμῖν.

LXXXVII. "Ἀλλὰ μήτε ὑμεῖς, ὦ Καμαριναῖοι,
ταῖς τῶνδε διαβολαῖς ἀναπείθεσθε μήτε οἱ ἄλλοι·
εἰρήκαμεν δ' ὑμῖν πᾶσαν τὴν ἀλήθειαν περὶ ὧν
ὑποπτευόμεθα, καὶ ἔτι ἐν κεφαλαίοις ὑπομνή-
2 σαντες ἀξιώσομεν πείθειν. φαμὲν γὰρ ἄρχειν μὲν
τῶν ἐκεῖ, ἵνα μὴ ὑπακούωμεν ἄλλου, ἐλευθεροῦν
δὲ τὰ ἐνθάδε, ὅπως μὴ ὑπ' αὐτῶν βλαπτώμεθα,
πολλὰ δ' ἀναγκάζεσθαι πράσσειν, διότι καὶ πολλὰ
φυλασσόμεθα, ξύμμαχοι δὲ καὶ νῦν καὶ πρότερον
τοῖς ἐνθάδε ὑμῶν ἀδικουμένοις οὐκ ἄκλητοι, παρα-
3 κληθέντες δὲ ἥκειν. καὶ ὑμεῖς μήθ' ὡς δικασταὶ
γενόμενοι τῶν ἡμῖν ποιουμένων μήθ' ὡς σωφρο-

[1] τε, Hude reads δέ with M.

---

[1] πολλὰ πράσσειν, as well as πολυπραγμοσύνη below, is used
in a good sense, characterizing the policy of the Athenians at
their acme, as described by Pericles in the funeral oration,
ii. 40, 41.

prevent these things and who up to this time have kept Sicily from being under their dominion, as though you were without sense. But it is to a safety far more real that we in our turn invite you, begging you not to throw away that safety which we both derive from one another; and to consider that for them, even without allies, the way is always open against you because of their numbers, whereas for you the opportunity will not often present itself to defend yourselves with the help of so great an auxiliary force. But if through your suspicions you suffer this force to depart with its object unaccomplished, or, worse still, defeated, you will hereafter wish that you could see even the merest fraction of it when its presence will no longer avail you aught.

LXXXVII. "Nay, be not moved, men of Camarina, either you or the other peoples of Sicily, by the calumnies of these men. We have told you the whole truth concerning the matters of which we are suspected, and now again briefly recalling to your minds the chief points of our argument, we fully expect to convince you. We say, namely, that we hold sway over the cities in Hellas in order that we may not have to obey some other power, but that we are trying to free those here, in order that we may not be injured by them. We are obliged to be active in many matters,[1] because we have many dangers to guard against; and we come as allies, now as before, to those of you here who are wronged, not uninvited, but by your express invitation. And do not you, by constituting yourselves either judges of our conduct or by tutoring us in moderation[2]—a hard task at

---

[2] σωφρονισταί as in III. lxv. 3 ; VIII. xlviii. 6 ; cf. Plato, Rep. 471 a εὐμενῶς σωφρονιοῦσιν, οὐκ ἐπὶ δουλείᾳ κολάζοντες, οὐδ᾽ ἐπ᾽ ὀλέθρῳ, σωφρονισταὶ ὄντες, οὐ πολέμιοι.

νισταί, ὃ χαλεπὸν ἤδη, ἀποτρέπειν πειρᾶσθε, καθ'
ὅσον δέ τι ὑμῖν τῆς ἡμετέρας πολυπραγμοσύνης
καὶ τρόπου τὸ αὐτὸ ξυμφέρει, τούτῳ ἀπολαβόντες
χρήσασθε, καὶ νομίσατε μὴ πάντας ἐν ἴσῳ βλάπτειν αὐτά, πολὺ δὲ πλείους τῶν Ἑλλήνων καὶ
4 ὠφελεῖν. ἐν παντὶ γὰρ πᾶς χωρίῳ, κἂν ᾧ μὴ
ὑπάρχομεν, ὅ τε οἰόμενος ἀδικήσεσθαι καὶ ὁ ἐπι-
βουλεύων διὰ τὸ ἑτοίμην[1] ὑπεῖναι ἐλπίδα τῷ
μὲν ἀντιτυχεῖν ἐπικουρίας ἀφ' ἡμῶν, τῷ δέ, εἰ
ἥξομεν, μὴ ἀδεεῖ εἶναι κινδυνεύειν, ἀμφότεροι
ἀναγκάζονται ὁ μὲν ἄκων σωφρονεῖν, ὁ δ' ἀπραγ-
5 μόνως σῴζεσθαι. ταύτην οὖν τὴν κοινὴν τῷ τε
δεομένῳ καὶ ὑμῖν νῦν παροῦσαν ἀσφάλειαν μὴ
ἀπώσησθε, ἀλλ' ἐξισώσαντες τοῖς ἄλλοις μεθ'
ἡμῶν τοῖς Συρακοσίοις, ἀντὶ τοῦ αἰεὶ φυλάσσεσθαι
αὐτούς, καὶ ἀντεπιβουλεῦσαί ποτε ἐκ τοῦ ὁμοίου
μεταλάβετε."

LXXXVIII. Τοιαῦτα δὲ ὁ Εὔφημος εἶπεν. οἱ
δὲ Καμαριναῖοι ἐπεπόνθεσαν τοιόνδε. τοῖς μὲν
Ἀθηναίοις εὖνοι ἦσαν, πλὴν καθ' ὅσον[2] τὴν
Σικελίαν ᾤοντο αὐτοὺς δουλώσεσθαι, τοῖς δὲ
Συρακοσίοις αἰεὶ κατὰ τὸ ὅμορον διάφοροι· δεδιότες δ' οὐχ ἧσσον τοὺς Συρακοσίους ἐγγὺς ὄντας
μὴ καὶ ἄνευ σφῶν περιγένωνται, τό τε πρῶτον
αὐτοῖς τοὺς ὀλίγους ἱππέας ἔπεμψαν καὶ τὸ λοιπὸν
ἐδόκει αὐτοῖς ὑπουργεῖν μὲν τοῖς Συρακοσίοις

---

[1] διὰ τὸ ἑτοίμην ὑπεῖναι ἐλπίδα ... σῴζεσθαι, the text is
probably corrupt. Hude follows van Herwerden in reading
ἀν[τι]τυχεῖν, and, with Krüger, emends ἀδεεῖς of the MSS. to
ἀδεεῖ, and deletes κινδυνεύειν. Steup, as also Stahl, adopts
Reiske's conjecture ἀδεές and deletes κινδυνεύειν.
[2] εἰ, after καθ' ὅσον in MSS., deleted by Reiske, followed
by Krüger.

this late day!—make any attempt to divert us, but in so far as anything in our busy activity and our character is at the same time to your interest, take this and make use of it; and think, not that these qualities of ours are hurtful alike to all, but that they are even profitable to far the greater part of the Hellenes. For everyone in every place, even where we are not already present, both he that thinks he will suffer wrong, and he that plots to do wrong—on account of the certain prospect that is ever present in their minds, in the one case that he will obtain succour from us in return for his allegiance, in the other that, if we shall come, he will run the risk of not escaping unscathed for his wrongdoings—are both alike under constraint, the latter to be moderate however unwilling, the former to be saved without effort of his own. This common safety, then, which is now offered to anyone who may ask for it as well as to you, reject not; but availing yourselves of it as others do, join forces with us and instead of having always to be on your guard against the Syracusans, change your course and at length plot against them even as they have plotted against you."

LXXXVIII. Thus Euphemus spoke. But what the Camarinaeans had felt was this: They were well disposed to the Athenians, except in so far as they thought that these would enslave Sicily; but with the Syracusans, as is usual with next-door neighbours, they were always at variance. And it was because they were more afraid of the Syracusans, as being so near, that they had in the first instance sent them the few horsemen,[1] lest they might prove superior to the Athenians even without their aid; and they

---

[1] Ch. lxvii. 2.

μᾶλλον ἔργῳ, ὡς ἂν δύνωνται μετριώτατα, ἐν δὲ
τῷ παρόντι, ἵνα μηδὲ τοῖς Ἀθηναίοις ἔλασσον
δοκῶσι νεῖμαι, ἐπειδὴ καὶ ἐπικρατέστεροι τῇ μάχῃ
2 ἐγένοντο, λόγῳ ἀποκρίνασθαι ἴσα ἀμφοτέροις. καὶ
οὕτω βουλευσάμενοι ἀπεκρίναντο, ἐπειδὴ τυγχάνει
ἀμφοτέροις οὖσι ξυμμάχοις σφῶν πρὸς ἀλλήλους
πόλεμος ὤν, εὔορκον δοκεῖν εἶναι σφίσιν ἐν τῷ
παρόντι μηδετέροις ἀμύνειν. καὶ οἱ πρέσβεις
ἑκατέρων ἀπῆλθον.

3   Καὶ οἱ μὲν Συρακόσιοι τὰ καθ' ἑαυτοὺς ἐξηρτύ-
οντο ἐς τὸν πόλεμον, οἱ δ' Ἀθηναῖοι ἐν τῇ Νάξῳ
ἐστρατοπεδευμένοι τὰ πρὸς τοὺς Σικελοὺς ἔπρασσον, ὅπως αὐτοῖς ὡς πλεῖστοι προσχωρήσονται.
4 καὶ οἱ μὲν πρὸς τὰ πεδία μᾶλλον τῶν Σικελῶν,
ὑπήκοοι ὄντες τῶν Συρακοσίων, οὐ[1] πολλοὶ ἀφει-
στήκεσαν· τῶν δὲ τὴν μεσόγειαν ἐχόντων αὐτόνομοι
οὖσαι καὶ πρότερον αἰεὶ αἱ[2] οἰκήσεις εὐθύς, πλὴν
ὀλίγοι, μετὰ τῶν Ἀθηναίων ἦσαν, καὶ σῖτόν τε
κατεκόμιζον τῷ στρατεύματι καὶ εἰσὶν οἳ καὶ
5 χρήματα. ἐπὶ δὲ τοὺς μὴ προσχωροῦντας οἱ
Ἀθηναῖοι στρατεύσαντες τοὺς μὲν προσηνάγκαζον,
τοὺς δὲ καὶ ὑπὸ τῶν Συρακοσίων, φρουρούς τ'
ἐσπεμπόντων καὶ βοηθούντων, ἀπεκωλύοντο. τόν
τε χειμῶνα μεθορμισάμενοι ἐκ τῆς Νάξου ἐς τὴν
Κατάνην καὶ τὸ στρατόπεδον ὃ κατεκαύθη ὑπὸ
τῶν Συρακοσίων αὖθις ἀνορθώσαντες διεχείμαζον.
6 καὶ ἔπεμψαν μὲν ἐς Καρχηδόνα τριήρη περὶ φιλίας,
εἰ δύναιντό τι ὠφελεῖσθαι, ἔπεμψαν δὲ καὶ ἐς
Τυρσηνίαν, ἔστιν ὧν πόλεων ἐπαγγελλομένων καὶ

---

[1] Canter's correction for οἱ πολλοί of the MSS.
[2] αἱ added by Bekker.

now resolved for the future to keep on giving to them rather than to the Athenians assistance in fact, though as moderately as possible, and for the present, in order that they might not seem to show less favour to the Athenians, especially since these had proved the stronger in the battle, to give in word the same answer to both. Having thus determined, they made answer, that, as they were allies of both parties that were at war, it seemed to them to be consistent with their oath to aid neither at present. So the envoys of both sides went away.

The Syracusans on their side were getting ready for the war, while the Athenians who were encamped at Naxos were negotiating with the Sicels, in the effort to bring over as many of them as possible. Now, of the Sicels that lived more toward the flat country and were subjects of the Syracusans not many [1] had revolted; but the Sicel settlements in the interior, which even before had always been independent, with few exceptions straightway sided with the Athenians, bringing down grain for the army and in some cases money also. Against those that did not come over the Athenians took the field, and compelled some to do so, but were kept from compelling others by the Syracusans, who sent garrisons to their relief. Removing also the anchorage of their fleet from Naxos to Catana, and restoring the camp which had been burned by the Syracusans, they passed the winter there. They sent also a trireme to Carthage on a mission of friendship, in the hope that they might be able to get some aid; and they sent one also to Tyrrhenia, as some of the cities there offered of

---

[1] Or, retaining οἱ πολλοί, "most had held aloof," *i.e.* from the alliance with the Athenians.

αὐτῶν ξυμπολεμεῖν. περιήγγελλον δὲ καὶ τοῖς
Σικελοῖς καὶ ἐς τὴν Ἔγεσταν πέμψαντες ἐκέλευον
ἵππους σφίσιν ὡς πλείστους πέμπειν, καὶ τἆλλα
ἐς τὸν περιτειχισμόν, πλινθία [1] καὶ σίδηρον, ἡτοί-
μαζον, καὶ ὅσα ἔδει, ὡς ἅμα τῷ ἦρι ἑξόμενοι τοῦ
πολέμου.

7 Οἱ δ' ἐς τὴν Κόρινθον καὶ Λακεδαίμονα τῶν
Συρακοσίων ἀποσταλέντες πρέσβεις τούς τε Ἰταλιώτας ἅμα παραπλέοντες ἐπειρῶντο πείθειν μὴ
περιορᾶν τὰ γιγνόμενα ὑπὸ τῶν Ἀθηναίων, ὡς καὶ
ἐκείνοις ὁμοίως ἐπιβουλευόμενα, καὶ ἐπειδὴ ἐν τῇ
Κορίνθῳ ἐγένοντο, λόγους ἐποιοῦντο ἀξιοῦντες
8 σφίσι κατὰ τὸ ξυγγενὲς βοηθεῖν. καὶ οἱ Κορίνθιοι, εὐθὺς ψηφισάμενοι αὐτοὶ πρῶτοι ὥστε πάσῃ
προθυμίᾳ ἀμύνειν, καὶ ἐς τὴν Λακεδαίμονα ξυναπ-
έστελλον αὐτοῖς πρέσβεις, ὅπως καὶ ἐκείνους
ξυναναπείθοιεν τόν τε αὐτοῦ πόλεμον σαφέστερον
ποιεῖσθαι πρὸς τοὺς Ἀθηναίους καὶ ἐς τὴν Σικελίαν
9 ὠφελίαν τινὰ πέμπειν. καὶ οἵ τε ἐκ τῆς Κορίνθου
πρέσβεις παρῆσαν ἐς τὴν Λακεδαίμονα καὶ Ἀλκιβιάδης μετὰ τῶν ξυμφυγάδων, περαιωθεὶς τότ'
εὐθὺς ἐπὶ πλοίου φορτικοῦ ἐκ τῆς Θουρίας ἐς
Κυλλήνην τῆς Ἠλείας πρῶτον, ἔπειτα ὕστερον
ἐς τὴν Λακεδαίμονα αὐτῶν τῶν Λακεδαιμονίων
μεταπεμψάντων ὑπόσπονδος ἐλθών· ἐφοβεῖτο γὰρ
10 αὐτοὺς διὰ τὴν περὶ τῶν Μαντινικῶν πρᾶξιν. καὶ
ξυνέβη ἐν τῇ ἐκκλησίᾳ τῶν Λακεδαιμονίων τούς
τε Κορινθίους καὶ τοὺς Συρακοσίους τὰ αὐτὰ καὶ
τὸν Ἀλκιβιάδην δεομένους πείθειν τοὺς Λακεδαιμονίους. καὶ διανοουμένων τῶν τε ἐφόρων καὶ

---

[1] Hude writes πλινθεῖα, after the Schol. Patm. (τὰ ἐν τύποις
ξύλα, οἷς τὰς πλίνθους κατεσκεύαζον).

themselves to join them in the war. They also despatched messengers to the various Sicel tribes, and sending to Egesta urged them to send as many horses as possible ; and they were getting ready for the circumvallation bricks and iron and whatever else was needful, with a view to taking the war in hand as soon as spring opened.

Meanwhile the Syracusan envoys, who had been sent to Corinth and Lacedaemon, as they sailed along the coast tried to persuade the Italiots [1] not to tolerate the conduct of the Athenians, as the plot was aimed equally against them; and when they reached Corinth they made an appeal to the Corinthians, urging them to send them aid on grounds of kinship. And the Corinthians at once took the lead in voting to aid them with all zeal themselves, and also sent envoys along with them to Lacedaemon, to help in persuading them not only to prosecute the war at home more openly against the Athenians, but also to send aid in some form to Sicily. Accordingly there were present at Lacedaemon these envoys from Corinth, and also Alcibiades with his fellow-exiles. He had, at the time of which we have spoken,[2] at once crossed over on a freight-boat from Thuria, going first to Cyllene in Elis, and had afterwards, on the summons of the Lacedaemonians themselves, come to Lacedaemon under safe-conduct; for he feared them on account of his intrigues in the affair of the Mantineans. So it happened that in the Lacedaemonian assembly the Syracusans, the Corinthians, and Alcibiades, making the same appeal, were prevailing upon the Lacedaemonians. The ephors indeed and others in

[1] Greek colonists settled in the part of Italy called Magna Graecia.   [2] cf. ch. lxi. 6.

τῶν ἐν τέλει ὄντων πρέσβεις πέμπειν ἐς Συα-
κούσας κωλύοντας μὴ ξυμβαίνειν Ἀθηναίοις,
βοηθεῖν δὲ οὐ προθύμων ὄντων, παρελθὼν ὁ Ἀλκιβιάδης παρώξυνέ τε τοὺς Λακεδαιμονίους καὶ
ἐξώρμησε λέγων τοιάδε.

LXXXIX. "'Αναγκαῖον περὶ τῆς ἐμῆς διαβολῆς πρῶτον ἐς ὑμᾶς εἰπεῖν, ἵνα μὴ χεῖρον τὰ
2 κοινὰ τῷ ὑπόπτῳ μου ἀκροάσησθε. τῶν δὴ ἐμῶν
προγόνων τὴν προξενίαν ὑμῶν κατά τι ἔγκλημα
ἀπειπόντων αὐτὸς ἐγὼ πάλιν ἀναλαμβάνων ἐθερά-
πευον ὑμᾶς ἄλλα τε καὶ περὶ τὴν ἐκ Πύλου
ξυμφοράν. καὶ διατελοῦντός μου προθύμου ὑμεῖς
πρὸς Ἀθηναίους καταλλασσόμενοι τοῖς μὲν ἐμοῖς
ἐχθροῖς δύναμιν, δι᾽ ἐκείνων πράξαντες, ἐμοὶ δὲ
3 ἀτιμίαν περιέθετε. καὶ διὰ ταῦτα δικαίως ὑπ᾽
ἐμοῦ πρός τε τὰ Μαντινέων καὶ Ἀργείων τραπο-
μένου καὶ ὅσα ἄλλα ἠναντιούμην ὑμῖν ἐβλάπτεσθε·
καὶ νῦν, εἴ τις καὶ τότε ἐν τῷ πάσχειν οὐκ εἰκότως
ὠργίζετό μοι, μετὰ τοῦ ἀληθοῦς σκοπῶν ἀναπει-
θέσθω· ἢ εἴ τις, διότι καὶ τῷ δήμῳ προσεκείμην
μᾶλλον, χείρω με ἐνόμιζε, μηδ᾽ οὕτως ἡγήσηται
4 ὀρθῶς ἄχθεσθαι. τοῖς γὰρ τυράννοις αἰεί ποτε
διάφοροί ἐσμεν (πᾶν δὲ τὸ ἐναντιούμενον τῷ δυνα-
στεύοντι δῆμος ὠνόμασται), καὶ ἀπ᾽ ἐκείνου ξυμ-
παρέμεινεν ἡ προστασία ἡμῖν τοῦ πλήθους. ἅμα
δὲ καὶ τῆς **πόλεως δημοκρατουμένης τὰ πολλὰ**

authority were already intending to send envoys to Syracuse to prevent their making terms with the Athenians, but were not disposed to send them aid; Alcibiades, however, coming forward, inflamed the Lacedaemonians and goaded them on, speaking as follows:

LXXXIX. "It is necessary first of all to speak to you about the prejudice against me, in order that you may not through suspicion of me give a less favourable hearing to matters of public concern. When my ancestors on account of some complaint had renounced their office as your proxenoi, I myself, seeking to revive the relationship, courted your favour in other matters and especially in regard to your misfortune at Pylos.[1] And although I continued zealous, you, in making peace with the Athenians, by negotiating through my personal enemies conferred power upon them but brought dishonour upon me. For these reasons you deserved the injury you suffered when I turned to the side of the Mantineans and Argives, and when I opposed you in other matters.[2] And if anyone at the actual moment of suffering was unduly angry at me, let him now look at it in the light of the truth and be led to a different conviction; or if anyone thought worse of me because I was more inclined to the cause of the people, let him not even on that ground suppose that he was rightly offended. For my family have always been at variance with tyrants, and as all that is opposed to despotic power has the name of democracy, so from the fact of that opposition of ours the leadership of the people has remained with us. Besides, while the city was a democracy, it was necessary in

[1] cf. v. xliii. 2.   [2] cf. v. liii. ff.

5 ἀνάγκη ἦν τοῖς παροῦσιν ἔπεσθαι. τῆς δὲ ὑπαρχούσης ἀκολασίας ἐπειρώμεθα μετριώτεροι ἐς τὰ
πολιτικὰ εἶναι. ἄλλοι δ' ἦσαν καὶ ἐπὶ τῶν πάλαι
καὶ νῦν οἳ ἐπὶ τὰ πονηρότερα ἐξῆγον τὸν ὄχλον·
6 οἵπερ καὶ ἐμὲ ἐξήλασαν. ἡμεῖς δὲ τοῦ ξύμπαντος
προύστημεν, δικαιοῦντες ἐν ᾧ σχήματι μεγίστη ἡ
πόλις ἐτύγχανε καὶ ἐλευθερωτάτη οὖσα καὶ ὅπερ
ἐδέξατό τις, τοῦτο ξυνδιασῴζειν (ἐπεὶ[1] δημοκρατίαν
γε ἐγιγνώσκομεν οἱ φρονοῦντές τι, καὶ αὐτὸς
οὐδενὸς ἂν χείρον, ὅσῳ καὶ† λοιδορήσαιμι· ἀλλὰ
περὶ ὁμολογουμένης ἀνοίας οὐδὲν ἂν καινὸν λέγοιτο), καὶ τὸ μεθιστάναι αὐτὴν οὐκ ἐδόκει ἡμῖν
ἀσφαλὲς εἶναι ὑμῶν πολεμίων προσκαθημένων.

XC. "Καὶ τὰ μὲν ἐς τὰς ἐμὰς διαβολὰς τοιαῦτα
ξυνέβη· περὶ δὲ ὧν ὑμῖν τε βουλευτέον καὶ ἐμοί,
2 εἴ τι πλέον οἶδα, ἐσηγητέον, μάθετε ἤδη. ἐπλεύ-
σαμεν ἐς Σικελίαν πρῶτον μέν, εἰ δυναίμεθα,
Σικελιώτας καταστρεψόμενοι, μετὰ δ' ἐκείνους
αὖθις καὶ Ἰταλιώτας, ἔπειτα καὶ τῆς Καρχη-
3 δονίων ἀρχῆς καὶ αὐτῶν ἀποπειράσοντες. εἰ δὲ
προχωρήσειε ταῦτα ἢ πάντα ἢ καὶ τὰ πλείω, ἤδη
τῇ Πελοποννήσῳ ἐμέλλομεν ἐπιχειρήσειν, κομίσαντες ξύμπασαν μὲν τὴν ἐκεῖθεν προσγενομένην
δύναμιν τῶν Ἑλλήνων, πολλοὺς δὲ βαρβάρους
μισθωσάμενοι καὶ Ἴβηρας καὶ ἄλλους τῶν ἐκεῖ
ὁμολογουμένως νῦν βαρβάρων μαχιμωτάτους,

---

[1] Hude writes ἐπεὶ δημοκρατίας γε καταγιγνώσκομεν οἱ φρονοῦντές τι, καὶ αὐτὸς οὐδενὸς ἂν χείρον, ὅσῳ κἂν λοιδορήσαιμι,
which must be about the meaning of the passage.

most respects to conform to existing conditions. We
tried, however, to pursue a moderate course in politics
in contrast with the prevailing licence. But there have
been others, both in the time of our forefathers and
now, who led the masses into more evil ways; and
these are the very men who have driven me out.
But it was of the whole people that we were leaders,
deeming it right to help to preserve that form of
government under which the state had, as it chanced,
attained its highest greatness and completest freedom,
and which had come down to us—for as to democracy
of course, all of us who have any sense well understood
what it was, and I better than anyone, inasmuch as
I have greater cause to abuse it; but indeed nothing
new can be said about an admitted folly—and it did
not seem to us wise to change our democratic constitution when you, our enemies, were waiting at
our gates.

XC. " With regard, then, to the prejudices against
me, that is how things fell out; but with reference
to the matters about which you must take counsel and
which I, if I have any superior knowledge, must bring
to your notice, give me now your attention. We sailed
to Sicily, first, to subdue the Siceliots, if we could,
and after them the Italiots also; and then to make
an attempt upon the empire of the Carthaginians
and upon the city itself. If these things, either all,
or at least the greater part of them, succeeded, then
we intended to attack the Peloponnesus, bringing
here the whole Hellenic force that had joined us
there, hiring besides many barbarians, both Iberians
and others of the peoples there that are admittedly
the most warlike of the barbarians at the present

τριήρεις τε πρὸς ταῖς ἡμετέραις πολλὰς ναυπηγη-
σάμενοι, ἐχούσης τῆς Ἰταλίας ξύλα ἄφθονα, αἷς
τὴν Πελοπόννησον πέριξ πολιορκοῦντες καὶ τῷ
πεζῷ ἅμα ἐκ γῆς ἐφορμαῖς τῶν πόλεων τὰς μὲν
βίᾳ λαβόντες, τὰς δ᾽ ἐντειχισάμενοι ῥᾳδίως ἠλπί-
ζομεν καταπολεμήσειν καὶ μετὰ ταῦτα καὶ τοῦ
4 ξύμπαντος Ἑλληνικοῦ ἄρξειν. χρήματα δὲ καὶ
σῖτον, ὥστε εὐπορώτερον γίγνεσθαί τι αὐτῶν,
αὐτὰ τὰ προσγενόμενα ἐκεῖθεν χωρία ἔμελλε
διαρκῆ ἄνευ τῆς ἐνθένδε προσόδου παρέξειν.

XCI. "Τοιαῦτα μὲν περὶ τοῦ νῦν οἰχομένου
στόλου παρὰ τοῦ τὰ ἀκριβέστατα εἰδότος ὡς
διενοήθημεν ἀκηκόατε· καὶ ὅσοι ὑπόλοιποι στρατηγοί, ἢν δύνωνται, ὁμοίως αὐτὰ πράξουσιν. ὡς
δέ, εἰ μὴ βοηθήσετε, οὐ περιέσται τἀκεῖ, μάθετε
2 ἤδη. Σικελιῶται γὰρ ἀπειρότεροι μέν εἰσιν, ὅμως
δ᾽ ἂν ξυστραφέντες ἀθρόοι καὶ νῦν ἔτι περι-
γένοιντο· Συρακόσιοι δὲ μόνοι μάχῃ τε ἤδη
πανδημεὶ ἡσσημένοι καὶ ναυσὶν ἅμα κατειργό-
μενοι ἀδύνατοι ἔσονται τῇ νῦν Ἀθηναίων ἐκεῖ
3 παρασκευῇ ἀντίσχειν. καὶ εἰ αὕτη ἡ πόλις
ληφθήσεται, ἔχεται καὶ ἡ πᾶσα Σικελία, καὶ
εὐθὺς καὶ Ἰταλία· καὶ ὃν ἄρτι κίνδυνον ἐκεῖθεν
4 προεῖπον, οὐκ ἂν διὰ μακροῦ ὑμῖν ἐπιπέσοι. ὥστε
μὴ περὶ τῆς Σικελίας τις οἰέσθω μόνον βουλεύειν,
ἀλλὰ καὶ περὶ τῆς Πελοποννήσου, εἰ μὴ ποιήσετε
τάδε ἐν τάχει, στρατιάν τε ἐπὶ νεῶν πέμψετε
τοιαύτην ἐκεῖσε οἵτινες αὐτερέται κομισθέντες
καὶ ὁπλιτεύσουσιν εὐθύς, καὶ ὃ τῆς στρατιᾶς ἔτι

day, and building many triremes in addition to our own, as Italy has timber in abundance. Laying a blockade with these triremes round the Peloponnesus, and at the same time attacking it with our infantry by land, having thus taken some of its cities by assault and walled in others, we expected easily to reduce it, and after that to have sway over the whole Hellenic race. As to money and food, for making any of these projects more feasible, the additional territory acquired in Sicily would of itself furnish these in sufficient quantity, independently of our home revenues.

XCI. "That such were the objects of the expedition which has sailed, you have heard now from one who knows most accurately what we purposed; and the rest of the generals will, if they can, carry out these plans without change. But that the people over there cannot hold out unless you aid them, let me now show you. The Siceliots have indeed less military experience than the Athenians, yet if they were united in one body they could, even as it is, gain the victory. But the Syracusans alone, being already worsted in battle with their full force and at the same time hemmed in at sea, will be unable to withstand the army of the Athenians now there. And if this city shall be taken, all Sicily is theirs, and so presently will Italy be also; nor will it be long before the danger which I have just now predicted from that quarter would fall upon you. Therefore let nobody think that you are deliberating about Sicily only, but about the Peloponnesus also, unless you do quickly the following things: send thither by ship such a body of troops as, after working their own passage at the oar, can at once serve as hoplites; also what I

χρησιμώτερον εἶναι νομίζω, ἄνδρα Σπαρτιάτην
ἄρχοντα, ὡς ἂν τούς τε παρόντας ξυντάξῃ καὶ
τοὺς μὴ 'θέλοντας προσαναγκάσῃ· οὕτω γὰρ οἵ
τε ὑπάρχοντες ὑμῖν φίλοι θαρσήσουσι μᾶλλον
5 καὶ οἱ ἐνδοιάζοντες ἀδεέστερον προσίασιν. καὶ
τὰ ἐνθάδε χρὴ ἅμα φανερώτερον ἐκπολεμεῖν, ἵνα
Συρακόσιοί τε νομίζοντες ὑμᾶς ἐπιμέλεσθαι μᾶλλον ἀντέχωσι καὶ Ἀθηναῖοι τοῖς ἑαυτῶν ἧσσον
6 ἄλλην ἐπικουρίαν πέμπωσιν. τειχίζειν τε χρὴ
Δεκέλειαν τῆς Ἀττικῆς, ὅπερ Ἀθηναῖοι μάλιστα
αἰεὶ φοβοῦνται καὶ μόνου αὐτοῦ νομίζουσι τῶν ἐν
τῷ πολέμῳ οὐ διαπεπειρᾶσθαι. βεβαιότατα δ᾽
ἄν τις οὕτως τοὺς πολεμίους βλάπτοι, εἰ, ἃ μάλιστα δεδιότας αὐτοὺς αἰσθάνοιτο, ταῦτα σαφῶς
πυνθανόμενος ἐπιφέροι· εἰκὸς γὰρ αὐτοὺς ἀκριβέστατα ἑκάστους τὰ σφέτερα αὐτῶν δεινὰ ἐπι-
7 σταμένους φοβεῖσθαι. ἃ δ᾽ ἐν τῇ ἐπιτειχίσει
αὐτοὶ ὠφελούμενοι τοὺς ἐναντίους κωλύσετε,
πολλὰ παρεὶς τὰ μέγιστα κεφαλαιώσω. οἷς τε
γὰρ ἡ χώρα κατεσκεύασται, τὰ πολλὰ πρὸς ὑμᾶς
τὰ μὲν ληφθέντα, τὰ δ᾽ αὐτόματα ἥξει· καὶ τὰς
τοῦ Λαυρείου τῶν ἀργυρείων μετάλλων προσ-
όδους καὶ ὅσα ἀπὸ γῆς καὶ δικαστηρίων νῦν ὠφε-
λοῦνται εὐθὺς ἀποστερήσονται, μάλιστα δὲ τῆς
ἀπὸ τῶν ξυμμάχων προσόδου ἧσσον ἂν φορου-

---

[1] The occupation of Deceleia took place in 413 B.C. (cf.
VII. xix.).

[2] i.e. a fortress built to dominate an enemy's territory.

consider even more indispensable than the army, a
Spartan as commander, that he may organize the
forces already present and press into service those
that are unwilling. For in this way the friends you
have already will be encouraged, and those who are
in doubt will come over with less misgiving. And
the war here you must at the same time prosecute
more openly, in order that the Syracusans,
convinced that you are really concerned, may offer
greater resistance, and the Athenians be less able
to send reinforcements to their own troops. You
ought likewise to fortify Deceleia in Attica,[1] the
very thing the Athenians are always most in dread
of and reckon the only peril of which they have not
made full trial in this war. And the surest way in
which anyone can hurt his enemies is this: acting on
certain information, he should inflict upon them that
which he perceives they most fear; for it is natural
that every man should have the most accurate knowledge of his own dangers and should fear them
accordingly. But as to the benefits which you
yourselves will gain by this menacing stronghold [2] and
will prevent your opponents from obtaining, I will
pass over many and sum up only the most important.
Whatever their country is stocked with will for the
most part come into your hands, either by capture
or by voluntary surrender.[3] And the revenues of
the Laureian silver mines and whatever profits they
now derive from their land and from their courts,[4]
they will at once be deprived of, and above all
of the tribute from their allies, that would be less

---

[3] αὐτόματα, refers to slaves, who were part of the "stock."
[4] The fees and fines arising from the adjudication of cases
brought by the allied states.

μένης, οἳ τὰ παρ' ὑμῶν νομίσαντες ἤδη κατὰ
κράτος πολεμεῖσθαι ὀλιγωρήσουσιν.

XCII. "Γίγνεσθαι δέ τι αὐτῶν καὶ ἐν τάχει
καὶ προθυμότερον ἐν ὑμῖν ἐστιν, ὦ Λακεδαιμόνιοι,
ἐπεὶ ὥς γε δυνατά (καὶ οὐχ ἁμαρτήσεσθαι οἶμαι
2 γνώμης) πάνυ θαρσῶ. καὶ χείρων οὐδενὶ ἀξιῶ
δοκεῖν ὑμῶν εἶναι, εἰ τῇ ἐμαυτοῦ μετὰ τῶν πολε-
μιωτάτων, φιλόπολίς ποτε δοκῶν εἶναι, νῦν
ἐγκρατῶς ἐπέρχομαι, οὐδὲ ὑποπτεύεσθαί μου ἐς
3 τὴν φυγαδικὴν προθυμίαν τὸν λόγον. φυγάς τε
γάρ εἰμι τῆς τῶν ἐξελασάντων πονηρίας καὶ οὐ
τῆς ὑμετέρας, ἢν πείθησθέ μοι, ὠφελίας· καὶ
πολεμιώτεροι οὐχ οἱ τοὺς πολεμίους που βλά-
ψαντες ὑμεῖς ἢ οἱ τοὺς φίλους ἀναγκάσαντες
4 πολεμίους γενέσθαι. τό τε φιλόπολι οὐκ ἐν ᾧ
ἀδικοῦμαι ἔχω, ἀλλ' ἐν ᾧ ἀσφαλῶς ἐπολιτεύθην.
οὐδ' ἐπὶ πατρίδα οὖσαν ἔτι ἡγοῦμαι νῦν ἰέναι,
πολὺ δὲ μᾶλλον τὴν οὐκ οὖσαν ἀνακτᾶσθαι. καὶ
φιλόπολις οὗτος ὀρθῶς, οὐχ ὃς ἂν τὴν ἑαυτοῦ
ἀδίκως ἀπολέσας μὴ ἐπίῃ, ἀλλ' ὃς ἂν ἐκ παντὸς
τρόπου διὰ τὸ ἐπιθυμεῖν πειραθῇ αὐτὴν ἀναλαβεῖν.
5 οὕτως ἐμοί τε ἀξιῶ ὑμᾶς καὶ ἐς κίνδυνον καὶ ἐς
ταλαιπωρίαν πᾶσαν ἀδεῶς χρῆσθαι, ὦ Λακεδαιμόνιοι, γνόντας τοῦτον δὴ τὸν ὑφ' ἁπάντων
προβαλλόμενον λόγον ὡς, εἰ πολέμιός γε ὢν
σφόδρα ἔβλαπτον, κἂν φίλος ὢν ἱκανῶς ὠφελοίην,
ὅσῳ τὰ μὲν Ἀθηναίων οἶδα, τὰ δ' ὑμέτερα ἤκαζον,

regularly brought in; for these, convinced that the war is now being prosecuted on your part with all your might, will take their obligations lightly.

XCII. "The accomplishment of any of these projects promptly and more zealously depends, men of Lacedaemon, upon you, for that they are possible— and I do not think that I shall prove wrong in my judgment—I am fully assured. And I claim that no one of you shall think more harshly of me because I, who seemed once to be a lover of my city, now make assault with all my might upon her, in concert with her bitterest enemies; nor do I think that my word should be suspected on the score of the outcast's zeal. For outcast as I am from the villainy of those that expelled me, I am not ousted from doing you good service, if you will but hearken to me; and the worse enemies are not those who, like you, have merely hurt their enemies, but those who have forced their friends to become foes. And as to love of country— I have it not when I am wronged, but had it when I possessed my civil rights in security. And it is not, as I conceive, against a country still my own that I am now going, but far rather one no longer mine that I am seeking to recover. And the true patriot is not the man who, having unjustly lost his fatherland, refrains from attacking it, but he who in his yearning for it tries in every way to get it back. So I urge you, Lacedaemonians, to use me without misgiving for any danger and for any hardships, recognising that, according to the saying which is on everybody's lips, if as an enemy I did you exceeding injury, I might also be of some sufficient service to you as a friend, in so far as I know the affairs of the Athenians, while I could only conjecture yours. And I urge, too,

καὶ αὐτοὺς νῦν, νομίσαντας περὶ μεγίστων δὴ τῶν
διαφερόντων βουλεύεσθαι, μὴ ἀποκνεῖν τὴν ἐς
τὴν Σικελίαν τε καὶ ἐς τὴν Ἀττικὴν στρατείαν,
ἵνα τά τε ἐκεῖ βραχεῖ μορίῳ ξυμπαραγενόμενοι
μεγάλα σώσητε καὶ Ἀθηναίων τήν τε οὖσαν καὶ
τὴν μέλλουσαν δύναμιν καθέλητε, καὶ μετὰ
ταῦτα αὐτοί τε ἀσφαλῶς οἰκῆτε καὶ τῆς ἁπάσης
Ἑλλάδος ἑκούσης καὶ οὐ βίᾳ, κατ᾽ εὔνοιαν δὲ
ἡγῆσθε."

XCIII. Ὁ μὲν Ἀλκιβιάδης τοσαῦτα εἶπεν. οἱ
δὲ Λακεδαιμόνιοι διανοούμενοι μὲν καὶ αὐτοὶ
πρότερον στρατεύειν ἐπὶ τὰς Ἀθήνας, μέλλοντες
δὲ ἔτι καὶ περιορώμενοι, πολλῷ μᾶλλον ἐπερ-
ρώσθησαν διδάξαντος ταῦτα ἕκαστα αὐτοῦ καὶ
νομίσαντες παρὰ τοῦ σαφέστατα εἰδότος ἀκη-
2 κοέναι· ὥστε τῇ ἐπιτειχίσει τῆς Δεκελείας προσ-
εῖχον ἤδη τὸν νοῦν καὶ τὸ παραυτίκα καὶ τοῖς ἐν
τῇ Σικελίᾳ πέμπειν τινὰ τιμωρίαν. καὶ Γύλιπ-
πον τὸν Κλεανδρίδου προστάξαντες ἄρχοντα τοῖς
Συρακοσίοις ἐκέλευον μετ᾽ ἐκείνων καὶ τῶν Κορινθίων βουλευόμενον ποιεῖν ὅπη ἐκ τῶν παρόντων
μάλιστα καὶ τάχιστά τις ὠφελία ἥξει τοῖς ἐκεῖ.
3 ὁ δὲ δύο μὲν ναῦς τοὺς Κορινθίους ἤδη ἐκέλευέν
οἱ πέμπειν ἐς Ἀσίνην, τὰς δὲ λοιπὰς παρασκευά-
ζεσθαι ὅσας διανοοῦνται πέμπειν καί, ὅταν καιρὸς
ᾖ, ἑτοίμας εἶναι πλεῖν. ταῦτα δὲ ξυνθέμενοι
ἀνεχώρουν ἐκ τῆς Λακεδαίμονος.

that you yourselves now, convinced that you are deliberating about interests that are of the greatest importance, shrink not from sending an expedition into Sicily, and also into Attica, in order that, by keeping a small detachment on the island, you may preserve the large interests you have over there and may overthrow the power of the Athenians both present and prospective, and after that may yourselves live in security and be accepted by all the Hellenes of their free will, not by force but through affection, as their leaders."

XCIII. Such was the speech of Alcibiades; and the Lacedaemonians, who had already before this been disposed to make an expedition against Athens, but were still hesitating and looking about them, were now far more encouraged when Alcibiades himself explained these matters in detail, thinking that they had heard them from the one man who had most certain knowledge. And so they now turned their attention to the fortification of Deceleia and, in particular, to sending immediately some assistance to the Sicilians. Having appointed Gylippus son of Cleandridas commander of the Syracusan forces, they ordered him, in consultation with the envoys of the Syracusans and Corinthians, to devise how under present circumstances help might come to the Syracusans in the best and quickest way. And Gylippus bade the Corinthians send to him at once at Asine[1] two ships, and to equip all the rest they intended to send, and to be ready to sail whenever opportunity offered. Having made these arrangements the envoys left Lacedaemon and set out for home.

[1] Probably the harbour in Messenia (IV. xiii. 1).

4 Ἀφίκετο δὲ καὶ ἡ ἐκ τῆς Σικελίας τριήρης τῶν
Ἀθηναίων, ἣν ἀπέστειλαν οἱ στρατηγοὶ ἐπί τε
χρήματα καὶ ἱππέας. καὶ οἱ Ἀθηναῖοι ἀκούσαντες ἐψηφίσαντο τήν τε τροφὴν πέμπειν τῇ
στρατιᾷ καὶ τοὺς ἱππέας. καὶ ὁ χειμὼν ἐτελεύτα,
καὶ ἕβδομον καὶ δέκατον ἔτος τῷ πολέμῳ ἐτελεύτα τῷδε ὃν Θουκυδίδης ξυνέγραψεν.

XCIV. Ἅμα δὲ τῷ ἦρι εὐθὺς ἀρχομένῳ τοῦ
ἐπιγιγνομένου θέρους οἱ ἐν τῇ Σικελίᾳ Ἀθηναῖοι
ἄραντες ἐκ τῆς Κατάνης παρέπλευσαν ἐπὶ Μεγάρων,[1] οὓς ἐπὶ Γέλωνος τοῦ τυράννου, ὥσπερ καὶ
πρότερόν μοι εἴρηται, ἀναστήσαντες Συρακόσιοι
2 αὐτοὶ ἔχουσι τὴν γῆν. ἀποβάντες δὲ ἐδῄωσαν
τούς τε ἀγροὺς καὶ ἐλθόντες ἐπὶ ἔρυμά τι τῶν
Συρακοσίων καὶ οὐχ ἑλόντες αὖθις καὶ πεζῇ καὶ
ναυσὶ παρακομισθέντες ἐπὶ τὸν Τηρίαν ποταμὸν
τό τε πεδίον ἀναβάντες ἐδῄουν καὶ τὸν σῖτον
ἐνεπίμπρασαν, καὶ τῶν Συρακοσίων περιτυχόντες
τισὶν οὐ πολλοῖς καὶ ἀποκτείναντές τέ τινας καὶ
τροπαῖον στήσαντες ἀνεχώρησαν ἐπὶ τὰς ναῦς.
3 καὶ ἀποπλεύσαντες ἐς Κατάνην, ἐκεῖθεν δὲ ἐπι-
σιτισάμενοι πάσῃ τῇ στρατιᾷ ἐχώρουν ἐπὶ Κεν-
τόριπα, Σικελῶν πόλισμα, καὶ προσαγαγόμενοι
ὁμολογίᾳ ἀπῆσαν, πιμπράντες ἅμα τὸν σῖτον τῶν
4 τε Ἰνησσαίων καὶ τῶν Ὑβλαίων. καὶ ἀφικόμενοι ἐς Κατάνην καταλαμβάνουσι τούς τε ἱππέας
ἥκοντας ἐκ τῶν Ἀθηνῶν πεντήκοντα καὶ διακοσίους ἄνευ τῶν ἵππων μετὰ σκευῆς, ὡς αὐτόθεν

[1] τῶν ἐν τῇ Σικελίᾳ, after Μεγάρων in MSS., deleted by
Krüger.

354

At this time also there arrived at Athens from Sicily the trireme that had been sent by the generals for money and cavalry. And the Athenians, hearing their request, voted to send to the army both the supplies and the cavalry. And the winter ended, and with it the seventeenth year of this war of which Thucydides wrote the history.

XCIV. At the very beginning of the following spring, the Athenians in Sicily set out from Catana and proceeded along the coast toward Megara, from which, as has been stated before,[1] the Syracusans in the time of the tyrant Gelon had expelled the inhabitants, holding their territory themselves. Here they landed and ravaged the fields; then, attacking a stronghold of the Syracusans without success, they went back again along the coast with both land-force and fleet to the river Terias, and going inland ravaged the plain and set fire to the grain. Meeting with a small force of Syracusans, they killed some of them and after setting up a trophy withdrew to their ships. Having sailed back then to Catana and supplied themselves with provisions from there, they advanced with their whole army to Centoripa,[2] a Sicel town; and when they had brought it over by capitulation they returned, burning at the same time the grain of the Inessians[3] and Hyblaeans.[4] On their arrival at Catana they found that the horsemen had come from Athens, two hundred and fifty in number—with accoutrements but without the horses, for it was expected that horses would be procured

414 B.C.

---

[1] cf. ch. iv. 2.
[2] Now Centorbi, twenty-seven miles north-west from Catana and near Mt. Aetna.
[3] The site of Inessa is doubtful (cf. III. ciii. 1).
[4] Hybla Geleatis (ch. lxii. 5).

ἵππων πορισθησομένων, καὶ ἱπποτοξότας τριάκοντα καὶ τάλαντα ἀργυρίου τριακόσια.

XCV. Τοῦ δ' αὐτοῦ ἦρος καὶ ἐπ' Ἄργος στρατεύσαντες Λακεδαιμόνιοι μέχρι μὲν Κλεωνῶν
ἦλθον, σεισμοῦ δὲ γενομένου ἀπεχώρησαν. καὶ
Ἀργεῖοι μετὰ ταῦτα ἐσβαλόντες ἐς τὴν Θυρεᾶτιν
ὅμορον οὖσαν λείαν τῶν Λακεδαιμονίων πολλὴν
ἔλαβον, ἣ ἐπράθη ταλάντων οὐκ ἔλασσον πέντε
2 καὶ εἴκοσι. καὶ ὁ Θεσπιῶν δῆμος ἐν τῷ αὐτῷ
θέρει οὐ πολὺ ὕστερον ἐπιθέμενος τοῖς τὰς
ἀρχὰς ἔχουσιν οὐ κατέσχεν, ἀλλὰ βοηθησάντων
Θηβαίων[1] οἱ μὲν ξυνελήφθησαν, οἱ δ' ἐξέπεσον
Ἀθήναζε.

XCVI. Καὶ οἱ Συρακόσιοι τοῦ αὐτοῦ θέρους
ὡς ἐπύθοντο τούς τε ἱππέας ἥκοντας τοῖς Ἀθηναίοις καὶ μέλλοντας ἤδη ἐπὶ σφᾶς ἰέναι, νομίσαντες, ἐὰν μὴ τῶν Ἐπιπολῶν κρατήσωσιν οἱ
Ἀθηναῖοι, χωρίου ἀποκρήμνου τε καὶ ὑπὲρ τῆς
πόλεως εὐθὺς κειμένου, οὐκ ἂν ῥᾳδίως σφᾶς, οὐδ'
εἰ κρατοῖντο μάχῃ, ἀποτειχισθῆναι, διενοοῦντο
τὰς προσβάσεις αὐτῶν φυλάσσειν, ὅπως μὴ κατὰ
2 ταῦτα λάθωσι σφᾶς ἀναβάντες οἱ πολέμιοι· οὐ
γὰρ ἂν ἄλλῃ γε αὐτοὺς δυνηθῆναι. ἐξήρτηται
γὰρ τὸ ἄλλο χωρίον, καὶ μέχρι τῆς πόλεως ἐπι-
κλινές τέ ἐστι καὶ ἐπιφανὲς πᾶν ἔσω· καὶ
ὠνόμασται ὑπὸ τῶν Συρακοσίων διὰ τὸ ἐπιπολῆς
3 τοῦ ἄλλου εἶναι Ἐπιπολαί. καὶ οἱ μὲν ἐξελ-

---

[1] Θηβαίων, so B alone correctly against Ἀθηναίων of all the
other MSS., which gives no satisfactory sense ; for in case of
a real interference on the part of the Athenians, which
would have meant an infraction of existing peace relations
with the Boeotians (cf. v. xxxii. 5), more exact information
was to be expected.

in Sicily—as well as thirty mounted archers and three hundred talents [1] of silver.

XCV. During the same summer the Lacedaemonians, making an expedition to Argos, got as far as Cleonae, but when an earthquake occurred they retired. After this the Argives invaded the Thyreatis, which lies on their borders, and took much booty from the Lacedaemonians, which was sold for not less than twenty-five talents.[2] And in the course of the same summer, not long afterwards, the people of Thespiae attacked the government but did not succeed; for succour came from Thebes and some were arrested, while others fled for refuge to Athens.

XCVI. During the same summer the Syracusans, on learning that the Athenians had received their cavalry and that they were about to march against them immediately, thinking that unless the Athenians should get possession of Epipolae, a precipitous place lying directly above the city, they themselves, even if they were defeated in battle, could not easily be walled in, determined to guard the approaches to it, in order to prevent the enemy from ascending secretly by that way, since they could not possibly do so by any other road. For at all other points the place overhangs the city and slopes right down to it, the whole height being visible from it; and it is called Epipolae by the Syracusans because it lies as an upper surface above the rest of the country. So they went out at daybreak in full

---

[1] £60,000, $291,600. [2] £5,000, $24,300.

θόντες πανδημεὶ ἐς τὸν λειμῶνα τὸν¹ παρὰ τὸν
Ἄναπον ποταμὸν ἅμα τῇ ἡμέρᾳ (ἐτύγχανον γὰρ
αὐτοῖς καὶ οἱ περὶ τὸν Ἑρμοκράτη στρατηγοὶ
ἄρτι παρειληφότες τὴν ἀρχήν), ἐξέτασίν τε
ὅπλων ἐποιοῦντο καὶ ἐξακοσίους λογάδας τῶν
ὁπλιτῶν ἐξέκριναν πρότερον, ὧν ἦρχε Διόμιλος,
φυγὰς ἐξ Ἄνδρου, ὅπως τῶν τε Ἐπιπολῶν εἶεν
φύλακες καί, ἢν ἐς ἄλλο τι δέῃ, ταχὺ ξυνεστῶτες
παραγίγνωνται.

XCVII. Οἱ δὲ Ἀθηναῖοι ταύτης τῆς νυκτός,
ἢ² τῇ ἐπιγιγνομένῃ ἡμέρᾳ ἐξητάζοντο, ἔλαθον³
αὐτοὺς παντὶ ἤδη τῷ στρατεύματι ἐκ τῆς Κατάνης σχόντες κατὰ τὸν Λέοντα καλούμενον, ὃς
ἀπέχει τῶν Ἐπιπολῶν ἓξ ἢ ἑπτὰ σταδίους, καὶ
τοὺς πεζοὺς ἀποβιβάσαντες ταῖς τε ναυσὶν ἐς τὴν
Θάψον καθορμισάμενοι· ἔστι δὲ χερσόνησος μὲν
ἐν στενῷ ἰσθμῷ προύχουσα ἐς τὸ πέλαγος, τῆς
δὲ Συρακοσίων πόλεως οὔτε πλοῦν οὔτε ὁδὸν
2 πολλὴν ἀπέχει. καὶ ὁ μὲν ναυτικὸς στρατὸς τῶν
Ἀθηναίων ἐν τῇ Θάψῳ διασταυρωσάμενος τὸν
ἰσθμὸν ἡσύχαζεν· ὁ δὲ πεζὸς ἐχώρει εὐθὺς δρόμῳ
πρὸς τὰς Ἐπιπολὰς καὶ φθάνει ἀναβὰς κατὰ τὸν
Εὐρύηλον πρὶν τοὺς Συρακοσίους αἰσθομένους ἐκ
τοῦ λειμῶνος καὶ τῆς ἐξετάσεως παραγενέσθαι.
3 ἐβοήθουν δὲ οἵ τε ἄλλοι ὡς ἕκαστος τάχους εἶχε
καὶ οἱ περὶ τὸν Διόμιλον ἐξακόσιοι· στάδιοι δὲ
πρὶν προσμεῖξαι ἐκ τοῦ λειμῶνος ἐγίγνοντο αὐτοῖς
4 οὐκ ἔλασσον ἢ πέντε καὶ εἴκοσι. προσπεσόντες
οὖν αὐτοῖς τοιούτῳ τρόπῳ ἀτακτότερον καὶ μάχῃ
νικηθέντες οἱ Συρακόσιοι ἐπὶ ταῖς Ἐπιπολαῖς

---

¹ Added by Krüger. ² Added by Madvig.
³ καί, before ἔλαθον in the MSS., deleted by Madvig.

force to the meadow along the river Anapus—for Hermocrates and his fellow-generals, as it chanced, had just come into office—and proceeded to hold a review of the hoplites. And they selected first six hundred picked men of these, under the command of Diomilus, a fugitive from Andros, that these might be a guard for Epipolae, and if there were need of them anywhere else might be quickly at hand in a body.

XCVII. And the Athenians during the night preceding the day on which the Syracusans held their review, came from Catana with their whole force and put in unobserved at the place called Leon, which is six or seven stadia distant from Epipolae, disembarking the land-force there and anchoring their ships at Thapsus. That is a peninsula, with a narrow isthmus, extending into the sea and not far distant from the city of Syracuse, either by sea or by land. The naval force of the Athenians, having run a stockade across the isthmus, lay quiet on Thapsus; but the land-force advanced at once at a run to Epipolae, and got up by way of Euryelus before the Syracusans, when they became aware of it, could come up from the review which they were holding in the meadow. They brought aid, however, everyone with what speed he could, the others as well as the six hundred under Diomilus; but they had not less than twenty-five stadia to go, after leaving the meadow, before they reached the enemy. Consequently the Syracusans fell upon the Athenians in considerable disorder, and being defeated in battle

THUCYDIDES

ἀνεχώρησαν ἐς τὴν πόλιν· καὶ ὅ τε Διόμιλος
5 ἀποθνῄσκει καὶ τῶν ἄλλων ὡς τριακόσιοι. καὶ
μετὰ τοῦτο οἱ Ἀθηναῖοι τροπαῖόν τε στήσαντες
καὶ τοὺς νεκροὺς ὑποσπόνδους ἀποδόντες τοῖς
Συρακοσίοις, πρὸς τὴν πόλιν αὐτὴν τῇ ὑστεραίᾳ
ἐπικαταβάντες, ὡς οὐκ ἐπεξῇσαν αὐτοῖς, ἐπανα-
χωρήσαντες φρούριον ἐπὶ τῷ Λαβδάλῳ ᾠκοδό-
μησαν ἐπ' ἄκροις τοῖς κρημνοῖς τῶν Ἐπιπολῶν
ὁρῶν πρὸς τὰ Μέγαρα, ὅπως εἴη αὐτοῖς, ὁπότε
προΐοιεν ἢ μαχούμενοι ἢ τειχιοῦντες, τοῖς τε
σκεύεσι καὶ τοῖς χρήμασιν ἀποθήκη.

XCVIII. Καὶ οὐ πολλῷ ὕστερον αὐτοῖς ἦλθον
ἔκ τε Ἐγέστης ἱππῆς τριακόσιοι καὶ Σικελῶν
καὶ Ναξίων καὶ ἄλλων τινῶν ὡς ἑκατόν· καὶ
Ἀθηναίων ὑπῆρχον πεντήκοντα καὶ διακόσιοι, οἷς
ἵππους τοὺς μὲν παρ' Ἐγεσταίων καὶ Καταναίων
ἔλαβον, τοὺς δ' ἐπρίαντο, καὶ ξύμπαντες πεντή-
2 κοντα καὶ ἑξακόσιοι ἱππῆς ξυνελέγησαν. καὶ
καταστήσαντες ἐν τῷ Λαβδάλῳ φυλακὴν ἐχώρουν
πρὸς τὴν Συκὴν οἱ Ἀθηναῖοι, ἵναπερ καθεζόμενοι
ἐτείχισαν τὸν κύκλον διὰ τάχους. καὶ ἔκπληξιν
τοῖς Συρακοσίοις παρέσχον τῷ τάχει τῆς οἰκοδο-
μίας· καὶ ἐπεξελθόντες μάχην διενοοῦντο ποι-
3 εῖσθαι καὶ μὴ περιορᾶν. καὶ ἤδη ἀντιπαρατασ-
σομένων ἀλλήλοις οἱ τῶν Συρακοσίων στρατηγοὶ
ὡς ἑώρων σφίσι τὸ στράτευμα διεσπασμένον τε
καὶ οὐ ῥᾳδίως ξυντασσόμενον, ἀνήγαγον πάλιν ἐς

on Epipolae, retired into the city, Diomilus and about
three hundred of the rest being slain. After this
the Athenians, having set up a trophy and given up
their dead under truce to the Syracusans, next day
went down against the city itself; but when the
enemy did not come out against them they withdrew
and built a fort at Labdalum, on the verge of the
bluffs of Epipolae looking towards Megara, that it
might serve as a magazine for their baggage and
stores whenever they advanced either to fight or
to work at the wall.

XCVIII. Not long afterwards there came from
Egesta three hundred horsemen, and from the Sicels,
Naxians, and some others about one hundred; and the
Athenians had already two hundred and fifty, for
whom they received some horses from the Egestaeans
and Catanaeans and purchased others; so that altogether six hundred and fifty cavalry were mustered.
Placing a garrison at Labdalum, the Athenians advanced to Syce, where they took position and built
the round fort[1] with all speed. The Syracusans
were struck with consternation by the rapidity of their
building; and they went out against them, determined to give battle and not look on idly. And
when they were already drawing up for the conflict
the generals of the Syracusans, seeing that their own
army had become disordered and did not readily get
into line, led them back to the city, all save a

---

[1] Syke (*i.e.* a place set with fig-trees; see Steph. *s.v*
Συκαί) is probably to be located in the middle of the plateau
of Epipolae. Here the Athenians built first a circular fort,
which later was the starting-point for the wall of circumvallation extending northward towards Trogilus and south-
ward to the Great Harbour. See Map, and also Holm
ii. 387 and Freeman, *Sic.* iii. 662 ff.

τὴν πόλιν πλὴν μέρους τινὸς τῶν ἱππέων· οὗτοι
δὲ ὑπομένοντες ἐκώλυον τοὺς Ἀθηναίους λιθο-
4 φορεῖν τε καὶ ἀποσκίδνασθαι μακροτέραν. καὶ
τῶν Ἀθηναίων φυλὴ μία τῶν ὁπλιτῶν καὶ οἱ
ἱππῆς μετ' αὐτῶν πάντες ἐτρέψαντο τοὺς τῶν
Συρακοσίων ἱππέας προσβαλόντες, καὶ ἀπέκτεινάν τέ τινας καὶ τροπαῖον τῆς ἱππομαχίας
ἔστησαν.

XCIX. Καὶ τῇ ὑστεραίᾳ οἱ μὲν ἐτείχιζον τῶν
Ἀθηναίων τὸ πρὸς βορέαν τοῦ κύκλου τεῖχος, οἱ
δὲ λίθους καὶ ξύλα ξυμφοροῦντες παρέβαλλον
ἐπὶ τὸν Τρώγιλον καλούμενον, αἰεὶ ᾗπερ βραχύτατον ἐγίγνετο αὐτοῖς ἐκ τοῦ μεγάλου λιμένος
2 ἐπὶ τὴν ἑτέραν θάλασσαν τὸ ἀποτείχισμα. οἱ δὲ
Συρακόσιοι οὐχ ἥκιστα Ἑρμοκράτους τῶν στρατηγῶν ἐσηγησαμένου μάχαις μὲν πανδημεὶ πρὸς
Ἀθηναίους οὐκέτι ἐβούλοντο διακινδυνεύειν, ὑπο-
τειχίζειν δὲ ἄμεινον ἐδόκει εἶναι ᾗ ἐκεῖνοι ἔμελλον
ἄξειν τὸ τεῖχος καί, εἰ φθάσειαν, ἀποκλήσεις
γίγνεσθαι, καὶ ἅμα καὶ ἐν τούτῳ εἰ ἐπιβοηθοῖεν,
μέρος ἀντιπέμπειν αὐτοῖς[1] τῆς στρατιᾶς· καὶ
φθάνειν ἂν τοῖς σταυροῖς προκαταλαμβάνοντες
τὰς ἐφόδους, ἐκείνους δὲ ἂν παυομένους τοῦ ἔργου
3 πάντας ἂν πρὸς σφᾶς τρέπεσθαι. ἐτείχιζον οὖν
ἐξελθόντες ἀπὸ τῆς σφετέρας πόλεως ἀρξάμενοι,
κάτωθεν τοῦ κύκλου τῶν Ἀθηναίων ἐγκάρσιον
τεῖχος ἄγοντες, τάς τε ἐλάας ἐκκόπτοντες τοῦ
4 τεμένους καὶ πύργους ξυλίνους καθιστάντες. αἱ

---

[1] αὐτοῖς, Bekker's conjecture, for αὐτούς of the MSS.

part of the cavalry. These remained behind and
tried to prevent the Athenians from bringing stones
and scattering to any great distance. But one tribal [1]
division of the Athenian hoplites, and with these all
their cavalry, attacked and routed the Syracusan
cavalry, killed some, and set up a trophy of the
cavalry fight.

XCIX. On the next day some of the Athenians proceeded to build the wall to the north of the round fort,
while others brought together stones and wood and
began to lay these down along the line towards the
place called Trogilus, in which direction the line of
circumvallation would be shortest from the Great
Harbour to the outer sea. But the Syracusans, at
the suggestion of their generals, and especially of
Hermocrates, were no longer inclined to risk pitched
battles with their whole force against the Athenians.
It seemed better to build a wall across the line where
the Athenians were going to bring their wall, so that
if they got ahead of them the Athenians would be
blocked off, and they decided at the same time, if
the Athenians should attack them while at this
work, to send a part of the army against them; and
they expected that they would get ahead of the
Athenians in occupying the approaches with their
stockades, and that they would cease from their
work and all turn against them. Accordingly they
went out and proceeded to build, starting from the
city and carrying a cross-wall below the round fort
of the Athenians, chopping down the olive-trees
of the precinct and setting up wooden towers. The

---

[1] φυλή is here used for τάξις, the term being borrowed
from the civil classification. Each of the ten tribes furnished
a division (τάξις).

δὲ νῆες τῶν Ἀθηναίων οὔπω ἐκ τῆς Θάψου
περιεπεπλεύκεσαν ἐς τὸν μέγαν λιμένα, ἀλλ' ἔτι
οἱ Συρακόσιοι ἐκράτουν τῶν περὶ τὴν θάλασσαν,
κατὰ γῆν δὲ ἐκ τῆς Θάψου οἱ Ἀθηναῖοι τὰ
ἐπιτήδεια ἐπήγοντο.

C. Ἐπειδὴ δὲ τοῖς Συρακοσίοις ἀρκούντως
ἐδόκει ἔχειν ὅσα τε ἐσταυρώθη καὶ ᾠκοδομήθη
τοῦ ὑποτειχίσματος, καὶ οἱ Ἀθηναῖοι αὐτοὺς οὐκ
ἦλθον κωλύσοντες, φοβούμενοι μὴ σφίσι δίχα
γιγνομένοις ῥᾷον μάχωνται, καὶ ἅμα τὴν καθ'
αὑτοὺς περιτείχισιν ἐπειγόμενοι, οἱ μὲν Συρακόσιοι φυλὴν μίαν καταλιπόντες φύλακα τοῦ
οἰκοδομήματος ἀνεχώρησαν ἐς τὴν πόλιν, οἱ δὲ
Ἀθηναῖοι τούς τε ὀχετοὺς αὐτῶν, οἳ ἐς τὴν πόλιν
ὑπονομηδὸν ποτοῦ ὕδατος ἠγμένοι ἦσαν, διέ-
φθειραν, καὶ τηρήσαντες τούς τε ἄλλους Συρακοσίους κατὰ σκηνὰς ὄντας ἐν μεσημβρίᾳ καί
τινας καὶ ἐς τὴν πόλιν ἀποκεχωρηκότας καὶ τοὺς
ἐν τῷ σταυρώματι ἀμελῶς φυλάσσοντας, τριακοσίους μὲν σφῶν αὐτῶν λογάδας καὶ τῶν ψιλῶν
τινας ἐκλεκτοὺς ὡπλισμένους προύταξαν θεῖν
δρόμῳ ἐξαπιναίως πρὸς τὸ ὑποτείχισμα, ἡ δὲ
ἄλλη στρατιὰ δίχα, ἡ μὲν μετὰ τοῦ ἑτέρου
στρατηγοῦ πρὸς τὴν πόλιν, εἰ ἐπιβοηθοῖεν, ἐχώρουν, ἡ δὲ μετὰ τοῦ ἑτέρου πρὸς τὸ σταύρωμα τὸ
2 παρὰ τὴν πυλίδα. καὶ προσβαλόντες οἱ τριακόσιοι αἱροῦσι τὸ σταύρωμα· καὶ οἱ φύλακες
αὐτὸ ἐκλιπόντες κατέφυγον ἐς τὸ προτείχισμα τὸ
περὶ τὸν Τεμενίτην. καὶ αὐτοῖς ξυνεσέπεσον οἱ
διώκοντες, καὶ ἐντὸς γενόμενοι βίᾳ ἐξεκρού-
σθησαν πάλιν ὑπὸ τῶν Συρακοσίων, καὶ τῶν

Athenian ships had not yet sailed round from Thapsus into the Great Harbour, but the Syracusans were still masters of the parts about the sea, and the Athenians brought their supplies from Thapsus by land.

C. When it seemed to the Syracusans that enough of their counter-wall had been constructed with stone-work and stockade,[1] and the Athenians did not come to hinder them—for they feared that the enemy might more easily deal with them if their forces were divided, and at the same time they were pushing on their own wall of circumvallation—leaving one division as a guard for their cross-wall, they withdrew to the city. Meanwhile the Athenians destroyed their pipes which ran underground into the city and supplied it with drinking-water. Then watching when most of the Syracusans were in their tents at midday—some of them having even gone to their homes in the city—and when those at the stockade were guarding the place carelessly, they stationed in front three hundred picked Athenians and a chosen body of the light-armed troops in heavy armour to go at a run suddenly against the counter-wall; while the rest of the army advanced in two divisions, one with one general against the city, in case they should come to the rescue, the other with the other general to that part of the stockade which is by the postern gate. The three hundred attacked and took the stockade, the guards leaving it and fleeing to the outwork around Temenites.[2] And their pursuers burst in with them; but these, after getting in, were forced out again by

---

[1] The ὑποτείχισμα seems to have consisted partly of palisading and partly of stone-work.   [2] cf. ch. lxxv. 1.

Ἀργείων τινὲς αὐτόθι καὶ τῶν Ἀθηναίων οὐ
3 πολλοὶ διεφθάρησαν. καὶ ἐπαναχωρήσασα ἡ
πᾶσα στρατιὰ τήν τε ὑποτείχισιν καθεῖλον καὶ
τὸ σταύρωμα ἀνέσπασαν καὶ διεφόρησαν τοὺς
σταυροὺς παρ' ἑαυτούς, καὶ τροπαῖον ἔστησαν.

CI. Τῇ δ' ὑστεραίᾳ ἀπὸ τοῦ κύκλου ἐτείχιζον
οἱ Ἀθηναῖοι τὸν κρημνὸν τὸν ὑπὲρ τοῦ ἕλους, ὃς
τῶν Ἐπιπολῶν ταύτῃ πρὸς τὸν μέγαν λιμένα
ὁρᾷ, καὶ ᾗπερ αὐτοῖς βραχύτατον ἐγίγνετο κατα-
βᾶσι διὰ τοῦ ὁμαλοῦ καὶ τοῦ ἕλους ἐς τὸν λιμένα
2 τὸ περιτείχισμα. καὶ οἱ Συρακόσιοι ἐν τούτῳ
ἐξελθόντες καὶ αὐτοὶ ἀπεσταύρουν αὖθις ἀρξάμενοι ἀπὸ τῆς πόλεως διὰ μέσου τοῦ ἕλους· καὶ
τάφρον ἅμα παρώρυσσον, ὅπως μὴ οἷόν τε ᾖ τοῖς
3 Ἀθηναίοις μέχρι τῆς θαλάσσης ἀποτειχίσαι. οἱ
δ', ἐπειδὴ τὸ πρὸς τὸν κρημνὸν αὐτοῖς ἐξείργαστο,
ἐπιχειροῦσιν αὖθις τῷ τῶν Συρακοσίων σταυρώματι καὶ τάφρῳ, τὰς μὲν ναῦς κελεύσαντες περι-
πλεῦσαι ἐκ τῆς Θάψου ἐς τὸν μέγαν λιμένα τὸν
τῶν Συρακοσίων, αὐτοὶ δὲ περὶ ὄρθρον καταβάντες ἀπὸ τῶν Ἐπιπολῶν ἐς τὸ ὁμαλὸν καὶ
διὰ τοῦ ἕλους, ᾗ πηλῶδες ἦν καὶ στεριφώτατον,
θύρας καὶ ξύλα πλατέα ἐπιθέντες καὶ ἐπ' αὐτῶν
διαβαδίσαντες, αἱροῦσιν ἅμα ἕῳ τό τε σταύρωμα
πλὴν ὀλίγου καὶ τὴν τάφρον, καὶ ὕστερον καὶ τὸ
4 ὑπολειφθὲν εἷλον· καὶ μάχη ἐγένετο, καὶ ἐν αὐτῇ
ἐνίκων οἱ Ἀθηναῖοι· καὶ τῶν Συρακοσίων οἱ μὲν
τὸ δεξιὸν κέρας ἔχοντες πρὸς τὴν πόλιν ἔφυγον,
οἱ δ' ἐπὶ τῷ εὐωνύμῳ παρὰ τὸν ποταμόν. καὶ
αὐτοὺς βουλόμενοι ἀποκλῄσασθαι τῆς διαβάσεως
οἱ τῶν Ἀθηναίων τριακόσιοι λογάδες δρόμῳ
5 ἠπείγοντο πρὸς τὴν γέφυραν. δείσαντες δὲ οἱ

the Syracusans, some of the Argives and a few of
the Athenians being slain there. Then the whole
army withdrew and pulled down the counter-wall
and tore up the stockade, bringing the stakes over
to their own lines, and set up a trophy.

CI. The next day the Athenians, starting from
the round fort, began to fortify the bluff which is
above the marsh,[1] where on this side of Epipolae
it looks toward the Great Harbour, and where
they would find the line of circumvallation shortest
as they came down through the level ground and
the marsh to the harbour. The Syracusans meanwhile also went out and proceeded to build another
stockade, starting from the city, through the middle
of the marsh; and they dug at the same time a
ditch alongside, that it might not be possible for
the Athenians to complete their wall to the sea.
But the latter, when their wall to the bluff was
finished, again attacked the stockade and ditch of
the Syracusans, having ordered their ships to sail
around from Thapsus into the Great Harbour at
Syracuse and themselves gone down about daybreak
from Epipolae to the level ground. Laying down
doors and planks through the marsh where the soil
was clayey and firmest and crossing over on these,
they took at daylight the ditch, and all but a little
of the stockade, and later the remaining part. A
battle occurred also, in which the Athenians were
victorious, those of the Syracusans on the right
wing fleeing to the city, those on the left along
the river. Wishing to cut off the latter from the
crossing, the three hundred picked men of the
Athenians pushed on at a run to the bridge. But

[1] The Lysimeleia.

Συρακόσιοι (ἦσαν γὰρ καὶ τῶν ἱππέων αὐτοῖς οἱ
πολλοὶ ἐνταῦθα) ὁμόσε χωροῦσι τοῖς τριακοσίοις
τούτοις, καὶ τρέπουσί τε αὐτοὺς καὶ ἐσβάλλουσιν
ἐς τὸ δεξιὸν κέρας τῶν Ἀθηναίων. καὶ προσπε-
σόντων αὐτῶν ξυνεφοβήθη καὶ ἡ πρώτη φυλὴ
6 τοῦ κέρως. ἰδὼν δὲ ὁ Λάμαχος παρεβοήθει ἀπὸ
τοῦ εὐωνύμου τοῦ ἑαυτῶν μετὰ τοξοτῶν τε οὐ
πολλῶν καὶ τοὺς Ἀργείους παραλαβών, καὶ
ἐπιδιαβὰς τάφρον τινὰ καὶ μονωθεὶς μετ' ὀλίγων
τῶν ξυνδιαβάντων ἀποθνήσκει αὐτός τε καὶ πέντε
ἢ ἓξ τῶν μετ' αὐτοῦ. καὶ τούτους μὲν οἱ Συρακόσιοι εὐθὺς κατὰ τάχος φθάνουσιν ἁρπάσαντες
πέραν τοῦ ποταμοῦ ἐς τὸ ἀσφαλές, αὐτοὶ δὲ
ἐπιόντος ἤδη καὶ τοῦ ἄλλου στρατεύματος τῶν
Ἀθηναίων ἀπεχώρουν.

CII. Ἐν τούτῳ δὲ οἱ πρὸς τὴν πόλιν αὐτῶν τὸ
πρῶτον καταφυγόντες ὡς ἑώρων ταῦτα γιγνόμενα,
αὐτοί τε πάλιν ἀπὸ τῆς πόλεως [1] ἀναθαρσήσαντες
ἀντετάξαντο πρὸς τοὺς κατὰ σφᾶς Ἀθηναίους,
καὶ μέρος τι αὐτῶν πέμπουσιν ἐπὶ τὸν κύκλον
τὸν ἐπὶ ταῖς Ἐπιπολαῖς, ἡγούμενοι ἐρῆμον αἱρή-
2 σειν. καὶ τὸ μὲν δεκάπλεθρον προτείχισμα
αὐτῶν αἱροῦσι καὶ διεπόρθησαν, αὐτὸν δὲ τὸν
κύκλον Νικίας διεκώλυσεν· ἔτυχε γὰρ ἐν αὐτῷ δι'
ἀσθένειαν ὑπολελειμμένος· τὰς γὰρ μηχανὰς καὶ
ξύλα ὅσα πρὸ τοῦ τείχους ἦν καταβεβλημένα,
ἐμπρῆσαι τοὺς ὑπηρέτας ἐκέλευσεν, ὡς ἔγνω
ἀδυνάτους ἐσομένους ἐρημίᾳ ἀνδρῶν ἄλλῳ τρόπῳ
3 περιγενέσθαι. καὶ ξυνέβη οὕτως· οὐ γὰρ ἔτι
προσῆλθον οἱ Συρακόσιοι διὰ τὸ πῦρ, ἀλλὰ
ἀπεχώρουν πάλιν. καὶ γὰρ πρός τε τὸν κύκλον

[1] ἀπὸ τῆς πόλεως, omitted by Hude with C.

the Syracusans became alarmed, and, as most of their cavalry was there, closed with these three hundred, routed them, and attacked the right wing of the Athenians. On their charge the first division of this wing also became involved in the panic. And Lamachus, seeing this, came to their aid from his own place on the left wing, with a few bowmen and the Argives, whom he took with him; and advancing across a ditch and being cut off with a few of those who had crossed with him, he was killed himself and five or six of his followers. These the Syracusans at once hastily snatched up and succeeded in carrying over the river to safety, themselves retreating when the rest of the Athenian army began now to advance.

CII. Meanwhile those of them who had fled at first to the city, seeing what was going on, themselves took courage, and coming back from the city drew up against the Athenians in front of them; and they sent a part of their number against the round fort on Epipolae, thinking that they would find it without defenders and be able to take it. And they did indeed take and demolish their outwork of one thousand feet in length, but the round fort itself Nicias prevented their taking; for he happened to have been left behind there on account of illness. He ordered the attendants to set fire to the engines and wood that had been thrown down before the wall, seeing that they would be unable through lack of men to be saved in any other way. And it turned out so; for the Syracusans, coming no nearer because of the fire, now retreated. And, besides, reinforcements were already coming up to

βοήθεια ἤδη κάτωθεν τῶν Ἀθηναίων ἀποδιω-
ξάντων τοὺς ἐκεῖ ἐπανῄει, καὶ αἱ νῆες ἅμα αὐτῶν
ἐκ τῆς Θάψου, ὥσπερ εἴρητο, κατέπλεον ἐς τὸν
4 μέγαν λιμένα. ἃ ὁρῶντες οἱ ἄνωθεν κατὰ τάχος
ἀπῇσαν καὶ ἡ ξύμπασα στρατιὰ τῶν Συρακοσίων
ἐς τὴν πόλιν, νομίσαντες μὴ ἂν ἔτι ἀπὸ τῆς παρούσης σφίσι δυνάμεως ἱκανοὶ γενέσθαι κωλῦσαι
τὸν ἐπὶ τὴν θάλασσαν τειχισμόν.

CIII. Μετὰ δὲ τοῦτο οἱ Ἀθηναῖοι τροπαῖον
ἔστησαν καὶ τοὺς νεκροὺς ὑποσπόνδους ἀπέδοσαν τοῖς Συρακοσίοις καὶ τοὺς μετὰ Λαμάχου καὶ αὐτοὶ ἐκομίσαντο. καὶ παρόντος ἤδη
σφίσι παντὸς τοῦ στρατεύματος, καὶ τοῦ ναυτικοῦ καὶ τοῦ πεζοῦ, ἀπὸ τῶν Ἐπιπολῶν καὶ τοῦ
κρημνώδους ἀρξάμενοι ἀπετείχιζον μέχρι τῆς
2 θαλάσσης τείχει διπλῷ τοὺς Συρακοσίους. τὰ δ᾽
ἐπιτήδεια τῇ στρατιᾷ ἐσήγετο ἐκ τῆς Ἰταλίας
πανταχόθεν. ἦλθον δὲ καὶ τῶν Σικελῶν πολλοὶ
ξύμμαχοι τοῖς Ἀθηναίοις, οἳ πρότερον περιεω-
ρῶντο, καὶ ἐκ τῆς Τυρσηνίας νῆες πεντηκόντεροι
τρεῖς. καὶ τἆλλα προυχώρει αὐτοῖς ἐς ἐλπίδας.
3 καὶ γὰρ οἱ Συρακόσιοι πολέμῳ μὲν οὐκέτι ἐνόμιζον ἂν περιγενέσθαι, ὡς αὐτοῖς οὐδὲ ἀπὸ τῆς
Πελοποννήσου ὠφελία οὐδεμία ἧκε, τοὺς δὲ
λόγους ἔν τε σφίσιν αὐτοῖς ἐποιοῦντο ξυμβα-
τικοὺς καὶ πρὸς τὸν Νικίαν· οὗτος γὰρ δὴ μόνος
4 εἶχε Λαμάχου τεθνεῶτος τὴν ἀρχήν. καὶ κύρωσις
μὲν οὐδεμία ἐγίγνετο, οἷα δὲ εἰκὸς ἀνθρώπων
ἀπορούντων καὶ μᾶλλον ἢ πρὶν¹ πολιορκουμένων,
πολλὰ ἐλέγετο πρός τε ἐκεῖνον καὶ πλείω ἔτι

---

¹ πρὶν, Hude omits, with C.

the round fort from the Athenians below, who had chased away the enemy there, and their ships at the same time were sailing down, as they had been ordered, from Thapsus into the Great Harbour. Seeing these things, the men on the heights and the main army of the Syracusans hastily withdrew into the city, thinking that with the force they then had at their disposal they could no longer prevent the building of the wall to the sea.

CIII. After this the Athenians set up a trophy and restored their dead to the Syracusans under truce, themselves getting back the bodies of Lamachus and his men. The whole of their armament being now present, both fleet and land-force, starting from the bluff of Epipolae they proceeded to cut off the Syracusans by a double wall down to the sea. Provisions were coming in for the army from all quarters of Italy. And there came also as allies to the Athenians many of the Sicels, who before had been hesitating, and from Tyrrhenia three fifty-oared galleys. And other matters were progressing according to their hopes. For the Syracusans no longer thought they could win at war, as no aid had come to them even from the Peloponnesus; and indeed they were discussing terms of agreement, not only among themselves, but even with Nicias, who now since the death of Lamachus had sole command. No decision was reached; but, as is natural when men are in perplexity and more straitly besieged than before, many proposals were made to

κατὰ τὴν πόλιν. καὶ γάρ τινα καὶ ὑποψίαν ὑπὸ
τῶν παρόντων κακῶν ἐς ἀλλήλους εἶχον, καὶ τοὺς
στρατηγούς τε ἐφ' ὧν αὐτοῖς ταῦτα ξυνέβη ἔπαυ-
σαν, ὡς ἢ δυστυχίᾳ ἢ προδοσίᾳ τῇ ἐκείνων
βλαπτόμενοι, καὶ ἄλλους ἀνθείλοντο, Ἡρακλείδην καὶ Εὐκλέα καὶ Τελλίαν.

CIV. Ἐν δὲ τούτῳ Γύλιππος ὁ Λακεδαιμόνιος
καὶ αἱ ἀπὸ τῆς Κορίνθου νῆες περὶ Λευκάδα ἤδη
ἦσαν, βουλόμενοι ἐς τὴν Σικελίαν διὰ τάχους
βοηθῆσαι. καὶ ὡς αὐτοῖς αἱ ἀγγελίαι ἐφοίτων
δειναὶ καὶ πᾶσαι ἐπὶ τὸ αὐτὸ ἐψευσμέναι ὡς ἤδη
παντελῶς ἀποτετειχισμέναι αἱ Συράκουσαί εἰσι,
τῆς μὲν Σικελίας οὐκέτι ἐλπίδα οὐδεμίαν εἶχεν ὁ
Γύλιππος, τὴν δὲ Ἰταλίαν βουλόμενος περι-
ποιῆσαι, αὐτὸς μὲν καὶ Πυθὴν ὁ Κορίνθιος ναυσὶ
δυοῖν μὲν Λακωνικαῖν, δυοῖν δὲ Κορινθίαιν ὅτι
τάχιστα ἐπεραιώθησαν τὸν Ἰόνιον ἐς Τάραντα,
οἱ δὲ Κορίνθιοι πρὸς ταῖς σφετέραις δέκα Λευκα-
δίας δύο καὶ Ἀμπρακιώτιδας τρεῖς προσπληρώ-
2 σαντες ὕστερον ἔμελλον πλεύσεσθαι. καὶ ὁ μὲν
Γύλιππος ἐκ τοῦ Τάραντος ἐς τὴν Θουρίαν
πρῶτον πρεσβευσάμενος κατὰ τὴν τοῦ πατρὸς
ποτε πολιτείαν καὶ οὐ δυνάμενος αὐτοὺς προσαγαγέσθαι, ἄρας παρέπλει τὴν Ἰταλίαν, καὶ ἁρ-
πασθεὶς ὑπ' ἀνέμου,[1] ὃς ἐκπνεῖ ταύτῃ μέγας κατὰ
βορέαν ἑστηκώς, ἀποφέρεται ἐς τὸ πέλαγος, καὶ
πάλιν χειμασθεὶς ἐς τὰ μάλιστα τῷ Τάραντι
προσμίσγει· καὶ τὰς ναῦς ὅσαι ἐπόνησαν ὑπὸ τοῦ
3 χειμῶνος ἀνελκύσας ἐπεσκεύαζεν. ὁ δὲ Νικίας
πυθόμενος αὐτὸν προσπλέοντα ὑπερεῖδε τὸ πλῆθος

---

[1] κατὰ τὸν Τεριναῖον κόλπον, in MSS. after ἀνέμου, deleted
by Goeller.

him, and still more were discussed in the city. For under their present evils they had some suspicion even of one another; and the generals under whose lead these things had happened were deposed, on the ground that their disasters were due to their ill-luck or treachery, and in their stead were chosen Heracleides, Eucles, and Tellias.

CIV. Meanwhile Gylippus the Lacedaemonian and the ships from Corinth[1] were already at Leucas, proposing to bring aid to Sicily in all haste. As the reports that were coming to them were alarming and all to the same false purport, that Syracuse had already been completely walled off, Gylippus no longer had any hope of Sicily, but wishing to save Italy, he himself and Pythen the Corinthian, with two Laconian vessels and two Corinthian, crossed the Ionian gulf to Tarentum as quickly as possible; while the Corinthians, after manning, in addition to their own ten, two Leucadian and three Ambracian ships, were to sail later. From Tarentum, Gylippus, after first going on a mission to Thuria, on account of his father having been once a citizen there,[2] and failing to win them over, weighed anchor and sailed along the coast of Italy. Caught by a wind, which settling in the north blows violently in that region, he was carried out to sea, and then after a most violent storm again reached Tarentum; and there hauling ashore all of his ships that had suffered from the storm he set to repairing them. But Nicias, although he heard that he was sailing up, despised

---

[1] cf. ch. xciii. 3.
[2] Or, reading, with BH, καὶ τὴν τοῦ πατρὸς ἀνανεωσάμενος, "and having revived the sometime citizenship of his father."

τῶν νεῶν, ὅπερ καὶ οἱ Θούριοι ἔπαθον, καὶ λῃστι-
κώτερον ἔδοξε παρεσκευασμένους πλεῖν καὶ οὐδεμίαν φυλακὴν πω ἐποιεῖτο.

CV. Κατὰ δὲ τοὺς αὐτοὺς χρόνους τούτου τοῦ
θέρους καὶ Λακεδαιμόνιοι ἐς τὸ Ἄργος ἐσέβαλον
αὐτοί τε καὶ οἱ ξύμμαχοι καὶ τῆς γῆς τὴν πολλὴν
ἐδῄωσαν. καὶ Ἀθηναῖοι Ἀργείοις τριάκοντα
ναυσὶν ἐβοήθησαν, αἵπερ τὰς σπονδὰς φανερώ-
τατα τὰς πρὸς Λακεδαιμονίους αὐτοῖς ἔλυσαν.
2 πρότερον μὲν γὰρ λῃστείαις ἐκ Πύλου καὶ περὶ
τὴν ἄλλην Πελοπόννησον μᾶλλον ἢ ἐς τὴν Λακωνικὴν ἀποβαίνοντες μετά τε Ἀργείων καὶ Μαντινέων ξυνεπολέμουν, καὶ πολλάκις Ἀργείων
κελευόντων ὅσον σχόντας μόνον ξὺν ὅπλοις ἐς
τὴν Λακωνικὴν καὶ τὸ ἐλάχιστον μετὰ σφῶν
δῃώσαντας ἀπελθεῖν οὐκ ἤθελον· τότε δὲ Πυ-
θοδώρου καὶ Λαισποδίου καὶ Δημαράτου ἀρχόντων ἀποβάντες ἐς Ἐπίδαυρον τὴν Λιμηρὰν καὶ
Πρασιὰς καὶ ὅσα ἄλλα ἐδῄωσαν τῆς γῆς, καὶ τοῖς
Λακεδαιμονίοις ἤδη εὐπροφάσιστον μᾶλλον τὴν
αἰτίαν ἐς τοὺς Ἀθηναίους τοῦ ἀμύνεσθαι ἐποίη-
3 σαν. ἀναχωρησάντων δὲ τῶν Ἀθηναίων ἐκ τοῦ
Ἄργους ταῖς ναυσὶ καὶ τῶν Λακεδαιμονίων οἱ
Ἀργεῖοι ἐσβαλόντες ἐς τὴν Φλειασίαν τῆς τε γῆς
αὐτῶν ἔτεμον καὶ ἀπέκτεινάν τινας, καὶ ἀπῆλθον
ἐπ᾽ οἴκου.

the small number of his ships, just as the Thurians had done, and thinking they were coming equipped rather as privateers than as men-of-war, he took as yet no precautions.

CV. About the same time in this summer, the Lacedaemonians and their allies invaded Argos and ravaged most of the country. And the Athenians brought succour to the Argives with thirty ships, an act which violated their treaty with the Lacedaemonians in the most overt manner. For before this they waged the war, in cooperation with the Argives and Mantineans, by predatory excursions from Pylos and by making landings round the rest of the Peloponnesus rather than in Laconia; and although the Argives frequently urged them only to make a landing with arms on Laconian territory, devastate in concert with them even the least part, and then go away, they refused. But at this time, under the command of Pythodorus, Laespodias, and Demaratus, they landed at Epidaurus Limera, Prasiae, and other places, and laid waste some of their territory, and so gave the Lacedaemonians from now on a more plausible excuse for defending themselves against the Athenians. After the Athenians had withdrawn from Argos with their ships, and the Lacedaemonians also had retired, the Argives made an incursion into Phliasia, ravaging part of their land and killing some of the inhabitants, and then returned home.

PRINTED IN GREAT BRITAIN BY
RICHARD CLAY AND COMPANY, LTD.,
BUNGAY, SUFFOLK

THE LOEB CLASSICAL LIBRARY

VOLUMES ALREADY PUBLISHED

Latin Authors

AMMIANUS MARCELLINUS. Translated by J. C. Rolfe. 3 Vols. (3rd Imp., revised.)

APULEIUS: THE GOLDEN ASS (METAMORPHOSES). W. Adlington (1566). Revised by S. Gaselee. (8th Imp.)

S. AUGUSTINE: CITY OF GOD. 7 Vols. Vol. I. G. E. McCracken.

ST. AUGUSTINE, CONFESSIONS OF. W. Watts (1631). 2 Vols. (Vol. I. 7th Imp., Vol. II. 6th Imp.)

ST. AUGUSTINE, SELECT LETTERS. J. H. Baxter. (2nd Imp.)

AUSONIUS. H. G. Evelyn White. 2 Vols. (2nd Imp.)

BEDE. J. E. King. 2 Vols. (2nd Imp.)

BOETHIUS: TRACTS and DE CONSOLATIONE PHILOSOPHIAE. Rev. H. F. Stewart and E. K. Rand. (6th Imp.)

CAESAR: ALEXANDRIAN, AFRICAN and SPANISH WARS. A. G. Way.

CAESAR: CIVIL WARS. A. G. Peskett. (6th Imp.)

CAESAR: GALLIC WAR. H. J. Edwards. (11th Imp.)

CATO: DE RE RUSTICA; VARRO: DE RE RUSTICA. H. B. Ash and W. D. Hooper. (3rd Imp.)

CATULLUS. F. W. Cornish; TIBULLUS. J. B. Postgate; PERVIGILIUM VENERIS. J. W. Mackail. (13th Imp.)

CELSUS: DE MEDICINA. W. G. Spencer. 3 Vols. (Vol. I. 3rd Imp. revised, Vols. II. and III. 2nd Imp.)

CICERO: BRUTUS, and ORATOR. G. L. Hendrickson and H. M. Hubbell. (3rd Imp.)

[CICERO]: AD HERENNIUM. H. Caplan.

CICERO: DE FATO; PARADOXA STOICORUM; DE PARTITIONE ORATORIA. H. Rackham (With De Oratore. Vol. II.) (2nd Imp.)

CICERO: DE FINIBUS. H. Rackham. (4th Imp. revised.)

CICERO: DE INVENTIONE, etc. H. M. Hubbell.

CICERO: DE NATURA DEORUM and ACADEMICA. H. Rackham. (3rd Imp.)

CICERO: DE OFFICIIS. Walter Miller. (7th Imp.)

CICERO: DE ORATORE. 2 Vols. E. W. Sutton and H. Rackham. (2nd Imp.)

CICERO: DE REPUBLICA and DE LEGIBUS; SOMNIUM SCIPIONIS. Clinton W. Keyes. (4th Imp.)

CICERO: DE SENECTUTE, DE AMICITIA, DE DIVINATIONE. W. A. Falconer. (6th Imp.)

CICERO: IN CATILINAM, PRO FLACCO, PRO MURENA, PRO SULLA. Louis E. Lord. (3rd Imp. revised.)

CICERO: LETTERS TO ATTICUS. E. O. Winstedt. 3 Vols. (Vol. I. 7th Imp., Vols. II. and III. 4th Imp.)

CICERO: LETTERS TO HIS FRIENDS. W. Glynn Williams. 3 Vols. (Vols. I. and II. 4th Imp., Vol. III. 2nd Imp. revised.)

CICERO: PHILIPPICS. W. C. A. Ker. (4th Imp. revised.)

CICERO: PRO ARCHIA, POST REDITUM, DE DOMO, DE HARUS-PICUM RESPONSIS, PRO PLANCIO. N. H. Watts. (3rd Imp.)

CICERO: PRO CAECINA, PRO LEGE MANILIA, PRO CLUENTIO, PRO RABIRIO. H. Grose Hodge. (3rd Imp.)

CICERO: PRO CAELIO, DE PROVINCIIS CONSULARIBUS. PRO BALBO. R. Gardner.

CICERO: PRO MILONE, IN PISONEM, PRO SCAURO, PRO FONTEIO. PRO RABIRIO POSTUMO, PRO MARCELLO, PRO LIGARIO, PRO REGE DEIOTARO. N. H. Watts. (3rd Imp.)

CICERO: PRO QUINCTIO, PRO ROSCIO AMERINO, PRO ROSCIO COMOEDO, CONTRA RULLUM. J. H. Freese. (3rd Imp.)

CICERO: PRO SESTIO, IN VATINIUM. R. Gardner.

CICERO: TUSCULAN DISPUTATIONS. J. E. King. (4th Imp.)

CICERO: VERRINE ORATIONS. L. H. G. Greenwood. 2 Vols. (Vol. I. 3rd Imp., Vol. II. 2nd Imp.)

CLAUDIAN. M. Platnauer. 2 Vols. (2nd Imp.)

COLUMELLA: DE RE RUSTICA. DE ARBORIBUS. H. B. Ash, E. S. Forster and E. Heffner. 3 Vols. (Vol. I. 2nd Imp.)

CURTIUS, Q.: HISTORY OF ALEXANDER. J. C. Rolfe. 2 Vols. (2nd Imp.)

FLORUS. E. S. Forster and CORNELIUS NEPOS. J. C. Rolfe. (2nd Imp.)

FRONTINUS: STRATAGEMS and AQUEDUCTS. C. E. Bennett and M. B. McElwain. (2nd Imp.)

FRONTO: CORRESPONDENCE. C. R. Haines. 2 Vols. (3rd Imp.)

GELLIUS, J. C. Rolfe. 3 Vols. (Vol. I. 3rd Imp., Vols. II. and III. 2nd Imp.)

HORACE: ODES and EPODES. C. E. Bennett. (14th Imp. revised.)

HORACE: SATIRES, EPISTLES, ARS POETICA. H. R. Fairclough. (9th Imp. revised.)

JEROME: SELECTED LETTERS. F. A. Wright. (2nd Imp.)

JUVENAL and PERSIUS. G. G. Ramsay. (8th Imp.)

LIVY. B. O. Foster, F. G. Moore, Evan T. Sage, and A. C. Schlesinger and R. M. Geer (General Index). 14 Vols. (Vol. I. 5th Imp., Vol. V. 4th Imp., Vols. II.–IV., VI. and VII., IX.–XII. 3rd Imp., Vol. VIII., 2nd Imp. revised.)

LUCAN. J. D. Duff. (4th Imp.)

LUCRETIUS. W. H. D. Rouse. (7th Imp. revised.)

MARTIAL. W. C. A. Ker. 2 Vols. (Vol. I. 5th Imp., Vol. II. 4th Imp. revised.)

MINOR LATIN POETS: from PUBLILIUS SYRUS to RUTILIUS NAMATIANUS, including GRATTIUS, CALPURNIUS SICULUS, NEMESIANUS, AVIANUS, and others with "Aetna" and the "Phoenix." J. Wight Duff and Arnold M. Duff. (3rd Imp.)

Ovid: THE ART OF LOVE and OTHER POEMS. J. H. Mozley.
(4th Imp.)

Ovid: FASTI. Sir James G. Frazer. (2nd Imp.)

Ovid: HEROIDES and AMORES. Grant Showerman. (7th Imp.)

Ovid: METAMORPHOSES. F. J. Miller. 2 Vols. (Vol. I. 11th
Imp., Vol. II. 10th Imp.)

Ovid: TRISTIA and EX PONTO. A. L. Wheeler. (4th Imp.)

PERSIUS. Cf. JUVENAL.

PETRONIUS. M. Heseltine, SENECA APOCOLOCYNTOSIS.
W. H. D. Rouse. (9th Imp. revised.)

PLAUTUS. Paul Nixon. 5 Vols. (Vol. I. 6th Imp., II. 5th Imp.,
III. 4th Imp., IV. and V. 2nd Imp.)

PLINY: LETTERS. Melmoth's Translation revised by W. M. L.
Hutchinson. 2 Vols. (7th Imp.)

PLINY: NATURAL HISTORY. H. Rackham and W. H. S. Jones.
10 Vols. Vols. I.–V. and IX. H. Rackham. Vols. VI. and
VII. W. H. S. Jones. (Vol. I. 4th Imp., Vols. II. and III.
3rd Imp., Vol. IV. 2nd Imp.)

PROPERTIUS. H. E. Butler. (7th Imp.)

PRUDENTIUS. H. J. Thomson. 2 Vols.

QUINTILIAN. H. E. Butler. 4 Vols. (Vols. I. and IV. 4th
Imp., Vols. II. and III. 3rd Imp.)

REMAINS OF OLD LATIN. E. H. Warmington. 4 vols. Vol. I.
(ENNIUS AND CAECILIUS.) Vol. II. (LIVIUS, NAEVIUS,
PACUVIUS, ACCIUS.) Vol. III. (LUCILIUS and LAWS OF XII
TABLES.) (2nd Imp.) (ARCHAIC INSCRIPTIONS.)

SALLUST. J. C. Rolfe. (4th Imp. revised.)

SCRIPTORES HISTORIAE AUGUSTAE. D. Magie. 3 Vols. (Vol. I.
3rd Imp. revised, Vols. II. and III. 2nd Imp.)

SENECA: APOCOLOCYNTOSIS. Cf. PETRONIUS.

SENECA: EPISTULAE MORALES. R. M. Gummere. 3 Vols.
(Vol. I. 4th Imp., Vols. II. and III. 3rd Imp.)

SENECA: MORAL ESSAYS. J. W. Basore. 3 Vols. (Vol. II.
4th Imp., Vols. I. and III. 2nd Imp. revised.)

SENECA: TRAGEDIES. F. J. Miller. 2 Vols. (Vol. I. 4th Imp.
Vol. II. 3rd Imp. revised.)

SIDONIUS: POEMS AND LETTERS. W. B. Anderson. 2 Vols.
(Vol. I. 2nd Imp.)

SILIUS ITALICUS. J. D. Duff. 2 Vols. (Vol. I. 2nd Imp.
Vol. II. 3rd Imp.)

STATIUS. J. H. Mozley. 2 Vols. (2nd Imp.)

SUETONIUS. J. C. Rolfe. 2 Vols. (Vol. I. 7th Imp., Vol. II.
6th Imp. revised.)

TACITUS: DIALOGUES. Sir Wm. Peterson. AGRICOLA and
GERMANIA. Maurice Hutton. (7th Imp.)

TACITUS: HISTORIES AND ANNALS. C. H. Moore and J. Jackson.
4 Vols.. (Vols. I. and II. 4th Imp. Vols. III. and IV. 3rd Imp.)

TERENCE. John Sargeaunt. 2 Vols. (Vol. I. 8th Imp., Vol.
II. 7th Imp.)

TERTULLIAN: APOLOGIA and DE SPECTACULIS. T. R. Glover.
MINUCIUS FELIX. G. H. Rendall. (2nd Imp.)

VALERIUS FLACCUS. J. H. Mozley. (3rd Imp. revised.)

3

VARRO: DE LINGUA LATINA. R. G. Kent. 2 Vols. (*3rd Imp. revised.*)

VELLEIUS PATERCULUS and RES GESTAE DIVI AUGUSTI. F. W. Shipley. (*2nd Imp.*)

VIRGIL. H. R. Fairclough. 2 Vols. (Vol. I. 19*th Imp.*, Vol. II. 14*th Imp. revised.*)

VITRUVIUS: DE ARCHITECTURA. F. Granger. 2 Vols. (Vol. I. 3*rd Imp.*, Vol. II. 2*nd Imp.*)

Greek Authors

ACHILLES TATIUS. S. Gaselee. (*2nd Imp.*)

AELIAN: ON THE NATURE OF ANIMALS. 3 Vols. Vols. I. and II. A. F. Scholfield.

AENEAS TACTICUS, ASCLEPIODOTUS and ONASANDER. The Illinois Greek Club. (*2nd Imp.*)

AESCHINES. C. D. Adams. (*3rd Imp.*)

AESCHYLUS. H. Weir Smyth. 2 Vols. (Vol. I. 7*th Imp.*, Vol. II. 6*th Imp. revised.*)

ALCIPHRON, AELIAN, PHILOSTRATUS LETTERS. A. R. Benner and F. H. Fobes.

ANDOCIDES, ANTIPHON, Cf. MINOR ATTIC ORATORS.

APOLLODORUS. Sir James G. Frazer. 2 Vols. (*3rd Imp.*)

APOLLONIUS RHODIUS. R. C. Seaton. (*5th Imp.*)

THE APOSTOLIC FATHERS. Kirsopp Lake. 2 Vols. (Vol. I. 8*th Imp.*, Vol. II. 6*th Imp.*)

APPIAN: ROMAN HISTORY. Horace White. 4 Vols. (Vol. I. 4*th Imp.*, Vols. II.–IV. 3*rd Imp.*)

ARATUS. Cf. CALLIMACHUS.

ARISTOPHANES. Benjamin Bickley Rogers. 3 Vols. Verse trans. (*5th Imp.*)

ARISTOTLE: ART OF RHETORIC. J. H. Freese. (*3rd Imp.*)

ARISTOTLE: ATHENIAN CONSTITUTION, EUDEMIAN ETHICS, VICES AND VIRTUES. H. Rackham. (*3rd Imp.*)

ARISTOTLE: GENERATION OF ANIMALS. A. L. Peck. (*2nd Imp.*)

ARISTOTLE: METAPHYSICS. H. Tredennick. 2 Vols. (*4th Imp.*)

ARISTOTLE: METEOROLOGICA. H. D. P. Lee.

ARISTOTLE: MINOR WORKS. W. S. Hett. On Colours, On Things Heard, On Physiognomies, On Plants, On Marvellous Things Heard, Mechanical Problems, On Indivisible Lines, On Situations and Names of Winds, On Melissus, Xenophanes, and Gorgias. (*2nd Imp.*)

ARISTOTLE: NICOMACHEAN ETHICS. H. Rackham. (*6th Imp. revised.*)

ARISTOTLE: OECONOMICA and MAGNA MORALIA. G. C. Armstrong; (with Metaphysics, Vol. II.). (*4th Imp.*)

ARISTOTLE: ON THE HEAVENS. W. K. C. Guthrie. (*3rd Imp. revised.*)

ARISTOTLE: ON THE SOUL, PARVA NATURALIA, ON BREATH. W. S. Hett. (*2nd Imp. revised.*)

ARISTOTLE: ORGANON—Categories, On Interpretation, Prior Analytics. H. P. Cooke and H. Tredennick. (3rd Imp.)
ARISTOTLE: ORGANON—Posterior Analytics, Topics. H. Tredennick and E. S. Forster.
ARISTOTLE: ORGANON—On Sophistical Refutations.
On Coming to be and Passing Away, On the Cosmos. E. S. Forster and D. J. Furley.
ARISTOTLE: PARTS OF ANIMALS. A. L. Peck; MOTION AND PROGRESSION OF ANIMALS. E. S. Forster. (4th Imp. revised.)
ARISTOTLE: PHYSICS. Rev. P. Wicksteed and F. M. Cornford. 2 Vols. (Vol. I. 2nd Imp., Vol. II. 3rd Imp.)
ARISTOTLE: POETICS and LONGINUS. W. Hamilton Fyfe; DEMETRIUS ON STYLE. W. Rhys Roberts. (5th Imp. revised.)
ARISTOTLE: POLITICS. H. Rackham. (4th Imp. revised.)
ARISTOTLE: PROBLEMS. W. S. Hett. 2 Vols. (2nd Imp. revised.)
ARISTOTLE: RHETORICA AD ALEXANDRUM (with PROBLEMS. Vol. II.). H. Rackham.
ARRIAN: HISTORY OF ALEXANDER and INDICA. Rev. E. Iliffe Robson. 2 Vols. (3rd Imp.)
ATHENAEUS: DEIPNOSOPHISTAE. C. B. Gulick. 7 Vols. (Vols. I.–IV., VI. and VII. 2nd Imp., Vol. V. 3rd Imp.)
ST. BASIL: LETTERS. R. J. Deferrari. 4 Vols. (2nd Imp.)
CALLIMACHUS: FRAGMENTS. C. A. Trypanis.
CALLIMACHUS, Hymns and Epigrams, and LYCOPHRON. A. W. Mair; ARATUS. G. R. Mair. (2nd. Imp.)
CLEMENT of ALEXANDRIA. Rev. G. W. Butterworth. (3rd Imp.)
COLLUTHUS. Cf. OPPIAN.
DAPHNIS AND CHLOE. Thornley's Translation revised by J. M. Edmonds; and PARTHENIUS. S. Gaselee. (4th Imp.)
DEMOSTHENES I.: OLYNTHIACS, PHILIPPICS and MINOR ORATIONS. I.–XVII. AND XX. J. H. Vince. (2nd Imp.)
DEMOSTHENES II.: DE CORONA and DE FALSA LEGATIONE. C. A. Vince and J. H. Vince. (3rd Imp. revised.)
DEMOSTHENES III.: MEIDIAS, ANDROTION, ARISTOCRATES, TIMOCRATES and ARISTOGEITON, I. AND II. J. H. Vince (2nd Imp.)
DEMOSTHENES IV.–VI.: PRIVATE ORATIONS and IN NEAERAM. A. T. Murray. (Vol. IV. 3rd Imp., Vols. V. and VI. 2nd Imp.)
DEMOSTHENES VII.: FUNERAL SPEECH, EROTIC ESSAY, EXORDIA and LETTERS. N. W. and N. J. DeWitt.
DIO CASSIUS: ROMAN HISTORY. E. Cary. 9 Vols. (Vols. I. and II. 3rd Imp., Vols. III.–IX. 2nd Imp.)
DIO CHRYSOSTOM. J. W. Cohoon and H. Lamar Crosby. 5 Vols. (Vols. I.–IV. 2nd Imp.)
DIODORUS SICULUS. 12 Vols. Vols. I.–VI. C. H. Oldfather. Vol. VII. C. L. Sherman. Vols. IX. and X. R. M. Geer. Vol. XI. F. Walton. (Vol. I. 3rd Imp., Vols. II.–IV. 2nd Imp.)
DIOGENES LAERTIUS. R. D. Hicks. 2 Vols. (5th Imp.).
DIONYSIUS OF HALICARNASSUS: ROMAN ANTIQUITIES. Spelman's translation revised by E. Cary. 7 Vols. (Vols. I.–V. 2nd Imp.)

EPICTETUS. W. A. Oldfather. 2 Vols. (*3rd Imp.*)
EURIPIDES. A. S. Way. 4 Vols. (Vols. I. and IV. *7th Imp.*, Vol.
II. *8th Imp.*, Vol. III. *6th Imp.*) Verse trans.
EUSEBIUS: ECCLESIASTICAL HISTORY. Kirsopp Lake and
J. E. L. Oulton. 2 Vols. (Vol. I. *3rd Imp.*, Vol. II. *5th Imp.*)
GALEN: ON THE NATURAL FACULTIES. A. J. Brock. (*4th Imp.*)
THE GREEK ANTHOLOGY. W. R. Paton. 5 Vols. (Vols. I.–IV.
5th Imp., Vol. V. *3rd Imp.*)
GREEK ELEGY AND IAMBUS with the ANACREONTEA. J. M.
Edmonds. 2 Vols. (Vol. I. *3rd Imp.*, Vol. II. *2nd Imp.*)
THE GREEK BUCOLIC POETS (THEOCRITUS, BION, MOSCHUS).
J. M. Edmonds. (*7th Imp. revised.*)
GREEK MATHEMATICAL WORKS. Ivor Thomas. 2 Vols. (*3rd
Imp.*)
HERODES. Cf. THEOPHRASTUS: CHARACTERS.
HERODOTUS. A. D. Godley. 4 Vols. (Vol. I. *4th Imp.*, Vols.
II. and III. *5th Imp.*, Vol. IV. *3rd Imp.*)
HESIOD AND THE HOMERIC HYMNS. H. G. Evelyn White.
(*7th Imp. revised and enlarged.*)
HIPPOCRATES and the FRAGMENTS OF HERACLEITUS. W. H. S.
Jones and E. T. Withington. 4 Vols. (Vol. I. *4th Imp.*,
Vols. II.–IV. *3rd Imp.*)
HOMER: ILIAD. A. T. Murray. 2 Vols. (*7th Imp.*)
HOMER: ODYSSEY. A. T. Murray. 2 Vols. (*8th Imp.*)
ISAEUS. E. W. Forster. (*3rd Imp.*)
ISOCRATES. George Norlin and LaRue Van Hook. 3 Vols.
(*2nd Imp.*)
ST. JOHN DAMASCENE: BARLAAM AND IOASAPH. Rev. G. R.
Woodward and Harold Mattingly. (*3rd Imp. revised.*)
JOSEPHUS. H. St. J. Thackeray and Ralph Marcus. 9 Vols.
Vols. I.–VII. (Vol. V. *4th Imp.*, Vol. VI. *3rd Imp.*, Vols. I.–IV.
and VII. *2nd Imp.*)
JULIAN Wilmer Cave Wright. 3 Vols. (Vols. I. and II.
3rd Imp., Vol. III. *2nd Imp.*)
LUCIAN. A. M. Harmon. 8 Vols. Vols. I.–V. (Vols. I. and
II. *4th Imp.*, Vol. III. *3rd Imp.*, Vols. IV. and V. *2nd Imp.*)
LYCOPHRON. Cf. CALLIMACHUS.
LYRA GRAECA. J. M. Edmonds. 3 Vols. (Vol. I. *5th Imp.*
Vol. II *revised and enlarged*, and III. *4th Imp.*)
LYSIAS. W. R. M. Lamb. (*3rd Imp.*)
MANETHO. W. G. Waddell: PTOLEMY: TETRABIBLOS. F. E.
Robbins. (*3rd Imp.*)
MARCUS AURELIUS. C. R. Haines. (*4th Imp. revised.*)
MENANDER. F. G. Allinson. (*3rd Imp. revised.*)
MINOR ATTIC ORATORS (ANTIPHON, ANDOCIDES, LYCURGUS,
DEMADES, DINARCHUS, HYPEREIDES). K. J. Maidment and
J. O. Burtt. 2 Vols. (Vol. I. *2nd Imp.*)
NONNOS: DIONYSIACA. W. H. D. Rouse. 3 Vols. (*2nd Imp.*)
OPPIAN, COLLUTHUS, TRYPHIODORUS. A. W. Mair. (*2nd Imp.*)
PAPYRI. NON-LITERARY SELECTIONS. A. S. Hunt and C. C.
Edgar. 2 Vols. (*2nd Imp.*) LITERARY SELECTIONS.
(Poetry). D. L. Page. (*3rd Imp.*)

PARTHENIUS. Cf. DAPHNIS AND CHLOE.

PAUSANIAS: DESCRIPTION OF GREECE. W. H. S. Jones. 5 Vols. and Companion Vol. arranged by R. E. Wycherley. (Vols. I. and III. *3rd Imp.*, Vols. II., IV. and V. *2nd Imp.*)

PHILO. 10 Vols. Vols. I.–V.; F. H. Colson and Rev. G. H. Whitaker Vols. VI.–IX.; F. H. Colson. (Vols I–II., V.–VII., *3rd Imp.*, Vol. IV. *4th Imp.*, Vols. III., VIII., and IX. *2nd Imp.*)

PHILO: two supplementary Vols. (*Translation only.*) Ralph Marcus.

PHILOSTRATUS: THE LIFE OF APPOLLONIUS OF TYANA. F. C. Conybeare. 2 Vols. (Vol. I. *4th Imp.*, Vol. II. *3rd Imp.*)

PHILOSTRATUS: IMAGINES; CALLISTRATUS: DESCRIPTIONS. A. Fairbanks. (*2nd Imp.*)

PHILOSTRATUS and EUNAPIUS: LIVES OF THE SOPHISTS. Wilmer Cave Wright. (*2nd Imp.*)

PINDAR. Sir J. E. Sandys. (*8th Imp. revised.*)

PLATO: CHARMIDES, ALCIBIADES, HIPPARCHUS, THE LOVERS, THEAGES, MINOS and EPINOMIS. W. R. M. Lamb. (*2nd Imp.*)

PLATO: CRATYLUS, PARMENIDES, GREATER HIPPIAS, LESSER HIPPIAS. H. N. Fowler. (*4th Imp.*)

PLATO: EUTHYPHRO, APOLOGY, CRITO, PHAEDO, PHAEDRUS. H. N. Fowler. (11*th Imp.*)

PLATO: LACHES, PROTAGORAS, MENO, EUTHYDEMUS. W. R. M. Lamb. (*3rd Imp. revised.*)

PLATO: LAWS. Rev. R. G. Bury. 2 Vols. (*3rd Imp.*)

PLATO: LYSIS, SYMPOSIUM GORGIAS. W. R. M. Lamb. (*5th Imp. revised.*)

PLATO: REPUBLIC. Paul Shorey. 2 Vols. (Vol. I. *5th Imp.*, Vol. II. *4th Imp.*)

PLATO: STATESMAN, PHILEBUS. H. N. Fowler; ION. W. R. M. Lamb. (*4th Imp.*)

PLATO: THEAETETUS and SOPHIST. H. N. Fowler. (*4th Imp.*)

PLATO: TIMAEUS, CRITIAS, CLITOPHO, MENEXENUS, EPISTULAE. Rev. R. G. Bury. (*3rd Imp.*)

PLUTARCH: MORALIA. 14 Vols. Vols. I.–V. F. C. Babbitt. Vol. VI. W. C. Helmbold. Vol. VII. P. H. De Lacy and B. Einarson. Vol. X. H. N. Fowler. Vol. XII. H. Cherniss and W. C Helmbold. (Vols. I.–VI. and X. *2nd Imp.*)

PLUTARCH: THE PARALLEL LIVES. B. Perrin. 11 Vols. (Vols. I., II., VI., VII., and XI. *3rd Imp.*, Vols. III.–V. and VIII.–X. *2nd Imp.*)

POLYBIUS. W. R. Paton. 6 Vols. (*2nd Imp.*)

PROCOPIUS: HISTORY OF THE WARS. H. B. Dewing. 7 Vols. (Vol. I. *3rd Imp.*, Vols. II.–VII. *2nd Imp.*)

PTOLEMY: TETRABIBLOS. Cf. MANETHO.

QUINTUS SMYRNAEUS. A. S. Way. Verse trans. (*3rd Imp.*)

SEXTUS EMPIRICUS. Rev. R. G. Bury. 4 Vols. (Vol. I. *4th Imp.*, Vols. II. and III. *2nd Imp.*)

SOPHOCLES. F. Storr. 2 Vols. (Vol. I. 10*th Imp.* Vol. II. 6*th Imp.*) Verse trans.

STRABO: GEOGRAPHY. Horace L. Jones. 8 Vols. (Vols. I., V., and VIII. 3rd Imp., Vols. II., III., IV., VI., and VII. 2nd Imp.)
THEOPHRASTUS: CHARACTERS. J. M. Edmonds. HERODES, etc. A. D. Knox. (3rd Imp.)
THEOPHRASTUS: ENQUIRY INTO PLANTS. Sir Arthur Hort, Bart. 2 Vols. (2nd Imp.)
THUCYDIDES. C. F. Smith. 4 Vols. (Vol. I. 5th Imp., Vols. II. and IV. 4th Imp., Vol. III., 3rd Imp. revised.)
TRYPHIODORUS. Cf. OPPIAN.
XENOPHON: CYROPAEDIA. Walter Miller. 2 Vols. (Vol. I. 4th Imp., Vol. II. 3rd Imp.)
XENOPHON: HELLENICA, ANABASIS, APOLOGY, and SYMPOSIUM. C. L. Brownson and O. J. Todd. 3 Vols. (Vols. I. and III 3rd Imp., Vol. II. 4th Imp.)
XENOPHON: MEMORABILIA and OECONOMICUS. E. C. Marchant (3rd Imp.)
XENOPHON: SCRIPTA MINORA. E. C. Marchant. (3rd Imp.)

IN PREPARATION

Greek Authors

ARISTOTLE: HISTORY OF ANIMALS. A. L. Peck.
PLOTINUS: A. H. Armstrong.

Latin Authors

BABRIUS AND PHAEDRUS. Ben E. Perry.

DESCRIPTIVE PROSPECTUS ON APPLICATION

London   WILLIAM HEINEMANN LTD
Cambridge, Mass.   HARVARD UNIVERSITY PRESS

8